Protest Public Relations

T0358870

Global movements and protests from the Arab Spring to the Occupy Movement have been attributed to growing access to social media, while without it, local causes like #bringbackourgirls and the ice bucket challenge may have otherwise remained unheard and unseen.

Regardless of their nature – advocacy, activism, protest or dissent – and beyond the technological ability of digital and social media to connect support, these major events have all been the results of excellent communication and public relations. But PR remains seen only as the defender of corporate and capitalist interests, and therefore resistant to outside voices such as activists, NGOs, union members, protesters and whistle-blowers.

Drawing on contributions from around the world to examine the concepts and practice of "activist," "protest" and "dissent" public relations, this book challenges this view. Using a range of international examples, it explores the changing nature of protest and its relationship with PR and provides a radical analysis of the communication strategies and tactics of social movements and activist groups and their campaigns. This thought-provoking collection will be of interest to researchers and advanced students of public relations, strategic communication, political science, politics, journalism, marketing, and advertising, and also to PR professionals in think tanks and NGOs.

Ana Adi is a Professor of Public Relations/Corporate Communications at Quadriga University of Applied Sciences in Berlin. When not analysing public relations from a critical perspective, Dr Adi's research, teaching and consultancy focuses on the strategic uses of digital and social media in a variety of communication fields. You can find more about her work on www.anaadi.net.

Routledge New Directions in Public Relations and Communication Research

Edited by Kevin Moloney

Current academic thinking about public relations (PR) and related communication is a lively, expanding marketplace of ideas and many scholars believe that it's time for its radical approach to be deepened. *Routledge New Directions in PR & Communication Research* is the forum of choice for this new thinking. Its key strength is its remit, publishing critical and challenging responses to continuities and fractures in contemporary PR thinking and practice, tracking its spread into new geographies and political economies. It questions its contested role in market-orientated, capitalist, liberal democracies around the world, and examines its invasion of all media spaces, old, new, and as yet unenvisaged. We actively invite new contributions and offer academics a welcoming place for the publication of their analyses of a universal, persuasive mind-set that lives comfortably in old and new media around the world.

Books in this series will be of interest to academics and researchers involved in these expanding fields of study, as well as students undertaking advanced studies in this area.

Corporate Social Responsibility, Public Relations & Community Development
Emerging Perspectives from Southeast Asia
Marianne D. Sison and Zeny Sarabia-Panol

Social Media, Organizational Identity and Public Relations
The Challenge of Authenticity
Amy Thurlow

Protest Public Relations
Communicating Dissent and Activism
Edited by Ana Adi

For more information about the series, please visit www.routledge.com/ Routledge-New-Directions-in-Public-Relations–Communication-Research/ book-series/RNDPRCR

Protest Public Relations

Communicating Dissent and Activism

Edited by Ana Adi

Routledge
Taylor & Francis Group

LONDON AND NEW YORK

First published 2019
by Routledge
2 Park Square, Milton Park, Abingdon, Oxon OX14 4RN

and by Routledge
52 Vanderbilt Avenue, New York, NY 10017, USA

First issued in paperback 2020

Routledge is an imprint of the Taylor & Francis Group, an informa business

British Library Cataloguing-in-Publication Data
A catalogue record for this book is available from the British Library

Library of Congress Cataloging-in-Publication Data
A catalog record has been requested for this book

ISBN 13: 978-0-367-66498-5 (pbk)
ISBN 13: 978-0-8153-8699-5 (hbk)

Typeset in Sabon
by Wearset Ltd, Boldon, Tyne and Wear

Contents

Figures

Tables

Contributors

Ana Adi (PhD, @ana_adi on Twitter; www.anaadi.net) is a Professor of Public Relations and Corporate Communications at Quadriga University of Applied Sciences in Berlin, Chair of the Digital Communication Awards, and part of the core research team of the Asia-Pacific Communication Monitor. She is also part of the organizing committee of MediAsia. Prior to editing *Protest Public Relations: Communicating dissent and activism* (Taylor & Francis), Dr Adi co-edited *#rezist – Romania's 2017 anti-corruption protests: causes, development and implications* (www.romanianprotests.info with Darren G. Lilleker) and *Corporate Social Responsibility in the Digital Age* (2015, Emerald with Georgiana G. Grigore and Alin Stancu). Originally from Romania, Dr Adi obtained her PhD from the University of the West of Scotland. Her research, teaching and consultancy focus on issues related to digital communication, CSR and PR, looking in particular at storytelling and measurement.

Kara Andrade is a PhD candidate at American University's School of Communication. She is a researcher, journalist and entrepreneur who focuses on Latin America, media, technology and society. She is also the Innovation Specialist for Counterpart International's Innovation for Change Initiative, which supports and starts-up regional innovation hubs in six regions: Latin America and the Caribbean, Middle East and North Africa, Africa, South Asia, Central Asia, and East Asia and Pacific. During her work as an Ashoka fellow and co-founder of HablaCentro Informatics NFP and LLC, she created a network of citizen journalism and information sharing hubs in Latin America that shared reliable and timely updates from the ground during crisis. Both her work through her social venture and at Counterpart focuses on the adoption and implementation of innovations to solve common democracy problems.

Nguyen Hoang Anh is currently in charge of communication and public relations, and branding at the Center for Communication and Public Relations at Hanoi University of Science and Technology, one of the leading technical universities in Vietnam. She is also a PhD candidate, visiting lecturer at the Faculty of Journalism and Communication, University of Social Sciences and Humanities, which is a member of Vietnam National University in Hanoi. She has eight years of experience in research and professional practice in the field of Journalism and Public Relations. In 2010, she graduated with a bachelor's degree in journalism after four years of study at the University of Social Sciences and Humanities, followed by a master's degree at the same institution per her excellent academic results. In 2011, she was the reporter as well as correspondent editor of channel VTC 14, which is a digital TV specialized in environmental problems in Vietnam. In 2012, she was among the first people who professionally in charge in branding for Hanoi University of Science and Technology. In 2013, she received a master's degree in Journalism from Hanoi University of Science and Technology, her research topic was entitled "Communication campaign on food hygiene and safety in the national target program." The article on this topic was later published in Vietnam's *Journal of Propaganda*. In 2015, passionate about research and teaching, she again enrolled as a PhD candidate of Journalism. She has successfully guided students to complete three thesis topics, two papers, and research on the online newspapers and social media in Vietnam. As a person working in media and public relations in Vietnam, she has special interests in theoretical as well as practical issues in public relations in Vietnam such as communication campaigns, public relations via using social media, activist PR related to social problems, etc. *Contact PhD candidate Nguyen Hoang Anh online via e-mail: hoanganhbc22@gmail.com, anh.nguyenhoang@ hust.edu.vn, or Facebook: Nguyeễn Hoàng Anh.*

A. Banu Bıçakçı (PhD) is an Associate Professor of Public Relations. She obtained her doctoral degree from Anadolu University, Turkey, in 2009. From 2002 to 2017 she was an academic at Yeditepe University's Public Relations and Publicity Department. Dr Bıçakçı has been a guest lecturer at the international MBA Communication and Leadership program, Quadriga University of Berlin for two semesters. At present she is engaged in a research project on digital media and migration. Dr Bıçakçı has a wide range of research interests including history of public relations, city branding and activist PR. Her work has been published in various public relations and communication management journals and in edited collections. She is currently on the advisory boards of *Public Relations Review* and *Journal of Public Relations Research*'s special issues on PR History and in the action committee of *International History of Public Relations Conference*. She is a member of EUPRERA, ECREA and IAMCR.

Ernesto Castañeda (PhD, Columbia 2010) is the author of *A Place to Call Home: Immigrant Exclusion and Urban Belonging in New York, Paris, and Barcelona* (Stanford University Press, 2018); co-author with Charles

Tilly and Lesley Wood of *Social Movements 1768–2018* (Routledge, 2018); editor of *Immigration and Categorical Inequality: Migration to the City and the Birth of Race and Ethnicity* (Routledge 2018); and co-editor with Cathy L. Schneider of *Collective Violence, Contentious Politics, and Social Change: A Charles Tilly Reader* (Routledge, 2017). He is an Assistant Professor of Sociology at American University, in Washington, DC.

Robert Crawford (PhD) is a Professor of Advertising in the School of Media and Communication at RMIT University. His research has focused on the growth and development of the advertising, marketing, and public relations industries across Australia, Oceania, and South East Asia. Professor Crawford's most recent publications include *Behind Glass Doors: The World of Australian Advertising Agencies 1959–89* (UWAP, 2016 – co-authored with Jackie Dickenson) and *Global Advertising Practice in a Borderless World* (Routledge, 2017 – co-edited with Linda Brennan and Lukas Parker).

Camelia Crişan (PhD) is a lecturer at the National University for Political Studies and Public Administration (NUPSPA) in Bucharest, Romania where she teaches courses on Leadership and Corporate Social Responsibility. She is also the Executive Director of the Progress Foundation, Romania, a foundation acting as an innovation boutique offering solutions for staff and organizational development, performs research studies on cultural consumption and design thinking. Within 2009–2015 Camelia has led the training department of the national program Biblionet, a Global Libraries initiative funded by the Bill and Melinda Gates Foundation (BMGF). Camelia has provided consultancy and support for the National Library of Columbia, VAKE Mediatheka (Georgia) and the Novateca Program (Moldova) as well as for a large number of Romanian public and private entities. Camelia holds a PhD in Sociology from the National University for Political Studies and Public Administration (NUPSPA), a BA in Communication Science and a BA in Psychology and leads the courses in Corporate Social Responsibility, Leadership and Organizational Development within NUPSPA.

Maria De Moya (PhD) is an Associate Professor of Public Relations in DePaul's University College of Communication, where she also serves as Academic Director of the master's program in Public Relations and Advertising, and Director of the Latino Media and Communication program. She holds a PhD in Mass Communication from the University of Florida, and a MA in Business and Economic Journalism from New York University, where she was a Fulbright scholar. Her research interests center on international and ethnic public relations, with a specific focus on questions of community, identity and advocacy. Her work intersects with the fields of public diplomacy and communication for social change.

Luis Rubén Díaz-Cepeda completed his PhD in moral and political philosophy in 2016 at the Universidad Autónoma Metropolitana-Iztapalapa in Mexico City, Mexico under the direction of Enrique Dussel. He holds master's degrees in Philosophy and Sociology from the University of Texas at El Paso, where he occasionally serves as a Visiting Scholar and Lecturer in the Philosophy Department. He is an Assistant Professor in the Humanities Department at the Universidad Autónoma de Ciudad Juárez-Cuauhtémoc in Mexico. His research focuses on ethics, borders, social movements, critical theory, and philosophy of liberation. Luis has organized international conferences in El Paso, Ciudad Juarez, and Mexico City. Published in Mexico, Argentina and The United States, recent works include "#Yo Soy 132: A Networked Social Movement of Mexican Youth," in *Waves of Social Movement Mobilizations in the Twenty-First Century: Challenges to the Neo-Liberal World Order and Democracy* (Lexington Books). He is currently working on a manuscript titled, *Latin American Philosophy and Social Movements: From Ciudad Juárez to Ayotzinapa*. He can be reached at luisdiazuam@gmail. com.

Barika Göncü (PhD) a former communication consultant in the private sector, is a full time lecturer (since 2011) of public relations at the School of Communication at Istanbul Bilgi University, also lecturing in the Public Relations and Corporate Communication Graduate Program (PRCC) of the same institution. She specializes in reputation management, public relations ethics, crisis management and communication, and issues management. Her research interests include external communication consulting, issues management, critical PR, activist PR, public relations ethics, crisis management, and communication. She is currently a member of the Media and Communication Council of Union of Chambers and Commodity Exchanges of Turkey (TOBB).

Oleksandra Gudkova is a PhD candidate conducting research on women's political activism in the public sphere, supervised by Professor Katharine Sarikakis. Specifically she is interested in Eastern European feminist activism. One of the central questions in her project is how women's activism is represented by printed media. She earned her bachelor's and master's degree at Taras Shevchenko National University of Kyiv, Ukraine, in International Journalism and International Information Management, from the International Relations Faculty. At the University of Vienna she studied Communication Science at the Department of Communication. Her MA thesis, supervised by Professor Katharine Sarikakis, investigated the media coverage of Eastern European feminist activism. Throughout the years of studying she also gained working experience as an intern at the Department of Public Information at the United Nations both in New York and Vienna, and the International Atomic Energy Agency Headquarters in Vienna.

Adam Howe (www.achowe.com) is completing his PhD in Sociology at the University of British Columbia. His research focuses on Canadian policy networks related to climate change. The project is part of a larger international project comparing national climate change policies. Using computational and social network analysis, Adam seeks to understand the overall structure of the policy network, the relationships among different segments of the network, and how these positions relate to informal processes of influence and power in policymaking. Adam has a second book chapter published in *Reading Sociology: Canadian Perspectives*, and a number of publications currently under review. He has also published a number of academic book reviews (one in *Mobilization*, one at *Mobilizing Ideas*) and an op-ed mobilizing public sociology. He recently organized a panel on Indigenous Theorizing, as part of a one-day symposium preceding the Annual Congress of the International Sociological Association. The symposium is being held by the theory cluster of the Canadian Sociological Association. Adam is originally from Ontario, Canada and completed his master's degree at McMaster University.

Pelin Hürmeriç is an Associate Professor and currently Vice Dean and Head of the Department of Public Relations and Publicity at the Faculty of Communication, Yeditepe University, İstanbul, where she has been a faculty member since 2001. She is on the editorial board of *Global Media Journal Turkish Edition*, and *International History of Public Relations Conference*. Her research interests include history of public relations, corporate communication and integrated marketing communication.

Nguyen Thi Thanh Huyen (PhD) has more than 20 years of teaching and researching experiences in the field of journalism and public relations; she was retained as a fulltime lecturer by the University of Social Sciences and Humanities, which is a member of Vietnam National University in Hanoi immediately after graduating from university excellently in Journalism (1995). In 2010, she became the first Vietnamese doctor in Public Relations after five years study in Sogang University, South Korea. In 2011, she was appointed as Head of Department of Public Relations and Advertising, as well as an associate Dean of the Faculty of Journalism and Communication in the University of Social Sciences and Humanities. As a pioneer in Public Relations in Vietnam, she actively designs and implements many training and research programs in Public Relations as well as widens the international cooperation in the field of her expertise for many universities in Vietnam. Her research interest are theories and practices of public relations, including national image communication, public relations training, public relations using social media, media relations, public relations in Vietnam, etc. She now directly manages a fulltime undergraduate program in Public Relations, and an International Master program in Media Management, which is a joint program between the University of Social Communication and Humanities with the University of Stirling (UK). These courses bring together the communications students and directors of many large enterprises in Vietnam. She is also author of her book "Public Relations – Theory and Practice" (2014) published in Vietnamese language, considered as the core textbook for those who attend the public relations undergraduate curriculums, and is the author of dozens of scientific papers published in journals at home and abroad, or conference proceedings. She can be contacted via e-mail: huyenanh02@yahoo.com, ntthuyen@ussh.edu.vn, or Facebook: Nguyễn Thanh Huyền, or Viber number: 84.(0)91.995.0698.

Dean Kruckeberg (PhD) APR, Fellow PRSA, is a professor in the Department of Communication Studies at the University of North Carolina at Charlotte. He was Executive Director of the Center for Global Public Relations in that department from 2008 to 2013. From 1983 through 2008, Dr Kruckeberg was a public relations professor in the Department of Communication Studies at the University of Northern Iowa, serving most of those years as coordinator of the Public Relations Degree Program or of the Mass Communication Division. He is co-author of the book, *Public Relations and Community: A Reconstructed Theory*, which won the first annual PRIDE Award from the National Communication Association Public Relations Division, and he is the author and co-author of book chapters, articles, and papers dealing with international public relations and its ethics. Dr Kruckeberg is co-author of *This Is PR: The Realities of Public Relations*, which has a global English edition and translation editions in several languages worldwide. In 2016, he was presented the NCA Public Relations Division Lifetime Achievement Award for Contributions in Public Relations Education. Dr Kruckeberg was recipient of the 2013 Atlas Award for Lifetime Achievement in International Public Relations, was the 1995 national "Outstanding Educator" of the Public Relations Society of America, and was awarded the Jackson Jackson & Wagner Behavioral Research Prize in 2006. He was the 1997 recipient of the Pathfinder Award presented by the Institute for Public Relations. From 1997 to 2012, Dr Kruckeberg was Co-Chair of the Commission on Public Relations Education.

Kylie Message is an Associate Professor and Senior Fellow in the Humanities Research Centre at the Australian National University. She is the author of books including *The Disobedient Museum: Writing at the Edge* (Routledge 2018), *Museums and Racism* (Routledge 2018), and *Museums and Social Activism: Engaged Protest* (Routledge 2014). She is series editor of Routledge's new *Museums in Focus* book series.

Michaela O'Brien is a principal lecturer at the University of Westminster and co-leader of the pioneering MA in Media, Campaigning and Social

Change, which she co-founded in 2014. Michaela previously worked in consultancy and strategic communications roles for nonprofits including Business in the Community, Gingerbread, Amnesty International, War on Want, Carers UK, British Library and the Refugee Council. Her research interests include power and the history of campaign communications.

Emily Robertson is a Lecturer in Communication in the Faculty of Art and Design, University of Canberra. Her work focuses upon the relationship between propaganda, ideology and morality. She has also published work on the history of public relations in Australia and is currently examining the impact of digital technology upon propaganda dissemination and reception. Upcoming publications include a chapter about atrocity propaganda in Great Britain and Australia during the Great War for *The Sage Handbook of Propaganda*.

Erkan Saka (PhD) is an Associate Professor of Media and Journalism Studies at the School of Communication at Istanbul's Bilgi University. He teaches on Digital Journalism, New Media Cultures, and Cyber-Anthropology. He is currently the Director of MA Program, Public Relations, and Corporate Communications. He earned his BA and MA degrees at the Sociology Department of Boğaziçi University, Istanbul. He received his PhD at the Anthropology Department of Rice University (Houston, USA). He has been a political blogger (Erkan's Field Diary, since June 2004). He is a co-coordinator of a Citizen Journalism Training Programs at Bilgi Eğitim, and he coordinated and presented a TV show, SosyalKafa, on social media cultures. His recent and current research topics include online information fact-checking and verification issues, digital web archiving and internet histories, ethnography of cryptocurrency circles in Turkey.

Katharine Sarikakis (PhD) is Professor of Communication Science with specialization in Media Governance, Media Organisation and Media Industries at the Department of Communication, University of Vienna (Vice-Director of the Doctoral Programmes of the Faculty of Social Sciences in 2011–2016). She leads the Media Governance and Industries Research Lab, which aims to research and analyze issues, contexts, actors and impacts of media and cultural governance and their under-explored interconnections to citizenship, autonomy and control as they are articulated in the shapes of media landscapes and the relation of citizens-at-large to dimensions of interlocution. She is the founding and twice elected Chair of the Communication Law and Policy Section of the European Communication Research and Education Association. She is an elected Jean Monnet Chair of European Media Governance and Integration. She is currently an elected member to the ECREA Executive Board. Katharine is also an elected Member of the International Council of IAMCR. She is the Co-Editor of the International Journal of Media and Cultural Politics.

Anıl Sayan (MA) is currently a research assistant at the public relations program at the School of Communication at Istanbul Bilgi University and a PhD Student at the Faculty of Communication, Istanbul University. His research interests include critical public relations, sociology of leisure and new media cultures in social sciences. His most recent research has been published by IGI Global Publications.

Thomas Stoeckle (@thomasstoeckle1 on Twitter) is an independent consultant and researcher in the areas of media intelligence and public communication. Previously he led strategic business development at LexisNexis Business Insight Solutions (BIS). Prior to joining LexisNexis, he was Group Director and Global Analytics Lead at W2O Group, and Managing Director at Report International (now CARMA). Originally from Germany, Thomas has been living and working in London since 2000, and enjoys traveling and learning about the world, both for business, and pleasure. Forever a digital Neanderthal among digital natives, he is keenly aware that adequate solutions to business communication problems demand fluency in the three languages of humans, machines, and business. Thomas hosts the SmallDataForum podcast, together with Neville Hobson and Sam Knowles. He is co-chair of the Institute for Public Relations Measurement Commission, editorial advisory board member of the Public Relations Journal, and a jury member of the Digital Communication Awards, hosted by Quadriga University Berlin.

Photini Vrikki (PhD) is a Research Fellow in Digital Humanities at Brunel University London. Her current research traces the digital representations of contemporary social media infused movements, with a focus on radical and anti-racism actions. Photini completed her PhD in Digital Culture and Society at King's College London in 2017, where she focused on the storytelling affordances of social media for social movements. Her research interests span from the politics of data and data storytelling to the identity politics, social movements, and solidarities forming in social media networks and digital environments such as VR and podcasts.

Marina Vujnovic (PhD) is an Associate Professor of Journalism in the Department of Communication at Monmouth University. Native of Croatia, Dr Marina Vujnovic, came to United States in 2003 to pursue her graduate education in journalism and mass communication. Before coming to United States she worked as a journalist before becoming a research assistant at the University of Zagreb. She also worked as a PR practitioner for Cyprian based PR agency Action Global Communications. She received her PhD at the University of Iowa in 2008. She is an author of *Forging the Bubikopf Nation: Journalism, Gender and Modernity in Interwar*

Yugoslavia, co-author of *Participatory Journalism: Guarding Open Gates at Online Newspapers*, and co-editor of *Globalizing Cultures: Theories, Paradigms, Actions*. Her research interest focuses on international communication and global flow of information, journalism studies; explorations of the historical, political-economic and cultural impact on media, class, gender, and ethnicity.

C. Kay Weaver (PhD) is a Professor and Dean of the School of Graduate Research at the University of Waikato in New Zealand. She has published many journal articles and book chapters advocating critical approaches to the examination of public relations and strategic communication theory and practice. She also researches and writes about gender, new technologies, and representations of violence. She is co-editor of *Public Relations in Global Contexts* (2011) and *Critical Readings: Violence and the Media* (2006), and is co-author of *Violence and the Media* (2003), *Women Viewing Violence* (1992) and *Cameras in the Commons* (1990). Kay has taught across the fields of public relations, communication, media, culture, and film in the UK and New Zealand.

Rima Wilkes (PhD) is Professor of Sociology at the University of British Columbia. She is also the current President of the Canadian Sociological Association (2017–2018) and the past editor of the Canadian Review of Sociology (2013–2015). Her research focuses on collective action, trust and race, and Indigenous politics. She currently holds a Social Science and Humanities Research Council of Canada grant to study ethnicity and trust and is part of an international team studying trust funded by the Swedish Tercientenary Foundation. This work has recently been published in Social Science Research, Social Forces and the Canadian Review of Sociology.

Protest public relations

Communicating dissent and activism – an introduction

Ana Adi

The first two decades of the twenty-first century were marked in quick succession by major political and social events, many of which have been attributed to the increased access to and rising popularity of digital and social media. From 2010 to 2012 alone there were "the Arab Spring, anti-austerity protests in Greece and Spain, student protests in Chile, Canada and the UK, and the rise (and fall) of Wikileaks, not to mention the global Occupy Movement" (Hensby, 2014). More recently, access to digital media and the absence of gatekeepers has been credited with the rise of both alternative right and left discourses and so called anti-establishment candidates in Europe, the USA or Japan, but also with the increased support and visibility to what otherwise would have been local and perhaps unheard causes: the women's march in Washington following President Trump's inauguration and the Dakota pipeline sacred land protests in the USA, or the recent #rezist anti-corruption and anti-establishment protests in Romania. Similarly, digital media is also seen as having played a major role in spreading support for advocacy and activist group sponsored causes, #bucketchallenge, #bringbackourgirls, or #heforshe being among them.

Regardless of their nature – advocacy, activist, protest or dissent – and beyond their effective use of technology and social media to connect and aggregate support, these major events have all been the result of excellent communication and public relations.

However, it is only recently that any of these actions and events would have been considered public relations in the traditional sense, the practice in these terms being something afforded only by corporations and organizations with big budgets. In this context, public relations sits in a position of power and influence (of mass-media and of the masses); however, it faces numerous challenges: from defining itself and hence justifying and legitimizing its activity to the wider aspirations of having an (equal) seat on the board (Demetrious, 2013). To achieve the status it deserves, Grunig in his lifetime work and his supporters suggest that PR should strive for symmetry, and mutual and equal dialogue between the organization and its stakeholders.

Speaking of symmetry and dialogue critics argue that, at times, they are impossible to achieve as stakeholders might have either conflicting demands or their positions are unethical from the outset (Cancel et al., 1999; Kent & Taylor, 2002). Moreover, the wider criticism of public relations as the "hired by big money function" is that it serves to stifle voices that are essential to democracy and active citizenship through their efforts to "mold people" into desired patterns of consumption or behavior (Achbar & Abbott, 2003 in Demetrious, 2013, p. 9).

Undesired and disruptive as it may be, the involvement of activists (and by extension of all the other groups mentioned) through pressure tactics, and redirecting and remobilizing resources has come to be praised by traditionalists for their help improving the functioning of organizations and their influence of management processes (Grunig & Grunig, 1997).

Instead of seeing the relationship between activism (activists/civil society) and organization permanently in this conflictual dichotomy, critical scholars suggest instead that both are recognized as equal. By doing so, Coombs and Holladay (2012b) quite optimistically indicate that the attention given to alternative perspectives, "offers hope that once marginalized pluralistic approaches, especially critical public relations, may disrupt the colonization of the orthodoxy and infiltrate mainstream public" (p. 880). Moreover, by considering that all these actors (be they organizational or activist) are doing "propaganda" as Moloney (2006) suggests, that is one sided, selective and manipulative communication that is nevertheless inevitable because it is rooted "in the pluralist, self-advantaging promotional culture associated with liberal democracy" (p. 168), what the critical scholars are doing is to invite investigation of "other forms of organizational communication occurring (...) that are largely unnamed, undescribed and unacknowledged" (Demetrious, 2013, p. 5) yet are "bold, inventive and effective" (Demetrious, 2013, p. 2).

This is very widely the aim of this book.

Envisaged as an edited collection containing contributions from established and emerging scholars around the world, and positing itself along the critical scholarship of public relations, this book invites a discussion and debate about these yet unnamed, undescribed and unacknowledged forms of communication. The international pool of contributors engaged in this discussion extends beyond public relations and into journalism, sociology and social movements. This brings diversity both into the topics and perspectives covered, the methodologies used and the questions raised.

Public relations has been associated with activism before, in its sense of "collective challenges <brought forward (n.ed)> by people with common purposes and solidarity in sustained interaction with elites, opponents and authorities" (Tarrow, 1994 cited in Kim & Sriramesh, 2009, p. 86). Perhaps one of the first to make the association was Cutlip, who wrote about the "unseen power" of PR (1994) arguing that PR has operated on the premise that the most effective PR is invisible PR. This view seems to be shared by Miller and Dinan's (2008) less flattering account of PR's journey to its position of power in *A Century of Spin*.

The scholars agree that historically PR existed before its corporate "service" and perhaps started (at least in the USA) with progressive reform movements such as the Muckrakers (albeit unknowingly) (Coombs & Holladay, 2012b), and continued with social movements such as feminism, environmentalism, consumer and gay rights. All these movements used the attention they created to achieve their goals and change policy to their advantage (Moloney, 2000). Demetrious (2013) uses a similar argument in her work about environmental groups and their actions in Australia over the 1993–2003 period.

Bennett (2003), on the other hand, is more concerned with the changing outlook of global activism under the direct influence of digital media, while Reber and Kim (2006) and Adi (2015) have looked at how activists use their websites for PR purposes. Cottle and Lester (2011) do the same, their contributors giving multiple examples of the relationship and interplay between media (traditional and new) and transnational protest movements. Their book is perhaps an echo of Della Porta and Tarrow's (2005) anthology dedicated to transnational protest and global activism. The latter do touch on communication practices of activist groups; however, overall, the book is more focused on the social movements and contentious politics aspect of protest and their progression to a global stage through diffusion, domestication and externalization.

Activism is also treated as a practice for PR professionals working inside corporate bodies. Advanced initially by Berger and Reber (2005) and then later elaborated upon by Holtzhausen (2007, 2013), this professional stance promotes the idea that the PR person should act as the conscience of the organization, urging management to behave ethically. In doing so, the authors argue, the PR practitioners can carry out internal resistance.

There are other scholars writing about protest, activism and public relations: Dozier and Lauzen (2000), Karlberg (1996), Kim and Sriramesh (2009), Smith and Ferguson (2001), Taylor, Kent and White (2001) and many others.

However, in speaking about activism and protest, the scholars generally use the terms interchangeably. Equally, the definitions advanced for activism and social movements come from political sciences or sociology (see Kim & Sriramesh, 2009 or Demetrious, 2013). Although there is great merit in using definitions that have already been accepted, these definitions make the clarification of how activist communication applies strategy and tactics difficult. In this sense, this book suggests that more attention should be given to the different conceptualization of activist, protest and dissent PR advanced by Adi and Moloney (2012).

Dissent PR is about bringing attention to new thinking and new behaviors in areas of national life. It promotes ideas for change and for retention in the political economy and civil society. It is PR promoting the ideas of public intellectuals, academics, experts, people of faith found in both progressive and conservative philosophical circles. It is PR techniques designed to bring attention to these thinkers and their arguments in order to change the policy climate, the political weather. Protest PR, on the other hand, is a consequence of the dissent PR. It is also persuasive communication but not principally about ideas, behaviors and policies. Instead, it persuades via occupations, demonstrations, strikes, public speaking and other forms of non-violent and violent protest in order to implement those ideas, behaviors and policies into law, regulation and other forms of executive action.

(Adi & Moloney, 2012, pp. 103–104)

So this book not only aims to uncover unnamed, undescribed and unacknowledged forms of communication, it also challenges contributors to engage with the definitions of protest, dissent and activist public relations, asking how they would define them and whether there is a need for them in the PR lexicon. This is addressed in three ways: engagement with theoretical paradigms, exploration of history and analysis of protests, cases, situations and movements from this perspective.

The chapters of this book

In Chapter 1, C. Kay Weaver explores how different theoretical paradigms speak of activism in relation to public relations. Her chapter starts with the definitions of activism as "the other" for public relations continuing her discussion with perspectives about public relations as activism, activism as public relations only to finish with an overview of public relations as the "other" for activism. She covers thus a rich theoretical terrain encompassing socio-cultural, critical, Marxist and postcolonial perspectives, among others. Not only does her chapter question in whose interest it is that activism and public relations would be conflated, but it also brings attention to how highly value-laden the attempt to define public relations and activism is:

how we define public relations and activism, and the relationships between the two, is determined by our own world views, theoretical and political positions and beliefs, and allegiances.

(p. 24)

In Chapter 2, Emily Robertson and Robert Crawford take us back in time, to the Australia of the First World War and the conscription debate of 1916. In following both the pro-conscription and anti-conscription campaigns, the two bring attention to the similarity of tactics and tools used by both campaigns, as well the similarity in intended outcomes: obtain public support. Arguably, both campaigns were a necessary part of the democratic process, which is why Robertson and Crawford argue recognizing activism as an essential part of PR history is vital to reshaping how public relations is understood.

In Chapter 3, Michaela O'Brien revisits some of the theoretical arguments surrounding protest and public relations with a greater focus on the historical development of protest public relations. In a sense, O'Brien asks the same questions as Weaver does about the relationship and role of public relations in society, only she does it from a historical perspective. In this sense she focuses on the type of actors driving communicative activities and the social issues they are communicating – from class-based debates (gender, race, labor) to universalist topics (peace, environment) – as well as the media context facilitating these debates. She takes a closer look at the suffragettes and their innovative tactics: coordinated branding, stunts and photo opportunities, celebrity endorsements to name a few. These, as we'll see in other chapters in this book, are tactics that continue to bring success to current protests and activist campaigns.

In Chapter 4, A. Banu Bıçakçı and Pelin Hurmeric focus on the tactics employed in Turkey during the second-wave feminism. In particular, they demonstrate how the activists' use of tactics, such as consciousness raising groups, demonstrations, festivals, petitions, magazines, periodicals and books influenced both policy and cultural changes. Bıçakçı and Hurmeric qualify many of the second-wave feminists' activities as dissent PR, subscribing thus to Moloney's (2012) definition of promoting ideas for change in the political economy and civil society.

Feminism is also in focus in Chapter 5. Here, Gudkova and Sarikakis compare two contemporary feminist groups, Femen from Ukraine and Pussy Riot from Russia. Like Bıçakçı and Hurmeric in Chapter 4, the authors reference the suffragettes and their communicative legacy. They also consider Femen's and Pussy Riot's communications to be part of dissent public relations. While both groups share similar views and objectives, and employ similar tactics of shock and provocation, their implementation is completely different. While the authors here too share support for the critical PR perspective advocating for the benefit of including activist voices into the history of public relations, what it is more valuable here and perhaps less developed as an argument are their references to dissent and power, and the fact that stunt-like activities are a necessary evil when one wants to draw attention to a non-mainstream cause.

Chapter 6 also focuses on dissent, this time on a contemporary case featuring the Haitian and Dominican diasporas in the US opposing a Dominican naturalization law. In retracing the development of the case, De Moya highlights how the diasporas kept international media attention on this issue, despite the Dominican government's efforts to put it to rest.

To record its evolution, the chapter presents the framing of the issue by both government and diaspora and investigates the media advocacy outcomes concluding:

> If the efforts of the Diaspora and the Dominican authorities is seen as a contest to gain and shape media coverage (as is the goal of mediated diplomacy and media advocacy), then the Diaspora was the one victorious.
>
> (p. 120)

Chapter 7 presents a case that would fit Moloney's (2012) description of activist PR as it features both spontaneous activities (protests) as well as long-term, planned ones (dissent) addressing multiple stakeholders. In retracing the moving and painful story of Ayotzinapa's 43 disappeared students (Mexico), Luis Rubén Díaz-Cepeda, Ernesto Castañeda and Kara Andrade also focus on the framing "battle" between authorities and the students. Their rendition of the students' networking and organization, including access to, training of and use of digital media to mobilize (themselves and others) is worthy to note here and so is their recoding of the way in which various campaigns supported one another online and offline (from hashtag campaigns to staged events). Yet, the authors argue:

> regardless the efficient use of communication technology and their savvy PR tactics (…) the political class overpowered the protests and diminished the movement.
>
> (p. 143)

Chapter 8 analyzes how activist groups utilized public relations strategies and tactics during Gezi Demonstrations from 2013. The Gezi Park protesters used tactics that other activist groups have successfully deployed: performances, plays and collective acts. However, the chapter by Barika Göncü, Erkan Saka and Anıl Sayan argues that the protest's relative success was due to their embracing of non-violent, collective actions, their use of humor and their efforts toward dialogue. Like the other movements and groups covered in previous chapters, the Gezi protesters were also media savvy to the point that in the absence of coverage they used a livestreaming channel.

Chapter 9 shifts focus from the "battle" between activists and governments to the internal struggle of a social movement. In examining the activities of the Occupy Archives Working Group, "which was one of more than a hundred working groups that existed within and contributed to the 2011 Occupy Wall Street movement that occurred in New York's Zuccotti Park" (p. 170), Kylie Message captures the conflict and debate faced by activists when faced with the choice of controlling their image, and recording and in this case archiving their "footprints." These debates are indicative of the problematic relationship between public relations and activism, and the outright refusal of the former to identify with the latter despite their use of similar tools.

Chapter 10 displays a similar broken relationship between activists, PR and their tools. In using the Romanian #rezist protests of 2017, Camelia Crişan seeks to identify what motivates activists and what are the main differences, in the activists'/protesters' view, between an activist and a PR practitioner? While driven by intrinsic motivations (personal development, patriotism), but mostly motivations connected to establishing fair power relations, Crişan's interviewees, all self-described activists and participants to the #rezist protests, contend that

> the values, behaviors and content of public relations for companies and social causes are different, i.e., tactics needed to promote a product or a brand are not necessarily useful to promote a cause. Also, personal emotions are stronger when promoting a cause than when promoting a product.
>
> (p. 201)

Chapter 11 reinforces the idea that activists use PR tools to achieve their goals. In their analysis of Vietnam's first and successful Facebook driven protest, Nguyen Thi Thanh Huyen and Nguyen Hoang Anh, investigate both the motivations of the individuals setting up Facebook pages and groups related to the project, and their strategy. They also analyze the groups and pages users' comments and discussions to identify key themes. In Vietnam's case, poor preparation on the authorities' side, coupled with the ubiquitous presence of Facebook as a social network in Vietnam, are credited with the protests' success. Similar to Crişan's activists, the individuals interviewed in Huyen and Anh's chapter display strong intrinsic motivations. However, unlike Crişan's activists, the Vietnamese activists are at times surprised, if not overwhelmed, by their success. Although not the central focus of this book, the effects and influence of social media on turning "outspoken" individuals into activists is something that should perhaps be looked into more carefully in the future.

Chapter 12 returns to Occupy, this time focusing on the movement's use of storytelling on Twitter. Photini Vrikki's chapter explores these public relations paths, both theoretically and empirically. Vrikki's

> final section analyses the four micro-narratives that formed the big narrative of the eviction: 1. Honoring the First Amendment, 2. Use of force, 3. Communication failure of authorities, and 4. Arrests. By telling the story of the eviction through the micro-narratives presented on Twitter this chapter analyses the ways in which OWS' eviction day can be seen as a public relations model for the ways in which

contemporary social movements can spread information and gather support through Twitter.

(p. 223)

Chapter 13 addresses environmental activism. In using social movement framing perspective (SMFP) to analyze the case of Clayoquot Sound in British Columbia, Canada, Adam Howe and Rima Wilkes provide PR scholars with a new tool to explicate framing processes.

The final two chapters of the book take readers into new directions both in public relations research and into practice.

Marina Vujnovic's and Dean Kruckeberg's chapter brings again into focus the definitions of protest, dissent and activist PR considering the specificities of the current media and digital environment communicators operate in. In drawing connections between journalism as activism and PR as activism – because it has been increasingly difficult to discern which is which in the new media environment – the chapter raises further valuable questions that scholars and practitioners could ponder on.

Finally, Thomas Stoeckle's concluding chapter (Chapter 15) not only considers the current digital environment PR operates in, which he calls the attention economy, but it also considers future challenges. In doing so, he proposes an activist reformation of PR which

> is one that considers the yin and yang of the liberation and suppression of dissenting voices through social media; it is one that considers protest and counter-protest movements from the perspective of their social context; it looks at concepts of PR as evolving from modernist, excellent models, to critical, postmodern positions, and then toward a metamodern idea, conceding that positions have become blurred as the present media ecosystem allows and enables more volatility and fluid alignments.
>
> (p. 279)

Stoeckle proposes we move on from current perspectives to metamodernist ones that remove the barriers between activists and PR practitioners, as they are united by common tools and practices: a good conclusion and invitation to think beyond the current state of the profession.

Defining protest, dissent, and activist PR

The contributors to this book have been invited to consider questions about protest, dissent and activist public relations: their definition, their description and their application. Despite the international background and the varied academic background, most contributors adopt Moloney's (2012) and Moloney and McKie's (2016) definitions of protest. In this sense, there is agreement that activist PR includes protest and dissent, where the first one is punctual, emotional and the second more strategic and long term. The differentiation between the two continues with the tactics they would be more prone to use, with die-ins, sit-ins, occupations, strikes, marches, rallies more likely to be attributed to protest PR, and discussions, fairs, books, debates to dissent PR.

Dissent, however, in the perception of this book's contributors is more closely related to advocacy, as it is more often associated to political and policy opposition. The adversarial relationship between activists and governments (in this case, their communication departments who would be likely to be involved in monitoring and responding to the issues raised) continues to be perpetuated in this book, not by desire or design, but rather as an outcome of the analyses provided: either due to the framing and counter-framing of issues, or due to the activists' own perceptions of PR.

The cases presented in this book are generally successful with each group and movement managing to obtain the change desired. Yet, it is the cases highlighting the weaknesses and shortcomings of the cases that strengthen this book's invitation to engage more with critical, non-corporate, non-mainstream stories. Occupy's failure to self-archive and concerns about their legacy and history reflects yet again the struggles that I have identified when comparing smaller occupations (Adi & Moloney, 2012), or when analyzing the web presence of bigger groups (Adi, 2015). Ayotzinapa's political overpowering by the political elites (Chapter 7), comes only to support Weaver's (Chapter 1) questions about who benefits from PR, and how does PR benefit others. It also highlights the fact that the concept of power cannot be ignored when embarking on the exploration of such cases.

Finally, the contributors of this book show that media (both mass-media and digital) continues to be an important element in activist (including dissent and protest) communication. Both mass-media and digital media coverage are desirable for their potential to amplify messages and frames, yet digital media provides control (see, in particular, the effort to either set up their own streaming, or TV channels – Chapters 4 and 10). Unlike governments, organizations and institutions, activist groups and social movements are more likely to use disruptive tactics (including shock – see Chapters 2 to 7) to attract media attention, the primary purpose being to attract attention, and then inform and persuade. In this sense, Gudkova and Sarikakis (Chapter 5) are right in indicating that protest groups and activists are social movements and would thus be more likely to use one-way asymmetrical communication (Grunig & Hunt, 1984).

Conclusion

This book has challenged its contributors (coming from a variety of fields including journalism and sociology) to engage with the definitions of protest, dissent and activist public relations, asking how they would define them and whether there is a need for them in the PR lexicon. Not only did they do that, but they brought forward a variety of examples, from world renowned to locally powerful. In doing so, they provided their own arguments into what they perceive the benefit of investigating persuasive communication from a critical perspective to be: from enriching history to enlarging horizons and to, what I might add, improving the profession and its perception.

In the end, both professional communicators and activists use similar tools: from stakeholder analysis to media outreach (so media relations and public information), yet each continues to be dismissive of the other. Acknowledging their coexistence and highlighting their commonalities more might help improve the practice and its perceptions overall (Adi & Stoeckle, 2018).

References

Adi, A. (2015). Occupy PR: an analysis of online media communications of Occupy Wall Street and Occupy London. *Public Relations Review*, 41(4), 508–514.

Adi, A. & Moloney, K. (2012). The importance of scale in Occupy movement protests: a case study of a local Occupy protest as a tool of communication through Public Relations and Social Media. *Revista Internacional de Relaciones Publicas*, 4(II), 97–122.

Adi, A. & Stoeckle, T. (2018). Fit for the 21st and digital century: PR should abandon its managerial dreams and focus more on achieving its promises. *PRConversations*. Retrieved on May 30, 2018 from www.prconversations.com/pr-fit-for-the-21st-and-digital-century/.

Bennett, W. (2003). Communicating global activism. *Information, Communication & Society*, 6(2), 143–168.

Berger, B. & Reber, B. (2005). *Gaining influence in public relations: the role of resistance in practice*, Mahwah, NJ: Lawrence Erlbaum Associates.

Cancel, A. E., Mitrook, M. A., & Cameron, G. (1999). Testing the contingency theory of accommodation in public relations. *Public Relations Review*, 25(2): 171–197.

Coombs, W. T. & Holladay, S. J. (2012a). Privileging an activist vs. a corporate view of public relations history in the U.S. *Public Relations Review*, 38: 347–353.

Coombs, W. T. & Holladay, S. J. (2012b). Fringe public relations: how activism moves critical PR towards the mainstream. *Public Relations Review*, 38(5), 880–887.

Cottle, S. R. & Lester, E. A. (2011). *Transnational protests and the media*. New York: Peter Lang.

Cutlip, S. (1994). *The unseen power: public relations: a history*. New York: Routledge.

Della Porta, D. & Tarrow, S. G. (2005). *Transnational protest and global activism*. Lanham, MD: Rowman & Littlefield.

Demetrious, K. (2013). *Public relations, activism, and social change: speaking up*. New York: Routledge.

Dozier, D. & Lauzen, M. (2000). Liberating the intellectual domain from the practice: public relations activism, and the role of the scholar. *Journal of Public Relations Research*, 12, 3–22.

Grunig, J. E. & Grunig, L. A. (1997). *Review of a program of research on activism: incidence in four countries, activist publics, strategies of activist groups, and organizational responses to activism.* Paper presented to the Fourth Public relations Research Symposium, Managing Environmental Issues, Lake Bled, Slovenia.

Grunig, J. E. & Hunt, T. (1984). *Managing public relations*. Belmont, CA: Wadsworth.

Hensby, A. (2014). Book review: Protest Inc.: the corporatization of activism edited by Peter Dauvergne and Genevieve LeBaron. Available from: http://blogs.lse.ac.uk/lsereviewofbooks/2014/05/17/protest-inc-the-corporatization-of-activism/, Accessed March 14, 2017.

Holtzhausen, D. R. (2007). Activism. In E. L. Toth (Ed.), *The future of excellence in public relations and communication management* (357–379). Mahwah, NJ: Lawrence Erlbaum Associates.

Holtzhausen, D. R. (2013). *Public relations as activism: postmodern approaches to theory & practice*. New York: Routledge.

Karlberg, M. (1996). Remembering the publics in public relations research: from theoretical to operational symmetry. *Journal of Public Relations Research*, 8, 263–278.

Kent, M. L. & Taylor, M. (2002). Toward a dialogic theory of public relations. *Public Relations Review*, 28: 21–37.

Kim, J.-N. & Sriramesh, K. (2009). Activism and public relations. In K. Sriramesh & D. Vercic (Eds.), *The global public relations handbook, revised and expanded edition: theory, research and practice*. New York: Routledge.

Miller, D. & Dinan, W. (2008). *A century of spin: how public relations became the cutting edge of corporate power*. London: Pluto Press.

Moloney, K. (2000). *Rethinking public relations*. London: Routledge.

Moloney, K. (2006). *Rethinking public relations: PR propaganda and democracy*, 2nd ed. London: Routledge.

Moloney, K. (2012). What is "dissent PR" and its related term "protest PR"? Are they terms that usefully describe some public relations work? Media School seminar on Protest PR, Bournemouth University, June 19, 2012.

Moloney, K. & McKie, D. (2016). Radical turns in PR theorisation. In J. L'Etang, D. McKie, N. Snow, & J. Xifra (Eds.), *Routledge handbook of critical public relations* (150–161). London and New York: Routledge.

Reber, B. H. & Kim, J. K. (2006). How activist groups use websites in media relations: evaluating online press rooms. *Journal of Public Relations Research*, 18, 313–334.

Smith, M. E. & Ferguson, D. P. (2001). Activism. In R. L. Heath (Ed.), *Handbook of public relations* (291–300). Thousand Oaks, CA: Sage.

Taylor, M., Kent, M. L., & White, W. J. (2001). How activist organizations are using the Internet to build relationships. *Public Relations Review*, 27, 263–284.

1 The slow conflation of public relations and activism

Understanding trajectories in public relations theorising

C. Kay Weaver

Activism has become a popular focus in public relations research and theorising, with an increasing number of public relations scholars writing about activism, civil society protest, and culture jamming activities as public relations, or forms of public relations (e.g., Adi, 2015; Coombs & Holladay, 2012a, 2012b; Curtin, 2016; Curtin, Gaither & Ciszeck, 2016; Heath & Waymer, 2009; Sommerfeldt, Kent & Taylor, 2012; Weaver, 2010, 2014). Others have assessed how organisations respond to activism (Demetrious, 2013; Stokes & Rubin, 2010; Veil et al., 2015; Wolf 2013; Zoller & Tener, 2010). Others still argue that public relations practitioners do, or should, perform the role of activists in organisations (Berger, 2005; Holtzhausen, 2007, 2012).

There is, unquestionably, a blurring of strategies and tactics across the arenas of activism and organisational-interest based public relations. Activists and activist organisations can be extremely adept at developing complex media strategies, public education and government lobbying campaigns, and many have adopted the organisational structures and aims of corporate entities (Dauvergne & LeBaron, 2014). Equally, corporations have drawn on guerrilla communication tactics of the types associated with protest and activism to emotionally engage audiences and publics (Bogost, 2016). Yet there are a variety of differing perspectives on activism in the public relations literature, some which position activism and public relations as quite different and even diametrically opposed in their aims, objectives, and communicative approaches, and others which conflate the two and claim they have a mutual history. How can we understand and make sense of these sometimes very different and even opposing perspectives on the relationship between public relations and activism?

This chapter examines the evolution of the theoretical conceptualising of activism in public relations scholarship and the socio-political and theoretical underpinnings of that work. It focuses on how activism and public relations are variously defined in these discussions, and why scholars might be at pains to position public relations and activism in opposition to each other, or to suggest that they are the same, but differently dressed activity. An important precursor in this undertaking is to consider how public relations and activism can be variously defined.

Defining public relations and activism

How the relationship between public relations and activism has been represented and theorised in scholarly literature is greatly dependent on, and influenced by, how each is defined. There is no commonly agreed definition of public relations; what it is and does differs according to the world view (Grunig & White, 1992) of who is defining it, for what purposes, and where. Grunig and Hunt's (1984) simple definition of public relations as the "management of communication between an organization and its publics" (p. 6) has maintained significant currency among normative and US-based researchers. In tertiary educational contexts Cutlip, Center and Broom's (2000) text-book definition of public relations as "the management function that establishes and maintains mutually beneficial relationships between an organization and the publics on whom its success or failure depends" (p. 6), has held considerable sway. Their definition, like Grunig and Hunt's, privileges an idealist view of public relations as an ethical and reciprocal, two-way relational process. It also, as Hutton (1999) has pointed out, is a definition that excludes consideration of "individuals or groups of people who are not formally organized" (p. 202) as public relations practitioners and audiences. Hutton consequently proposed that public relations be much more broadly defined as "managing strategic relationships" (p. 208). More recently Edwards (2012) proposed an even broader definition – one that does not presuppose that public relations work is always embedded in organisational contexts. She positions public relations as:

> the flow of purposive communication produced on behalf of individuals, formally constituted and informally constituted groups, through their continuous trans-actions with other social entities. It has social, cultural, political and economic effects and local, national and global levels.
>
> (p. 21)

It is generally the broader definitions of public relations of the types offered by Hutton and Edwards, as is discussed further below, which have opened the door for consideration of activism as a form, genre, or type of public relations.

As there are many definitions of public relations, so there are of activism, a practice embraced by a vast array of different groups, organisations, peoples and individuals, for an equally vast array of causes across the gamut of political and social-cultural spectra, and including an abundance of communicative methods. Defining activism requires acknowledging its place within social movements. Cammaerts (2015) explains that:

> A social movement is a social process through which collective actors articulate their interests, voice grievances and critiques, and proposed solutions to identified problems by engaging in a variety of collective actions.
>
> (p. 1027)

Thus, activism comprises intentional *actions* conducted in an effort to bring about social change. Yet, as Ganesh and Zoller (2012) usefully explain:

> definitions of activism vary, and different bodies of knowledge even appear to diverge in their collective emphasis on the importance of defining activism, which underscores the political functions of definitions in constituting key knowledge interests.... Across perspectives and disciplines, however, one finds an emphasis, on contestation as a core aspect of activist communication, and key concepts such as advocacy, conflict and transgression do appear to be central to activism.
>
> (p. 69)

Staples (2016) provides a good example of this in stating that:

> Social Action brings people together to convince, pressure, or coerce external decision makers to meet collective goals either to act in a specified manner or to modify or stop certain activities.
>
> (p. 11)

Such activism can be found from the grassroots level, where activists campaign for local change, to transnational levels involving "coordinated international campaigns on the part of networks of activists against international actors, other states, or international institutions" (Della Porta & Tarrow, 2005, p. 7).

Already apparent in this sketch of some definitions, is that normative characterisations of public relations are likely to privilege communicative relationship building. In contrast, definitions of activism emphasise activity taken against, or in conflict with, prevailing social structures, organisations, policies, and/or relations. Indeed, it was in light of these *apparent* differences in approach to the management of issues, that the discussion of activism entered the emerging discipline of public relations in the 1980s and 1990s.

Pluralism, public relations and activism and as "the other"

Early writing about activism in the public relations literature identified a relationship of cause and effect between the two activities. James Grunig (1989), in an effort to develop a predictive theory to "explain membership and participation in activist groups" (p. 7) asserted: "Activist groups produce conflict between organizations and their environments, and it is the presence of conflict that creates the need for public relations" (p. 4). In this work Grunig exhibits acute awareness of the idealism of laissez-faire market capitalist liberal-pluralism. This posits power as dispersed in a democracy and different groups as capable of gaining social representation and influence. Grunig's work also acknowledges Marxist arguments which, to the contrary, assert that elite privileged groups maintain their grip on financial and social power and actively work to prevent others from successfully challenging that power. Attempting to carve a pathway between these two positions, Grunig, argued that the notion of "issue-group liberalism" best reflected how the American political landscape was operating, with activist-issue groups across the political left and right variously attempting to pressurise corporations and governments to support their interests and causes. According to Grunig, interest activist groups play a crucial role "in limiting organisational autonomy" (1989, p. 22), and forcing organisations to engage in public relations work. Indeed, the voices of diverse special interest groups are welcomed into democratic public debate where it is argued that, in the marketplace of ideas, the public will evaluate competing messages and claims and come to decide which position best fits with their interests.

Larissa Grunig (1992), in an early attempt "to help public relations practitioners deal in more than an ad hoc way with the opposition their organizations often face from activist groups" (p. 504) used a variety of terms to describe these groups – from pressure groups, consumer groups, to interest groups. She defined "An activist public [a]s a group of two or more individuals who organize in order to influence another public or publics through action that may include education, compromise, persuasion, pressure tactics or force" (p. 504). Although positioning activist publics as needing to be monitored and managed, she did encourage organisations to adopt a two-way dialogic approach to negotiate a win–win compromise in relation to the concerns that activists were protesting about. How realistic such a compromise is when, as Larissa Grunig acknowledged, activists and business organisations often pursue diametrically opposed agendas (she used the example of businesses wanting to profit from coal mining and environmentalists wanting to protect the environment), is doubtful. Furthermore, the realities of public relations practice, which are "driven by competitive urges to triumph more than normative ideals" (Brown, 2015, p. vxi), do nothing to justify or encourage dialogue between an organisation and activists who seek to change that organisation's behaviour or even challenge its very existence. Yet what Larissa Grunig's (1992) argument demonstrates is how, within early excellence writings, activists were conceived of as a particular type of public – an obstacle with which organisations potentially have to contend in order to achieve their goals. Activists were positioned as limiting the autonomy and effectiveness of organisations and working to increase the legitimacy gap between public perceptions and social expectations of those organisations, sometimes to the point that their operations could be threatened with government and/or legal regulation (see also, Crable & Vibbert, 1985; Hallahan, 2001; Heath, 1997). Thus, in the context of the evolving issues management literature, "Activists appear to be constructed as problematic in public relations. They are *the other*, the implied organizational opponents" (L'Etang, 2008, p. 84, emphasis in original).

However, some scholars working within the excellence framework advocated for more inclusive consideration of activism. Dozier and Lauzen (2000) argued that researching activism in the public relations discipline provided an opportunity to explore the problem of "irreconcilable difference" given that excellence models emphasised the need to *reconcile* differences between an organisation and its publics. This was an important argument, reflective of evolving views that the relationship between public relations and activism could be considered from a wider range of perspectives, and that activism could be seen as making a positive contribution to deliberative democracies, organisational priorities, and decision making.

Public relations subjectivities: practitioners as activists

As a greater range of perspectives have been brought to bear on theorising of public relations in the twenty-first century, some scholars have argued that public relations practitioners have a role and even duty to ensure that the organisations they work for and represent behave ethically, and "do the right thing". In these terms they have positioned public relations professionals themselves as activists within organisations. This idea drew on critical social theories and involved considering the relations and structures of power that public relations practitioners are part of, participate in, and which they may be able to resist, or to which they may have to conform.

Berger (2005) advocated that public relations practitioners, and especially those who are part of the "dominant coalition", should use their managerial influence and, if necessary, unsanctioned forms of resistance, to ensure that organisations act for the greater good of society. He states that "practitioner resistance and activism may offer the best hope for professionals to do the right thing and to actualize the possibilities of a practice serving the interests and voices of the many" (p. 6). However, Berger's research with public relations professionals illustrated the very real difficulties they experienced in challenging, balancing, resisting, and even countering dominant organisational power and strategic and economic objectives. His empirical investigations demonstrated how the context of organisational power relations (power over) that a public relations employee operates in, makes it extremely difficult to step outside of their own role as representative and voice for that organisation. That is, the power of the organisation and the subjectivity this imposes on the paid public relations employee, restricts their ability to act as an agent and advocate for other interests.

Holtzhausen (2012) contests this argument, asserting from a post-modern perspective that the decentred fragmented reflexive subject – the public relations practitioner, has agency, and a responsibility to "move us toward justice in organisations" (p. 230). Previously, Holtzhausen, who has consistently made a case for conceptualising public relations practitioners as activists, had defined the public relations practitioner-activist as playing the role of "conscience in the organization" (Holtzhausen & Voto, 2002, p. 64). This role involves resisting dominate power structures and advocating for interests other than those of management – promoting "new ways of thinking and problem solving through dissensus and conflict" (p. 64).

More recently, Holtzhausen (2012) moved away from a fixed definition of the public relations practitioner as activist, and instead framed the role as (among others) to "challenge statements of absolute truth and resist becoming the tools through which truth is fixed, as in the case of managerialist discourse" (p. 235). In these terms she argues that public relations practitioners, and indeed other organisational employees, like members of social movements, have an important role to play in bearing witness and giving voice to the stories of others and "fighting for justice" (p. 239). While few other public relations scholars have consistently advocated this perspective or built on it, Holtzhausen's arguments are often cited in detail in public relations literature (see for example, Toledano, 2016). Doubts have been raised, however, about whether her theorising of a postmodern subjectivity for public relations practitioners has any grounding in reality when, as the saying goes, "he who pays the pier calls the tune" – which was Berger's (2005) conclusion. Rather than focusing on whether public relations practitioners can be considered as taking on activist roles in organisations, using a range of social-cultural perspectives other researchers have turned to assess how activists might be operating like public relations practitioners and using public relations techniques to achieve their goals (e.g., Coombs & Holladay, 2012a, 2012b; Curtin, 2016; Curtin, Gaither & Ciszeck, 2016; Heath & Waymer, 2009; Weaver, 2010, 2014).

Social-cultural perspectives: activism as public relations

As the public relations discipline has developed, it has moved away from a predominantly corporate managerial control organisational focus and increasingly acknowledged the value of critical social theories to understanding the role that public relations plays in social culture. These theories have contributed to a major epistemological shift in the public relations discipline, with public relations communication coming to be considered a dynamic, fluid, social co-creative process, rather than an organised linear stimulus response approach to managing stakeholders and their perceptions.

Interestingly, it is in the context of pluralist understandings of public relations that the last decade has seen a trend towards conflating the practices of public relations and activism. Indeed, some theorists argue that activists should be considered to be performing the same function in society as public relations practitioners. For example, Coombs and Holladay (2007) state that "Activism can be seen 'as' modern public relations.... [There is a] need for making the transition from viewing the activist 'as obstacle' to viewing the activist 'as practitioner'" (p. 53). This call to move away from corporate-centric views of what constitutes public relations in order to accommodate activism within the field is closely echoed by Heath and Waymer (2009). They argue that:

> If we think that public relations is limited to business promotion, we can ignore the promotional efforts by activists to call attention to, frame, and advocate one or more many issue positions ... we would be remiss if we ignore the promotional aspects of activism by only addressing their issue engagement.
>
> (p. 195)

A further step that Smith and Ferguson (2010) make in identifying similarities between and conflating activism and public relations is to position both as playing an important role in the public sphere, in democratic debate, and dialogue. They argue that

> the perspective that activism is a legitimate public relations practice, contributing to the marketplace of ideas essential to the development of a fully functioning society, has not been fully embraced by either scholars or practitioners.
>
> (p. 405)

Public relations scholars have increasingly advocated this liberal pluralist market position and focused their attentions on researching activism as a form of public relations. Moreover, so much has public relations scholarship embraced activism that Moloney and McKie (2016) suggest this trend "might almost earn the title of 'an activist turn' in its own right for it places activists at the core of public relations" (p. 154). Certainly, in the context of social media, which has given activists unprecedented access to audiences that journalistic gatekeepers and a lack of economic resources had denied them in previous times, has opened a vast new line of enquiry for researchers interested in how activists communicate strategically. It has also allowed assessment of what might be regarded as a more honest consideration of public relations as a practice that involves deliberate, tactical and embattled contestation of irreconcilable differences across interest groups, organisations, and peoples rather than attempts to reach negotiated compromises.

Yet this interest in activist use of public relations techniques is not confined to examining current trends in strategic communication. In an extraordinary turn-around from activists being "othered" as opponents to be overcome, Coombs and Holladay (2007) claim that the first practitioners of public relations were, in fact, *activists*. They describe how in the nineteenth century women's temperance and slavery abolitionist movements were using the kind of tactics now associated with public relations to promote social change:

> The activists in the First Reform Era were strategically using communication in a sustained effort to combat the social evils of alcohol by influencing public opinion. We need to consider these early activists as practicing public relations.
>
> (p. 65)

Since Coombs and Holladay made this argument, there have been a number of studies which have made the case that activist communication practices are types of public relations (e.g., Curtin, 2016; Heath & Waymer, 2009; Weaver, 2010, 2014).

Some recent theorising of social movements as working in the public interest and activism as a form of public relations is underpinned by critical social theory perspectives. Beck's (1992) notion of risk society, which conceptualises social development and technology as creating a vast array of risks to people's livelihoods and wellbeing in an increasingly socially disconnected world, encouraged further thinking about activist communication in the context of public relations. Drawing on Beck's theories, Kirsten Demetrious (2006) declared:

> activism is the dynamic new edge of the newly defined area of public communication. It is precisely because activists are perceived to be independent of any economic self-interest that they have gained legitimacy to dissect and describe and advocate social, economic, and cultural impacts in the public sphere.
>
> (p. 99)

Demetrious called for greater attention to be paid to the use of public communication by grassroots activists, predicting that "They will become adept in the traditional areas of public relations such as relationship management and the use of specialised communication tactics" (p. 99). Similarly, calling for activism to be embraced in public relations scholarship, rhetorical theorists Heath and Waymer (2009) positioned it as playing an important function in social debate and decision making. They declared that "the role of the activist organization in the issue dialogue ... is a vital part of issues management" (p. 195–196). Smith and Ferguson (2010) presented the same argument, asserting that "activists are co-creators of the relationships between organizations and their public, contributing to the development and resolution of issues and, ultimately, to social good" (p. 396).

This notion of co-creation is important in considering how activists can utilise techniques and technologies of communication to disrupt the status quo and further their interests, as it positions public relations within a wider context of social cultural relations, practices and dynamics. Much current theorising of activism within public relations has focused on exploring these cultural dynamics.

From a cultural-economic model (CEM), which draws on Foucault and theorises public relations as a culture producing discursive practice, and combining this with Hall's (2006) theory of articulation, Curtin (2016) has also made a case for activists to be viewed as practicing public relations. She asserts that

> Of note is that articulation theory expands the notion of public relations practitioner to encompass those who articulate relations to achieve public opinion goals and legitimize their positions – including activists.
>
> (p. 3)

This aligns with Curtin, Gaither and Ciszek's (2016) claim that:

> If public relations practice is conceived as embedded in and formative of cultural, social and economic discourses in part by how power shapes their contours, then public relations practice cannot be separated from issues of social justice.
>
> (p. 45)

Thus, through a CEM lens which posits that all moral truth claims, ethics, and values are relative, and which rejects what the authors' position as "the reductionism of false dichotomies" (p. 45), both the corporate-centred public relations representative and the progressive activist are theorised as undertaking social justice work. This argument is based on an interpretation of Foucault's (1980) theories of truth, power, and discourse as a case for conceiving society as pluralistic, and any position one might adopt on the political spectrum as a position on social justice.

There are also a number of scholars, who while not going so far as to define activists as public relations practitioners, have identified them as using the same communication methods as public relations. Ciszek (2015) states that "many of the tactics used by activists are public relations tactics, and their motives can be used as public relations strategies" (p. 447).

This is not a new argument; Larissa Grunig (1992) wrote about how activists use media relations, lobbying, public presentations, pseudo-events, and public education initiatives to get their message across to audiences. Weaver has also argued that where activist tactics are designed to perform a community building function, and where these tactics are used "as a vehicle for relationship management" (2010, p. 37), they represent a *genre* of public relations communication. This was in specific reference to humorous carnivalesque acts of protest designed to promote public dialogue and media interest in controversial issues. In these terms we can understand certain methods or tactics of communication as neutral tools of public relations (Moloney & McKie, 2016), which are commonly used by many different groups, individuals and/or larger organisations, be they public relations practitioners, activists, advocacy groups, politicians etc. This does not necessarily mean however, that those who use these tools should be labelled as practising public relations. This may be seen as hair splitting, but it has been a matter of concern for those who politically position public relations as "the other".

Public relations as "other": critical, Marxist and postcolonial perspectives

For some scholars, writing about public relations and activism it has been important not to subsume how activists communicate under the public relations umbrella, and to clearly label this as a very specific type of public relations. For example, Adi (2015), following Moloney, McQueen, Surowiec and Yaxley (2013), maintains a degree of separation in her analysis of the Occupy Movement's communication strategies and tactics, preferring to specify their work according to the terms "dissent PR", "protest PR" and "activist PR communications" (p. 511). She focuses in how activist groups apply public relations techniques in using social media to communicate with and influence "publics" – including media journalists and bloggers.

However, in direct contradiction to the pluralist trend of subsuming activism and activist public communication under the banner of public relations and/or articulating activism and public relations together, Wolf (2013) argues:

> Many of the tactics used and communication styles applied by activists *do not* mirror those used in public relations departments.... A characteristic example ... is the extensive use of humour which performs specific functions ... but also [negatively] impacts on activists' ability to influence external audiences, in particular business representatives, politicians and other industry-based power-holders, who are not familiar with humour and satire as a communications tool.
>
> (p. 274)

Wolf's critique of the conflating of public relations and activism tactics is based on an ethnographic study of the Western Australian anti-nuclear debate, and included interviews with a large number of anti-nuclear activists. Challenging the trend in critical public relations to position activists as public relations practitioners, Wolf concludes that, in the corporate organisational context:

> … ultimately, PR staff are employed to deliver specific and measurable outcomes related to corporate goals. Consequently the PR function is required to demonstrate its value, guaranteeing return on investment (ROI) and ensuring its contribution to the organisation's bottom line…. In larger not-for-profit organisations a similar arrangement may exist in the form of a staff member having to fundraise the equivalent of his or her salary. However, … this study suggests that grassroots movements are devoid of any comparable requirement.
>
> (p. 277)

Wolf makes other useful observations that some critical public relations scholars do not consider in relation to activist communication. These include her findings that: "'activists' alliance lies with the cause and not the organisation or group they may represent at a given point in time"; that "the activist group or organisation is a means to an end" (p. 273); and that "[d]ue to activist organisations' changeable structure and flexible composition … it is impossible to develop and guard a grassroots brand or image" (p. 274). In these terms being an activist, and working with or for an activist group – certainly a grassroots group – is very different to being a public relations practitioner working for, or on behalf of, an organisation. Certainly, as stated above, activists can and do use some of the same communication methods as public relations practitioners, but activism, by definition, also involves other communication approaches that have been given comparatively much less attention, and most notably those of communication of contestation and transgression. Clearly, notions of contestation and transgression do not fit well with normative models of ideal public relations practice. This highlights how the desire to iron out the differences between public relations and activism and present them as essentially two sides of the same coin is generally only found in public relations literature. It is not an approach found in social movement literature where public relations is often positioned as an oppositional other (DeLaure & Fink, 2017; DeLuca & Peebles, 2002). As Demetrious (2006) has written

> "public relations" has specific connotations for activists as a self-serving capitalist activity deeply rooted in exploitative corporate history and tradition. "PR" for activists is therefore a loaded term.
>
> (p. 107)

Indeed, social movement theorists and activists themselves appear to find nothing of interest or value in how public relations scholars theorise what they do. This is not to say that there is no merit in examining similarities between activism and public relations. L'Etang (2016) has asserted that "Framing public relations as an element within social movements … challenges those within social movements/activism to acknowledge and face critiques of persuasive communication and propaganda" (p. 33). However, recognising and respecting why some social theorists argue for maintaining strict divisions between public relations and activism is important.

The Marxist perspective on public relations regards and defines public relations as primarily an industry intimately intertwined with the evolution and ideological interests of capitalism. While not denying the importance of culture in considering how public relations techniques might be used in a variety of contexts and by a variety of different individuals and groups, Marxist theorists focus on the economic structures of power that public relations has worked to support since its birthing in the early years of the twentieth century (Miller & Dinan, 2000, 2003, 2008).

Postcolonial theorists tend to adopt a similar position. Dutta (2012), for example, whose critique of capitalism is underpinned by postcolonial perspectives, states that "Public relations has emerged on the political economy of transnational capitalism as a key actor in the management of public opinion, public policies, and resources at a global level" (p. 202).

The issue of who has access to the resources and infrastructures to promote their interests and messages through public relations activities is a key concern within Marxist and postcolonial approaches. Consequently, where such theorists have explored the connections between public relations and activism, it has tended to be in terms of actively encouraging left-wing orientated human and equal rights social justice groups and voices, to monitor, challenge, or protest against corporate and government public relations activities. David Miller and William Dinan, who have a history of sociological critique of public relations (see, 2000, 2003, 2008), are founder members of Spinwatch,[1] a group dedicated to "investigat[ing] the way that the public relations (PR) industry and corporate and government propaganda distort public debate and undermine democracy". Journalists and academics who work through Spinwatch have themselves actively campaigned to expose, for example, how corporate organisations lobby governments to ensure that their interests and operations are not threatened with changes in the regulatory environments. In turn, Kim and Dutta (2009) have advocated the value of subaltern frameworks for considering how grass roots activist, community organisations, groups and individuals resist dominant public relations crisis and issues management narratives. They argue that:

> resistance provides a key theoretical lens for looking at the ways in which meanings are negotiated in the realm of crises. The articulation of subaltern voices resists the dominant structures that otherwise

silences subaltern voices by presenting managerial interests, and through their presence, create epistemological and ontological possibilities for exploring the ways in which activism emerges amidst crises.

(p. 161)

What we do not see in Marxists and postcolonial approaches to activism in public relations literature is any tendency to represent activists as public relations practitioners, or utilising public relations methods. Rather, at the heart of these critical perspectives is a concern with investigating structures of power, and how these structures work to marginalise and oppress certain groups and peoples while elevating the power of others. Such work maintains the original transformative goal of critical theory (Kincheloe & McLaren, 2005) to support the articulation and emancipation of oppressed voices, peoples and groups. It does not seek to frame the resistance work of these groups as utilising the methodologies of their oppressors.

Conclusion

It is important to carefully reflect on our aims and motives in theorising activism within the public relations discipline. Public relations and activist activities do cover a vast and wide diversity of interests, ideological positions, beliefs and counter beliefs, and there are commonalities across the groups and interests represented by each. Yet how we define public relations and activism, and the relationships between the two, is determined by our own world views, theoretical and political positions and beliefs, and allegiances. Often, these allegiances, and how they conceive of how society is appropriately governed, how civil debate is conducted, and how power is negotiated, obtained and maintained, has been insufficiently articulated and interrogated in research and writing about activism in the public relations field.

When we examine and theorise activism, we need to be clear about how we are defining it, as well as about how we are defining public relations. We also need to clearly articulate our understanding of power and power-relations in society, our own theoretical and political world views, and what evidence there is to support our beliefs that these worldviews translate to actual social practice. Furthermore, we need to bring into this work many more voices of the people that we claim to speak for and about – activists. As Wolf (2018) urges, we also need to bring a more diverse range of activist voices into our research, including grassroots activists, those from different socio-economic groups, nationalities, ethnicities, age, gender and sexualities. Rather than defining what they do as public relations, and framing the way they communicate in terms of the tactics and strategies of public relations, we need to seek more of their reflections on how and why they attempt to engage in public debate, and how they might draw on and differ in their communicative practices compared to other types of social groups, organisations and/or individuals. We should ask what challenges activists face in contesting and transgressing the dominant discourses that frame their social concerns. We should ask how they identify as groups, organisations and individuals using different methods of communication and in their efforts to persuade others to align with their causes. It is a positive development that activists are no longer seen by many in the public relations discipline as "the other", and instead as an important contributors to social engagement, dialogue, public debate and change. We also need to respect what is often their opposition to the public relations industry and the dichotomies that they construct in marking out their own world views, cultural practices and identities.

Activism also brings new opportunities to explore how public relations practice and theory might be redefined in the context of digital and mobile communications, by peoples and groups which now have the means to communicate with vast audiences which they were historically unable to access when traditional mass media dominated public communication architectures. Perhaps what is most exciting here is how the practice and scholarly discipline of public relations could be completely disrupted and re-imagined outside of the confines of corporate and government communications in the context of its use by actual *active publics*.

Note

1 www.spinwatch.org.

References

Adi, A. (2015). Occupy PR: An analysis of online media communications of Occupy Wall Street and Occupy London. *Public Relations Review*, 41(4), 508–514.

Beck, U. (1992). *Risk society: Towards a new modernity*. London: Sage.

Berger, B. K. (2005). Power over, power with, and power to relations: Critical reflections on public relations, the dominant coalition and activism. *Journal of Public Relations Research*, 17(1), 5–28.

Bogost, I. (2016). Things you can't talk about in a Coca-Cola ad. *The Atlantic* 28 January. Retrieved from www.theatlantic.com/technology/archive/2016/01/things-you-cant-talk-about-in-a-coca-cola-ad/431628/.

Brown, R. E. (2015). *The public relations of everything: The ancient, modern and postmodern dramatic history of an idea*. New York and Oxon: Routledge.

Cammaerts, B. (2015). Social media and activism. In R. Mansell & P. Hwa (Eds), *The international encyclopedia of digital communication and society* (pp. 1027–1034). Oxford: Wiley-Blackwell.

Ciszek, E. L. (2015). Bridging the gap: Mapping the relationship between activism and public relations. *Journal of Public Relations Review*, 41(4), 447–455.

Coombs, T. W. & Holladay, S. J. (2012a). Fringe public relations: How activism moves critical PR toward the mainstream. *Public Relations Review*, 38, 880–887.

Coombs, T. W. & Holladay, S. J. (2012b). Privileging an activist vs. a corporate view of public relations history in the US. *Public Relations Review*, 38, 347–353.

Coombs, T. W. & Holladay, S. J. (2007). *It's not just PR: Public relations in society*. Malden, Oxford and Carlton: Blackwell Publishing.

Crable, R. E. & Vibbert, S. L. (1985). Managing issues and influencing public policy. *Public Relations Review*, 11(2), 3–16.

Curtin, P. A. (2016). Exploring articulation in internal activism and public relations theory: A case study. *Journal of Public Relations Research*. Online first. DOI: 10.1080/1062726X.2015.1131696.

Curtin, P. A., Gaither T. K. & Ciszek, E. (2016). Articulating public relations practice and critical/cultural theory through a cultural-economic lens. In J. L'Etang, D. McKie, N. Snow & J. Xifra (Eds), *Routledge handbook of critical public relations* (pp. 41–53). London and New York: Routledge.

Cutlip, S. M., Center, A. H. & Broom, G. (2000). *Effective public relations* (8th ed.). Upper Saddle River, MJ: Prentice Hall.

Dauvergne, P. & LeBaron, G. (2014). *Protest inc. The corporatization of activism*. Cambridge: Polity Press.

DeLaure, M. & Fink, M. (2017). *Culture jamming: Activism and the art of cultural resistance*. New York: New York University Press.

DeLuca, K. M. & Peebles, J. (2002). From public sphere to public screen: Democracy, activism, and the "violence" of Seattle. *Critical Studies in Communication*, 19(2), 125–151.

Della Porta, D. & Tarrow, S. (2005). *Transnational protests and global activism*. Lanham: Rowan & Littlefield.

Demetrious, K. (2006). Active voices. In J. L'Etang, & M. Pieczka (Eds), *Public relations: Critical debates and contemporary practice* (pp. 93–107). London: Lawrence Erlbaum.

Demetrious, K. (2013). *Public relations, activism, and social change: Speaking up*. London: Routledge.

Dozier, D. M. & Lauzen M. M. (2000). Liberating the intellectual domain from the practice: Public relations, activism, and the role of the scholar. *Journal of Public Relations Research*, 12(1), 3–22.

Dutta, M. J. (2012). Critical interrogations of global public relations: Power, culture and agency. In K. Sriramesh & D. Vercic (Eds), *Culture and public relations: Links and implications* (pp. 202–217). New York and London: Routledge.

Edwards, L. (2012). Defining the "object" of public relations research: A new starting point. *Public Relations Inquiry*, 1(1), 7–30.

Foucault, M. (1980). *Power/knowledge: Selected interviews and other writings 1972–1977*. New York: Pantheon.

Ganesh, S. & Zoller, H. M. (2012). Dialogue, activism, and democratic social change. *Communication Theory*, 22(1), 66–91.

Grunig, J. E. (1989). Sierra club study shows who become activists. *Public Relations Review*, 15(3), 3–24.

Grunig, L. A. (1992). Activism: How it limits the effectiveness of organizations and how excellent public relations departments respond. In J. E. Grunig (Ed.), *Excellence in public relations and communication management* (pp. 503–530). Hillsdale: Lawrence Erlbaum.

Grunig, J. E. & Hunt, T. (1984). *Managing Public Relations.* New York: Holt Rinehart & Winston.

Grunig, J. E., & White, J. (1992). The effect of worldviews on public relations theory and practice. In J. E. Grunig (Ed.), *Excellence in public relations and communication management* (pp. 31–64). Hillsdale: Erlbaum.

Hall, S. (2006). Encoding/decoding. In M. G. Durham & D. M. Kellner (Eds), *Media and cultural studies: Key works* (pp. 163–173). Malden, Oxford and Carlton: Blackwell Publishing.

Hallahan, K. (2001). The dynamics of issues activation and response: An issues processes model. *Journal of Public Relations Research*, 13(1), 27–59.

Heath, R. L. (1997). *Strategic issues management: Organizations and public policy challenges.* Thousand Oaks: Sage.

Heath, R. L. & Waymer, D. (2009). Activist public relations and the paradox of the positive: A case study of Frederick Douglass' "Fourth of July Address". In R. Heath, E. L. Toth, & D. Waymer (Eds), *Rhetorical and critical approaches to public relations* (pp. 195–215). New York: Routledge.

Holtzhausen, D. R. (2007). Activism. In E. L. Toth (Ed.), *The future of excellence in public relations and communication management* (pp. 357–379). Mahwah, NJ: Lawrence Erlbaum Associates.

Holtzhausen, D. R. (2012). *Public relations as activism: Postmodern approaches to theory and practice.* New York and London: Routledge.

Holtzhausen, D. R. & Voto, R. (2002). Resistance from the margins: The postmodern public relations practitioner as organizational activist. *Journal of Public Relations Research*, 14(1), 57–84.

Hutton, J. G. (1999). The definition, dimensions, and domain of public relations. *Public Relations Review*, 25(22), 199–214.

Kincheloe, J. L. & McLaren, P. (2005). Rethinking critical theory and qualitative research. In K. Denzin & Y. S. Lincoln (Eds), *Handbook of qualitative research* (3rd ed., pp. 303–342). Thousand Oaks: Sage.

Kim, I. & Dutta, M. J. (2009). Studying crisis communication from the subaltern studies framework: Grassroots activism in the wake of Hurricane Katrina. *Journal of Public Relations Research*, 21(2), 142–164.

L'Etang, J. (2008). *Public relations: Concepts, practice and critique.* London: Sage.

L'Etang, J. (2016). Public relations, activism and social movements: Critical perspectives. *Public Relations Inquiry*, 5(3), 207–2011.

Miller, D. & Dinan, W. (2000). The rise of the PR industry in Britain, 1979–98. *European Journal of Communication*, 15(1), 5–35.

Miller, D. & Dinan, W. (2003). Global public relations and global capitalism. In D. Demers (Ed.), *Terrorism, globalization and mass communication: Papers presented at the 2002 Center for global media studies conference* (pp. 193–214). Spokane: Marquette Books.

Miller, D. & Dinan, W. (2008). *A century of spin: How public relations became the cutting edge of corporate power.* London: Pluto Press.

Moloney, K. & McKie, D. (2016). Radical turns in PR theorisation. In J. L'Etang, D. McKie, N. Snow & J. Xifra (Eds), *Routledge handbook of critical public relations* (pp. 150–161). London & New York: Routledge.

Moloney, K., McQueen, D., Surowiec, P. & Yaxley, H. (2013). Dissent and protest public relations. *Papers and discussion from the dissent and public relations seminar series, October–December 2012.* Public Relations Research group:

The Media School, Bournemouth University. Retrieved from: https://research. bournemouth.ac.uk/wp-content/uploads/2013/10/Dissent-and-public-relations-Bournemouth-University.pdf.

Smith, M. F. & Ferguson, D. (2010). Activism 2.0. In R. L. Heath (Ed.), *The SAGE handbook of public relations* (pp. 395–408). London: Sage.

Sommerfeldt, E. J., Kent, M. L. & Taylor, M. (2012). Activist practitioner perspectives of website public relations: Why aren't activist websites fulfilling the dialogic promise? *Public Relations Review*, 38, 303–312.

Spinwatch: Public Interest Investigations. About us. www.spinwatch.org/index. php/about/about-spinwatch. Retrieved 14 January 2018.

Staples, L. (2016). *Roots to power: A manual for grassroots organising*. Santa Barbara. Praeger.

Stokes. A. Q. & Rubin, D. (2010). Activism and the limits of symmetry: The public relations battle between Colorado GASP and Philip Morris. *Journal of Public Relations Research*, 22(1), 26–48.

Toledano, M. (2106). Advocating for reconciliation: Public relations, activism, advocacy and dialogue. *Public Relations Inquiry*, 5(3), 277–294.

Veil, S. R., Reno, J., Freihaut, R. & Oldham, J. (2015). Online activists vs. Kraft foods: A case of social media. *Public Relations Review*, 41, 103–108.

Weaver, C. K. (2010). Carnivalesque activism as a public relations genre: A case study of the New Zealand group Mothers Against Genetic Engineering. *Public Relations Review*, 36(1), 35–41.

Weaver, C. K. (2014). Mothers, bodies, and breasts: Organising strategies and tactics in women's activism. In C. Daymon & K. Demetrious (Eds), *Gender and public relations: Critical perspectives on voice, image and identity* (pp. 108–131). London & New York: Routledge.

Wolf, K. (2013). Activism and symbolic capital in Western Australia: An ethnographic study of the anti-nuclear movement. PhD Thesis. Murdoch University, Australia.

Wolf, K. (2018). Power struggles: A sociological approach to activist communication. *Public Relations Review*, 44(2), 308–316.

Zoller, H. & Tener, M. (2010). Corporate proactivity as a discursive fiction: Managing environmental health activism and regulation. *Management Communication Quarterly*, 24(3), 391–418.

2 Activist nation

Australia and the 1916 conscription referendum

Emily Robertson and Robert Crawford

In January 1916, Brisbane's *Daily Standard* published a query from "a puzzled correspondent," who asked whether

> The coming into vogue of the word activist, usually applied to advocates of intervention, raises the question as to whether it is right to call a militant advocate of peace, an activist pacifist and, if so, is it right at the same time to call one who believes in peace movement but who does nothing to further its aims a passivist pacifist.[1]

Despite its tongue-in-cheek style, the musing reveals the currency of the term in wartime Australia. Significantly, the sense that pressure can be exerted on organizations, institutions and publics to elicit political goals is also consistent with contemporary definitions of activism (Ciszek, 2015, p. 447).

Activism as practised in Australia during the First World War contributed to a participatory democracy, which challenged the dominant voices of federal and state governments, and created a rich, if at times bombastic, dialogue within the electorate (Deetz, 1992). Undertaken by individuals and organizations across the political spectrum and across different professions, the activism involved in Australia's wartime conscription debates presents a unique opportunity to reconsider the historical relationship between activism and public relations, as well as its broader impact on national issues.

PR's antipathy to activists and activism has meant that their contribution to PR has, until recently, largely been ignored. Functional interpretations of PR have historically dismissed activists as "constraints or problems that public relations must address" (Coombs & Holladay, 2012, p. 882). Critical PR scholarship has challenged the view that PR is a mere tool of commerce and encouraged researchers to consider its operation within a broader social and political context (Ciszek, 2017, p. 881). Arguing that "the history of public relations' does not simply involve 'corporate reactions to activists,'" Coombs and Holladay contend the societal change wrought by activism effectively resituates PR from being "a *reaction* to activist activities" to an activity that was formulated *by* activists (2012, pp. 348–349).

The impact of the functionalist model has been less evident in Australian PR historiography. This reflects the importance of the Colonial, State, and Federal governments in Australian affairs as well as their willingness to invest in PR practices to communicate to publics (Crawford & Macnamara, 2014; Sheehan, 2014). In their outline of PR development in Australia prior to the Second World War, Crawford and Macnamara briefly point to activism around the conscription debates in Australia during the Great War (2014, pp. 277–281). By delving more deeply into these activities and strategies, notably the conscription referendum conducted in 1916, this chapter underscores the importance of adopting a critical approach.

Well outside the concerns of the market environment, activism in wartime Australia was practised within a strictly political environment, where the need to support the Empire was contrasted against the cost of mounting casualties. PR activism "facilitated democracy" and created social capital within the public sphere, as it was characterized by a need to persuade people about moral imperatives associated with the conflict (Sommerfeldt, 2013, p. 280). The broad range of Australians engaged in activist work during the war – and the conscription campaigns in particular – provide an excellent example of how dominant actors (such as a government prosecuting a war) do not necessarily possess the power to dictate outcomes, irrespective of the comparative power they possess. During the war, the Federal government used both censorship and persuasive tactics to promote recruiting and attempt introduce conscription. However, its failure to secure universal support for either aim underscores how complex the power relations were between activists and the government. The unique experiences of Australian activists during the First World War demonstrate that the Habermasian perspective of public relations – that it could, to paraphrase, "engineer consent" – struggles when sufficient numbers of citizens engage in activism in order to present multiple perspectives on key political issues (Rodney, 2008). By examining the activist campaigns waged by both pro-conscriptionists and anti-conscriptionists during the referendum of 1916, this chapter not only demonstrates the need to recast activism as an essential part of PR history, it also underscores the contribution that activism has made to broader democratic processes.

Establishing the tactics, networks and rhetoric

On October 28, 1916, Australians went to the ballot box to decide whether or not they supported the implementation of conscription for the purposes of overseas service. Australian losses had been steadily mounting, and Australia's Prime Minister, William ("Billy") Hughes, feared that Australia would fail in its commitment to Great Britain to supply them with troops. Addressing a public meeting in Launceston just days before the vote, Hughes pleaded the case for implementing conscription:

> We were not asked to do too much, and we are not asked to do more than half as much proportionately as Great Britain herself has done. This war is going to determine the destiny of every man and woman in Australia.[2]

Failure at the ballot box, he argued, would result in a German victory. Australians did not necessarily share these fears. A narrow victory for the anti-conscription vote in 1916 meant that a second referendum would be staged in 1917. Both campaigns would prove violently divisive, virulent and destructive (Beaumont, 2014). While Australian First World War historians have examined the issues underpinning the campaign as well as the key protagonists, and labor historians have explored the infrastructure of anti-conscription activism and its impact upon public debate, pro-conscription activism has been neglected. So too, has the nature of activist networks and their relationship to other areas of activism during the war.[3] Campaigners for and against conscription both drew upon a variety of networks that had been established at different times – before the war, during the war, and during the referendum campaign.

The issue of conscription in Australia was first raised in the early twentieth century. Concerns about Australia's poorly coordinated defense systems had seen the emergence of groups such as the Australian National Defence League (ANDL). In contrast to the Victorian division of the ANDL, the New South Wales (NSW) chapter supported conscription (Barrett, 1979). They were canny and enthusiastic activists who sought to influence political outcomes; during the federal election in 1910 they published a list of 80 candidates "whose attitude was considered to be sound," and also provided propaganda material to influential figures such as British Field Marshal and pro-conscriptionist Lord Kitchener before his visit to Australia in 1909 (Barrett, p. 48).

The ANDL's journal, *Call*, was indicative of the organization's efforts to mobilize publicity material to realize its aims. Highly militaristic in its outlook, the *Call* was sent "to all members of parliament ... newspapers, judges, mayors, landowners, principal ministers of religion: free of charge." The cover of the *Call's* 1911–1912 annual publication featured the work of prominent artist Norman Lindsay. Depicting a rugged Australian soldier and his iconic slouch hat looking out to sea where the enemies of Australia are gathering, the image anticipated many of the tropes that Lindsay would produce for the Australian magazine the *Bulletin* during the conscription referenda. Thus, even before the Great War, the *Call* magazine emphasized that military service was integral to the defense of both Australia and the British Empire. This imperial ethos would become a key argument in pro-conscription material during the conflict.

Although the ANDL largely dissolved after compulsory military training was achieved, its legacy was a lasting one. ANDL membership had included prominent wartime pro-conscription Labor politicians, such as William Holman (NSW Premier during the War) and wartime Prime Minister William Hughes. Its impact was also discernible in the formation and activities of the Universal Service League (USL). The losses being sustained by Australian forces at Gallipoli placed tremendous pressure on the voluntary system, and in September 1915 the USL was formed "to advocate the adoption for the period of the present war of the principle of universal compulsory war service."[4] F.B. Smith described the USL as "a powerful pressure group," and noted that its membership included politicians from both major political parties, trade union leaders, and a range of representatives from all of the church denominations in Australia (1965, p. 8). Involvement in both organizations thus meant that many pro-conscription activists were therefore well-versed in activist tactics and were ready to mobilize them when the Government announced that it would be staging a referendum.

Like the pro-conscriptionists, anti-conscription activists also drew on a range of networks, tactics and rhetoric that had been established before the war. Robin Archer (2016) has pointed out that the language used by anti-conscriptionists pre-dated the First World War. Liberal elements within the labor movement traditionally abhorred militarism, which was regarded as "the antithesis of a free society" with "conscription as the paradigm characteristic of militarism" (p. 41). Frank Bongiorno (2016) also notes that anti-conscriptionists were often "guided by well-developed understandings of British liberty" (p. 68). In 1913, John F. Hills of the Australian Freedom League published a pamphlet that declared:

> Tyranny is none the less tyranny when it is exercised by the many than by one … the Almighty as left free the human soul prayerfully to decide what is right for it to do in the course of its earthly life. Shall man strive to shackle what the maker has formed free?
>
> (*c.*1913, p. 14)

The Australian Freedom League was formed in 1912 with the aim of bringing about the "abolition of the compulsory clauses of the Commonwealth Defense Act" irrespective of party politics.[5] While the League continued to agitate against conscription during the First World War, it also adopted a more politically partisan stance by attaching itself to the unions. In a letter read out at a conscription meeting in Bendigo, the League's Commonwealth organizer bound together the League's anti-militarism perspective with that of the unions, stating that "military conscription" was "the cloak for industrial conscription" and a means through which the labor movement would be undermined.[6]

For many trade unions, there was a seamless transition from their stance against the power of industrialists, and their stance against conscription.

They considered the fight against conscription to be a continuation of their fight to safeguard workers' rights. In its 1916 manifesto against conscription, the Australian Council of Trade Unions directly connected conscription to the silencing of the rights to speak and act out against the forces of capitalism:

> the trade unionists of Australia have taken steps to guard the rights achieved by long years of sacrifice and toil. They will not lightly let them go. They will contend with all the powers at their disposal and the resources at their command against the enactment in Australia of practices and conditions imposed, under the pretence of national salvation, upon the workers of other countries.
>
> (p. 5)

With its strong ties to the Australian Labor Party, the union movement inevitably looked to use its influence within the party structure to promote its views. The conscription referendum in 1916 thus saw a shift in power within the Labor Party, as trade unionists leveraged "the issue to assert control" over "its moderate political leaders" and passed anti-conscription resolutions in several states. "Politicians," Sammut writes, "had no choice but to toe the industrialists' anti-militarist line or face expulsion as class traitors" (2005, p. 168). Sammut observes that pro-conscription stood in direct opposition to their "traditional" view, which was that conscription was a "means through which 'old world militarism' would be introduced and destroy democracy and trades unionism" (p. 164). The union movement's activism against the pro-conscription members of the Labor Party contributed to the spectacular split of the party in September 1916, with the Prime Minister Hughes himself being expelled from the NSW branch of the party. (Hughes and other pro-conscription Labor party members in the Federal government would form a coalition with the opposition, called the Nationalist Party.)

The groups that had a direct interest in the issue of conscription before the war were not the only source of ready-made conscription activists. Many had developed skills working as pro-war or anti-war activists. While it is certainly the case that many of those who were pro-war were not necessarily pro-conscription (Premier Ryan of Queensland being a notable example of a pro-war politician who opposed conscription), it was nonetheless the case that some of the most prominent activists during the 1916 conscription referendum emerged from groups that were firmly in either the pro-war or the anti-war camps. Significantly, many were engaged in publicity activities for those causes.

Several prominent anti-war organizations would redeploy their anti-war rhetoric and tactics during the war. The Industrial Workers of the World (IWW) were one of the most notorious groups to oppose both the war and conscription. Along with "other radicals," they formed an

Anti-Conscription and Anti-Militarist League (Bongiorno, p. 70). Their stance against militarism saw them opposing conscription and the war more generally. The Women's Peace Army (WPA), founded by Vida Goldstein in 1915, similarly combined its opposition to the war with the anti-conscription cause (Coleman, 1996). The WPA leveraged negative media to gain maximum publicity. In 1915 Adela Pankhurst (daughter of British suffragette Emmeline Pankhurst) (Hogan, 1990) and Cecilia John campaigned against the war using an American pacifist song, "I didn't Raise my Son to be a Soldier." During a trip down the Brisbane River on a government steamer, the two dissidents distributed copies of the song while singing it. Pankhurst and John were condemned as disloyal both by the media and Queensland parliament.[7] Capitalizing on the widespread publicity their activities had elicited, the WPA would reprint the song for distribution during the conscription referendum of 1916.[8]

In the case of pro-conscription campaigners, some networks grew from the pre-existing State Recruiting Committees. These bodies had been established during the war with the aim of gaining recruits within the voluntary system. For many of these recruiters, there was an abiding concern that the voluntary system would inevitably fail to produce the number of enlistments needed to replace the wounded and dead at the battle front. As Australian casualties mounted, these concerns heightened. In April 1916, the Queensland Recruiting Committee publicly joined voices calling for conscription when they passed a resolution stating that "the committee, having exhausted every effort in the endeavor to maintain the quota of recruits required of this district, now realize that it is impossible to do so."[9] However, it would be incorrect to assume that State Recruiting Committees were inherently pro conscription. J.H. Catts, for example, was the organizing secretary of the New South Wales Recruiting Committee. Catts would lead the no-conscription campaigns in NSW in both referenda. His position was never anti-war; rather, it was based on a concern that conscription would make Australia vulnerable to invasion from Japan (Hoyle, 1979).

The multitude of organizations engaged directly or indirectly in conscription debates in the pre-war period and the early stages of the war reveal that the conscription campaign of 1916 did not emerge from an ideological vacuum. A significant number of conscription activists were able to draw on their previous involvement with these groups. Their experiences in devising, organizing, and implementing a range of strategies and communication initiatives to persuade stakeholders and publics informed the nature of their activism during the lead up to the conscription referendum.

Pro-conscription activism and government recruiting committees

Since the outbreak of war, the state Recruitment Committees were charged with the task of maintaining Australia's commitment to the war effort. They had progressively built up nationwide networks that could efficiently organize speakers, events, and publicity materials. Pro-conscriptionists involved in these organizations understood the scope of these networks and were only too willing to use them to assist with the distribution of pro-conscription messages across the country. The Recruitment Committees thus became ad hoc sites from which pro-conscription activism occurred. Falling under the auspices of both state and federal governments, the Recruitment Committees were closely connected to the machinery of the civil arm of the military. As their official role was to persuade young men to enlist, the Committees were expected to remain neutral over the issue of conscription. However, Prime Minister Hughes' decision to use the recruiting networks of the Committees to promote the pro-conscription message effectively politicized them.

On September 20, 1916, Hughes sent a telegram to Frank Wilson, the Premier of Western Australia. Hughes requested that the Labor MP Jabez E. Dodd, the Vice Chairman of the Western Australian Recruiting Committee (WARC), assist him with forming the Western Australian division of the National Referendum Committee (NRC).[10] The purpose of the NRC was solely to "carry" the pro-conscription campaign "to a successful issue."[11] While the WA government sought to appear to be neutral over the issue, WARC had several members who were more than happy to promote the pro-conscription cause. Frank Rea, Mayor of Perth and a prominent WARC member, thus had little qualm in reaching out to the public. In a letter to a member of the public he wrote, "Whilst I agree with you that the referendum should not be taken, I feel the only course open to us in the circumstances is to endeavor to secure an overwhelming vote in the affirmative."[12]

The involvement of official recruiting bodies in pro-conscription activism proved to be exceedingly problematic for Donald Mackinnon, the Director General of Recruiting. The problem was twofold. On the one hand, the specter of conscription had seen enlistments decline, as many young men opted to delay enlistment and wait to be formally called up. On the other, the blurring of lines between recruitment and conscription obscured the Committees' primary role – both during the campaign and in the referendum's aftermath. Following the electorate's rejection of conscription, the Chairman of the Queensland State Recruiting Committee (QSRC) Colonel Thynne, publicly advocated for conscription. Mackinnon castigated Thynne after he and other QSRC members had engaged in a number of public pro-conscription meetings where the voluntary system was publicly labelled a "failure."[13] "Great publicity was given to these Queensland meetings," wrote Mackinnon, "and the [recruiting] work in other States was being seriously interfered with."[14]

Mackinnon was also concerned over the QSRC's circulation of pro-conscription propaganda within Queensland parliament. In a letter to another outspoken QSRC pro-conscriptionist, Captain Dash, Mackinnon observed that "Public opinion [in Queensland] is so bitter."[15] The QSRC's circulation of a pro-conscription pamphlet amongst Queensland parliamentarians therefore angered Mackinnon greatly, as he believed that such actions were directly undermining the voluntary recruiting system. "As a bit of a conscription propaganda, the report is a meritorious bit of work," Mackinnon wrote, "But its use for recruiting purposes was practically nil and it should never have been circulated in the way in which it was."[16]

In the highly charged political climate surrounding conscription, the blurring of the lines between the conscription issue and the task of increasing recruitment numbers led QSRC's prominent pro-conscription activists to take dramatic action to further their cause. In June 1917 the QSRC's "advocacy of conscription," which had "worried the Commonwealth Recruiting Committee not a little," had tendered their resignation to Mackinnon. In August 1917, Mackinnon was forced to accept their resignations because they had "never deviated one jot from" their "affirmed belief that conscription was necessary and long overdue."[17] Their role as pro-conscription activists, stated Mackinnon, rendered their recruiting work less effective.[18] Despite Mackinnon's attempts to create a unified recruiting campaign by 1918, the voluntary recruiting messages had been severely undermined by pro-conscription activists. Fatigue, economic hardship and the rise of militant unionism did little to improve his capacity to maintain enlistment numbers, let alone the efforts of anti-conscription activists.

Anti-war activists and the anti-conscription movement – leveraging negative publicity

The activities of the anti-conscription activists took place within the context of the censorship regime that was established under the *War Precautions Act*. Irrespective of affiliation, any individual or organization that voiced objections to the war (or conscription) risked coming under the scrutiny of Military Intelligence. Over 1915 and 1916, the *War Precautions Act* had been specifically strengthened to target anti-war activists. Section 30(f) listed "endangering the successful prosecution of the war" as an offence, and it was under this section and another (which forbade the spreading of "public alarm") that anti-war and anti-conscriptionists were prosecuted (Fewster, 1980, p. 46 and p. 127).

Despite the strength of the Act, and the enthusiasm with which it was enforced, dissenting views continued to be expressed. Indeed, it could be argued that the *War Precautions Act* itself served to amplify these voices, rather than silence them. Reports in the mainstream press documenting the views of those being persecuted thus proved to be an effective means of publicity. A newspaper report on the prosecution of South Australia state politician John Francis Hills under the War Precautions Act in 1915 illustrates this situation. Charged with having made statements "by word of mouth" that were "likely to prejudice the recruiting of His Majesty's subjects," the report recounted the words that had hitherto been audible only to a small audience: "If your Government brings in a Conscription Act let them shoot you down before you shoot the Germans. You can still refuse."[19] Verbatim reports of speakers' speeches at local rallies would prove an effective way of communicating to a broader audience. The efforts of anti-conscriptionists who successfully deployed their messages illustrate the use of PR as a form of participatory democracy envisaged by Deetz – where activists could circumvent the "managerialism" of the pro-conscriptionist lobby (who had much of the support of the government behind them) and fought to present alternative perspectives to voters.

Despite the authorities' best efforts, many anti-conscription activists continued to publish and distribute anti-war and anti-conscription propaganda throughout the conscription campaign and, indeed, beyond. The news article titled "The Lottery of Death," for example, had been initially written by Henry Earnest Boote for the *Worker*. While the article was banned, anti-conscriptionists sought to republish the article in pamphlet form to reach a wider audience while ensuring that the *Worker* would avoid any further prosecution.[20] Others opted for outright defiance. Being "convicted on several counts for breaches of the War Precautions Regulations" did not deter Melbourne publisher Fraser and Jenkinson from publishing its views.[21] The fact that the names of prohibited publications could not even be read out in parliament "in the interests of public safety" scarcely deterred the publisher from producing a lengthy pamphlet listing the banned works.[22]

Media coverage of the prosecutions of publishers and distributors of illegal publications again served to enhance and extend the reach of seditious messages. In January 1916, the Censor's Office combined forces with Military Intelligence in a raid on the headquarters of the No Conscription Fellowship (Cain, 1983, p. 111). They seized a number of pamphlets, some urging potential recruits to ignore the federal government's census on eligible men, others (accurately) warning of the government's plan to implement conscription. In June 1916, Samuel Ross, a member of the No Conscription Fellowship, was tried for producing the pamphlet. At the close of the trial, the *Age* repeated the contents of the pamphlet despite the fact that the government had deemed it prejudicial to recruiting, thereby expanding the reach of the pamphlet from the original 10,000 to the entire State of Victoria and, indeed, nationally.[23]

The IWW were arguably the most notorious anti-conscriptionists (and anti-war activists) of the Great War. Their very credo – that of anarcho-syndicalism, which advocated "the general strike as an instrument of revolution" – was even regarded as extreme by those within the general labor movement (Bongiorno, p. 71). Its vituperative language, expressed through the newspaper *Direct Action*, attracted the ire of Hughes. Throughout September 1916, Australia's federal police rounded up numerous IWW activists, drawing upon the *Treason Felony Act*, a piece of colonial legislation established in 1848 (Cain, 1983). While the legislation facilitated the arrest of key members of the IWW, it would have significant unintended and positive consequences for the anti-conscription movement. First, as Verity Burgmann (2015) speculates, the extreme language used by the IWW made the majority of anti-conscriptionists seem very mild in comparison (and easier to sympathize with). Second, the jailed IWW members came to be regarded as martyrs by those within the union movement – particularly as such imprisonment was seen as a way to silence the anti-conscription message. In 1917, the Amalgamated Miners' Association thus asked:

> if the advocates of One Big Union for the working class are to be cast into the dungeons for their propaganda, how long will it be before all unionism is crushed in the dust under the iron heel of capitalism.
>
> (AMA, 1917, p. 2)

Here again, the authorities' active efforts to repress and silence dissenting views ultimately proved counterproductive.

The Women's Peace Army (WPA) was another notorious anti-conscription activist group, which similarly sought to capitalize on publicity to advance their cause. Adela Pankhurst, in particular, was a persistent and indefatigable anti-war and anti-conscription activist well before the 1916 conscription referendum campaign. In 1915, a parliamentarian complained about Pankhurst's articles in *Woman Voter* and demanded that the Attorney General prevent it from producing seditious articles.[24] During the conscription campaign, the WPA's stance attracted further attention. Verbal abuse directed at a WPA speaker from soldiers at anti-conscription meetings attracted attention. The theft and subsequent public airing of her private correspondence by the Prime Minister garnered significant publicity. A week before the 1916 referendum, Hughes used a letter from Pankhurst to the editor of the IWW's newspaper *Direct Action* to smear the reputation of the WPA. The IWW, thundered Hughes, was the "curse of unionism" and had "wormed their way" into anti-conscription leagues. Hughes seized upon Pankhurst's words, "I know what the IWW has done in New South Wales. The outside organizations have really forced the Labor Party into the fight against conscription," to conflate the divide within the Labor Party with the claims that the IWW was essentially a terrorist organization.[25] Although the latter claims were proven to be false, the press seized on the salacious private correspondence – one article used the headline "Syndicalists and Anarchists in No-conscription Company."[26]

This could have been very damaging. However, the negative publicity had one advantage; it allowed the activists to spread their message beyond activist channels simply because there was sufficient controversy for their viewpoint to be published in the mainstream media. For example, *The Advertiser* provided space for Vida Goldstein's rebuttal of Hughes' allegations, reporting her speech thus:

> believe[s] that the charges levelled against these men were true, and you see how this letter has been twisted and turned to show that we are associated with a deadly, revolutionary body. The answer Miss Pankhurst received was that these charges were a deliberate frame up. There is no doubt about it, those in high places will stick at nothing to try and throw odium upon those opposing them.[27]

In drawing attention to Hughes' attempts to silence anti-conscription voices, Goldstein's public statement effectively established a space for activists, outside of trade union and peace activist publications, to state their position about conscription. Such media coverage underscores Hughes' inability to fully silence the voice of the activists in the public sphere.

As activist groups, the WPA and the IWW may have had less impact if Hughes and the censorship authorities had simply ignored them. Authorities sought to silence both anti-war and anti-conscription groups using a combination of force, legislation, and smear campaigning. However, the drama and emotion surrounding such measures only served to draw attention to those subjected to these tactics. Having largely been confined to disseminating their views in the pages of the trade union and peace movement press, as well as the local meetings, activists like the IWW and the WPA understood the importance of the media as well as its potential. By using publicity in the mainstream press as a platform to extend the reach of their message, these activists strategically enhanced their presence in the public sphere.

Conclusion

On October 28, 1916, Australians finally cast their vote. Pro-conscriptionists assured themselves that their loyalty to King and Country would readily appeal to the majority of voters during wartime – victory would therefore stem from their capacity to ensure their message was heard. This was PR's role. And, with the weight of the government both supporting their cause and restricting their opponents' voice, the "Yes campaigners expected to win" (Damousi 2016, p. 26). However, the result went the other way, with 1,160,033 voters (51.61 percent) voting against conscription. In the aftermath of the counting, Brisbane's *Leader* mused:

No one can have taken an active part in the recent Referendum campaign without learning a great deal in relation to the political life of the Commonwealth, and the forces which are behind that life, also the motives which appear to influence it.[28]

While the *Leader* linked voting patterns to socio-economic demographics rather than activists' campaigning strategies, there were nevertheless important lessons to be gleaned about activism and its relationship with PR.

Both pro-conscription and anti-conscription campaigners revealed that they possessed an innate understanding of PR. Many drew on their previous experiences as communicators. While organizational structures, rallies, speeches, publicity, and pamphlets had long been used to promote a particular cause or ideology, their deployment during the conscription campaign was both different and significant. This in part reflects the uniqueness of the conscription debate. This was a highly divisive and intensely emotional issue that necessitated direct action from the entire nation. Within this highly charged atmosphere, both sides increasingly incorporated activist strategies and tactics as a way of efficiently and effectively persuading large audiences. The activism of pro-conscription and anti-conscription campaigners illustrates the degree to which they were engaging with PR, as well as the need to recognize activism's contribution to PR history.

In noting that activism is not "necessarily a homogenous category" and that "activists range in scale, across the ideological spectrum, and are often in direct opposition to each other" (2016, p. 207), Jacquie L'Etang not only offers an important reminder of diversity of activists, she also underscores the importance of adopting a broader view of them and their contribution. By exploring both sides of the conscription campaign, this chapter has revealed how activism not only enables us to access further developments in PR's history, it also offers insights into PR's contribution to a functioning deliberative democracy. Despite the imposition of censorship under the *War Precautions Act*, activists continued to influence public opinion. The different pro-conscriptionist organizations similarly used PR to maintain their calls for Australia to implement conscription. Their persistence, coupled with the continuing decline in voluntary enlistments, ultimately led to another conscription referendum in 1917, which would be fought with even greater urgency than the first. Despite the animosity of the campaigns, Australia would survive the war intact; this was not a fate that was shared by other nations, such as Germany and Russia. While the war and the bitter animosity around conscription resulted in Australian being what Joan Beaumont labels a "broken nation," it nevertheless provided Australians with an opportunity to engage in a national issue and to participate as PR activists rather than through violence. This important lesson has since remained a mainstay of Australia's political landscape.

Notes

1 "The Daily Mirror," *Daily Standard*, January 8, 1916, 4.
2 "Conscription," *Argus*, October 14, 1916, 17.
3 Bongiorno 2016; Burgmann 2015; Holloway 1966; Sammut 2005.
4 "Universal Service," *Argus*, September 11, 1915, 7.
5 "Manifesto of Neutrality," *Register*, May 11, 1912, 14.
6 "Conscription," *Bendigo Advertiser*, April 22, 1916, 8.
7 Ibid., 67; "An Unpatriotic Circular," *Gympie Times and Mary River Mining Gazette*, November 27, 1915, 1.
8 Riley Collection, NLA.
9 "Recruiting: War Card Vagaries," *Telegraph*, April 1, 1916, 2.
10 Telegram from Prime Minister William Hughes to WA Premier Frank Wilson, *c.* September 20, 1916, State Records Office WA, 1496 1916/0228.
11 "Referendum Notes," *Maryborough Chronicle, Wide Bay and Burnett Advertiser*, September 25, 1916, 4.
12 Correspondence from Frank Rea to E.F. Brady, September 21, 1916, State Records Office of WA, 3054 1918/0380.
13 "Recruiting Conference in Brisbane: Conscription Advocated," *Maryborough Chronicle, Wide Bay, and Burnett Advertiser*, August 10, 1917, 3.
14 Donald Mackinnon, Director General of Recruiting to Colonel A. Thynne, Chairman, QSRC, October 30, 1917, NAA Melbourne, MP 367/1 609/30/700.
15 Ibid.
16 Ibid.
17 "Resignation of Recruiting Committee," *Gympie Times and Mary Mining River Gazette*, August 25, 1917, 1.
18 "Recruiting Committee: Director-General's Action," *Daily Mail*, August 25, 1917, 8.
19 "Anti-war Speaker," *Express & Telegraph*, August 19, 1915, 4.
20 People Printery: "The Lottery of Death," 1917, Riley Collection, NLA. Henry Earnest Boote, publisher, printer and editor of the "Worker" was prosecuted for publishing the article as it was deemed prejudicial to recruiting (see: "Editor of 'The Worker' Prosecuted," *The Australian Worker*, November 30, 1917, 6.
21 Brigadier-General, 3d Military District to Secretary, Department of Defence, June 26, 1917, NAA Melbourne, MP367/1 B570/12/269.
22 "Prohibited Publications," Melbourne, Fraser and Jenkinson, *c.*1915–1918, Mitchell Library.
23 "Prominent Socialist in Court. Charge Dismissed," *The Age*, June 10, 1916, 12.
24 "The Name 'Pankhurst': Mr Hughes Had Heard of It," *The Ballarat Courier*, May 8, 1915, 4.
25 "'The Curse of Unionism': Miss Pankhurst and Tom Barker," *Barrier Miner*, October 20, 1916, 1.
26 "Syndicalists and Anarchists in No-conscription Company," *The Sydney Stock and Station Journal*, October 20, 1916, 14.
27 "Miss Pankhurst and the IWW," *The Advertiser*, October 19, 1916, 6.
28 "The Referendum Campaign – and After," *Leader*, November 10, 1916, 1.

References

Amalgamated Miners' Association (AMA). (1917). *Solidarity Sentenced: The Conscription Aftermath: Labor Agitators Get 150 Years Gaol: Sensational Disclosure*. Broken Hill: New South Wales.

Archer, R. (2016). Labour and Liberty: The Origins of the Conscription Referendum. In R. Archer, J. Damousi, M. Goot & S. Scalmer (Eds.), *The Conscription Conflict and the Great War*. Melbourne: Monash University Publishing.

Australian Trade Union Congress. (1916). *Australian Trade Unionism and Conscription: Being Report of Proceedings of Australian Trade Union Congress Together with the Manifesto of the National Executive*. Melbourne: Labor Call Print.

Barrett, J. (1979). *Falling in: Australians and "Boy Conscription" 1911–1915*. Sydney: Hale & Ironmonger.

Beaumont, J. (2014). *Broken Nation: Australians in the Great War*. New South Wales: Allen & Unwin.

Bongiorno, F. (2016). Anti-Conscription in Australia: Individuals, Organisations and Arguments. In R. Archer, J. Damousi, M. Goot & S. Scalmer (Eds.), *The Conscription Conflict and the Great War*. Melbourne: Monash University Publishing.

Burgmann, V. (2015). Syndicalist and Socialist Anti-Militarism 1911–18: How the Radical Flank Helped Defeat Conscription. In P. Deery & J. Kimber (Eds.), *Fighting Against War: Peace Activism in the Twentieth Century*. Melbourne: Leftbank Press.

Cain, F. (1983). *The Origins of Political Surveillance in Australia*. Australia: Angus & Robertson.

Ciszek, E.L (2015). Bridging the Gap: Mapping the Relationship between Activism and Public Relations. *Public Relations Review*, 41(4), pp. 447–455.

Ciszek, E.L. (2017). Public Relations, Activism and Identity: A Cultural-Economic Examination of Contemporary LGBT Activism. *Public Relations Review*, 43(4), pp. 809–816.

Coleman, V. (1996). *Adela Pankhurst: The Wayward Suffragette, 1885–1961*. Melbourne: Melbourne University Press.

Coombs, W.T. & Holladay, S.J. (2012). Fringe Public Relations: How Activism Moves Critical PR toward the Mainstream, *Public Relations Review*, 38(5), pp. 880–887.

Crawford, R. & Macnamara, J. (2014). An Agent of Change: Public Relations in Early Twentieth Century Australia. In B. St John III, M. Opdycke Lamme & J. L'Etang (Eds.), *Pathways to Public Relations: Histories of Practice and Profession*. London and New York: Routledge.

Damousi, J. (2016). Universities and Conscription: The "Yes" Campaigns and the University of Melbourne. In R. Archer, J. Damousi, M. Goot & S. Scalmer (Eds.), *The Conscription Conflict and the Great War*. Melbourne: Monash University Publishing.

Deetz, S. (1992). *Democracy in an Age of Corporate Colonisation: Developments in Communication and the Politics of Everyday Life*. New York: State University of New York Press.

Fewster, K.J. (1980). *Expression and Suppression: Aspects of Military Censorship in Australia during the Great War* (PhD thesis). University of New South Wales, Australia.

Hills, J.F. (*c.*1913). *Child Conscription: Our Country's Shame*. Sydney: Australian Freedom League.

Hogan, S. (1990). Pankhurst, Adela Constantia (1885–1961). In *Australian Dictionary of Biography*. National Centre of Biography: Australian National University, http://adb.anu.edu.au/biography/pankhurst-adela-constantia-9275, published first in hardcopy 1990, accessed online January 10, 2018.

Holloway, E.J. (1966). *The Australian Victory Over Conscription in 1916–17.* Melbourne: Australian Conscription Jubilee Committee.

Hoyle, A. (1979). Catts, James Howard (1877–1951). In *Australian Dictionary of Biography*. National Centre of Biography: Australian National University, http://adb.anu.edu.au/biography/catts-james-howard-5535, published first in hardcopy 1979, accessed February 2, 2018.

L'Etang, J. (2016). Public Relations, Activism and Social Movements: Critical Perspectives. *Public Relations Inquiry*, 5(3), pp. 207–211.

Rodney, B. (2008), Public Relations in the Public Sphere: Habermas, Bourdieu and the Question of Power, *Conference Papers – International Communication Association*, 2008 Annual Meeting, pp. 21–25.

Ryan, T. (n.p.). *National Preservation: A Plea*, Essendon, John Osborne Print, *c.*1916–1917, p. 11, Josiah Symons collection of First World War propaganda, S.L.S.A.

Sammut, J. (2005). "Busting" the Anti-conscription Legend. *Journal of the Royal Australian Historical Society*, 91(2), pp. 163–183.

Sheehan, M. (2014). Australasia. In T. Watson (Ed.), *Asian Perspectives on the Development of Public Relations: Other Views*. Basingstoke: Palgrave Macmillan.

Smith, F.B. (1965). *The Conscription Plebiscites in Australia 1916–17*. Melbourne: Melbourne University Press.

Sommerfeldt, E.J. (2013). The Civility of Social Capital: Public Relations in the Public Sphere, Civil Society, and Democracy. *Public Relations Review*, 39(4), pp. 280–289.

Archives and collections

- Riley Collection, National Library of Australia.
- National Archives of Australia.
- State Records Office of Western Australia.

3 Activists as pioneers in PR

Historical frameworks and the suffragette movement

Michaela O'Brien

Introduction

This chapter sets out to examine some of the ways in which public relations (PR) academics have sought to chart the historical development of PR, and to consider the relevance of those approaches for charting the historical development of *protest* PR. Many considerations of the historical development of PR assume a corporate subject and overlook non-profit actors such as charities, non-governmental organisations (NGOs), trades unions and social movements. One impact of this is to privilege the role of PR in supporting organisations over its role in society. The chapter suggests that Baringhorst's historical development framework (2009), drawn from political communications theory and pinned to developments in the media, may offer a more useful lens through which to assess protest PR. Finally, the communicative activities of the suffragettes are considered against Baringhorst's framework, using an historical analysis of archive material held at the Museum of London. This analysis identifies some of the ways in which the suffragettes were pioneers in their communicative activity.

Dominant historical frameworks overlook protest PR

The dominant view of the historical development of public relations (PR) comes from the functional US school of PR study. In common with many other early theoretical frameworks for PR that emerged from the American tradition, this historical model foregrounds a corporate subject. Authors from the critical school of PR including L'Etang (2009, 2015), Demetrious (2006, 2013), Coombs and Holladay (2012a), Edwards and Hodges (2011) and O'Brien (2018) have argued that PR literature has, until recently, shown a tendency to privilege the corporate voice and overlook or marginalise non-profit actors. L'Etang (2009) argues that:

> The dominant paradigm in public relations is firmly rooted in the concerns of US capitalism ... Activists appear to be constructed as

problematic in public relations. They are *the other*, the implied organisational opponents.

(p. 84)

Considering the historiography of public relations, she notes that (2015):

Part of the history of the discipline has been the privileging of US
accounts and paradigms – to the extent that these were widely and
uncritically promoted and adopted in a range of cultural contexts.

(p. 30)

L'Etang (2015) reminds us that the challenges of historical sociology
include being aware of one's own influences and being transparent about
them. With the dominant discourse within PR literature to this point
reflecting a corporate-centric approach, it is timely to look at its influence
on our understanding of the history of PR, and critically examine how far
this understanding applies to the genre of protest PR.

The early, dominant histories of PR foreground corporate examples,
with Broom and Cutlip (2013, p. 106) showcasing a "timeline of defining
events and people" that includes railroads, energy and other predominantly corporate organisations, along with the clients and career of the
"father of PR" Edward Bernays, whose torches of freedom parade for the
American Tobacco Company has been described as the first public relations stunt. Demetrious (2013) points to the influence of Edward Bernays
on our understanding of PR and its development, linking his portrayal of a
wise elite who manipulate the weak masses to our current understanding.
In particular, she claims that his influence built into the foundations of PR
theory false assumptions about power and public relations, presenting a
view of public relations that privileges the role of corporate actors, that
"others" activists and uses the notion of pluralism to defend the dominance of the corporate voice. Demetrious argues, drawing on Coombs and
Holladay (2012a), that pluralism entrenches the dominant corporate-
centric tradition of PR as it overlooks the discrepancy of power between
corporate actors and activists:

While pluralism may appear to offer tolerance and inclusion for activists, close examination reveals that it over simplifies questions of
power and access and also promotes an attitude towards activism that
enables business to dismiss … and marginalise it almost completely.

(2013, p. 23)

Grunig and Hunt's influential four models of PR (1984) also assume a corporate subject. They suggest a chronological progression that paints a
picture of an historical development from a less ethical "craft" PR following the press agentry and public information models, to a more ethical

"professional" PR in the twentieth and twenty-first centuries focusing on two-way dialogue, whether asymmetrical or symmetrical. Here historical development is presented as growth in professionalism and ethical practice; a claim contested by academics such as Laskin (2009) and L'Etang and Piezcka (2006). As with much of Grunig's work, the unstated assumption is that the PR protagonist is a corporate employee, whose objective is to promote the products or services and reputation of their business. Thus his "modern" symmetrical two-way dialogue, posited as the aspirational model for all PR practitioners to follow, involves negotiations between a business pursuing profit and its stakeholders including employees, customers, government and NGOs, stakeholders who have varying but different priorities including societal well-being. This model, like the later mixed motive model developed by Grunig (2001) in response to criticism that the two-way symmetrical model was idealistic, is based on an oppositional relationship between the organisational (read financial) success of a business and stakeholders with societal as well as organisational objectives. In this way a corporate focus is built into our understanding of both the historical development of PR and its aspirations: namely to enhance the status of an organisation. Protest PR as a legitimate specialism of PR, with aspirations to support progressive social change as well as or instead of enhancing an organisation, does not feature in Grunig's work. NGOs, charities and social movements are almost entirely presented as "the other", and usually as an active risk or threat to the corporate protagonist.

The assumptions behind this historical framework limit its usefulness as a lens through which to understand the development of protest PR, which tends to focus on highlighting social problems, suggesting solutions and promoting social justice (these are the "demands" of the protestors, whether seeking tax justice or votes for women). This focus may include or result in an oppositional relationship between the protestors and business or government, but the oppositional relationship is not a necessary starting point for understanding protest PR or its history.

Some PR academics have sought to address this corporate bias in the documented history of PR. L'Etang's history of the development of PR in the UK (2004) breaks with the US corporate-centric tradition, and identifies the genesis of PR in the public sector in the 1920s, before the emerging profession was taken up first by government and then by the private sector. Gregory and Halff (2014) identify the same trend in Europe, charting the historical development of PR within Europe from late nineteenth century origins in the public sector to adoption by government in the early twentieth century and finally take up by the corporate sector. Based on a literature review of 51 histories of PR in Asia, Gregory and Halff (2014) also suggest three strands of the historical development of PR in Asian countries, moving from postcolonial nation building by governments, to growth by governments, and global corporate PR. They identify the corporate bias of the US models, and like L'Etang include government and public sector as PR actors. Other non-profit actors, however, are largely overlooked.

Coombs and Holladay (2012b) explicitly set out to counter the dominant, corporate-centric history of PR in the US. Their focus is on acknowledging the role of activist PR in contributing to the development of public relations as a profession overall, and their argument is that public relations can thus claim a societal role wider than simply the promotion of business interests, and in doing so repair its sometimes flawed reputation. Their discussion of the written histories of the development of public relations shows how in many cases early protest PR in the US was innovative and in advance of the bulk of the profession, including corporate PR. They cite research by Stoker and Rawlins (2005, cited in Coombs & Holladay 2012b) claiming that US activists in the Progressive era looking for social reforms in the early 1900s led to the birth of public relations as a profession. The second wave of protest PR around environmental issues, civil rights and the peace movement prompted a second "growth spurt" in the wider profession, while the development of the Internet and the opportunities it provides activists to organise and publicise has prompted the development inside PR of online reputation management as a growing specialism. These three historical stages of social reform; the rise of public interest in universal issues; and technological developments within media platforms could provide a more useful framework through which to consider the historical development of protest PR.

In contrast to the organisation-centric and specifically corporate-centric approaches to PR history, Coombs and Holladay shift our focus to society, and PR's role within it. This approach is echoed by L'Etang (2015), Demetrious (2013), Baringhorst (2009) and Hilder et al. (2007).

Expanding the history of PR to include its role in society

L'Etang links the study of PR history to our understanding of "PR practices and operating assumptions" (2015, p. 28). She argues that academics need to broaden their methodological approaches, drawing on social theory to look at "interpretations of modernity, post-modernity, the public sphere, political economy, communicative action, governance and the social imaginary" (2015, p. 28) to help us to understand the role of PR in terms of not just activities and a profession, but also social development. Academics writing PR history should think about multiple levels of involvement and intersections, relationships between agents and actions, PR as a focus for conflict and the role of PR in society and in social change. This challenge "raises questions about where PR history is located: within institutional history, corporate history, political history, social history or economic history" (2015, p. 31). L'Etang suggest that "PR histories should be repositioned and embedded within histories of broader societal shifts" and considers the importance of moving away "from an organisational focus towards positioning public relations as societal change" (2015, p. 28).

Considering the history of protest PR is thus an opportunity to locate PR history outside of corporate history and so to enrich both our understanding and our aspirations for the profession. This approach not only gives the history of protest PR a place within the history of the profession, it also foregrounds protest PR within that history, since protest PR is inextricably linked to social justice and change. Whether conducted by a formal organisation such as an NGO or charity, or a more fluid unstructured grouping such as a social movement, all non-profit actors embed societal change within their communicative and other activities.

Demetrious (2013) considers the development of activist PR in the social context, drawing a distinction between activist PR and corporate PR that is grounded on an understanding of the role of activist PR in social and political activity.

Drawing on Giddens (2009, cited in Demetrious, 2013) and Burgmann (1993, cited in Demetrious, 2013), Demetrious considers the historical development of activist PR in terms of connections between the type of actors driving these communicative activities, and the social issues around which they were communicating. Before the 1960s, class-based political parties and trade unions were the most active organisations, communicating around class, workers' rights and poverty. In the 1960s, the growth of identity politics, including gender, sexuality and race, led to a different kind of communicative activity focusing less on negotiating with state power and more on building individual power. Simultaneously, the growth of national and international charities and NGOs saw the rise of a new category of activist PR actor, one with more claim to (and desire for) professionalism. By the end of the millennium, universalist types of movement on topics such as peace and the environment had started to flourish. This chronological progression foregrounds social context over organisational development and so echoes Coombs and Holladay (2012b) rather than Grunig and Hunt's four models (1984).

Demetrious (2013) cites the environmental campaigner Doyle, who differentiated cycles within the environment movement in Australia through their partnerships or relationships with other players. He identifies three cycles: the outsider radical approach sitting outside government and seeking to exert pressure over it; the insider corporatist approach working with government; and third an insider approach working with business.

These cycles continue to inform non-profit actors globally.[1] While they appear to resemble Grunig's mixed motive model (2001), they are informed by the different possibilities for progressive social change created by changing political and social contexts. They also echo L'Etang's idea (2015) of looking at relationships between actors in the social context.

Dietz and Garrelts (2014) identify modern actors in the environmental protest movement using a similar demarcation and including:

- radical actors calling for systemic change to the political and economic system e.g. La Via Campesina and Plane Stupid;
- modernisers who aim to solve climate change within existing institutions and power structures e.g. Friends of the Earth and 350.org; and
- others including market-based players (corporates including the renewable energy sector and corporate social responsibility or sustainability teams), state actors and scientists.

They point to historical periods of flux between these actors, for example following key policy milestones such as the COP (annual Conference of the Parties under the United Nations Framework Convention on Climate Change) (Dietz & Garrelts, 2014, p. 2). In the same handbook, Della Porta and Parks (in Dietz & Garrelts, 2014) point to the historical shift of communications and framing approaches within the environment movement to reframe the issue from climate change to climate justice to "broaden the view of the problem" (2014, pp. 22–23) because actors adopting insider approaches and working with international organisations and national governments were not making progress and more radical actors perceived the need for a broader, more justice-based coalition. In this case communications explicitly followed social and political shifts and relationships between actors.

The social change campaigner Paul Hilder et al. (2007) also link the historical development of protest PR to developments in the social (as well as media and political) context, identifying four key stages:

- origins of protest in the creation of a legal space for assembly, urbanisation and the founding of the mass media;
- an increased right to vote and improved rights for more of the population during the twentieth century;
- the impact of globalisation and the rise of consumerism and individualism as traits within Western society that create social problems and therefore the need for social campaigning protest; and,
- social network power, enabling online grassroots activism.

Drawing on L'Etang (2015), Demetrious (2013), Coombs and Holladay (2012b) and Hilder et al. (2007) we could argue that considering the history of protest PR reflects a way of seeing the world, and the place of communicative activities within it, that privileges societal justice and social impact over organisational reputation. Looking at changing social and political contexts rather than developments inside organisations or professional skills sets enhances this approach. In this way, studying the history of protest PR is a way to reclaim or challenge the corporate-centric nature of the history of PR up to this point.

The naming of this activity can be problematic. Baringhorst (2009), Demetrious (2013) and L'Etang (2015) acknowledge that activism and social movements have traditionally been the study of sociologists, but that their communicative work can also

> Be regarded as a form of public relations work concerned with advocacy, promotion, events, lobbying and public affairs, communicating with a wide range of publics, and are clearly directed towards change as a form of social action and the realisation of idealised goals.
>
> (L'Etang, 2015, p. 30)

Yet grassroots activists, social movements, charities, NGOs and individuals may all engage in these communicative activities without accepting the label of PR. L'Etang claims that their practices include "activities that may not be described as public relations, sometimes for ideological reasons" (2015, p. 37). Tom Watson (2013) distinguishes between proto-PR, which he defines as persuasive communication used across different civilisations up to the late nineteenth century; and the profession of PR, defined by a particular set of tactics and approaches, starting at the end of the nineteenth century as the media industry developed. However, some non-profit actors may actively avoid being described as part of a profession or professional. The pre-figurative approach adopted by many social movements includes new ways of organising such as, for example, consensus decision making around media liaison. Professionalisation may be viewed as problematic by those who value consensus, authenticity and connection to the issue over professional skills in communicative activities (L'Etang, 2015). Demetrious (2013) also claims that the term PR embodies the dominant corporate focus of the PR body of knowledge (at least until recently), and so many civil society actors make a conscious decision to avoid the use of the term PR, rejecting the corporate focus and the aspirations to professionalism along with the term itself. She suggests the use of the term public communications as a way to resolve these tensions. For the purposes of this chapter the term protest PR is used to represent these activities, and the term non-profit actors is used to denote the broad range of individuals and organisations working for progressive social change including charities, NGOs and social movements.

Historical developments and the media context

Moloney (2006) defines the factors that drive PR development as: a market economy, pluralism, democracy, a competitive media marketplace and consumer choice. Certainly free speech and the ability to influence political decision-making, along with a free media whose editorial policy is not dictated by political parties, enable strategic media management by organisations and by activists. However, social movements and other protest PR actors can also flourish in environments where these factors do not all exist. Palowski (1991, cited in Demetrious, 2013), identifies rather different conditions required for activism to occur, including rapid social change, opportunities for action, and an exclusion from government relative to the expectations of society. The suffragettes ran one of the most successful protest campaigns in history in the context of exclusion from democracy, to win the right to vote and through that the right to participate in that democracy. Additionally, non-profit actors, especially social movements, may work outside the media marketplace to avoid the constraints of the protest paradigm (McLeod 2007). Many rely on alternative media to connect directly with supporters or decision makers as part of what Rucht (2004) describes as the Quadruple A approach. This alternative media strategy can be seen to apply from the suffragettes' early twentieth-century newspaper *The Suffragette*, to the early use of websites to share campaign messages by Friends of the Earth in 1995, and videos produced by UK-based alternative news producer Undercurrents[2] who, staffed by activists and volunteers, produced alternative news videos on VHS in the 1990s and continue to provide alternative news footage from the activist perspective, unmediated by media companies, on a range of environmental and social issues.

Baringhorst's consideration of the development of political communication in connection with developments in the media landscape offers another media-driven perspective. She looks at the relationship between "changing modes of political campaigning and processes of modernization of media technology and media systems" (2009, p. 9). This is useful as a framework to consider the historical development of protest PR, as it is not explicitly tied to any particular sector or ideological approach. In addition, she includes non-profit organisations and social movements as legitimate actors in her analysis. Baringhorst's definition of campaigning can be applied also to protest PR:

> A series of communicative activities undertaken to achieve predefined goals and objectives regarding a defined target audience in a set time period with a given amount of resources.
>
> (2009, p. 10)

We can understand "predefined goals and objectives" to include delivering tangible progressive social change, in the form of legislation or policies, as well as the changes in attitudes, opinions and behaviours that are often a prerequisite to that change. This encompasses the different elements of protest PR that may include: to draw attention to an injustice, to mobilise support around that injustice and to press for a progressive solution.

Baringhorst argues that "changing media environments ... have ... direct as well as indirect implications for the historical development of political campaigning" (2009, p. 14). She draws on Norris (2000, cited in Baringhorst, 2009) who identified three stages of electoral campaigning – pre-modern, modern and post-modern. Baringhorst extends this to apply to a broader range of political actors including activists (2009, pp. 14–17) and to consider the historical development of their communicative activity:

- Pre-modern campaigns from nineteenth century to the 1950s, characterised by face-to-face communication using volunteers and grassroots activists, e.g. through door-to-door canvassing and rallies, as well as leaflets and some third party endorsement;
- Modern campaigns from the 1950s to the 1980s, characterised by a more national focus and by new television-friendly tactics such as stunts and photo opportunities, sound-bites for news programmes, celebrities and human interest/personalisation;
- Post-modern campaigns from the 1980s onwards, characterised by the pluralisation of channels creating niche audiences, more professionalisation, but also by bottom up structures and online media that enable participatory tactics and co-creation of content.

Looking at these three stages in terms of protest PR, we can see evidence for Coombs and Holladay's (2012a) claim that protest PR often innovated ahead of other sectors. The suffragettes in the UK, campaigning in the "premodern" period, used all the tactics Baringhorst described for that period but also developed more sophisticated approaches including several classified by Baringhorst as modern. For example, the suffragettes in England were using photo opportunities and stunts as early as the 1910s, staging mass demonstrations, seeking media coverage in the newly expanding national press, piloting a boat advertising their key campaign demand past the windows of the Houses of Parliament (Tickner, 1987) in what we could describe as a photo call, and developing what would today be called branding – a distinctive colour palette and easily recognised symbols and slogans, all consistently used across a range of campaign materials and merchandise, from posters and leaflets to badges, banners, sashes and tea-sets.

The suffragettes: historical analysis

To explore this further, an historical analysis of suffragette materials in the archive of the Museum of London was conducted to explore the notion that the suffragettes were pioneers who innovated outside frameworks used to describe PR or public communication of that period.

The suffragettes' campaign called for legislative change to extend the right to vote in British elections to women. Gradually developing momentum after the Reform Acts of 1867 and 1884 gave votes to the majority of men, but excluded women, the campaign reached its height at the beginning of the twentieth century and was eventually successful when some women were granted the right to vote in 1918 (Tickner, 1987). The Museum of London holds the largest collection in the world on the militant suffragette campaign (Kennedy, 2017). A selection of 437 items from the Museum of London

Figure 3.1 Badges such as this one from the Women's Social and Political Union were sold to raise funds, and also to help ensure that supporters wore the suffragette colours.

Source: the Museum of London.

archive was considered from the period 1903–1914, when the suffragettes suspended their campaign for the duration of the First World War. A broad qualitative analysis of items was undertaken through the museum's online collection, supplemented by analysis of selected physical items. While the research uses a coding approach, it is interpretivist rather than positivist and the research was driven by inductive reasoning (Daymon & Holloway, 2011). The overall research question was:

> To what extent do the tactics suggested by materials in the suffragette collection at the Museum of London align with Baringhorst's three identified periods of political communication?

As Daymon and Holloway note (2011, p. 196), one limitation of historical research is of projecting modern sensibility onto historical activities or events. This analysis can therefore only suggest insights. Following an initial sampling to establish key emerging themes, materials were coded by:

1   showing evidence of deliberate campaign branding (consistent colour palette, recurring symbols and slogans); and
2   illustrating the use of tactics associated with the modern and post-modern stages suggested by Baringhorst (including a national focus, stunts and photo opportunities, celebrity, human interest, co-creation and participatory tactics).

Clear themes were identified that indicate where the suffragettes used innovative tactics when considered against Baringhorst's modern and post-modern periods, in addition to using the pre-modern tactics appropriate for the time frame of the campaign. These innovative tactics include:

- Branding (not included in Baringhorst);
- National focus (modern campaign stage);
- Stunts and photo opportunities (modern campaign stage);
- Celebrity and human interest (modern campaign stage);
- Co-creation and participatory tactics (post-modern campaign stage).

Branding

A sophisticated branding identity is visible across suffragette materials, including a distinctive purple, white and green colour palette; slogans including Votes for Women and Deeds not Words; and symbols including the freedom angel. Elements of this identity are visible in half of the materials within the archive. Suffragette organisers asked women to wear the colour palette at all public demonstrations and activities, and sold a range of branded brooches, including cheap tin brooches at one penny, both for fundraising and to enable consistent and widespread branding at all events.[3]

Branding is not included by Baringhorst as a pre-modern characteristic. In a clear demonstration of the way protest PR may foreground the social issue rather than organisational interest, elements of this branding identity were used by several organisations within the broader movement, including the Women's Social and Political Union (WSPU), the Women's Freedom League and the Church League for Women's Suffrage, and materials do not always show an organisation's name. This can be considered as movement branding and not simply organisational branding, reflecting the social emphasis that helps characterise protest PR.

National focus and photo opportunities (modern)

The national focus of the suffragettes' campaign saw them target variously MPs and Parliament,[4] the King,[5] the Church of England[6] and iconic national assets such as the National Gallery.[7] Many demonstrations and processions brought women from across the country for national events, such as the Women's Coronation Procession of 1911, and the National Union of Women's Suffrage Societies procession on 13 June 1908, which chartered special trains for the purpose.[8] The desire to generate national media coverage is evident in, for example, suffragettes' frustration and direct action[9] when national newspapers failed to cover events, in letters to editors of national newspapers regarding the forcible feeding of hunger strikers and in references within suffragettes' correspondence to the amount of publicity generated by their activity. Front page national media coverage in the *Daily Mirror*[10] of the suffragettes' demonstration when David Lloyd George opened an institute in his childhood home village in Wales evidences an understanding of how to stage a photo opportunity in order to generate national media coverage.

Figure 3.2 National events such as the Women's Coronation Procession of 1911 increased pressure on national figures including, in this case, the new King.

Source: the Museum of London.

Figure 3.3 Suffragettes were keen to secure media coverage in the growing national newspaper market.

Source: the Museum of London.

This is a stunt that would not look out of place in a current social movement's repertoire of tactics. While Baringhorst associates a national focus and photo opportunities with modern campaigns from the 1950s to the 1980s, the suffragettes were ahead of this trend.

Celebrity and human interest (modern)

High-profile supporters of the suffragettes included a member of the Punjabi royal family, who was photographed selling *The Suffragette* newspaper.[11] The archive materials reveal an organised strategy to honour and celebrate suffragettes who participated in the campaign, creating suffrage celebrities and human interest. Badges were sold showing the faces of campaign leaders including Emmeline Pankhurst,[12] Christabel Pankhurst,[13] and Emmeline Pethick-Lawrence,[14] their names were prominently displayed on fliers[15] advertising events and they were celebrated in merchandising materials including packs of playing cards.[16] A hierarchy of celebrity is evident in the range of medals and brooches produced for those who had served

Figure 3.4 Medals awarded to suffragettes who had served prison sentences honoured the physical suffering endured by women like Florence Haig, presented with this medal after her third hunger strike, and helped create inspiring role models for the movement.

Source: the Museum of London.

prison sentences, presented at formal occasions in presentation boxes, and decorated variously with convict arrows,[17] bars marking periods of hunger strike,[18] and medals for periods of forced labour.[19]

Brooches were also sold to celebrate participation in mass window smashing campaigns.[20] This honouring of women's participation was extended to create empathy through human interest, for example including personal testimonies in leaflets about the effects of force feeding, and through the recreation of a prison cell at the 1909 Women's Exhibition, complete with suffragettes in replica prison costumes[21] re-enacting the activities they undertook while in prison and demonstrating the poor prison conditions.

Co-creation and participatory tactics (post-modern)

Suffragettes participated in numerous processions and demonstrations, in civil disobedience such as window smashing campaigns, and in fundraising events and strategies including running WSPU shops. Regional organisers such as Charlotte Marsh[22] worked to promote participation, in her case across Yorkshire, Nottingham and the South East.

Figure 3.5 The Artists' Suffrage League was an outlet for women to participate in designing and creating the movement's key campaign materials such as banners and posters.

Source: the Museum of London.

Suffragettes also participated in the design and co-creation of banners[23] that reflected their region, profession or other affiliation, through the Suffrage Atelier (Tickner, 1987) anticipating the modern interest in craftivism (Corbett, 2017). And Tickner cites evidence that the suffragettes used participatory tactics to choose the distinctive purple, white and green colour palette.[24]

The suffragettes' lesson for PR

The items in the suffragette collection at the Museum of London demonstrate the use of several tactics that Baringhorst identifies as common to the modern and post-modern periods, though these began more than 40 years after the suffragettes' campaign. Like the US activists identified by Coombs and Holladay (2012b) as innovating in advance of their peers, the suffragettes were pioneers. Their use of branding, a national media focus, the use of photo opportunities, generating celebrity and human interest, and building participatory tactics anticipate elements of the modern and post-modern stages of Baringhorst's framework. In addition, these archival items indicate that promoting the issue of women's suffrage often took precedence over promoting organisations, reflecting the social lens discussed by Demetrious and L'Etang. Finally, the suffragette movement was a forerunner 100 years ago for the issues-based movements that Burgmann (1993, cited in Demetrious, 2013) categorises as growing from the 1960s onwards. The Museum of London collection suggests that more research of protest PR and communicative activities is required to document the scale of innovation by non-profit actors.

Enduring trends: referencing protest history

While changing media and technological contexts require continual adaptation by non-profit actors to the tools and channels at their disposal, these changes have less impact on the communicative activities within protest PR than one might imagine. Some aspects persist over time, adapting themselves to changing contexts.

For example, if we consider the role of stunts, photo opportunities or pseudo-events (Boorstin, 1987), we can see certain themes or trends that recur throughout history. For at least 100 years, protesters have used the tactic of chaining oneself to an object or building that is the site of the power being challenged. The suffragettes chained themselves to the railings of Parliament[25] to signify their commitment to bringing the issue of female suffrage to the attention of political decision-makers. Environmental protestors opposed to the construction of the Newbury bypass in the 1990s camped high in trees and D-locked themselves inside tunnels on site to prevent bulldozers from operating. These tactics have the communicative purpose of providing a dramatic news hook that meets the news criteria of the mass media, while also visually telling the story or demand of the protesters.

The tactic of staging a mass die-in is another symbolic act that both demonstrates the fatal or potentially fatal impact of the issue being protested, alongside providing a visual news hook for the mass media to pick up, spreading the campaign or protest message, and also building a sense of community and commitment among the protesters. This tactic has been used since at least the 1960s, when the Campaign for Nuclear Disarmament staged mass die-ins to represent visually their core message that stockpiling nuclear weapons could lead to mass fatalities. The tactic has been used since by campaigners as diverse in their organisational style, issue and objective as cycling campaigners protesting unsafe road conditions in London, and the feminist social movement Sisters Uncut using the premiere of the film *Suffragette* to stage a stunt on the red carpet drawing attention to cuts to domestic violence refuges (Sisters Uncut, 2015).

This goes further than simply repackaging or reusing tactics. Some protest PR references its own history, embodying the message that protest can be and has been successful in bringing about progressive social change. UK Feminista consciously echo the successful suffragette movement in their communicative activities around gender and inequality (Rickman, 2012). The history of protest PR not only offers us insights into the role of protest PR within society, and the ways in which it challenges the corporate view of the role of PR and power, it also offers hope that can help to mobilise the next generation of protesters.

Conclusion

This chapter has argued that the dominant historical frameworks for the development of PR (e.g. Grunig & Hunt, 1984) overlook the development of protest PR. The history of activist and protest PR has largely been written out of the history of the profession. These dominant frameworks privilege an organisational and specifically a corporate-centric view of public relations activity. For these reasons, they are not the ideal lens through which to examine the historical development of protest PR.

Naming protest activity as PR and including it within historical frameworks can help to position PR as playing a role in societal issues and social change, enabling us to consider PR outside a narrow corporate or organisational focus. As L'Etang says:

> Placing public relations on a continuum that links it to propaganda and persuasion, and activism and social movements, positions it as one of a series of linked activities and terms engaged in the rhetorical and political contexts of societal conflict and change.
>
> (2015, p. 37)

Frameworks that foreground the social and political context of protest PR enable us to consider the role of PR within society, as called for by L'Etang (2015) and Demetrious (2013), and to move away from the organisational and corporate-centric focus of the dominant frameworks for considering the development of PR. A part of this social focus is to consider the changing issues around which nonprofit actors organise, the changing organisation types and platforms which they use to do so, and the changing relationships between them.

Considering the historical development of protest PR through the lens of changes in the media landscape (Baringhorst, 2009) allows us to see both the characteristics of protest PR which persist throughout time, such as stunts and photo calls, symbolic acts, mass mobilisation and identity building, and also the pattern of innovation within this activity as exemplified by the suffragettes. The suffragettes were early pioneers in developing strong campaign brands and in staging photo opportunities for the national media, employing activities in the 1900s and 1910s that anticipate the pre-modern period of the 1950s–1980s.

Overall then, we have the opportunity to understand the historical development of protest PR through several lenses:

1 changes in the media landscape;
2 changes in the social and political context;
3 the development and professionalisation of different protest PR actors; and
4 the changing issues around which protest and activist PR is enacted.

The impact of the varying contexts in different countries, regions, political regimes and cultures is also central to the analysis of protest PR.

The consistent thread that runs throughout examples of protest PR is a commitment to progressive social change and to the role of communicative activity in achieving this. The ability of communications to build collective identity, enable participatory action, and galvanize support for social change are behind the historic and continuing success of protest PR by non-profit actors.

Notes

1 E.g. see Stachowiak, S. (2013) *Pathways for change: 10 theories to inform advocacy and policy change efforts.* Centre for Evaluation Innovation.
2 See www.undercurrents.org/.
3 Museum of London (MoL) collections, WSPU badge (1908–1910) 50.82/1169, https://collections.museumoflondon.org.uk/online/object/43306.html.
4 MoL collections, Daily Mirror (1910) 2003.46/185, https://collections.museum oflondon.org.uk/online/object/748737.html.
5 MoL collections, Photograph (1911) 50.82/1383, https://collections.museumof london.org.uk/online/object/294039.html.

6 MoL collections, Suffrage Atelier banner (1909–1910) 81.113/42, https://collections.museumoflondon.org.uk/online/object/91750.html.

7 MoL collections, Photograph (1914) 50.82/1393, https://collections.museumoflondon.org.uk/online/object/294074.html.

8 MoL collections, Christina Broom photograph (1908) IN1271, https://collections.museumoflondon.org.uk/online/object/436952.html.

9 MoL collections, Whip (1911) 50.82/1205, https://collections.museumoflondon.org.uk/online/object/65663.html.

10 MoL collections, Newspaper cutting (1912) 2008.1/28, https://collections.museumoflondon.org.uk/online/object/773538.html.

11 MoL collections, Photograph (1913) 2003.46/108, https://collections.museumoflondon.org.uk/online/object/731598.html.

12 MoL collections, WSPU badge (1910) 50.82/1162, https://collections.museumoflondon.org.uk/online/object/43307.html.

13 MoL collections, WSPU badge (1910) 50.82/1161, https://collections.museumoflondon.org.uk/online/object/65676.html.

14 MoL collections, WSPU badge (1910) 50.82/1163, https://collections.museumoflondon.org.uk/online/object/65685.html.

15 MoL collections, WSPU handbill (1914) 50.82/737, https://collections.museumoflondon.org.uk/online/object/288618.html.

16 MoL collections, Panko game (1909) 50.82/1506, https://collections.museumoflondon.org.uk/online/object/48456.html.

17 MoL collections, Pin brooch (1909) 50.82/1150, https://collections.museumoflondon.org.uk/online/object/43310.html.

18 MoL collections, Medal (1912) 50.82/1160a, https://collections.museumoflondon.org.uk/online/object/752608.html.

19 MoL collections, Medal (1912) 2005.145/5, https://collections.museumoflondon.org.uk/online/object/744233.html.

20 MoL collections, Silver brooch (1912) 50.82/1188a, https://collections.museumoflondon.org.uk/online/object/65680.html.

21 MoL collections, Bonnet (1909–1914) 96.103/3, https://collections.museumoflondon.org.uk/online/object/143482.html.

22 MoL collections, Christina Broom photograph (1910) IN1350, https://collections.museumoflondon.org.uk/online/object/437266.html.

23 MoL collections, Photograph (1910) 50.82/1382, https://collections.museumoflondon.org.uk/online/object/294036.html.

24 More evidence of participatory organising tactics may be present in journals and other documents held in collections such as the National Archive, rather than in objects.

25 MoL collections, Belt and chain (c.1840) 61.186, https://collections.museumoflondon.org.uk/online/object/67530.html.

References

Baringhorst, S. (2009) Introduction: Political campaigning in changing media cultures. In S. Baringhorst, V. Kneip & J. Niesyto (eds) *Political campaigning on the web*. Bielefeld: Transcript Verlag.

Boorstin, D. (1987) *The image: a guide to pseudo-events in America*. New York: Athenaeum.

Broom, G. & Cutlip, S. (2013) *Cutlip and Center's effective public relations* 11th ed. Harlow: Person Education.

Coombs, W.T. & Holladay, S. (2012a) Fringe public relations: How activism moves critical PR towards the mainstream, *Public Relations Review*, 38 (5), 880–887.

Coombs, W.T. & Holladay, S. (2012b) Privileging an activist vs. a corporate view of public relations history in the U.S, *Public Relations Review* 38 (3), 347–353.

Corbett, S. (2017) *How to be a craftivist: the art of gentle protest*. London: Unbound.

Daymon, C. & Holloway, I. (2011) *Qualitative research methods in public relations and marketing communications* 2nd ed. New York: Routledge.

Della Porta, D. & Parks, L. (2014) Framing processes in the climate movement. In M. Dietz & H. Garrelts (eds) *Routledge handbook of the climate change movement*. London: Routledge, pp. 19–30.

Demetrious, K. (2006) Active voices. In J. L'Etang & M. Pieczka (eds) *Public relations: critical debates and contemporary practice*. London: Lawrence Erlbaum Associates, pp. 93–107.

Demetrious, K. (2013) *Public relations, activism and social change: speaking up: PR and activism*. London: Routledge.

Dietz, M. & Garrelts, H. (eds) (2014) *Routledge handbook of the climate change movement*. London: Routledge.

Edwards, L. & Hodges, C. (2011) *Public relations, society and culture*. London: Routledge.

Gregory, A. & Halff, G. (2014) Towards an historically informed Asian model of public relations, *Public Relations Review*, 40 (3), 397–407.

Grunig, J.E. (2001) Two-way symmetrical public relations: Past, present and future in *Handbook of Public Relations*, R. Heath (ed.). London: Sage.

Grunig, J.E. & Hunt, T. (1984) *Managing PR*. New York: Holt, Rinehart and Winston.

Hilder, P., Caulier-Grice, J. & Lalor, K. (2007) *Contentious citizens – civil society's role in campaigning for social change*. The Young Foundation.

Kennedy, M. (2017, 9 November) Museum of London exhibition will mark suffragettes' victory. *Guardian*. Retrieved from https://amp.theguardian.com/politics/2017/nov/09/museum-of-london-exhibition-will-mark-suffragettes-victory.

Laskin, A. (2009) The evolution of models of public relations: An outsider's perspective *Journal of Communication Management*, 13 (1), 37–54.

L'Etang, J. (2004) *Public relations in Britain: a history of professional practice in the 20th century*. London: Lawrence Earlbaum Associates.

L'Etang, J. (2009) *Public relations, concepts, practice and critique*. London: Sage.

L'Etang, J. (2015) History as the source of critique from the *Routledge handbook of critical public relations*. Oxon: Routledge, pp. 28–40 [online].

L'Etang, J. & Pieczka, M. (2006) *Public relations: critical debates and contemporary practice*. London: Lawrence Erlbaum Associates.

McLeod, D. (2007) News coverage and social protest: How the media's protest paradigm exacerbates social conflict. *Journal of Dispute Resolution*, 2007 (1), 185–194.

Moloney, K. (2006) *Rethinking public relations: PR propaganda and democracy* 2nd ed. London: Routledge.

Museum of London (n.d.) *Collections*. Retrieved from https://collections.museumoflondon.org.uk.

O'Brien, M. (2018) Non-profit issues management, a new approach to resist the label of 'risk'. In N. Garsten & I. Bruce (eds) *Communicating causes, strategic public relations for the non-profit sector*. London: Routledge, pp. 41–54.

Rickman, D. (2012, 24 October) Suffragettes storm Parliament as part of UK Feminista lobby. *The Huffington Post*. Retrieved from www.huffingtonpost.co.uk/2012/10/24/suffragettes-storm-parliament-feminism_n_2008361.html.

Rucht, D. (2004) The quadruple 'A': Media strategies of protest movements since the 1960s'. In W. Van de Donk, P.D. Loader, P.G. Nixon & D. Rucht (eds) *Cyberprotest: new media, citizens and social movements*. London and New York: Routledge, pp. 29–56.

Sisters Uncut (2015, 8 October) Why we stormed the Suffragette premiere. *The Daily Telegraph*. Retrieved from www.telegraph.co.uk/women/womens-life/11919707/Feminist-protestors-Why-we-stormed-the-Suffragette-premiere.html.

Stachowiak, S. (2013) *Pathways for change: 10 theories to inform advocacy and policy change efforts*. Centre for Evaluation Innovation.

Tickner, L. (1987) *The spectacle of women: imagery of the suffrage campaign 1907–14*. London: Chatto and Windus.

Watson, T. (2013) Keynote address presented at the International History of Public Relations Conference 2013, Bournemouth. Retrieved from https://microsites.bournemouth.ac.uk/historyofpr/proceedings/.

4 Second-wave feminist movement in Turkey through an activist PR perspective

A. Banu Bıçakçı and Pelin Hürmeriç

In the dawn of a big socio-economic and political change, the year 1980 marked a sharp turning point for Turkey. A military coup d'état over-threw the country's statist system, as the public became familiar with neo-liberalism. From the 1980s on the class structure, status and cultural groups of the country were diversified and restructured (Şimşek, 2004), whereas women enhanced their political activism in the public realm and began to redefine their relationship to the state (Y. Arat, 2008). Con-sequently, the second wave feminism of the West penetrated Turkey with 15–20 years of delay. Throughout the 1980s and 1990s, Turkish feminists protested against problems such as domestic violence and the amendment of the Turkish Civil Code, with a primary objective of gaining acceptance for women as individuals in control of their own lives in a patriarchal country (Y. Arat, 2000, 2008; Karagöz 2008; Sirman, 1989; Tekeli, 1986).

The idea of public relations is conceptualized with a focus on its role in social changes when examined as a social, cultural and political phenom-enon, and not only as a corporate position. Even if the mainstream per-spective defines PR as "a strategic communication process that builds mutually beneficial relationships between organizations and their publics" (About PR, 2018) and in doing so, serving the benefits of both the organ-ization and the society, the definition excludes its role in civil society as being the voice of disadvantaged groups. Moloney (2006) states, "civil society is an important social location for public relations" (p. 87). Holtzhausen (2012) notes, "public relations is political, no matter what the action" (p. 104), and it is vital to facilitate social change; without com-munication activities – to educate, influence, promote, engage, prod and persuade – social or political change would hardly occur (Martinelli, 2014, p. 208). Accordingly, the sub-field of activist public relations serves the development of the civil society.

Demetrious (2008) defines activist public relations as:

> A focused view of communication activity by politicized third sector groups such as social collectives, community action groups, and

nongovernmental organizations (NGOs) to foster their public legitimacy as voices for social change.

(p. 1)

Among activist groups there are also feminists that utilize various public relations techniques in the ideological war against patriarchal values, targeting the social norms which empower men to be counted as always powerful and legitimate. Although the feminist movement is a major field of study in sociology, political science and gender studies, there are only a few studies, if any, in the public relations field.

While there are numerous studies on the women's movement in Turkey, the research on the topic though the lens of public relations is limited only with the role of female practitioners in the field (see Deren van het Hof and Hoştut, 2016; Öksüz and Görpe, 2014; Tanyıldızı, 2011). This chapter traces the emergence of an organized and oppositional feminist movement in Turkey in the 1980s and examines the effects of this movement, both in the civil society and legislation, from an activist public relations perspective. The main goal of this chapter is to expand the historical understanding of public relations benefiting from the "dissent PR" and "protest PR" concepts (Moloney et al., 2012). Considering the historical research guide of McDowell (2002), this research informing this chapter is based on a review of 52 short articles (memories of feminist women) in a commemorative book, about 150 articles published in three major feminist magazines (*Soyut-4. Sayfa, Pazartesi and Kaktüs*), declarations and notes written by Turkish feminists between 1980–1990 along with relevant secondary sources such as news, statistics, reports and photos – most of which are obtained from the Women's Library and Information Center's[1] archives in İstanbul. In doing so, we try to find out how dissent and protest PR tactics intertwine and raise public consciousness in a critical issue. This approach is based on the definition of public relations "as a persuasive tool for strengthening democracy" (McQueen, 2013, p. 5), and public relations in its relationship to activism is seen as a meaning-making process. Regarding PR strategies and tactics, the study takes Ronald D. Smith's (2009) conceptualization and terminology into consideration. Exploring how Turkish women have used activist techniques to get their voices in the society, this discussion aims to contribute conceptualization of dissent PR and protest PR terms delving deep into the strategies and creative tactics before the social media era.

The intersection of public relations and activism

Since its first use, public relations has been defined in various ways based on its role and functions in a society. As public relations has historically been viewed as representative of those involved in maintaining the status quo – those in decision-making positions within or on behalf of organizations, corporations and governments – it has been largely left out of the social movement literature (Martinelli, 2014). Coombs and Holladay (2012, p. 349) state that, although there has been an increase in research that includes activists as practicing public relations, the contributions of activists still remain overlooked from a historical perspective.

Activism is identified through the actions of individuals advocating an issue and in so doing they become activists who are defined as individuals or groups seeking to influence public policy, organizational actions, social norms or values (Coombs and Holladay, 2010, p. 82). Kim and Sriramesh (2009, p. 82) define activism as the "coordinated effort of a group that voluntarily organizes in an effort to solve problems that threaten the common interest of members of the group." Ehling, on the other hand (as cited in Benedict, 2017, p. 15), argues that an activist public is a group of two or more individuals who organize in order to influence another public or publics through action that may include education, compromise, persuasion, pressure tactics or force. Ganesh and Zoller (2012) state that activist groups actively engage in dialogue, develop actions and analyze dialogue and contestation. Coombs and Holladay (2014, p. 2) link activism and public relations by giving examples of activists using public relations in the past such as Greenpeace, Labor behind the Label and PETA and later using new communication technology as it evolves. They underline that there is a history and tradition in activism that began in 1800s in the US, some time before the modern corporation. During that period, although the term public relations did not exist, activists of this era were using PR to create pressure for social change. One of the important roles of PR professionals is to serve public interest by informing and educating stakeholders on social issues, and thus, it can be argued that public relations is vital to facilitating social change (Martinelli, 2014).

Ciszek (2015) suggests that:

> Activists have been implementing public relations for at least 100 years. In fact, a modest body of literature indicates that many of the tactics used by activists are public relations tactics, and their motives can be viewed as public relations strategies.
>
> (p. 447)

In the 1960s activists utilized public relations to attract the attention of the corporate elite, developing and utilizing many of the modern tools of public relations (Coombs and Holladay, 2014, p. 63). Print media, public speeches, and pseudo-events were used to draw attention to and build support for causes. Reber and Berger (as cited in Benedict, 2017, p. 67) claim that many public relations scholars look at activism "as something to be managed or as something that forces corporations toward better public relations practice," but rarely as a communications process with its own strategies and tactics. Demetrious (2013, p. 34) supports this by stating that much public relations activity is preoccupied with monitoring, guiding against, or mending "damage" involving activism.

Postmodern public relations theorists suggest that PR professionals will act as an activist within the organization and thus taking a more activist stance will make the profession more ethical (Holtzhausen 2000, 2012; Holtzhausen and Voto, 2002 cited in Coombs and Holladay, 2014). Demetrious (2013) emphasizes this by claiming that "marginal groups and communication are necessary to achieve representational democracy" (p. 48) and that "the communication activities of public relations and activism and their relationship [is] centrally important to the democratic ideal" (p. 49). In order to underline the intersection of PR and activism, Martinelli (2014, p. 206) also states that in their struggles to gain the right to vote, women suffragists around the world instigated social change by using public relations strategies and tactics to educate, persuade, and motivate other women as well as male political elites.

It is evident that public relations is vital in democratic societies and as it plays an important role in facilitating social change, both dissent and protest PR strategies and tactics can be utilized in order to inform, educate and persuade target publics. Dissent PR is explained as the sharing of ideas, commentaries, and policies through strategic communication techniques in order to change current, dominant thinking and behavior in discrete economic, political and cultural areas of public life. Another term that is related with dissent PR is protest PR, and it is identified as a consequence of the dissent term. Protest PR is persuasive communication that aims to implement ideas, behaviors and policies into law, regulation and other forms of executive action (Moloney et al., 2012).

In the next part, the second wave feminist movement in Turkey will be analyzed through an activist PR perspective based on strategies and tactics that are observed under dissent and protest PR.

Second wave feminism in Turkey

Scholars point to the late 1960s and early 1970s as marking the beginning of the second wave feminist thinking in the Western societies, where feminism and women's activism have been often relegated to a sidebar of social movement histories of those years (Evans, 1998, 2008; Gilmore, 2008; Nicholson, 1997); however, in Turkey it was only in the 1980s when the feminist movement brought up issues common to second wave feminism in the West, such as the elimination of violence against women revealing the harassment that women faced in the family, the use of sexuality as a medium for male dominance, the misrepresentation of women in the media and the challenge against virginity tests – a common practice for women who were about to get married or who had been subject to a sexual attack (Diner and Toktaş, 2010, p. 41).

Despite divergent approaches in the periodization of the women's movement in Turkey (Y. Arat, 2008; Sirman, 1989; Tekeli, 2017; Yaraman, 2001), researchers agree that 1980 was a major breaking point in the historical development of the movement. Nevertheless, Turkish feminism has its roots in much earlier times, dating back to Ottoman periods. The first wave of feminism started in pre-republican times in the early twentieth century and as Y. Arat (2008) mentioned "the first generation of feminists protested through journals and cultivated their solidarity through associations, and feminists of later generations followed suit" (p. 389). When the country was going through major revolutions in the 1920s and 1930s, in the aftermath of the foundation of the new Turkish Republic, and following the War of Liberation[2] led by Mustafa Kemal Atatürk, a small number of women's organizations at the time aimed at equality in civic and political rights. The ideal of becoming a Westernized society required legal equality between all citizens regardless of gender. Thus, the women's organizations' statements, overlapped with nationalist considerations and the Kemalist reforms[3] (Z. F. Arat, 2008; Diner and Toktaş, 2010; Tekeli, 2017). As summarized by Coşar and Onbaşı (2008):

> In 1926, the Turkish Civil Code was adopted. It abolished polygamy, endorsed compulsory civil marriage and recognized the right of divorce for both partners, while also anticipating egalitarian inheritance laws – egalitarian relative to Ottoman times. In 1930 and 1934, women were given the right to participate in municipal and general elections.
>
> (p. 326)

However, this cannot be considered as a victory of the suffragists, since the women's suffrage was granted within the institutionalization of a secular nation-state (Y. Arat, 2008). The first wave of Turkish feminism that was marked with the colonization of the women's movement by the discourses on nation-state building lasted until the Turkish Women's Union (*Türk Kadınlar Birliği*)[4] was closed in 1935; after 1935, Turkish feminism has been dormant for the following 45 years.

Prior to 1980, Kemalism, the official political ideology, declared that the problems of women were solved by the state; Islam, the dominant social ideology assumed that women did not even suffer, and Marxism, the leftist ideology striving for hegemony, claimed that women did not have any problems except capitalist exploitation. However, in the Turkey of those times, gender playing a determining role with women of all classes suffering from sexual abuse, discrimination and domestic violence (Tekeli, 2017, p. 269). In 1980, only 36 percent of the economically active population was female and the female literacy rate was about 55 percent. The ratio of the women in parliament did not exceed 4.5 percent (this was partly due to the late acceptance of women into public office). And although there was an obvious discrepancy, women did not conduct any serious protest against the state discourse nor its practices toward women until the early 1980s (Y. Arat, 2008, p. 394).

According to Demetrious (2013), social movements are "purposeful collective actions which advocate with socio-political intent" (p. 34). The second wave of the women's movement in Turkey was closely associated with the social and political environment of those times, Diner and Toktaş (2010) summarizing well this context:

> This was the period after the military coup in 1980; all the political parties were closed down except those few which were newly founded and strictly controlled by the military; many of the leaders of the political parties, labor unions and political organizations were banned from politics; the youth and women's branches of banned political parties were also ruled to be illegal; and a new constitution was enacted in 1982 that outlined a very limited framework for individual rights and freedoms. (...) it was at this moment, when there were serious legal and political barriers to political expression and participatory civil society that an independent women's movement developed. (...) Those questioning women's status in society were mostly urban, middle-class, well-educated, professional women.
>
> (p. 45)

These women have had a stronger "gendered" worldview in comparison to the first wave. The second wave Turkish feminists directly targeted patriarchy, criticized male hegemony, utilized a radical tone and demanded the development of women's status not only in the public sphere but in the private sphere as well (Diner and Toktaş, 2010). They were against the discriminative social norms and laws such as the requirement that wives get permission from their husbands to be eligible for employment in the business sector, the use of the man's surname as the family name, men being recognized as head of the household and men's right to decide on the schooling of the children as well as on the house that the family will live in.

Throughout the 1980s the feminists had a negative attitude toward the state, as they perceived it as the main guardian of the patriarchal system; consequently, they refused to cooperate (Coşar and Onbaşı, 2008). However, Turkish state officials clearly misunderstood and underestimated the feminists' anti-statist political attitude as they assumed women were fighting for something the founders of the Republic had already legitimized by adopting the civil code and granting women's rights (Yeşilyurt Gündüz, 2004). This understanding paved the way for the second wave feminist activist movement.

Second wave feminism in Turkey, as an activist movement, utilized various tactics such as meetings, demonstrations, festivals, petitions and publications to enable a change both in the civil society and the laws that restricted the freedom of women. Those creative, interpersonal and news media tactics served as dissent and protest PR strategies.

Consciousness raising meeting: an awakening

Inspired by a form of activism known by the same name "the Consciousness-Raising Meetings" (see Eastman, 1973; Weitz, 1982) was one of the first actions of the second wave feminist movement in Turkey. These meetings were not an invention of second wave feminists, but an earlier form of rhetorical strategy (Sowards and Renegar, 2004). They were meant to bring attention to a new thinking, and inspire new behaviors in areas of national life and thus utilized in dissent PR. The participant women were encouraged to share personal experiences of gender discrimination in the conversations. It is through consciousness raising meetings that the ideas of second wave feminism were promoted and the Turkish women were awakened to take an action in changing the male dominance. Similar to their Western counterparts, Turkish feminists explained that the personal was political and that the state had to respect the private sphere.

> The "private is political" dictum is explanatory in this respect, since it constituted the main reference point for the first feminist initiatives after 1980. Consciousness-raising groups availed feminists in voicing the issues of sexual freedom, sexual harassment, rape, battering of women, and discrimination at the workplace as issues belonging to the political and public domains.
>
> (Coşar and Onbaşı, 2008, p. 330)

Consciousness raising meetings began in 1981 with the aim of politico-feminist resocialization of group members (Arat, 1994). These groups were made up of young women criticizing the leftist movements from the women's perspective, as well as the women who got back to the country after completing their educations abroad and young academics that had to resign after the coup. The primary audience of the meetings was the participant women rather than the women in general. Through the meetings those women tried to persuade themselves to consider adopting a feminist world-view and consolidate the feminist identity (i.e., Berktay, 2013; Devecioğlu, 2013; Erozan, 2013; Paker, 2013; Tınç, 2013). In order to build a stronger and fruitful relationships among the women and maintain them on a high level, the feminists aimed to increase participation and attendance to the meetings, the various communication techniques been utilized serving that purpose. Paker (2013) depicted the scene, as follows:

> I was living in the center of Istanbul with my little daughter, so my home was an ideal meeting venue for us. (...) It was very surprising

that those meetings in hustle, accompanied by coffee and wine, turned us upside down and empowered us to belong to that tiny community.

(p. 22)

Minu (2013) also mentions in her memories the importance of having meetings, after working hours, in one of her friends' workplace, an architectural office in Beşiktaş (a town at the heart of the city of Istanbul). They used to re-design the office before each meeting to allow the participants sit down face to face and see each other (p. 42). Designing the meeting place was efficient since seeing each other facilitated the interaction and acceptance of new ideas. As Thomas and Ralph (2009) state, the spoken message is more effective the closer the members of an audience sit to each other, i.e., as the "density" of the audience increases.

Besides providing effective interpersonal communication and involvement, watching movies such as *Stepford Wives* (1975) and *Kramer vs. Kramer* (1979) together helped the women to question the issues and consolidate their identity. Moreover, the writings, acts, the reforms and the success of their "sisters from the West" have become guiding lights in their struggle. The women have discovered their grandmothers' untold histories and have given priority to the issues unique to their society, as well (Tekeli, 2004).

Meanwhile, with Şirin Tekeli, Gülnur Savran and Stella Ovadia in lead, feminists started publishing in YAZKO (*Yazarlar Kooperatifi*, Cooperative of the Writers) in 1981 (Karakuş, 2018). Soon after, in May 1981, they organized two panels consecutively with the theme "literature and women problems." Question and answer sessions following the panels helped the audience participate the discussions regarding the feminist issues. Then the same team invited French feminist and activist Gisèle Halimi and organized a symposium in April 1982, during which the participants discussed the problems of women in a panel, even the symposium took place under police surveillance. This symposium was a milestone in the second wave Turkish feminism as it encouraged women to become more vocal and to spread the movement. This was later seen in the launch in 1985 of a book club, the Women's Circle (*Kadın Çevresi*) in which the books related to the Feminist Theory were translated into Turkish, the feminist ideology was spread to women from all ages and segments of the society and internalized within their discussions (Tekeli, 2017; Ergün, Güler and Tanyer, n.d.).

Tekeli (2017) stated

> Translation and publication of feminist classics including "Conversations with Simone de Beauvoir by Alice Schwarzer" enabled us to reach a wider community. As a result of the book club, seminars and the meetings our community expanded not only with the married women professionals in their 30s, but also with the younger women who were university students, workers, secretaries or saleswomen.
>
> (p. 273)

Information exchange tactics such as the consciousness raising meetings, the *Problems of Women Symposium* and the book club have enabled the women's movement to introduce issues considered private (i.e., sexual freedom, sexual harassment, rape, battering of women, and discrimination at the workplace) into the political public sphere. Interpersonal communication techniques served to fulfill dissent PR objectives targeting at the information-seeking publics that were the new feminist women. Audience participation inherent in the consciousness raising meetings and the clubs was a major proactive strategy in this phase, which lasted in the first half of 1980s. Subsequently problematizing women's lack of substantive rights allowed Turkish feminists for a transition to street actions and diverse forms of protests.

Demonstrations, festivals, petitions

In the second half of 1980s, feminists in Turkey were ready to be more vocal and visible in the society not only to spread the ideology "private is political" but also to change the articles of the Criminal Code that discriminated against women. In this phase they utilized both pro-active and reactive strategies for dissent and protest PR. Dissent PR strategies were generally pro-active and they included both action and communication. Special events such as festivals, meetings and various forms of publications were in charge to promote feminist ideas demanding change. Where protest PR is a consequence of dissent, feminists in Turkey utilized petitions, demonstrations on the streets, protest campaigns, press meetings and lobbying in the parliament in order to implement the feminist thought and policies in the law and regulation.

Turkey has signed the basic human rights conventions that shape the contemporary liberal democratic legal framework, including the UN Convention for the Elimination of any Discrimination Against Women (CEDAW),[5] which promotes women's rights (Arat, 2010). The Convention, signed and ratified in 1985, demands the realization of the same rights for men and women in all fields of life with conversions and revisions of law in areas that discriminate against women and the taking of necessary measures for the modification of everyday routines that support discrimination. Since Turkey has signed the Convention due to international pressure and concern about the international reputation of the country (Müftüler Baç, 2012; Yeşilyurt Gündüz, 2004), incorporation of the measures was deliberate. Hence, feminist groups from Ankara and Istanbul collaborated to launch a petition campaign in 1986, for the implementation of CEDAW (Arat, 1994). On March 7, a petition signed by 2,861 women was delivered to the Turkish assembly. The number of signatures grew to 6,000 soon after (Tekeli, 2015). This attempt was significant because of being the first collective protest PR activity of the feminists. As an example of newsworthy information strategy in protest

PR, the petition campaign received coverage in the national media on women's day (March 8) in 1986, which enabled the movement to reach masses and gain legitimacy.

Another cornerstone of the Turkish feminist movement was a demonstration against violence toward women, the first of its kind at the time. What initiated the demonstration was a judge's refusal to allow the divorce of a pregnant mother of three children, who was regularly beaten by her husband. The judge, citing a famous Turkish proverb, claimed "you should not leave a woman's back without a stick and her belly without a colt (baby)," which means that a husband should beat his wife constantly and he should also keep her pregnant all the time. Following the court decision, the women telegraphed protests to the court appealing for a trial against the decision that showed how domestic violence was considered legal. However, they did not stop there, and on May 17, 1987, more than 1,000[6] infuriated women demonstrated in Istanbul and protested the patriarchal system where the pivot was the discriminative decision of the judge. The protesters chanted slogans against domestic violence such as: "We do not want the paradise of violence!" "Women! Solidarity against violence," "There is no legal violence," "Violence is the reason to escape from home" (Arat, 1994; Feminist, 2018; Our Story, 2018). Seen from a protest PR perspective, this demonstration was a tactic of an offensive response strategy. The feminists' street demonstrations aimed to embarrass policy makers into changing the discriminative laws while also pointing out to the fallacies and failures of casuist judges.

The "Solidarity against beating" campaign, initiated in the same year, served both dissent and protest PR goals of the feminists. In the campaign violence toward women was not framed as an individual matter in the domestic realm but as a political topic that needed to be dealt with in the public realm. Among the campaign objectives were the establishment of a consultancy system and the creation of shelters for the women exposed to violence. It took several years but the campaign's objectives were reached in the 1990s (Müftüler-Baç, 2012).

In the course of the campaign, on October 4, an open-air festival was held in the garden of İstanbul Kariye Museum, an ancient Byzantine church. This one-day festival, organized by women aiming to share their thoughts on domestic violence, education of children, prostitution, and similar issues while having fun with concerts and theater shows, was a special event designed to achieve dissent PR objectives. As a proactive PR strategy of action, special events are appropriate to bring attention to the ideas of public intellectuals, academics and experts and their arguments to change the policy climate (Smith, 2009). Hence, the Kariye festival program featured a variety of activities: the pivotal name of the movement, Şirin Tekeli, gave an opening speech; feminist singers such as Deniz Türkali and Maria Rita Epik held concerts and chats with the participants; children were also taken care of with a variety of activities dedicated to them.

Also, during the festival women sold house-made products and crafts as a means of fundraising for their future projects (Figure 4.1).

Using the money thus collected, the "Scream, let them hear you" (*Bağır Herkes Duysun*) book, based on witness testimonies of women suffering violence, was published in 1988.

> The goal of this book was to underline the legitimacy behind violence against women in society openly, as it stressed that the use of domestic violence is supported by the state and is a part of male dominance.
>
> (Yeşilyurt Gündüz, 2004, p. 120)

Judging from the increasing interest of the media (Tekeli, 2015) the strategies of newsworthy information and the special events, have contributed to the campaign's success.

Figure 4.1 The poster of Kariye Women's Festival, adapted from the figure Catlakzemin.com (2017).

Source: https://catlakzemin.com/4-ekim-1987-kariyede-dayaga-karsi-kampanya-kadin-senligi-yapildi/.

The late 1980s witnessed more unconventional and radical protests and demonstrations in which feminists used offensive response strategies. On March 8, 1988, the "Temporary Museum of Women" (*Geçici Kadın Müzesi*), was opened in Cağaloğlu, İstanbul. Launched with the theme "Ancient times, new age, modern age and it is always the same age; nothing has changed in the domestic works of women for ages," the museum featured a statue of a housewife made up of natural materials such as tweezers, tampons, laundry lines, contraceptives, feeding bottles, cradles, cooking pots and detergents, in order to create an effect of alienation (via archive of Women's Library). In doing so, the museum aimed to embarrass the audience by highlighting many of the challenging aspects of women's everyday life such as the underestimated amount of housework, various unappreciated labors and menstruation. The museum itself was a dissent PR tactic too albeit embracing a reactive strategy. Reactive strategies are used in dissent PR when accusations or criticisms are made against the ideas that are meant to be disseminated.

In 1989, in the metropolitan cities of Izmir, Ankara and Istanbul, a campaign called "the Purple Needle" (*Mor İğne*) was launched. Feminists handed out needles with purple ribbons to women on the streets, to protest physical and sexual abuse on the streets and in public transportation vehicles. The needles would enable women to protect themselves while expressing their concerns over sexual violence (Y. Arat, 2008; Diner and Toktaş, 2010; Kardam, 2017). As the needles threatened the harassers, this offensive response strategy turned a traditionally private response into an effective protest PR tactic in the public realm.

Another demonstration during this period protested the Minister of Family Affairs' declaration that there was no difference between a woman's flirting with a man and the practice of prostitution (Diner and Toktaş, 2010). The last years of the 1980s were marked with protest campaigns against discriminative legislation; the feminists protested article 438 of Turkish ex-criminal code that diminished the severity of sentencing in a rape case by two thirds if the victim was a prostitute and article 159 of ex-civil code, which made women gain their husband's permission before they could work outside the house (Işık, 2007). The feminists utilized rather reactive protest PR methods where they aimed at tangible legal amendments.

In 1989, second wave feminists in Turkey declared a "Feminist Manifesto" in which they announced the resurgence of their contestation against the patriarchal system (Tekeli, 2015). Within this period, they have published significant periodicals, journals and books as to support and share feminist philosophy and thinking.

Magazines, periodicals and books

In public relations, various media and communication tactics can be utilized in order to achieve the stated objectives. The news media tactics are one of those tactics that can reach large audiences and may encompass most people who are interested in a specific topic (Smith, 2009). During the second wave feminism in Turkey, magazines, periodicals and books were published. It can be stated that those media are used as dissent PR tools, as dissent PR is the dissemination of ideas, commentaries, and policies through PR techniques in order to change current, dominant thinking and behavior in discrete economic, political and cultural areas of public life (Moloney et al., 2012).

Feminist alternative media, by which feminist discourses are created and feminist movement is extended, have become an important area within the women's publicity framework because women's media struggle is a mean for efforts of gaining a seat and in dominant patriarchal public space (Tekvar, 2017). During this period, feminist writing and publishing was an important tool of penetrating public consciousness. Feminists came to express what they thought and stood for by writing in journals, papers, and their own publications perhaps more than they did through mass demonstrations and public marches. According to Aslı Davaz-Mardin, 44 women's periodicals or magazines were published between 1980 and 1990 and 63 between 1990 and 1996 in Turkey. Considering that 195 women's periodicals came out between 1929 and 1996, the post-1980 period was prolific (Davaz-Mardin, 1998). In 1983, a "feminist women" page was published in the journal *Somut*. Even the duration of this publication was relatively short, its reflections in the feminist community was huge. Erozan (2013, p. 30) mentions, "*Somut* showed me that new questions might be asked and it was possible to make unlimited interrogations. And the greatest point was that you were starting this interrogation from yourself!"

Among the feminist publications published since women began identifying themselves as feminists in the 1980s, *Pazartesi* magazine has a unique place since it has been published for the longest period of time for the largest constituency (Arat, 2004).

Feminism in Turkey has reached a new exciting dimension in the last decade with the emergence of autonomous and different female voices. Duygu Asena, an editor and novelist, has much to do with paving the way for the emergence of these voices. With her controversial writings and independent lifestyle, she is an icon of Turkish feminism. As a protagonist of loyal individualism, she has not allied herself with any group or movement. But through her editorials in *Kadınca* (Womanly) and two controversial novels, *Kadının Adı Yok* (Woman Has No Name) and its sequel *Aslında Aşk da Yok* (In Reality Love Does Not Exist Either) that insist on female equality and autonomy, she has greatly shaped public opinion that has made the mobilization of other feminists possible (Erol, 1992).

Another writer who has influenced feminist women in this period is Erendiz Atasü. She played an important role in conveying the feminist values by her storybook, *Kadınlar da vardır* (Women Also Exist, 1983).

As women's magazines and periodicals proliferated in the 1980s, feminist ideas and values penetrated some of these. For example, *Kadınca*, published between 1978 and 1998, was a commercial women's magazine infused with feminist ideology. It reflected a feminist perspective pervading through stories and its choice of material covered. Contrasting other commercial women's magazines that maintained traditional female roles and values, it featured rather feminist issues such as dilemmas of professional women and the problem of domestic violence. However, it was restricted by commercial concerns and profit making which led it, for example, to thrive on advertisements stereotyping women's roles and promoting patriarchal values (Kırca, 2001; Öztürkmen, 1998).

Women who identified themselves as radical feminists published the journal *feminist* (feminist) and the socialist feminists published the *Sosyalist Feminist Kaktüs* (Socialist Feminist Cactus) (Yöney, 1995). The journal *feminist* was published for seven issues between 1987 and 1990 and *Kaktüs* for 12 issues between 1988 and 1990. Many women who brought out these two magazines later worked in *Pazartesi* (Monday) and many ideas that surfaced in the pages of *feminist* and *Kaktüs* were later fleshed out in *Pazartesi*. While *feminist* served as a medium where women experimented with divulging their private experiences of gender oppression and defining their feminism, *Kaktüs* acted more as a medium where women worked out the more academic questions of being socialist feminists. Yet both magazines had limited resources and the few issues published were slim pamphlets (Arat, 2004).

All of the above-mentioned magazines and books have played a significant role in explaining the importance of the women's movement and they have served as news media tactics of publicity, audience participation and newsworthy information strategies of the second wave feminist movement in Turkey.

Outcomes of the movement

There have been concrete outcomes of the second wave feminist movement in Turkey both in the civil life and in the regulation. Arat (1994) suggested that women's activism played a significant role in the transition from authoritarianism to democracy. In this section some of the major outcomes of the movement are stated.

As a result of the consciousness raising groups' meetings, the feminist movement reached a number of women, predominantly living in the metropolis. In the first half of the 1980s the new feminists were on a quest to find an identity that placed protection of women rights at the center. Exchanging their personal thoughts in the informal gatherings and writing articles in the lately sprouting feminist journals helped them reach their objectives of dissent.

In the second half of the 1980s the wind of courage blowing behind the new feminists enabled them to protest more actively and to seek substantial resolutions to their social, cultural and legal problems. The activities played a major role in sensitizing the public as well as pressuring government to take concrete steps. Besides the interest of mainstream media on the women issues, 44 women's periodicals or magazines were published between 1980 and 1990 in Turkey and the number increased gradually afterwards (Diner and Toktaş, 2010). In particular, the journal *Pazartesi* had contributed to challenging the traditional norms, which tolerated sexual harassment and expected women to be silent about it (Y. Arat, 2008). The media served to disseminate information and raise public consciousness concerning the feminist agenda.

As a consequence of the demonstrations and the campaign "Solidarity against Beatings" in 1987, a commission of law professors was assigned by the Ministry of Justice to prepare a draft legislation; while the process still continued several modifications had taken place (Kardam and Ertürk, 1999). For the first time, a separate unit for gender equality was established in the public sector; within the State Planning Organization an "Advisory Board for policies with regards to Women" was founded with the participation of representatives from public agencies, non-governmental organizations and universities (Müftüler-Baç, 2012). In January 1989 a telephone helpline was also launched released offering legal and practical support for the victims of domestic violence. The following year, the "Purple Roof Women's Shelter" was founded so as to go on consultations with women and to reinforce the battle against domestic violence (Tahaoğlu, 2017; Our Story, 2018).

As the 1980s came to end so did second wave feminism in Turkey after having set the scene for the third wave feminism. In particular, the 1990s saw a wide range of important initiatives coming into effect:

- Establishment of "the General Directorate of Women's Status" (*Kadının Statüsü Genel Müdürlüğü, KSGM*).
- Establishment of a Women's Library (*Kadın Eserleri Kütüphanesi ve Bilgi Merkezi Vakfı*), which collects scholarly and literary works on women and by women, in İstanbul.
- Universities started to establish research centers on women's issues and departments of women's studies at the graduate level (Istanbul University and Marmara University in Istanbul, Ankara University and Middle East Technical University in Ankara, 9 Eylül University in Izmir and Çukurova University in Adana opened women's studies programs – in the 1990s).
- The number of women's organizations started to increase throughout the country, with the highest increases being recorded mostly in urban areas.
- Article 438 of Turkish criminal code that diminished the severity of sentencing in rape case by two thirds if the victim was a prostitute, was deleted.

- Article 159 of Turkish civil code, which made women gain their husbands' permission to work outside, was abolished.

Even though the feminist activists of the early 1980s were scattered in the 1990s, the journal *Pazartesi* upheld the feminist banner and embedded feminism. By the end of the 1990s, feminism was recognized as a legitimate if marginal position in public life (Y. Arat, 2008). However, significant progress was still needed, particularly in the area of gender based violence (Müftüler Baç, 2012).

Conclusion

This chapter explored resurgence of a feminist contestation in Turkey from an activist PR perspective. According to Diner and Toktaş (2010), "the women's movement in Turkey has been greatly influenced by the political context" (p. 57). Thus, until the 1980s an independent women's movement could not arise. This second wave feminist movement was rather a critique of the patriarchal foundations of Turkish society.

Yaxley (2013) asserts that the concepts of dissent and protest PR are beneficial in expanding the historical understanding of public relations and they could also provide a focus on how women have used dissent and activist techniques to get their voices heard in society. Second wave Turkish feminism was vocal between 1980 and 1990 and it was shaped around the campaign against domestic violence. The campaign included many tactics such as meetings, demonstrations, festivals, petitions, panel discussions, articles in academic publications and popular magazines and lobbying activities.

Concerning the women's movement there were two major goals of the Turkish feminists in the beginning:

- Raise consciousness about gender discrimination and domestic violence in the society.
- Promote a new feminist identity among the women.

In order to reach these dissent PR goals, audience participation, special events, publicity and embarrassment strategies were followed.

Audience participation is a proactive action strategy and the following tactics are observed: consciousness raising meetings – sitting face-to face, movie sessions and storytelling facilitated participation-, Q/A sessions after the panels and the symposium, book-club and Q/A sections of women's magazines.

The second dissent PR strategy is special events; similar to the first one, this is another proactive action strategy. Panels, Problems of Women Symposium and Kariye Open-air Festival were among its observed tactics. During the festival, concerts, speeches, activities for the children and fundraising activities were spotted as the interpersonal communication tactics.

Publicity is the third dissent PR strategy. Special pages concerning women's issues in the periodicals, women's magazines and the books spreading the feminist thinking can be named among the tactics of this pro-active communication strategy.

The last strategy of dissent PR is the re-active offensive response strategy of embarrassment. The creative tactic called "Temporary Museum of Women" was aimed to embarrass the audience as to draw attention to the issue. Despite the majority of proactive strategies in dissent PR, reactive strategies might be used when accusations or criticisms are made against the ideas – like feminism – that are meant to be disseminated.

Success of these strategies and tactics enabled a transition to street actions. In the second half of the 1980s, while feminists went on promoting ideas for change, they also started striving for the implementation of these changes. Therefore both dissent and protest PR strategies were observed in this period. The main goal of protest PR was to change the discriminative norms and legislations.

There were three strategies observed: newsworthy information, embarrassment and threat.

Newsworthy information is a proactive communication strategy and the tactics observed are petition campaign, celebrity participation in the events, and published books (i.e., "Scream, Let them hear you"). Two other strategies are both reactive offensive response strategies. The embarrassment strategy's main tactic was street demonstrations and the threat strategy's main tactic was "the Purple Needle" campaign.

All of the above mentioned strategies and tactics are used in order to draw attention and foster an awareness regarding the second wave feminist movement in Turkey. The energy of the second wave of Turkish feminism initiated a number of attempts to institutionalize the women's movement in the following years. Observing the successful outcomes of the movement, we can claim that both dissent and protest PR strategies have been effective and the relevant tactics have been chosen adequately.

Notes

1 The Women's Library and Information Centre Foundation (WLICF) is the first and only women's library in Turkey. It was founded in Istanbul in 1989 and opened on April 14, 1990, mainly to assist research on the history of women. The library has assigned itself the mission of acquiring, protecting, and preserving the materials, statistics, laws, journal articles, photographs, letters, diaries, memoirs, newspaper clips, conference papers, proceedings of seminars and books written about the women and issues relating to women, as well as the statues and publications of women's organizations. http://kadineserleri.org/hakkimizda/.

2 Turkish War of National Liberation (or War of Independence – *Kurtuluş Savaşı*) led by Mustafa Kemal Atatürk between 1919–1923, has led the country to become the Republic of Turkey (for more information please refer to http://historyofturkey.com/independence/.

3 The reforms introduced by Mustafa Kemal Ataturk (referred to as Kemalist Reforms) after the founding of the Turkish Republic have been identified as parts of a broad policy of rapid Westernization (Z. F. Arat, 2008). These were a series of political, legal, religious, cultural, social, and economic policy changes that were designed to convert the new Republic of Turkey into a secular, modern nation-state.

4 The leaders of the Republic, rejected the founding of a women's party and recommended that she found a women's association instead. It was in this context that the Turkish Women's Union (*Türk Kadınlar Birliği*) was founded on February 7, 1924. www.turkkadinlarbirligi.org/kurumsal/Tarih%C3%A7e.

5 The Convention on the Elimination of all Forms of Discrimination Against Women (CEDAW) is an international treaty adopted in 1979 by the United Nations General Assembly. Described as an international bill of rights for women, it was instituted on September 3, 1981 and has been ratified by 189 states (www.un.org/womenwatch/daw/cedaw/).

6 Feminist references have given contradicting numbers regarding the number of participants whereas some have given numbers rising up to 3,000s, however when checked from other archival sources, it is observed that there were around 1,000 women in the demonstrations.

References

About PR. (2018, March 22). Retrieved from www.prsa.org/all-about-pr/.

Arat, Y. (1994). Women's movement of the 1980s in Turkey: radical outcome of liberal Kemalism. In Göçek, F. M. and Shiva, B. (Eds.), *Reconstructing Gender in Middle East: Tradition, Identity and Power* (pp. 100–112). New York: Columbia University Press.

Arat, Y. (2000). From emancipation to liberation: the changing role of women in Turkey's public realm, *Journal of International Affairs*, 54(1), 107–123.

Arat, Y. (2004). Rethinking the political: a feminist journal in Turkey, Pazartesi, *Women's Studies International Forum*, 27(3), 281–292.

Arat, Y. (2008). Contestation and collaboration: women's struggles for empowerment in Turkey. In Kasaba, R. (Ed.), *The Cambridge History of Turkey* (pp. 388–418). Cambridge: Cambridge University Press.

Arat, Y. (2010). Religion, politics and gender equality in Turkey: implications of a democratic paradox?, *Third World Quarterly*, 31(6), 869–884.

Arat, Z. F. (2008). Kemalism and Turkish women, *Women & Politics*, 14(4), 57–80.

Benedict, B. (2017). *Activism and Public Relations: Then and Now* (Master of Arts Dissertation). Retrieved from Proquest.

Berktay, F. (2013). Kendi sesini bulmak (Finding your own voice). In *Somut 4. Sayfa: İlk Feminist Yazılar 30.yıl kitabı*. Ankara: Kadın Kültür İletişim Vakfı, p. 27.

Ciszek, E. L. (2015). Bridging the gap: mapping the relationship between activism and public relations, *Public Relations Review*, 41(4), 447–455.

Coombs, W. T. and Holladay, S. J. (2010). *PR Strategy and Application: Managing Influence*. Singapore: Wiley-Blackwell.

Coombs, W. T. and Holladay S. J. (2012). Privileging an activist vs. a corporate view of public relations history in the U.S., *Public Relations Review*, 38(3), 347–353.

Coombs, W. T. and Holladay, S. J. (2014). *It's Not Just PR: Public Relations in Society* (2nd ed.). West Sussex: Blackwell Publishing Ltd.

Coşar, S. and Gençoğlu, Onbaşı F. (2008). Women's movement in Turkey at a crossroads: from women's rights advocacy to feminism, *South European Society & Politics*, 13(3), 325–344.

Davaz-Mardin, A. (1998). *Kadın Süreli Yayınları Bibliografisi: 1928–1996: Hanımlar Alemi'den Roza'ya*. Istanbul: Kadın Eserleri Kütüphanesi & Türkiye Ekonomik ve Toplumsal Tarih Vakfı.

Demetrious, K. (2008). Activist public relations. In Donsbach, W. (Ed.), *The International Encyclopedia of Communication*. Blackwell Publishing. Retrieved March 18, 2018 from www.communicationencyclopedia.com/subscriber/tocnode.html?id=g978140513199 5_yr2012_chunk_g97814051319956_ss76-1.

Demetrious, K. (2013). *Public Relations, Activism, and Social Change: Speaking up*. New York: Routledge.

Deren van Het Hof, S. and Hoştut, S. (2016). Pembe Getto: Türkiye'de Kurumsal İletişim Yöneticileri (Pink ghetto: corporate communications managers in Turkey), *Fe Dergi*, 8(2), 101–109.

Devecioğlu, A. (2013), Hikayenin en güzel tarafı (Best side of the story). In *Somut 4. Sayfa: İlk Feminist Yazılar 30.yıl kitabı*. Ankara: Kadın Kültür İletişim Vakfı, p. 21.

Diner, Ç. and Toktaş, Ş. (2010). Waves of feminism in Turkey: Kemalist, Islamist and Kurdish women's movements in an era of globalization, *Journal of Balkan and Near Eastern Studies*, 12(1), 41–57.

Eastman, P. C. (1973). Consciousness-raising as a resocialization process for women, *Smith College Studies in Social Work*, 43(3), 153–183.

Ergün, Y., Güler, B. and Tanyer, İ. (n.d.). Türkiye'de 80 Sonrası Kadın Hareketi. Retrieved on May 30, 2018 from https://kadinlarinkurtulusu.wordpress.com/yazdiklarimiz/turkiyede-80-sonrasi-kadin-hareketi/.

Erol, S. (1992). Feminism in Turkey, *New Perspectives on Turkey*, 8, 109–120.

Erozan, F. (2013). Sadece bir dergi aldığımı sanıyordum (I thought that I was buying only a magazine). *In Somut 4. Sayfa: İlk Feminist Yazılar 30.yıl kitabı*. Ankara: Kadın Kültür İletişim Vakfı, p. 30.

Evans, J. (1998). *Feminist Theory Today: An Introduction to Second Wave Feminism*. London: Sage.

Evans, S. M. (2008). Foreword. In Gilmore, S. (Ed.), *Historical Perspectives on Second Wave Feminism in the United States* (pp. vii–1). Illinois: University of Illinois Press.

Feminist (2018, March 20). [Data file]. Retrieved on May 30, 2018 from www.pazartesidergisi.com/pdf/Feminist3.pdf.

Ganesh, S. and Zoller, H. M. (2012). Dialogue, activism, and democratic social change, *Communication Theory*, 22(1), 66–91.

Gilmore, S. (2008). Thinking about feminist coalitions. In Gilmore, S. (Ed.), *Historical Perspectives on Second Wave Feminism in the United States* (pp. 1–19). Illinois: University of Illinois Press. p. 29.

Hakkımızda: Kadın Eserleri Kütüphanesi ve Bilgi Merkezi Vakfı: Kadın Merkezli Bir Kütüphane ve Arşiv. (2018, February 12). Retrieved on May 30, 2018 from http://kadineserleri.org/hakkimizda/.

Holtzhausen, D. R. (2000). Postmodern values in public relations, *Journal of Public Relations Research*, 12(1), 93–114.

Holtzhausen, D. R. (2012). *Public Relations as Activism: Postmodern Approaches to Theory and Practice.* New York: Routledge.

Işık, N. (2007). 1990'larda Kadına Yönelik Şiddetle Mücadele Hareketi İçinde Oluşmuş bazı Gözlem ve Düşünceler. In Aksu, B. and Günal, A. (Eds.), *90'larda Türkiye'de Feminizm* (2nd ed., pp. 43–46). İstanbul: İletişim Yayınları.

Karagöz, B. (2008). Türkiye'de 1980 Sonrası Kadın Hareketi'nin Siyasal Temelleri ve İkinci Dalga Uğrağı, *Memleket, Siyaset, Yönetim Dergisi,* 3(7), 168–190.

Karakuş, F. (2018, April 23). 23 Nisan 1982: Türkiye'de feminizm ilk kez kürsüden seslendi/YAZKO Sempozyumu. Retrieved on May 30, 2018 from https://catlakzemin.com/23-nisan-1982-turkiyede-feminizm-ilk-kez-kursuden-seslendi-yazko-sempozyumu/.

Kardam, N. (2017). *Turkey's Engagement with Global Women's Human Rights.* New York: Routledge.

Kardam, N. and Ertürk, Y. (1999). Expanding gender accountability? Women's organizations and the state in Turkey, *International Journal of Organization Theory & Behavior,* 2(1/2), 167–197.

Kırca, S. (2001). Turkish women's magazines: the popular meets the political, *Women's Studies International Forum,* 24(3/4), 457–468.

Kim, I. and Sriramesh, K. (2009). Activism and public relations. In K. Sriramesh and D. Vercic (Eds.), *The Global Public Relations Handbook: Theory, Research and Practice* (pp. 79–97). New York: Routledge.

Martinelli, D. K. (2014). The intersection of public relations and activism: a multinational look at suffrage movements. In B. St. John III, M.O. Lamme and J. L'Etang (Eds.), *Pathways to public relations: histories of practice and profession.* (pp. 206–223). Oxon: Routledge.

McDowell, W. H. (2002). *Historical research: a guide.* Essex: Longman.

McQueen, D. (2013). Dissent and protest public relations. By Kevin Moloney, David McQueen, Pawel Surowiec and Heather Yaxley. Papers and discussions from the Dissent and Public Relations seminar series, October–December 2012. Available on https://microsites.bournemouth.ac.uk. Accessed on February 12, 2018.

Minu (2013). Nurser'in değerli anısına (To the valuable memory of Nurser). *In Somut 4. Sayfa: İlk Feminist Yazılar 30.yıl kitabı* (p. 42). Ankara: Kadın Kültür İletişim Vakfı.

Moloney, K. (2006). *Rethinking Public Relations* (2nd ed.). Oxon: Routledge.

Moloney, K., McQueen, D., Surowiec, P. and Yaxley, H. (2012). Dissent and protest public relations. Papers and discussion from the Dissent and Public Relations seminar series, October-December 2012. Bournemouth University. Retrieved on February 12, 2018 from https://microsites.bournemouth.ac.uk/cmc/files/2013/10/Dissent-and-publicrelations-Bournemouth-University.

Müftüler Baç, M. (2012). Gender equality in Turkey, monograph, The European Parliament, Brussels. Retrieved on March 22, 2018 from www.europarl.europa.eu/document/activities/cont/201202/20120207ATT37506/20120207ATT37506EN.pdf.

Nicholson, L. (1997). Introduction. In Nicholson, L. (Ed.), *A Reader in Feminist Theory: Part 1* (pp. 1–7). London: Routledge.

Our Story (2018, March 20). Retrieved on May 30, 2018 from www.morcati.org.tr/en/about-us/our-story.

Öksüz, B. and Görpe, S. (2014). Türkiye'de Halkla İlişkiler Alanında Kadının Yeri: Akademisyenler, Uygulamacilar ve Meslek Örgütü Temsilcilerinin Konuya Yaklaşimlari (Woman's place in the field of public relations in Turkey: perspectives of academics, practitioners, and representatives of professional organizations on it), *İstanbul Üniversitesi İletişim Fakültesi Dergisi*, 2014(II,47), 125–142.

Öztürkmen, A. (1998). A short history of Kadınca magazine and its feminism. In Z. Arat (Ed.), *Deconstructing Images of Turkish Women*. London: Macmillan.

Paker, B. (2013). Hala Sesini Duyuyoruz! (We still hear the voice!). In *Somut 4. Sayfa: İlk Feminist Yazılar 30.yıl kitabı* (p. 22). Ankara: Kadın Kültür İletişim Vakfı.

Şimşek, S. (2004). New social movements in Turkey since 1980, *Turkish Studies*, 5(2), 111–39.

Sirman, N. (1989). Feminism in Turkey: a short history, *New Perspectives on Turkey*, 3(1), 1–34.

Smith, R. D. (2009). *Strategic Planning for Public Relations* (3rd ed.). New York: Routledge.

Sowards, S. K. and Renegar, V. R. (2004). The rhetorical functions of consciousness – raising in third wave feminism, *Communication Studies*, 55(4), 535–552.

Tahaoğlu, Ç. (2017). Dayağa Karşı Yürüyüş'ün 30. Yıldönümünde Kadınlar Anlattı. Retrieved on May 30, 2018 from https://m.bianet.org/bianet/kadin/186540-dayaga-karsi-yuruyus-un-30-yildonumunde-kadinlar-anlatti.

Tanyıldızı, N. İ. (2011). Türkiye'de Halkla İlişkiler Mesleğinde Kadın (Women in Turkish public relations), *KMÜ Sosyal ve Ekonomik Araştırmalar Dergisi*, 13(20), 75–81.

Tekeli, Ş. (1986). Emergence of the feminist movement in Turkey. In D. Dahlerup (Ed.), *The New Women's Movement* (pp. 179–199). Sage: London.

Tekeli, Ş. (2004). On Maddede Türkiye'de Kadın Hareketi. Retrieved on May 30, 2018 from https://m.bianet.org/bianet/kadin/43145-on-maddede-turkiyede-kadin-hareketi.

Tekeli, Ş. (2015). *1980'ler Türkiyesi'nde Kadın Bakış Açısından Kadınlar (Women from the Women's Perspective in Turkey of 1980s)* (6th ed.). İstanbul: İletişim.

Tekeli, Ş. (2017). *Feminizmi Düşünmek (Thinking about the Feminism)*. İstanbul: İstanbul Bilgi Üniversitesi Yayınları.

Tekvar, S. O. (2017). Türkiye'de Feminist Alternatif Medyanın İşlevselliği: Bir Alternatif Medya Örneği "Kadınların Postası" Projesinin İncelenmesi, *İnsan ve Toplum Bilimleri Araştırmaları Dergisi*, 6(1), 537–552.

Thomas, G. L. and Ralph, D. C. (2009). A study of the effect of audience proximity on persuasion, *Speech Monographs*, 26(4), 300–307.

Tınç, F. (2013). Yazko bir özgürlük meydanıydı (Yazko was a square of freedom). In *Somut 4. Sayfa: İlk Feminist Yazılar 30.yıl kitabı* (p. 29). Ankara: Kadın Kültür İletişim Vakfı.

Weitz, R. (1982). Feminist consciousness raising, self-concept, and depression, *Sex Roles*, 8(3), 231–241.

Yaraman, A. (2001). *Resmi Tarihten Kadın Tarihine (From the Official History to the History of Women)*. İstanbul: Bağlam.

Yaxley, H. (2013). Dissent PR – the women's perspective: from suffragettes to slutwalks. In Moloney, K (Ed.), *Dissent and Protest Public Relations. Papers and Discussion from the Dissent and Public Relations Seminar Series*. Retrieved on

February 12, 2018 from https://microsites.bournemouth.ac.uk/cmc/files/2013/10/Dissent-and-publicrelations-Bournemouth-University.

Yeşilyurt Gündüz, Z. (2004). The women's movement in Turkey: from Tanzimat towards European Union Membership, *Perceptions*, Autumn, 115–134.

Yöney, S. (1995). Turkish feminist movement in the 80s: a study of two feminist journals: Kaktüs and Feminist, master's thesis, İstanbul, Boğaziçi University.

5   Public relations for social change

Shock tactics in feminist activism in Eastern Europe

Oleksandra Gudkova and Katharine Sarikakis

Historically, social movements have created transformational social change by relying in part on the power of the ways in which their message convinces the public to stand behind it *and* the policymakers to, at least, engage in conversation. The role of public relations and social movements sounds antithetical, even controversial when considering the perspectives of PR aims and social activists. Public relations has historically engaged professional communicators to further the benefits of a company, the state or an organization more generally, aiming predominantly at persuasion of the publics it addresses. To society, the image of PR is that of distortion of truth, manipulation and selfishness and has been associated with organized advocacy for private interests. Yet, much of PR theory and professional organizations' work point to the social role of PR to inform the public and to submit new ideas and information to the marketplace of ideas (Fitzpatrick & Bronstein, 2006). The ethics of PR in society and the public realm demand from PR professionals, beyond any regulatory obligations, commitment to the truth, dialogue with society, and objectivity in the messages they convey. Social movements' role as public communicators and contributors to democratic debate is historically seen as separate from PR, at least the professional and organization related practices. To that, social movements aiming for structural change, professional PR constitutes a set of practices not compatible with the aims of change. Hence, while advocacy is also a core element of any social movement public action, this is understood to be for the benefit of the common good and therefore of diffuse interests (Della Porta & Diani, 2006). In the past decade, however, increasing attention has been given to the intersections of PR and social movements and within this context, renewed interest in a global society and transnational movements and their ways of communicating has arisen. Here we discuss the ways in which modern feminist movements engage in public communication tactics of a public relations nature to put their message across, by providing counter-arguments, information and polemic in an effort to galvanize and mobilize both publics and policymakers, but also to impact public debate. The following discussion explores the feminist groups FEMEN and Pussy Riot, whose East-European origins expand in their impact and network to become transnational through their style and communication tactics based on *shock and surprise in public spaces*.

For this chapter, we analyzed actions by FEMEN and Pussy Riot and draw upon visual materials and newspapers articles, as well as personal interviews with FEMEN activists. For our purposes, discourse analysis is the most appropriate method, since it is an interdisciplinary tool for analyzing reality and corresponds to the contemporary specificity of political reality: its rootedness in language, multiplicity, subjectivity and dynamism. Personal interviews provided the in-depth understanding of the ways in which tactics of protest and dissent PR are used in feminist activism. This has allowed us to study the features of feminist discourse in activism PR.

Historical trajectories of "shock" communication in feminist movements

One of the most useful ways of thinking about public relations has been through the description of public relations models that identify the central ideas of public relations and the ways in which they are related to each other. The first to outline the now widely known four models of PR were Grunig and Hunt in 1984. In their work *Managing Public Relations* they presented the following PR models: press agentry/publicity; public information; two-way asymmetric and two-way symmetric (Grunig & Hunt, 1984, p. 22). In recent years, a strand of scholarship paid attention to protests as part of PR, whereby activists globally have used various strategies and tactics, including dissent and protest PR. Moloney et al. (2013) explore the meaning and uses of the terms *dissent* and *protest PR*, terms that are apparently new to the disciplinary lexicon. He differentiates the terms from *activism PR*. Dissent PR is the dissemination of ideas and policies through PR techniques, in order to bring about change in different areas of public life. It is about "bringing attention to new thinking and new behaviors in areas of national life. It promotes ideas for change and for retention in the political economy and civil society" (Adi & Moloney, 2012, p. 103). Protest PR aims to persuade in order to implement those ideas into regulation or other forms of executive actions and public policy (Moloney et al., 2013). It is

> not principally about ideas, behaviors and policies. Instead, it persuades via occupations, demonstration, strike, public speaking and other forms of non-violent and violent protest in order to implement those ideas, behaviors and policies into law, regulation and other forms of executive action.
>
> (Adi & Moloney, 2012, p. 104)

Using one-way communication method is vital for any kind of protest, as the information comes from the activists and goes to the public with the purpose of trying to influence the audience. In the one-way communication flow, the sender and a receiver are in an asymmetric relationship, since one exerts more control over the communication flow than the other (Mattoni, 2012). At the end of the day, whoever controls the narrative has the power. The concept of public relations as a "control mechanism" originates in public relations "social scientific foundation" where its purpose is to understand

> the communication behaviour of its publics in such a way that the messages created and the information disseminated can have an optimal and measurable outcome in terms of controlling those publics to the benefit of the organization they work for.
>
> (Holtzhausen, 2012, p. 185)

However, it is neither wise nor appropriate to compare activist groups to the practices, and resources, and power of corporate organizations, it is interesting to explore some more tactics through which feminist groups might be employing "cultural traits" of organizations where "the ethics of reciprocity" prevail. In other words, when symmetrical organizations care for their role in the environment or their impact on society, they seek to give back some of the benefits that derive from it (Grunig & Hunt, 1984).

Activism pursuing social justice aims to provide the tools to the public to demand policy change and force policymakers to face their responsibility for reciprocity. In other words, social justice activism aims to induce symmetry in an asymmetrical playing field of power inequalities. As the position of activism vis-a-vis corporations or state is hardly one of equality in resources, it is important to understand that activism must cover for this imbalance through forms of communication, which can reach the most people with the given means available. Therefore, although a social movement might behave in a symmetrical, i.e. responsible, conscientious and non-strictly hierarchical and non-conflictual manner in its internal affairs, the room for engaging in constant dialogue with society might be limited, especially due to shortage of resources. Hence, activists operate in an asymmetrical and public information one-way communication model, without this meaning the same as it does for an organization.

According to public relations scholar Karen Miller (2000), social movements adopted the same public relations techniques that were used by other organizations. Moreover, she notes that

> public relations texts give virtually no attention to the women who headed such movements, including Clara Barton, Margaret Sanger, Susan B. Anthony, Ida B. Wells, and Elizabeth Cady Stanton. Each of these women used public relations techniques of the day most effectively to inform the public about controversial issues despite the fact that their work is generally considered to be outside the business frame of the field.
>
> (Lattimore et al., 2004b, p. 31)

Feminism and dissent

Protest feminism, originated from the representatives of the suffragist move-ment – militants – in Great Britain at the end of the nineteenth century to the beginning of the twentieth century, and continued in the 1960–1980s with actions of the representatives of the "second wave" in the feminist move-ment development, and is a type of radical feminism. Women's suffrage and feminism is based on the aim to change society toward egalitarian treatment of women and for the powerless to confront the powerful. Protest plays an important role as a public act of challenging the status quo and as a reminder to the wider public about the issue at hand. Eastern Europe, in general and the post-Soviet space in particular, has witnessed decades-long struggles for change and social justice; the role of feminism as a force of transformation, however, has remained under-researched.

Just like the British suffragette movement in the early 1900s, con-temporary Eastern European feminist movements FEMEN and Pussy Riot use strategies and tactics of both dissent and protest PR in their actions. Interestingly, just like with dissent and protest PR, FEMEN and Pussy Riot seem to be turning to two models at once: the public information model, as it uses one-way communication techniques focused solely on distrib-uting organizational information; and the two way asymmetrical model whereas by using research into the audience, the organization use persua-sion of audiences to influence them (Grunig & Hunt, 1984).

FEMEN and Pussy Riot have demonstrated until now that they are interested in delivering social justice messages to the masses, in a clearly one-way manner: they do so by engaging in deploying short bursts of spec-tacle to deliver information and positions of critique against hegemonic politics.

Perhaps it is more effective to view FEMEN and Pussy Riot as tempo-rary and unintended or part-time public relations actors engaged in prac-tices closer to the cultural interpreter model and the personal influence model (Lattimore et al., 2004a). This chapter argues that the feminist movement in Eastern Europe has sought to overturn the mainstream PR approach of shock to attract attention in order to make a change in the society and leave a lasting impression in the spotlight.

Women engaged in organizing for change employ a variety of strategies, ranging from reformist to revolutionary, and strategies may be valid in specific circumstances and for particular purposes. The protests organized by Eastern European feminist self-organized activists are explored here through the cases of FEMEN in Ukraine and Pussy Riot in Russia. The chapter explores the ways in which Eastern European feminist movements have aimed to bring attention to neglected areas in public discourse, from authoritarian rule to the sex-industry, patriarchy and religion.

Feminist activism targets not only the conditions of work or legal issues in women's equality, but also seeks to improve the quality of life and the social status of women by changing perceptions about women and cultural values that keep women locked in a system of power inferiority. The beginning of the twentieth century witnessed the feminist movement; practically everywhere was transformed from the moderate to more radical stage. The militant period is, perhaps, the best-studied period in the history of British suffragist movement. However, scholars have not come to the common opinion regarding the militants' activity (its representatives were also called *suffragettes* in contradistinction to *suffragists*) and its evaluation.

The dissent PR model could also be applied to the suffragettes who championed female enfranchisement using protests and marches, combined with a level of civil disobedience, which, Lysack (2008) argues, gradually became more militant in its approach.

It is necessary to take into account that the concept of militancy changed during the period from 1850 to 1914. Generally, it has been connected with violent tactics in the activity of suffragettes. Using hammers, militants were breaking windows of houses and shops, damaging grounds for golf, cutting telegraph wires, setting fire and arranging explosions at railway stations and even in churches. The suffragettes' "symbolic violence" and "rage" were opposed to the power of the state. The contrast of "elegant" women who demonstratively tried to play a role not "inherent" in them was used to attract attention to the best moral qualities of human nature. Their "asocial" behavior and extremism were not always appreciated (Riddell, 2018).

Despite the most different attitudes of society toward suffragettes' tactics, an aim was achieved: their actions resulted in exciting the "public mind" as everyone talked about women's rights. The effectiveness of militants' activity can be subject to discussion, but, it looks morally justified, as the participants of the radical women's movement believed in their rightness and the fairness of their demands.

Founded in 1913 as the Congressional Union for Woman Suffrage (CU), the National Woman's Party (NWP) was instrumental in raising public awareness of the women's suffrage campaign. Using a variety of tactics, the party successfully pressured President Woodrow Wilson, members of Congress, and state legislators to support passage of a 19th Amendment to the US Constitution guaranteeing women nationwide the right to vote. In so doing, the NWP established a legacy defending the exercise of free speech, free assembly, and the right to dissent.

> The willingness of NWP pickets to be arrested, their campaign for recognition as political prisoners rather than as criminals, and their acts of civil disobedience in jail shocked the nation and brought attention and support to their cause.
>
> (Tactics and techniques of the National Woman's Party suffrage campaign, p. 2)

In the 1970–1980s, feminists experimented with various external theatre-like events, oriented to undermine the system of gender cultural norms, stereotypes, and values. The point of the transition to active measures became the famous feminist action "Miss America Protest" in Atlantic City in 1968 where the "Miss America" beauty competition took place. Over 150 feminists from different cities joined them to show how women were hurt by beauty competitions. During the demonstration, the participants made a "basket of freedom" where they threw their bras and waist belts as the symbols of women's enslavement by the violent and unrealistic standards of beauty. The action obtained wide and very negative media exposure, marking a day of mass "bra burning" in feminist history (Dow, 2003).

These PR tactics used in their campaign are integrated in the protests organized today by radical feminists all of over the world, including Eastern Europe. The Ukrainian group FEMEN and Russian group Pussy Riot are the most striking cases of modern feminist activism.

The "naked truth" of FEMEN

FEMEN emerged in Ukraine in 2008, and had become well known by the middle of 2009. Their actions are characterized by topless female activists, their bodies used as posters painted with slogans and crowned with flowers. The main goals of the organization are, in the short term, to publicize problems, which require public attention, and, in the long run, to achieve "complete victory over patriarchy" (FEMEN, 2018).

Sextremism, atheism and feminism are the ideological principles of this movement: the FEMEN manifesto states that the mission of the organization is to protest, and the weapon of protest are "naked breasts." Protest and bare breasts form "sextremism," which is considered by FEMEN participants as a "new form of feminist actionism" (Shevchenko, 2018), developed in the framework of their activities, nonviolent and aggressive form of provocation. Unofficial, unsanctioned actions, using female sexuality, are mostly directed against patriarchy. FEMEN believes that patriarchy has a theological basis – the belief that "man is better, man is steeper, man is the dominant species of people on Earth" (Diash, 2018). FEMEN struggles with this attitude, but is aware of the complexity of the task, because patriarchy is a centuries-old tradition. Activists metaphorically call the patriarchate a "three-headed dragon" – to refer to the powers of religion, politics and the sex industry (Diash, 2018). In the political sphere, there is a political exploitation of women, in the religious sphere – the spiritual, the sex industry is engaged in the economic exploitation of women.

One of the FEMEN leaders defines their activities as "provocative feminism" (Volokhov, 2012), with the main goal of the liberation of women from patriarchal oppression. The movement distanced itself from what they call "academic" interpretation of feminism and deliberately decided

Figure 5.1 Femen in Paris, March 31, 2012.

Source: Wikimedia Commons, the free media repository. https://commons.wikimedia.org/wiki/File:Femen_(6890661898).jpg.

to represent the ideology of pop feminism,[1] which is accessible to a wide audience and attractive to young people.

The participants, however, note that their actionism can be "too radical" for a traditionalist country as Ukraine and aimed to expand its actions in Western Europe (Shevchenko, 2018).

The organization uses shock as a PR tactic. The postmodern aspect is embodied in performances, kitsch, irony, and carnival parody. FEMEN justifies the adoption of shock as tactic arguing that the traditional forms of public mobilization are too serious and uninteresting; therefore not only do they fail to attract media attention but they are also easily forgotten by the audience. In Ukraine, public outcry is caused by the fact that the "naked protesting woman" is the most outrageous phenomenon for the patriarchate. This facilitates the dissemination of information about FEMEN as a media virus, due to its scandalous context, which becomes a tool to attract attention to serious problems.

Feminists define their organization as a radical women's movement. First of all, radicalism means "scandal." Gutsol notes, that it is necessary to act radically, and this means "topless" (Mayerchik & Plakhotnik, 2010). Naked bodies here are the main protest PR elements, which help attract the public's attention. They are also the symbol of liberation from patriarchy and revolution in the political and private spheres.

The theme of the first action of FEMEN in Khmelnytsky in 2008 was the death of several women due to medical error. Activists "stood with placards in the square, bursting into the office to the head of the regional administration" (Shevchenko, 2018). These events were filmed by TV crews, so the whole country learned about them. At this point, the FEMEN activists realized how they can "loudly say what they want to say" (Shevchenko, 2018). The starting point of the new strategy was the realization that their actions should be "interesting" for the media:

> In order to be heard, we must understand the rules of the game. If we want Ukraine to hear us, if we want to state a problem, then we must do something that will allow us to be heard, it should be a public action, we can invite journalists, not only local, but also all-Ukrainian media.
>
> (Shevchenko, 2018)

From that moment, the activists decided that they

> need to work out a scheme, a formula to be heard, we need to have a list of journalists, we need to find their phones, e-mails in order to send the press announcement of the action beforehand.
>
> (Shevchenko, 2018)

At the first stage of development of the organization in the small town in Ukraine, the format of the activity was round tables, in the framework of which actual problems were discussed (for example, stereotypes in advertising). They were not spectacular events. A participant and one of the founders of FEMEN, Shevchenko, defines the format of such meetings as "the girls gathered in the room to discuss the problem" (Shevchenko, 2018). At the stage of training, FEMEN activists consider the media's potential role for the action. The choice of the form of protest depends on how it will be presented in the media. Activists are not oriented to a separate media channel, but to the entire "classical media machine" (Diash, 2018). However, FEMEN activists are skeptical about social networks, in particular, Facebook. In their opinion, today they are not able to adequately display the actions: "Facebook is created by a man, does not support FEMEN, constantly bans accounts" (Diash, 2018). Although there does not seem to be any direct engagement of public relations professionals in these activist initiatives – the group clearly reflects on and displays an understanding of PR techniques in gaining the attention of media, politicians and the general public.

FEMEN actions are at the center of the press, which is the result of a thoughtful strategy of activists. The methods of representation in the media do not always correspond to the idea of a specific political event. If this happens, then the organizers blame only themselves, not the "bad" media:

It's our fault, we did something wrong. Our best actions are unambiguous. They are absolutely understandable and clear. Everybody sees what happened. We are working and we want to ensure that the media does not have the opportunity to treat the actions differently.

(Diash, 2018)

This approach indicates that the FEMEN organizers are familiar with the principles of the work of the media and take them into account when preparing the action. However, the strategy doesn't always work and sometimes, the radicalism of such actions can actually play a low-down trick.

The actions of FEMEN are so shocking in their form, that their contents are not perceived at all. People, primarily men, consider them as a performance with beautiful naked girls and do not listen to what these actions would like to convey.

(FEMEN: is "sextremism" bad for feminism?, 2012)

The world community observes the shock tactics of the Ukrainian activists as the naked body became the "visiting card" of the group.

Ironically it is those who dress in more provocative clothing, sometimes just their underwear, who attract media attention … Consequently, critics have argued the movement has focused on dress rather than power or deeper issues. Further criticism is that the approach reflects the "pornification of everything" and supports increased sexualisation of women.

(Yaxley, 2012, para. 17)

Modern examples of political behavior demonstrate the synthesis of PR and politics. Street protests use new forms of expression to enhance the effect, to create maximum resonance, and to draw attention to the existing problems in society with the help of PR tactics. Political action in the postmodern reality, based on the game, is fragmentary and provocative. An important manifestation of the postmodern era is self-expression of the individual with the help of creative forms of mass participation. Visualization and elements of the game strengthen the emotional coloring of political actionism. This has an impact on its effectiveness.

FEMEN defines the body as exclusively a women's weapon, which should demonstrate freedom from the stereotypes, imposed by men. The use of naked female bodies in street actions as a performative PR strategy is a unique practice for Eastern Europe (Teteryuk, 2013). Mayerchik and Plakhotnik note that activists are criticized for "objectified sexist stylistics," "trade by sexualized female corporeality" (Mayerchik & Plakhotnik, 2010, pp. 7–8). This criticism is caused by the use of marketing strategies, inherent in the society of consumption: the woman's body as an advertising tool, provocativeness as a way of presentation of social problems.

The nude stylistics of FEMEN protests is characterized by femininity – deliberately sexualized, stereotypical, formed according to the standards of magazines. Female model-like bodies are recognized as a universal product in the global or local market. Based on the market principle, FEMEN activists are trying to "sell" social and political topics by inserting subversion and shock through their message and publicness. Paradoxically, by repackaging femininity, FEMEN subverts all femininity traits: women not supposed to be loud in public, their bodies covered or uncovered according to male norms, their voices quiet and low, their place not in politics, their affiliation not to other women. By invading public spaces historically dominated and controlled by men, when it comes to politics, they use the body both to attract attention to its message for a few seconds of news coverage and for stirring up public debate especially on the question if the aim can justify the means.

Pussy Riot: "blasphemy" as provocation

Further challenging male spaces, Pussy Riot relies on artistic outrageousness: happenings, a game improvisation, proceeding as an action, is primarily provoked by its organizers. Happenings can be conducted in an open space, the most suitable for attracting the political interest of the public. The atmosphere of absurdity, inherent in happenings, is associated with the absurd phenomena in society happenings, which the group seeks to criticize (Honcharenko, 2013). The goal of happenings is to deliver a spontaneous, irrational performance. Therefore, the actions of participants are often considered as illogical and absurd, random. Happenings use the elements of plastic and spatial action: music, dance, recitation, and video demonstration, so well demonstrated by the Pussy Riot in Russia. Unlike performances, which can later be reproduced, happenings are unique, one-off events. For journalists, such a form of fine art as performance does not require "a special gift and diligent hard work, but gives the right to call oneself an artist. Shocking can instantly become famous" (Zolotukhina, 2013, para 16).

The actions of Russian radical feminist punk-rock band Pussy Riot caused a huge public response. Views on the protest actions of the group are sometimes diametrically opposed: from angry to enthusiastic. Punk-prayer at the Cathedral of Christ the Saviour in 2012 hit a vulnerable spot of the Russian state, and re-actualized a bulk of problems from the merging of the church and the state apparatus, to infringement of women's rights, the strengthening of the position of the church, and the increasingly conservative tendencies in society. Pussy Riot's protest actions can be observed from a variety of perspectives. Feminist ideas are inherent in them, they reflect world tendencies of protest movement and modern art practices, which see actionism as one of the most demanded forms of artistic expression.

Pussy Riot was created on November 7, 2011, when the band's first video appeared on social networks ("Pussy Riot: The story so far," 2013). As women activists say, the band was created due to the absence of "an explosive, effective punk feminist group that encourages citizens to develop a culture of protest" in Russia (Kharitonova, 2012). After studying the world trends of feminist art practices, having become acquainted with the work of feminist punk bands in the US and Western Europe, activists wanted to create a Russian analogue. Pussy Riot became world-known due to a combination of elements of actionism, contemporary art, shocking tactics, and feminism.

The activity of this group was based on conceptual grounds of open-air actionism at the grassroots level of culture. No less significant for the formation of actionism in the post-Soviet space is the action event of the art group "Э.Т.И," when the participants put out the word "DICK" with their bodies opposite the Mausoleum on Red Square in 1991. This action is considered the first in the post-Soviet space, which openly criticized the phallocenterism of power in the iconic public sphere.

Actionism as a form of contemporary art and PR presupposes direct actions of the artist in public. The format of Pussy Riot's actions as representatives of political, feminist art with elements of actionism is "a sudden appearance somewhere with musical instruments with the performance of a song" (Sobchak & Sokolova, 2012). Actions are held in the form of

Figure 5.2 Rehearsal of Pussy Riot, February 14, 2012.

Source: photo by Denis Bochkarev (Wikimedia Commons, the free media repository). https://commons.wikimedia.org/wiki/File:Pussy_Riot_-_Denis_Bochkarev_5.jpg.

exploration of a certain urban space. These include actions "Free the paving stones," "Kropotkin Vodka," "Death to prison, freedom to protest," "Putin Has Pissed Himself," "Virgin Mary, put Putin away!" The most famous and disputable Pussy Riot action is a punk-prayer "Virgin Mary, put Putin away!" held on February 21, 2012. At the Cathedral of Christ the Saviour the women actionists rose to the pulpit, where they were moving in a punk manner, crossing themselves, falling down on their knees, singing "Virgin Mary, put Putin away!" up to the moment they were moved out by the security. The message of the song was criticism of the alliance between the state and the church, the leadership of the Moscow Patriarchate, intelligent services and the President of Russia, Vladimir Putin.

The Union of Orthodox Women deemed Pussy Riot's performance a "blasphemous act [which] insulted not only the feelings of the faithful, but also the heroism of our ancestors" (Mason, 2018). Lind (2015) notes that

> precisely because of the transgressive character of the images, sounds and utterances, those who find the video offensive have a hard time seeing how it does anything but display disrespect toward faith, believers, and sacred symbols of the Russian Orthodox Church.
>
> (p. 9)

Maria Alekhina, Nadezhda Tolokonnikova, and Katerina Samutsevich were detained after a punk-prayer service, which they performed with two other unidentified members of Pussy Riot. Modern Russian conservative society perceived the punk-prayer as a desecration of the shrine. The venue of the action – the Cathedral of Christ the Saviour in Moscow – was destroyed by Soviet authorities at the beginning of 1930s and reconstructed in 1990s as a symbol of renunciation of the Stalinist past and return to "Christian values." Gradually, it turned into a major Church establishment, from where TV broadcasts of services are conducted during Orthodox holidays. The Cathedral of Christ the Savior, having become the main temple of Russia, in the opinion of activists, symbolizes the fusion of Church and state.

Before the performance of Pussy Riot in the Cathedral, few knew that the church pulpit was a forbidden place for women. N. Tolokonnikova believes that the pulpit is a place for a woman, because she is not a sinful creature; a woman should conduct worship services in the temples. At the trial, Tolokonnikova stated that "the official version of religion, headed by the current hierarchy of the ROC, is a pseudo-religion, just as Putin's regime is pseudo-democracy" ("Pussy Riot participants," 2012).

During the trial, the participants of Pussy Riot attracted global attention, despite the fact, that the band was created only several months before the prayer. The trial has caused a broad response around the world on the grounds of freedom of expression and artistic freedom. During the trial, the court stated that the actions of activists are "disorderly conduct based on religious hatred" and in August 2012 sentenced them to two years of imprisonment in a general regime colony. Thus, activists were convicted of a musical performance criticizing the Russian Orthodox Church and the Russian president.

There is the view, that the trial and the verdict are Putin's revenge for the action "Putin Has Pissed Himself,"[2] which was held by the group at the Lobnoye mesto[3] of Red Square in Moscow (Sobchak & Sokolova, 2012). Regardless, Pussy Riot became a landmark for Russian society, having provoked a discussion about the role of the Church in society. The punk-prayer caused fury of the leadership of the Moscow Patriarchate, Orthodox activists, politicians, and significant part of the public.

In the opinion of Pastukhov, the action of Pussy Riot

> hit precisely into the bare social nerve, any touch to which causes a convulsive and extremely painful reaction. Russia suffocated with anger and shame at the same time. Well, they should be thanked for the fact that they helped us to find the pressure point.
>
> (Pastukhov, 2012)

The fact that Pussy Riot activists are young women points to a new way of thinking of Russian youth. According to Alekhina, they did not want to offend anyone, but protested against the unification of political and spiritual elites (Zarubina, 2012). Their action criticizes the abuse by representatives of the hierarchy of the Moscow Patriarchate. The performance was of a political nature, and was not a protest against religion. Thus, the activists separate the political nature of the protest from the religious one. The object of protest is not the Orthodox Church, but its elite.

After the amnesty, Tolokonnikova and Alekhina launched social projects, they organize and take part in protest actions, as well as write books. Participants of Pussy Riot were offered a contract for a world tour, but "the girls abandoned millions, remaining true to the original concept: unexpected performances in unexpected places" (Barabanov, 2014). Despite this, Pussy Riot performed at the festival in Glastonbury, presented prizes at the Berlin Film Festival, starred in the series "House of Cards," and performed at a concert of Amnesty International together with Madonna.

Tolokonnikova and Alekhina are engaged in human rights activities, they implement the "Zone of Law" project, and have also founded the Internet resource "Mediazona." They also take part in the actions, support any form of protest in the country, where the demand for autocracy and Orthodoxy increased again due to propaganda. For example, during the Sochi Winter Olympic Games in 2014, they held an action against the background of the Olympic rings with the song "Putin Will Teach You How to Love the Motherland" (Tolokonnikov, 2014). In December 2017, Pussy Riot held an action near the Federal Security Services (FSB) building on Bolshaya Lubyanka Street in Moscow. On the day of the security forces and the 100th anniversary of the Russian special services, activists came to the FSB building and put up a banner with the words "Happy Birthday, Butchers" ("Maria Alekhina was arrested," 2017).

Since the Pussy Riot's punk prayer, the image of a girl in a balaclava and a dress of acid color has become one of the iconic images associated with Russian youth. The fact that a brief action has generated such a powerful and contradictory reaction, a lot of arguments, disputes, speaks about its significance. Some researchers believe that feminists held the action "at the most inappropriate moment, the period of pre-election hysteria" ("Pussy Riot: art or politics?" 2012); on the other hand, it can be interpreted as an exact hit in the political context.

The action in the Cathedral made it possible to demonstrate how various aspects of modern society can be reflected in one event. The case of Pussy Riot demonstrated the historical continuity of the feminist movement, political protest, the currents of avant-garde art and protest PR. The punk-prayer "Virgin Mary, put Putin away!" is connected to modern art (from futurism to Moscow actionism) by means of de-sacralization of space and sacred images, a certain gesture in the social space, outrageous behavior, and appearance, parodying, multilayered, sometimes unobvious idea of the action, relevance of the problems, theatricality of the action, and ambiguous public reaction.

The Pussy Riot action is an important part of the Russian cultural space. Tolokonnikova believes that the punk-prayer has already become a classic of modern art. The ambiguous reaction of the public to the action was due to the positioning of the performance as a manifestation of contemporary art. The gender aspect plays an important role in the self-identification of Pussy Riot participants, who consider themselves to be representatives of the third wave of feminism and supporters of "politicized feminism." As the activists say, the feminist theorists who influenced Pussy Riot are Simone de Beauvoir, Andrea Dworkin, Emmeline Pankhurst, Sulamith Firestone, Gayatri Chakravorti Spivak, bell hooks, Kate Millett, Rosie Braidotti, Judith Butler (Kharitonova, 2012). Among the women's movements that inspired the Pussy Riot activists to fight, it is necessary to single out suffragettes, radical feminists, feminist political, and artistic actions of the 1960s and 1970s.

The reason for the worldwide appeal of Pussy Riot is the use of an international language, the introduction of unique content and message with the help of well thought through PR strategies. The problems of artists in countries with authoritarian and totalitarian regimes are determined by the way they exist within the regimes. Pussy Riot as artists of an authoritarian country are the antipodes of power. For an artistic career, this is a profitable position. When the authorities began to pursue Pussy Riot, they became world stars (Kan, 2017).

So similar, yet so different

Actionism is considered as the practice of group or individual actions, aimed at creation of information message, which has the features of theatrical performance. Actionism is the generalized name of the "art of action," where the gesture, the act or the event are the pieces of work. Actionism is a show technology, used in the political sphere, which has become a means of forming the audience's worldview. Actionism is also one of the most important practices of socially critical art. Performance is a form of "action art," a kind of actionism (Robinson, 2015).

A large number of shocking performances are carried out by the Ukrainian women's organization FEMEN. Using the female body, this community oversteps the symbolic line of society's control over this body and the reclaiming of the body by women in their own terms, in order to draw attention to a wide range of problems. FEMEN explains its shocking nature by the fact that the traditional forms of activism are less effective in connecting with the public, especially these groups who would not think about sexism or the issues raised by FEMEN. Traditional activism, claims the group, appears too serious, so it does not meet with public response and is not covered in the media.

Concerning the popularity of the FEMEN movement, it should be noted that it managed to change the public discourse about the rights of women in Ukraine. They occupied the streets, used a naked female body, carnival humor, burlesque as arguments in political disputes (Chermalykh, 2013). Activists say that they are not only interested in the Ukrainian society. They struggle against "all manifestations of patriarchy, wherever they occur, throughout the world" (Diash, 2018). Participants are positioned as "women with no nationality," so they protest naked (Diash, 2018). Through the use of these universal codes, FEMEN activists have overcome geographical, cultural and national boundaries. The movement has followers in different countries, using the stylistics of FEMEN in protests.

Participants of Pussy Riot highlight their difference from the movement FEMEN, finding similarity neither in the form of protest, nor in the interpretation of feminism. Samutsevich believes that the fundamental difference between Ukrainian and Russian activists is that the participant of Pussy Riot

> is not a girl who undresses, because she wants to look attractive for men. FEMEN does not hide this and write that men want to see such women and that's what we are. Through images that men like, we will promote feminism.
>
> (Sobchak & Sokolova, 2012)

Pussy Riot has another approach: activists hide faces, they have an androgynous image of a creature in a dress and colored tights: "Somewhat like a woman, but without a woman's face, hair. Androgyne, like a hero from a cartoon, superhero." Animation and brightness of this character in many respects aesthetically predetermined the international success of Pussy Riot. According to Samutsevich, this character is universal:

> It can be anyone – a girl, a guy. Anyone can put on a balaclava, even a man. Here, too, is the idea of anonymity, the idea of an active action, not very typical for women. Dancing in balaclava is not what society expects from women.
>
> (Sobchak & Sokolova, 2012)

Another fundamental difference between Pussy Riot and FEMEN is seen in the various strategies they use to resist power. After the Cathedral performance of Pussy Riot, a line of defense was built that some of the members of the group are positioning themselves as Christians. While FEMEN consider themselves atheists and declare this position.

Shocking the public helped FEMEN and Pussy Riot to get their message across quickly and get a big response and coverage in the media. The concept of shock tactics originates from the notion that a sudden and brief shock can affect behavior in a positive way. While this may not always be the case, there is no denying that such tactics can help to put certain brand, group or organization on the map, to make their message heard and to leave a long-lasting impression.

Recent studies that have interpreted activism and protest as part of PR history is not without challenge or controversy.

> While some see activism and PR as ideologically distinct, others seek to integrate activism within PR canon or even to idealize activism as a form of PR that helps position PR more favorably within the moral universe.
>
> (L'Etang, 2016, p. 208)

Since PR is not going away, it is essential to rethink and analyze where activism and public relations articulate and intersect in their development. Today the reality remains that few studies have explored the possibility of studying the relation of public relations as tools and possibly ways of thinking for social movements. Rapid changes in technology and developments in communication require refinements in public relations theory

> to provide more adequate guides for those who are practicing or preparing to operate across the cultural, political, and economic boundaries that comprise comprehensive international public relations.
>
> (Wakefield, 2007, p. 138)

In conclusion, the concepts of dissent and protest PR could be useful in expanding the historical understanding of public relations. They could also provide a focus on how women have used dissent and activist techniques to get their voices heard in society. Overall, an initial consideration of the women's perspective on the example of Eastern European feminist activism indicates that the concepts of dissent and protest PR could open up new directions for research.

Notes

1 Pop feminism – is the penetration of feminist ideas into pop culture. Due to this, there is the attraction of attention of new audience.
2 On January 20, 2012, Pussy Riot performed the song "Riot in Russia – Putin Has Pissed Himself" at the Lobnoye mesto of Red Square in Moscow. After the performance, eight participants of the band were detained and released later the same day. Red Square was chosen as a performance venue due to its symbolism. The Kremlin is a symbol of power that is associated with Putin. Red Square has a rich tradition of actionism.
3 Lobnoye mesto – minor round platform, surrounded by a stone fence was primarily used for announcing the tsar's ukazes and for religious ceremonies.

References

Adi, A. & Moloney, K. (2012). The importance of scale in Occupy movement protests: a case study of a local Occupy protest as a tool of communication through Public Relations and Social Media. *Revista Internacional de Relaciones Públicas*, II(4), 97–122. Retrieved from https://goo.gl/j3EaiK.

Barabanov, B. (2014, April 2). Tallinn Music Week has ended. *Kommersant*. Retrieved from http://kommersant.ru/doc/2443772 (in Russian).

Chermalykh, N. (2013). Glimpse on global protest movements from American-Ukrainian perspective: from FEMEN to OCCUPY: discussion between Jessica Zihovych and Nataliya Chermalykh. *Ya*. 33, 15–18 (in Ukrainian).

Della Porta, D. & Diani, M. (2006). *Social movements: an introduction*. 2nd ed. London: Blackwell Publishing.

Diash, A. (2018, January 9). Personal interview.

Dow, B. (2003). Feminism, Miss America, and media mythology. *Rhetoric & Public Affairs*, 6, 127–149.

FEMEN: is "sextremism" bad for feminism? *Inosmi*. (2012). Retrieved from https://inosmi.ru/world/20121017/201039475.html (in Russian).

FEMEN Official Blog (2018). About us. Retrieved from https://femen.org/about-us/.

Fitzpatrick, K. & Bronstein, C. (eds.) (2006). *Ethics in public relations: Responsible advocacy*. Thousand Oaks, CA: SAGE Publications, Inc.

Grunig, J. E. & Hunt, T. (1984). *Managing public relations*. Belmont, CA: Wadsworth.

Holtzhausen, D. R. (2012). *Public relations as activism: Postmodern approaches to theory & practice*. London: Routledge.

Honcharenko, D. R. (2013), Performance-art as a phenomenon of postmodernism culture. *Current Problems of Art Practice and Art Science*, 5, 333–337 (in Ukrainian).

Kan, A. (2017, November 24). Pussy Riot, Pavlensky & others: post-Soviet actionism at Saatchi London Gallery. *BBC Russian*. Retrieved from www.bbc.com/russian/features-42070045 (in Russian).

Kharitonova, O. (2012). Phenomenon of Pussy Riot. Retrieved from http://krotov. info/history/21/2011/haritonova_2012.htm (in Russian).

Lattimore, D., Baskin, O., Heiman S., Toth, E., & Van Leuven, J. (2004a). Public relations: the profession and the practice. Chapter 3, *A theoretical basis of public relations*, pp. 50–69. Retrieved from http://highered.mheducation.com/sites/dl/ free/0073512052/930653/Chapter_3.pdf.

Lattimore, D., Baskin, O., Heiman S., Toth, E., & Van Leuven, J. (2004b). Public relations: the profession and the practice. Chapter 2, *History of public relations*, pp. 24–49. Retrieved from http://highered.mheducation.com/sites/dl/free/007351 2052/930653/Chapter_2.pdf.

L'Etang, J. (2016). Public relations, activism and social movements: critical perspectives. *Public Relations Inquiry*, 5(3), 207–2011. Sage Publications.

Lind, T. (2015). Blasphemy cries over Pussy Riot's "punk prayer." *Special Edition – Researching Music Censorship*, pp. 7–34. Retrieved from www.danishmusicology online.dk/arkiv/arkiv_dmo/dmo_saernummer_2015/dmo_saernummer_2015 _musikcensur_01.pdf.

Lysack, K. (2008). *Come buy, come buy: Shopping and the culture of consumption in Victorian women's writing.* New Brunswick, NJ: Rutgers University Press.

Maria Alekhina was arrested near FSB building on Lubyanka with a banner saying "Happy birthday torturers" (2017, December 20). *Mediazona*. Retrieved from https://zona.media/news/2017/12/20/happy-birthday (in Russian).

Mason, J. (2018). Pussy provocations: feminist protest and anti-feminist resurgence in Russia. *Feminist Encounters: A Journal of Critical Studies in Culture and Politics*, 2(1), 5. Retrieved from https://doi.org/10.20897/femenc.201805.

Mattoni, A. (2012). *Media practices and protest politics: How precarious workers mobilize.* London and New York: Routledge.

Mayerchik, M. & Plakhotnik, O. (2010). Radical FEMEN and new feminine activism. *Critics*, 11–12, 7–9 (in Ukrainian).

Miller, S. K. (2000). U.S. public relations history: knowledge and limitations. *Communication Yearbook*, 23, 381–420.

Moloney, K., McQueen, D., Surowiec, P., & Yaxley, H. (2013). *Dissent and protest public relations.* Public Relations Research Group, The Media School, Bournemouth University.

Pastukhov, V. (2012, July 5). Pussysteria. *Politru*. Retrieved from http://polit.ru/ article/2012/07/05/core/ (in Russian).

Pussy Riot: art or politics? (2012). *Look at me.* Retrieved from www.lookatme.ru/ mag/archive/experience-interview/159845-hlystom-i-pryanikom (in Russian).

Pussy Riot participants: our case is political (2012, August 6). *BBC*. Retrieved from www.bbc.com/russian/russia/2012/08/120806_pussy_riot_day_six (in Russian).

Pussy Riot: the story so far. (2013, December 23). *BBC*. Retrieved from www.bbc. com/news/world-europe-25490161.

Riddell, F. (2018, February 6). Suffragettes, violence and militancy. Retrieved from www.bl.uk/votes-for-women/articles/suffragettes-violence-and-militancy.

Robinson, H. (2015). *Feminism-art-theory: An anthology, 1968–2014*, 2nd ed. Chichester: Wiley Blackwell.

Shevchenko, A. (2018, January 28). Personal interview.

Sobchak, K. & Sokolova, K. (2012, October 19). Ekaterina Samutsevich. Non-uncovered. *Snob*. Retrieved from http://archive.is/8fVuv (in Russian).

Tactics and techniques of the National Woman's Party suffrage campaign. (n.p.). The Library of Congress. American memory. 1–12. Retrieved from www.loc.gov/collections/static/women-of-protest/images/tactics.pdf.

Teteryuk, M. (2013). Female body as a political instrument: media-representations of FEMEN actions. Naukovi zapysky NaUKMA. *Teoriia ta istoriia kultury*, 140, 55–59 (in Ukrainian).

Tolokonnikov, A. (2014, February 21). Putin fails to teach Pussy Riot to "love the Motherland" at the Sochi Olympics. *Huffington Post*. Retrieved from www.huffingtonpost.com/andrey-tolokonnikov/putin-fails-to-teach-pussy-riot-to-love-the-motherland_b_4831033.html.

Volokhov, S. (2012, March 26). Strip games. FEMEN gains sympathy from men and loses support from feminists. *Focus*. Retrieved from https://focus.ua/society/224236/ (in Russian).

Wakefield, R. I. (2007). Theory of international public relations, the internet, and activism: a personal reflection. *Journal of Public Relations Research*, 20(1), 138–157.

Yaxley, H. (2012, December 13). Dissent PR – from suffragettes to slut walks. *PR Conversations*. Global discussion of PR from local perspectives. Retrieved from www.prconversations.com/dissent-pr-from-suffragettes-to-slut-walks/.

Zarubina, T. (2012, April 13). Anna Zobnina: everyone should have defensive arguments for Pussy Riot. *Snob*. Retrieved from https://snob.ru/selected/entry/48011 (in Russian).

Zolotukhina, I. (2013, January 15). The truth about Pussy Riot: what main scandalists of 2012 achieve. *Segodnya*. Retrieved from www.segodnya.ua/investigations/Vsya-pravda-o-Pussy-Riot-chego-dobivayutsya-glavnye-skandalistki-2012-goda.html.

6 Protesting the homeland

Diaspora dissent public relations efforts to oppose the Dominican Republic's citizenship policies

Maria De Moya

In September 2013, a Dominican Republic Constitutional Court ruling threatened to revoke the citizenship rights of the children of foreign-born parents lacking a proper immigration status. Due to the contentious relationship with its neighbor, this ruling was seen to specifically target people of Haitian descent. In response, Haitian and Dominican Diaspora members organized to garner the international community's support in pressuring the Dominican government to revoke its decision. These efforts included public protests, letters to U.S. media editors and social media-organized protests aimed at protecting the citizenship rights of Dominicans of Haitian descents and the human rights of Haitian immigrants (De Moya & Bravo, 2018).

In response, the Dominican government revised their ruling to allow time for thousands of immigrants to retain their status, a temporary measure that offered respite to some, but still left thousands in a legal limbo (Amnesty International, 2015; Human Rights Watch, 2015). Therefore, the efforts to oppose the ruling and the new law continued, as both Diasporas ensured that the media did not forget the issue or the people being affected. Through this case study, the present chapter details how these two Diasporas engaged in dissent and protest public relations in their efforts try to influence national policies, presenting how Diasporas can become adversarial in their relationship with the homeland.

Foreign media and image of nations

A nation's image can be understood as the aggregate beliefs and attitudes that the public hold of that nation (Kotler, Haider & Rein, 1993). Images of other nations can "serve to justify a nation's desired reaction or treatment toward another" (Alexander, Levin & Henry, 2005, p. 28). This image can have a significant impact on tourism, foreign investment, as well as its cultural and diplomatic relationships (Anholt, 2006).

Nations attempt to shape their image as part of their international public relations or public diplomacy efforts.[1] These attempts include strategic efforts to shape and influence how they are portrayed in the media

(Entman, 2008). The evolution of media channels has opened the public sphere and created a context in which the image, reputation and credibility of a nation can be as valuable, if not more, than its other tangible resources (Gilboa, 2008).

A nation's image management efforts traditionally include media diplomacy. Gilboa (2002) defines media diplomacy as the use of the media to "express interest in negotiation, to build confidence, and to mobilize support for agreements" (p. 741). This can be done through the country's own media channels, like in the case of Venezuela, Japan, Russia and France (Chang & Lin, 2014), or through foreign media (Johnson, 2005; Lee, 2007; Rosendorf, 2014).

However, governments are not the only agents that can affect a nation's portrayal in international media, and hence, their image. Non-state actors such as corporations, grassroots movements and NGOs, have long been known to influence a nation's relationship with its partners and foreign publics (Gilboa, 1998; Zaharna, 2007). These actors shape public conversations by incorporating their own opinions and perspectives into the mix of information about that nation (Riley, 2014). When they are able to influence media coverage, these publics have "the potential to influence public opinion and the policy process" (Manheim & Albritton, 1984, p. 656).

Of these non-state actors one group that has proven very influential is Diasporas, which are "individual immigrants or communities who live outside the legal or recognized boundaries of the state or the homeland, but inside the reterrorized space of the dispersed nation" (Laguerre, 1998, p. 8). Today Diasporas have an important role to play in the public diplomacy and image management efforts of their homelands.

The importance of diasporas

Diasporas are a product of voluntary or forced migration. As Laguerre (1998) explains, the life of this immigrant community may be interpreted in terms of continuity and "*rerootedness*" (p. 8), which refers to their living in another state as well as their translational relationship with the homeland.

Diaspora members have increasingly become more involved in the political affairs of the homeland (Adén-Papadopoulos & Pantti, 2013; Mahieu, 2017). To some nations they have become allies contributing to the public diplomacy efforts of the homeland, while also helping the host country reach the home country's publics (Bravo, 2014). Additionally, in the past, diasporas have offered support to public diplomacy efforts by backing their nation's stance on international issues and helping advance their domestic policies (e.g., Cull, 2009; Zaharna, 2011). However, as Diaspora groups become involved in public diplomacy, the home country's government can lose control over the message and, thus, be left with no choice but to "accept critical voices as part of the project" (Attias, 2012, p. 482).

In their analysis of adversarial publics in public diplomacy, Zaharna and Uysal (2016) presented a typology of nation-to-public relational dynamics, which detailed how the nature of the relationships might differ in the efforts are public-based versus state-based. The authors explained that in public-based initiatives, i.e., those that are led by the public and attempt to meet the goals they have established for themselves (as opposed to those established by the homeland). This creates the possibility for a negative to adversarial relationship with the nation. In these cases, the public can be composed of people who are connected or not to each other, or the nation. Still, the context allows Diasporas to develop an oppositional relationship with the homeland, especially as they lead the communication efforts which are guided by their own goals.

For example, in his study of media production by Venezuelans in the United States, Shumow (2014) identified an opposition model of Diaspora journalism in which the journalists' main focus was on the events of the homeland and their firm opposition to then president, Hugo Chávez. In fact, the Diaspora journalist pursued stories for political-driven purposes, knowing that their work was being closely followed by audiences at home (Shumow, 2014). Similarly, in the case of the Syrian community in Italy, Al-Rawi and Fahmy (2018) found that the Diaspora used social media for political activism against the Assad government and to show solidarity with Syrian rebels. In cases like these, the Diaspora shifts from partner to opposition, appealing to the media in order to influence publics in the homeland and abroad.

Protesting the homeland

The importance of maintaining the nation's image, gives the Diaspora an opportunity not only to support the homeland, but also to publicly oppose it through the use of protests and media advocacy efforts, part of what is called dissent public relations. Moloney, McQueen, Suroweic and Yaxley (2012) define dissent public relations as

> the dissemination of ideas, commentaries, and policies through PR techniques in order to change current, dominant thinking and behavior in discrete economic, political and cultural areas of public life.
>
> (p. 2)

A related practice is protest public relations, which includes efforts to persuade in order to forward changes in laws and regulations (Moloney et al., 2012). Dissent and protest public relations can be, but are not always, used together. For example, Gantchev (2009) saw protests and other forms of direct action as a higher-cost and more confrontational tactic employed by activists when other attempts at engagement have failed. But this is not the only use of protests, as they can also be a way for activists to counterbalance the power dynamic of the groups they are opposing, such as governments or large corporations, by gaining the media's attention. In fact, Coombs and Holladay (2012) explain that activists tend to be marginalized and have less power than the organizations they are trying to influence, but by employing public relations strategies, they can attempt to build power and persuade organizations to change their behaviors and policies.

Media advocacy in dissent public relations

Media attention on issues in the public debate is a frequently sought by organizations trying to promote views or policies around these issues (Cottle, 2008). In reaching out to the media, the way the issue of dissent is presented, or framed, is key as it can influence public perception and motivate them to try to bring about change (McKeever, 2013). The media's framing "defines to a large extent, the boundaries of public discussion about an issue" (Wallack & Dorfman, 1996, p. 298).

Often, the key factor for a particular frame to become part of the media coverage is the power of the organization or actor that promotes it (Entman, 2008). Yet less-powerful advocates can also frame stories in ways that get journalists' attention by making their stories newsworthy, highlighting controversy, conflict or injustice, for example (Wallack & Dorfman, 1996).

One strategic use way of doing dissent public relations, through media advocacy, is for the opposition to directly target policy makers, including elected officials, regulatory agents, legislators or business people to bring about policy changes (Dorfman & Krasnow, 2014). Efforts to reach these actors, these elites, rely heavily on traditional media (Gibson, 2010) despite the proven usefulness of social media and the proliferation of new media tools (e.g., McKeever, 2013; Wilkinson, 2016).

Of course, the potential of these efforts to influence policy depends on the advocate's opposition's ability to attract media coverage (Gibson, 2010). For these purposes protests have proven useful. As Cottle (2008) explains protests are an "accepted political tactic for an expanded range of organizations, single-issue campaigns, new social movements and transnational advocacy networks" (p. 854).

The framework of dissent and protest public relations, including media advocacy, serves as a foundation for the present chapter, which presents an original case study on Diaspora opposition to policies of the homeland. The case in question is the revocation of citizenship rights of Dominicans of Haitian descent by the Dominican Republic as a result of the 2013 citizenship ruling (Hannam, 2014; Tribunal Constitucional, 2013). Since late September 2013, the Dominican and Haitian Diasporas in the United States have been working together to present open opposition to the Dominican Republic's new citizenship policies that affected Dominicans of Haitian descent (e.g., Dominicanos por Derecho, n.d.; Haitian American

Association of New York, n.d.: Reconoci.do, n.d.; The Haitian Community Land Trust, n.d.; We are all Dominican, n.d.). These efforts included both dissent and protests strategies.

Data for the case study was collected from a variety of sources including news articles, opinion pieces, news releases, social media posts, as well as videos transcripts over two years (September 2013 to September 2015). Additionally, reports on the topic published by international organizations that had been cited in the news were collected for a closer analysis. Finally, data was collected from official Dominican government sources including the office of the Presidency, the Constitutional Tribunal and the Dominican Embassy in the United States.[2] All the news coverage, information subsidies and reports containing the terms, "Dominican," "Haitian" and "Citizenship" and/or referencing the 2013 Dominican citizenship ruling or the 2014 naturalization law, were included in the sample.

Case study: opposing the 2013 Dominican citizenship ruling

The Dominican Republic and Haiti share the Caribbean island of Hispaniola, but they are significantly distinct nations. The Dominican Republic has a strong economy and has recently seen reductions in poverty (World Bank, 2017a), while Haiti is considered one of the poorest nations in the world (World Bank, 2017b). Also, the Dominican Republic is a Spanish-speaking nation (Embassy of the Dominican Republic, n.d.), while the official languages in Haiti are Haitian creole and French (Embassy of the Republic of Haiti, n.d.).

Despite having similar population numbers (9.4 million for the Dominican Republic, and 9.8 million for Haiti), Haiti has double the population density of the Dominican Republic (Jaramillo & Sancak, 2007), compounding its poverty issue.

Poverty is cited as the main reason Haitians immigrate to the Dominican Republic in search for jobs (García, 2013; Lamb & Dundes, 2017). A recent Dominican survey of immigrants, the first of its kind, estimated that there are in excess of 450,000 Haitian immigrants in the country, representing 87 percent of the total number of immigrants, and nearly 5 percent of the country's total population (Oficina Nacional de Estadística, 2013).

The relationship between both nations can be best described as complex. Despite being close economic partners, the Dominican Republic has a long history of anti-Haitian sentiment, often referred to as *antihaitianismo* (Hall, 2017; Sagas, 1993; Tavernier, 2008). In recent history, this often exemplified by Dominican Dictator Rafael Trujillo's deportation and assassination of dark-skinned Dominicans and Haitians in an effort to "whiten" the population (Sagas, 1993). Some have argued that Dominican and Haitian identities have been constructed as polar opposites so that "to be Dominican means to be not Haitian, and especially not black" (Tavernier, 2008, para. 4). In this historical context, the Dominican Republic's decision to re-interpret the citizenship rights to people born in the country to foreign parents, was seen by many as an intentional effort to strip Dominican of Haitian descent of their citizenship rights (Archibold, 2013; Amnesty International, 2015; Human Rights Watch, 2015; We Are All Dominican, 2013).

As a result of the 2013 Citizenship Ruling in the Dominican Republic, influential Haitian and Dominican Diaspora members and organizations appealed to the media through letters and interviews to bring attention to what they viewed as a grave injustice (e.g., Fiezer, 2013; We Are All Dominican, 2013). Both the Dominican Republic and Haiti have sizeable Diasporas in the United States. Over 500,000 Haitians live in the country, the majority in Florida and New York (Camarota, 2010). The Dominican population in the U.S. is estimated to be 1.8 million, with the largest communities also in New York and Florida (Pew Research Center, 2015).

Members of the Dominican Diaspora remain active in both the homelands and the host country's political life, leading nonprofit organizations to serve the community and participating in the business sector (Castro & Boswell, 2002; Paarlberg, 2017). Similarly, the Haitian Diaspora remains involved in the political landscape (Paarlberg, 2017) and have organized to help the country in times of crisis (Joseph, Irazábal, & Désir, 2018). However, the 2013 ruling presented a unique opportunity for the Diasporas to work together to advance mutual interest, since it affected Dominican nationals of Haitian descent disproportionately.

The 2013 citizenship ruling

On September 23, 2013, the Supreme Court of the Dominican Republic provided a definitive interpretation of the country's constitution, which states that citizenship is not awarded to the children of undocumented immigrants (Hannam, 2014; Tribunal Constitucional, 2013). The ruling specified "THAT NOT ALL BORN IN THE DOMINICAN REPUBLIC'S TERRITORY ARE BORN DOMINICAN" (Tribunal Constitucional, 2013, p. 7, capitalization as in the original). This ruling officially and irrevocably changed the existing practice of granting nationality to all born on Dominican territory, except for the children of diplomats and people in transit (Hannam, 2014). The first significant shift to this policy started in 2007 when a resolution by the Dominican Electoral Board prohibited awarding birth certificates and *cédulas* (the national identification and voter-registration cards) to those born of parents lacking an immigrant or citizenship status (Pérez, 2013). In response to this resolution, Juliana Deguis Pierre, a child of Haitian immigrants born in the Dominican Republic, appealed to courts when her *cédula* was denied because she was assumed to be the child of undocumented Haitians laborers (Tribunal Constitucional, 2013). The case reached the Constitutional Tribunal (Tribunal Constitucional, in Spanish), which ruled that Dominican citizenship is not awarded to the children of undocumented migrants and that their birth would have to be registered at their country of origin's diplomatic mission (Tribunal Constitucional, 2013, p. 7). The ruling further specified:

> That in respect to the children of illegal foreigners, the Central Electoral Board has applied the legal criteria established for the Constitution since nineteen ninety-nine (1929)[3] and ratified by the Supreme Court of Justice, through its sentence of December fourteen (14) two thousand five (2005), in relation to the unconstitutionality recourse against the General Immigration Law number 285–04, consistent in that (…) IS NOT BORN DOMINICAN; GIVEN THE REASON THAT THE CHILD OF A FOREIGN MOTHER CANNOT BE, IF AT THE MOMENT OF GIVING BIRTH SHE IS IN AN IRREGULAR SITUATION, AND THUS CANNOT JUSTIFY THEIR ENTRY AND PERMANECE in Dominican Republic.
> (Tribunal Constitucional, 2013, p. 8, capitalization as in the original)

By emphasizing the 1929 ratification of the Dominican Constitution, the ruling applied retroactively and therefore could revoke the nationality of people who had been declared Dominican citizenship at birth (Pérez, 2013). The judgement "ordered the administrative transfer of all birth certificates of people born in the Dominican Republic as children of 'foreigners in transit' from 1929–2007, to the birth registration book of foreigners" (Inter-American Commission of Human Rights 2015, p. 11). For these reasons, the ruling was condemned almost immediately by international organizations and the Dominican and Haitian Diasporas.

The Caribbean Community put out a statement condemning "the abhorrent and discriminatory ruling" (CARICOM, 2013, para. 1), calling on the international community to appeal to the Dominican government to ensure the ruling would not stand and to grant full citizenship rights to Dominicans of Haitian descent. Similarly, the Inter-American Commission of Human Rights (OAS, 2013) called on the Dominican authorities to respect a person's right to nationality. These reports, and others that followed, joined the voices of the Diaspora in calling for a revocation of the new law.

Diaspora response to the 2013 ruling

A few days after the ruling an article published by the *Washington Post* warned of a human rights crisis that could follow the ruling ("Rights crisis feared after court ruling," 2013), which set the tone for much of the coverage that was to follow. During the first couple of months following the Dominican court's decision, the US media and international wire services published several stories focusing on the human cost of the ruling (e.g., Archibald, 2013; Gonzalez, 2013; McCalister, 2013).

The Haitian and Dominican Diasporas, as well as the Haitian authorities, soon became an integral part of this story. In October 2013, the *New York Daily News* reported that a protest organized by Haitian activists was announced, listing the Haitian Embassy in Washington as the source for information and updates (McCalister, 2013). A *New York Times* piece following the protest started with the story of Nina Paulino, a Dominican-American citizen, as one of dozens who had shown up to denounce the ruling (Semple, 2013). Semple (2013) reported that the ruling had

> presented a particular emotional challenge to many in New York's Dominican Diaspora who have been forced to wrestle with two competing ideas: Loyalty to their native or ancestral country and a deep, visceral opposition to the court's decision.
>
> (para. 7)

Haitian and Dominican Diaspora members would continue to organize similar protests in the US and the homeland which garnered more media attention (EFE Newswire, 2014, 2015; Wallace, 2013), but they would also move to more proactive media advocacy efforts.

After a front-page *New York Times* article detailed the dire consequences the ruling would have on Dominicans of Haitian descent (Archibold, 2013), the paper published two letters to the editor; one from then Ambassador to the Dominican Republic in the US, Anibal de Castro, and another signed by American journalist, Mark Kurlansky; Dominican-American authors Junot Díaz and Julia Álvarez; and Haitian American author, Edwidge Danticat ("Two versions of a Dominican tale," 2013). The Ambassador's letter focused the nation's interest in regulating immigration and emphasized the nation's sovereignty and autonomy. de Castro argued that the Dominican Republic

> should not be pressured by outside actors and other countries to implement measures contrary to its own Constitution and that would be unacceptable to most other nations facing similar immigration pressures.
>
> ("Two versions of a Dominican tale," 2013, para. 2)

In direct opposition, the letter penned by Diaspora members referred to a history of abuse from Dominican authorities to Haitian immigrants and called the ruling racist, and emphasizing the human cost:

> The ruling will make it challenging for them to study; to work in the formal sector of the economy; to get insurance; to pay into their pension fund; to get married legally; to open bank accounts; and even to leave the country that now rejects them if they cannot obtain or renew their passport. It is an instantly created underclass set up for abuse.
>
> ("Two versions of a Dominican tale," 2013, para. 9)

In this first stage of the crisis, the media coverage continued to highlight the risk to people who would lose their citizenship rights. International organizations such as the Inter-American Commission of Human Rights (OAS, 2013), the Caribbean Community (CARICOM, 2013) as well as the United States Department of State (2013) denounced the ruling as a human rights violation. News coverage quoted Human Rights experts, Dominican-American, Haitian-American and Haitian-Dominican citizens and experts, with little attention given to the Dominican authority's views. For example, a *Washington Post* editorial ("Shun thy neighbor," 2013) explained the ruling as a decision that

> enshrines the deep-seated racism and discrimination suffered by Haitian migrants and their children, who have worked back-breaking jobs in Dominican sugar-cane fields and construction sites for many years.
>
> (para. 2)

The editorial closed with a call for US officials to press the issue through Diplomatic channels. Just a couple of days later, the *Los Angeles Times* published an opinion piece (the fourth on the issue since the ruling), penned by Kurlansky, Álvarez, Danticat and Díaz (2013). International organizations such as CARICOM (2013) and the United Nations Human Rights Council (2013) had joined in denouncing the ruling and urging the Dominican Republic to address the issue of statelessness.

The international outcry led Dominican President, Danilo Medina, to seek to appease critics, while keeping to the country's new law. The result was the 2014 Naturalization Law (Congreso Nacional, 2014).

The Dominican government's response: the 2014 naturalization law

In November, just two months after the ruling, President Medina submitted a decree proposing a law that would offer undocumented immigrants and those whose citizenship status was at risk a way to apply for a visa, permit or start a process of naturalization (Presidencia de la República Dominicana, 2013). The law was ratified by the Dominican congress in May 2014, re-establishing the citizenship rights of those inscribed in the Dominican citizenship records from June 16, 1929 to April 18, 2007 (Congreso Nacional, 2014). It also allowed for a period of 180 days for people to apply for naturalization (Congreso Nacional, 2014), which was extended by another 90 days and expired in February 2015 (Mejía, 2015).

Even before the law was ratified, it sparked criticism from the Diaspora. The main concern was that the law asked people who by birth would be entitled to Dominican citizenship, to apply for naturalization

(Inter-American Commission of Human Rights, 2015). Effectively, Dominicans of Haitian descent were being treated as foreigners by their homeland.

In the Dominican Republic, a group of citizens opposing the ruling and the proposed naturalization law convened in a manifestation at the Dominican national university ("La solidaridad con los desnacionalizados...," 2013) in early December. In the US an open letter to Dominican President Danilo Medina from a newly formed group called *We Are All Dominican*, detailed the position of the New York Diaspora and called for a solution to this "human problem" (para. 11). We Are All Dominican identified itself as "a group of students, educators, community activists and artists living in New York City, composed primarily of Dominican-Americans as well as allies" (We Are All Dominican, 2013, para. 1). In their letter they made a public statement of solidarity towards Dominicans of Haitian descent "who are at risk of losing not only their nationality but also the ability to lead full lives in their own country," promising continued support to "our Dominican brothers and sisters of Haitian descent" (para. 12).

The negative news coverage continued, supported by new reports by International and Human Rights organizations. For example, Human Rights Watch (2015) reported that the law had serious design and implementation flaws. As the Inter-American Commission of Human Rights (2015) concluded

> [it] cannot but express its rejection of the procedure that allows people born in the Dominican Republic and who under Dominican legislation were entitled to Dominican nationality, to be treated as foreigners and that the option given to them to retell their Dominican nationality is to apply for a naturalization process...
>
> (p. 15)

As a response, the Dominican Republic office of the president launched a social media campaign to communicate what they understood to be the progress made with the law (Presidencia de la República Dominicana, 2015c). In a news release announcing the social media campaign (Presidencia de la República Dominicana, 2015d) the Dominican government announced that over 288,000 "foreigners without papers" (para. 1) in the country had been inscribed in the regularization plan, and Dominican nationality was recognized for 55,000 people and their descendants.

Despite these efforts, news coverage remained negative. The two Dominican ambassadors who served during this time frame had some success in publishing opinion pieces to present the view of the country (de Castro, 2013, 2014; Pérez, 2015), but the majority of opinion articles and letters to the editor published after the naturalization law, continued to oppose the ruling, some authored by experts in Human Rights, Immigration or related fields (De Moya & Bravo, 2018). The Diaspora presented a counter argument for every message put forth by the Dominican authorities and had their positions magnified by the media. Table 6.1 summarizes the Dominican Presidency's frames and the corresponding Diaspora's opposition frames.

Media advocacy outcomes

Following the naturalization law, the Diaspora organized more protests, which continued to be featured in the media (Correal, 2015; EFE Newswire, 2014, 2015). Additionally, the Diaspora's position benefited from the support of international organizations and other powerful voices, such as Haitian and US officials, as evidenced in the news coverage of the issue.

For example, New York City mayor Bill De Blasio is quoted in a *New York Times* article saying: "It is clearly an illegal act, it is an immoral act, it is a racist act by the Dominican government" (Correal, 2015, para. 3) adding that he thought this was happening because Haitians are black. Additionally, in an article published in the *Miami Herald* by a former Ambassador of Haiti to the United States, the author retells a long history of abuse by Dominican authorities, starting with the colorism of the Dominican Republic (Joseph, 2015). The author compares conditions under which Haitians worked in the Dominican sugar cane fields as "akin to slave labor" (Joseph, 2015, para. 6), denounces the Dominican officials for having been "defiant in carrying out ethnic cleansing" (para. 13) and "imposing a system akin to apartheid" (para. 14). Not only was the Dominican official position not present in this piece but also, these claims are not directly addressed in the Dominican authority's messaging (see Table 6.1).

Opinion pieces continued to call for the Dominican Republic to change its policy and for international organizations to influence the country to do so. In an article penned by two Human Rights professors in *New York Times* (Altholz & Fletcher, 2015) the authors called on the Dominican Republic to "put a halt to the sporadic roundups and summary expulsions. If it doesn't, the international community must step in" (para. 14). Thus, despite their best efforts to explain the ruling and defend their image, the Dominican Republic did not succeed in gaining the support of the Diaspora, the media or the international organizations who had denounced it since the beginning.

Conclusion

The case of the Dominican citizenship ruling shows how Diasporas, the same communities that nations depend on to help advance foreign policy and shape a positive image of the homeland, can turn into a strong opposition force when it does not agree with the country's policies. The

Table 6.1 Competing frames in Dominican citizenship ruling media coverage

Dominican authority frames	Diaspora opposition frames
1 **Not stateless, Haitian.** Claims that these people were entitled to Haitian citizenship by birth. Also emphasized that Haiti should take responsibility for these people. *"Migrants from a supposedly democratic country such as Haiti cannot be stateless, as the editorial asserted; they carry the nationality of their country of birth."* (de Castro, 2013)	1 **Stripping citizenship/rendering stateless.** Highlighting that people who might have previously be considered Dominican lost their nationality, and this affected them. *"…the decision seeks to strip the citizenship and violate the rights of tens of thousands, and potentially hundreds of thousands, of Dominicans of Haitian descent that are recognized as Dominican nationals by the Article 18.2 of the country's 2010 Constitution."* (We are all Dominican, 2013)
2 **Need for regulating immigration.** Claim that, as a sovereign nation, the country had a legitimate interest in regulating immigration. *"The Dominican Republic has a legitimate interest in regulating immigration and having clear rules for acquisition of citizenship. It should not be pressured by outside actors and other countries to implement measures contrary to its own Constitution."* (de Castro, 2013)	

continued

Table 6.1 Continued

Dominican authority frames	Diaspora opposition frames
3 **A good neighbor.** Even when acknowledging the difficult relationship between the nations, this frame emphasized how the Dominican Republic treated its neighbor fairly, and even benevolently. *"Neither you, nor any other country in the world has done more than what the Dominican Republic has done in benefit to the Haitian people. The Dominican Republic just recognized the legal immigration status of more than 340 thousand Haitians, a number that added to the thousands that work and will continue to work in the tourism, agriculture and construction sector, could give you an idea of what has been our policy and the spirit of solidarity with relation to our neighbors."* (Pérez, 2015)	2 **A brutal history.** Mentions of the difficult history of the two countries and pasts abuses by the Dominican authorities against Haitians and people of Haitian descent. *"Such appalling racism is a continuation of a history of constant abuse, including the infamous Dominican massacre, under the dictator Rafael Trujillo, of an estimated 20,000 Haitians in five days in October 1937."* ("Two versions of a Dominican tale," 2013, para. 8)
4 **Respecting human rights.** Reaffirming their commitment to respecting the rights of all people and specially Haitians, as well as positioning their immigration policies and efforts to protect human rights. *"[...] the government of the Dominican Republic reinforces its commitment to continue working towards the adequate and accurate identification and regularization of those living in its territory, and to protect and guarantee the rights of all people."* (Presidencia de la República Dominicana, 2015a)	3 **Violating human rights.** Frames the decision as a human rights violation, emphasizing the effect on individuals. *"The court's action violates standards of international law and the Inter-American Court of Human Rights, which clearly state that people cannot be stripped of citizenship. Although the Constitutional Court cited a 2010 amendment on citizenship in its 38th Constitution in making the ruling, the decision violates Title II, Chapter 1, Article 38 of that same Constitution, which says all Dominicans are entitled to the same rights regardless of gender, religion, skin color or national origin."* (Kurlansky, Alvarez, Danticat & Díaz, 2013, para. 11)

4 **Redefining citizenship and identity.** Framed the country as redefining not only what it meant to be a citizen but also people's national identity.

"Officially the Dominican constitution grants citizenship to all who are born in the country, unless they are the children of people who are "in transit," such as tourists or diplomats. Which begs the question: Can one be in transit for 85 years? Even by the most exclusionary definitions of citizenship, this one puts it beyond the reach of most people."

(Danticat, 2013)

5 **Rounded up and deported en masse.** Presenting the visual of people being treated inhumanely, rounded up and deported to Haiti, despite possibly having no ties to that country.

"In effect, it also means that three generations of one family could be deported. Since the Sept. 23 ruling, deportations have begun: The Associated Press reported that over 300 people have been deported thus far, despite the Dominican government's assurance that there would be no large-scale removals."

(García-Peña, 2013)

5 **A path to citizenship.** Emphasizing that people residing in the country have legal options to become documented immigrants and a path to citizenship. This frame was used in their explanation of the 2014 naturalization law.

"The new law completes the government's framework for enacting a modern and transparent policy for registering national and immigrant residents in a way that respects each person's contribution to Dominican society."

(de Castro, 2014)

6 **Mass immigration/invasion.** Framing the issue of Haitian immigration as a problem for the Dominican Republic, giving the impression of a mass exodus from Haiti and invasion of the Dominican Republic.

"Every year, every month, every day, even more foreigners (Haitians) enter and stay in the Dominican Republic IRREGULARLY without any document control of any kind. From Haiti they FLEE AND CROSS, like Pedro in his home, to the Dominican Republic. Without papers…."

(Presidencia de la República Dominicana, 2015b)

Dominican Diaspora responded quickly to what they viewed as a crisis by mobilizing support through marches and protests in front of the Dominican embassy in New York and in the streets of Santo Domingo; engaging in social media and media advocacy; and clearly presenting their opposition to the court ruling and naturalization law. Diasporas are one of the many types of organizations or groups that "seek out media coverage for the wider dissemination and legitimation of their aims and claims, and they do so in a more complex media ecology and network of communication flows" (Cottler, 2008, p. 867). This new complex media ecology is also what makes it possible for them to gain attention and influence the framing of the issue.

Through their dissent and protests efforts, both Diasporas successfully framed the issue in a way that was closely tied to the international organizations who weighed in (in several cases anticipating these organizations' statements and reports) and were able to use their position as influential members of the Diaspora to mobilize others to action. In fact, it is doubtful that the 2014 naturalization law would have happened without the public statements from CARICOM (2013) and the OAS (2013), and it's likely that the Diasporas had some impact in calling these organizations' attention to the issue through their public outcry and manifestations. The Diasporas' advocacy strategy included tools that have proven successful in other cases such as appeals to reason and emotion (Gregory, 2011) and highlighting controversy, conflict and injustice (Wallack & Dorfman, 1996) to get and retain the media's attention.

The media coverage and the Diaspora framing of the issue were complementary. Newspapers in New York and Florida, where most of the Haitian and Dominican Diaspora reside, expressed their support for Haitian-Dominicans and Haitian-Americans through their editorial pages. If the efforts of the Diaspora and the Dominican authorities is seen as a contest to gain and shape media coverage (as is the goal of mediated diplomacy and media advocacy), then the Diaspora was the one victorious. Despite having counter messages to almost all claims made by the Diaspora and other anti-ruling advocates, the coverage continued to focus on the human cost of the ruling for Dominicans of Haitian descent and Haitian immigrants.

This case study contributes to the theoretical understanding of Diasporas as opposing publics in homeland public diplomacy efforts, building on the adversarial relationship type described in Zaharna and Uysal's (2016) research. As the authors explained, adversarial relations

> raise the possibility that public discourse and disagreement, distributed through personalized communication channels, may evolve into open and quite visible displays of physical confrontation that take place outside of formal spaces within civil society.
>
> (Zaharna & Uysal, 2016, p. 113)

In the case of the Dominican and Haitian Diasporas' advocacy against Dominican policies, the discourse evolved into protests, manifestations and international news coverage that created an image crisis for the Dominican Republic.

As Entman (2008) explains, often framing of an issue is influenced by powerful actors. Traditionally, this would give authority sources, such as the Dominican government, more influence on coverage. In this case, the combined efforts by the Diasporas and the support of vocal actors outside of the community allowed them to overcome any power disadvantage to present a strong counter to any efforts of the Dominican government to shift the conversation.

Notes

1 For previous research detailing the central role that public relations plays in public diplomacy programs see Gilboa, 2008; L'Etang, 2009; Signitzer and Coombs, 1992; or Yun, 2006.
2 This process resulted in a sample of 48 Spanish wire stories, 59 English wires stories, 41 U.S. news stories; five press releases from the Dominican government; 26 opinion pieces (including editorials and letters to the editor), five of which were authored by the Dominican government; seven reports by International nongovernmental organizations; and five information subsidies from advocacy organizations. In sum, 174 news articles and 17 information subsidies were analyzed.
3 The error in the year spelled out features in the original text in Spanish:

> Que, respecto a los hijos de extranjeros ilegales, la Junta Central Electoral ha aplicado el criterio jurídico establecido por la Constitución desde mil novecientos noventa y nueve (1929) y ratificado por la Suprema Corte de Justicia, mediante su sentencia del catorce (14) de diciembre de dos mil cinco (2005), relativo al recurso de inconstitucionalidad interpuesto contra la Ley General de migración núm. 285–04, consistente en que: (…) NO NACE DOMINICANO; QUE, CON MAYOR RAZÓN, NO PUEDE SERLO EL HIJO (A) DE LA MADRE EXTRANJERA QUE AL MOMENTO DE DAR A LUZ SE ENCUENTRA EN UNA SITUACIÓN IRREGULAR Y, POR TANTO, NO PUEDE JUSTIFICAR SU ENTRADA Y PERMANENCIA en la República Dominicana […].
>
> (Tribunal Constitucional, 2013, p. 8)

References

Adén-Papadopoulos, K. & Pantti, M. (2013). The media work of Syrian diaspora activists: Brokering between the protest and mainstream media. *International Journal of Communication* 7, 22.

Alexander, M. G., Levin, S. & Henry, P. J. (2005). Image theory, social identity, and social dominance: Structural characteristics and individual motives underlying international images. *Political Psychology* 26(1), 27–45.

Al-Rawi, A. & Fahmy, S. (2018). Social media use in the diaspora: The case of Syrians in Italy. In *Diaspora and Media in Europe* (pp. 71–96). Cham: Palgrave Macmillan.

Altholz, R. & Fletcher, L. E. (2015, July 5). The Dominican Republic must stop expulsions of Haitians. *New York Times*. Retrieved from: www.nytimes.com/2015/07/06/opinion/the-dominican-republic-must-stop-expulsions-of-haitians.html.

Amnesty International (2015). Without papers I'm no one: Stateless people in the Dominican Republic. Retrieved from www.amnesty.org/en/documents/amr27/2755/2015/en/.

Anholt, S. (2006). Why brand. Some practical considerations for nation branding. *Place Branding and Public Diplomacy* 2(2), 97–107.

Archibold, R. C. (2013, October). Dominicans of Haitian descent cast into legal limbo by court. *New York Times*. Retrieved from: www.nytimes.com/2013/10/24/world/americas/dominicans-of-haitian-descent-cast-into-legal-limbo-by-court.html.

Attias, S. (2012). Israel's new peer-to-peer diplomacy. *The Hague Journal of Diplomacy* 7, 473–482.

Bravo, V. (2014). The importance of diaspora communities as key publics for national governments around the world. In G. J. Golan, S. U. Yang & D. Kinsey (Eds.), *International public relations and public diplomacy: Communication and engagement*. New York: Peter Lang.

Camarota, S. A. (2010). Fact sheet on Haitian immigrants in the United States. Retrieved from: https://cis.org/Fact-Sheet/Fact-Sheet-Haitian-Immigrants-United-States.

CARICOM (2013). CARICOM statement on developments in the aftermath of the ruling of the constitutional court of the Dominican Republic on nationality. Retrieved from: www.caricom.org/jsp/pressreleases/press_releases_2013/pres265_13.jsp.

Castro, M. J. & Boswell, T. D. (2002). The Dominican Diaspora revisited: Dominicans and Dominican-Americans in a new century. *The North South Agenda Papers 53*, 1–25.

Chang, T. K. & Lin, F. (2014). From propaganda to public diplomacy: Assessing China's international practice and its image, 1950–2009. *Public Relations Review* 40(3), 450–458.

Congreso Nacional (2014). Ley No. 169–14. Presidencia de la República Dominicana. Retrieved from: https://presidencia.gov.do/themes/custom/presidency/docs/gobplan/gobplan-15/Ley-No-169-14.pdf.

Correal, A. (2015, June 25). De Blasio adds his voice to debate over Dominican deportation law. *New York Times*. Retrieved from: www.nytimes.com/2015/06/22/nyregion/de-blasio-is-criticized-after-denouncing-dominican-deportation-law.html.

Coombs, W. T. & Holladay, S. J. (2012). Fringe public relations: How activism moves critical PR toward the mainstream. *Public Relations Review* 38(5), 880–887.

Cottle, S. (2008). Reporting demonstrations: The changing media politics of dissent. *Media, Culture & Society* 30(6), 853–872.

Cull, N. J. (2009). Public diplomacy: Lessons from the past. *CPD Perspectives on Public Diplomacy* 2, 19. Retrieved from: http://stage.uscpublicdiplomacy.org/sites/uscpublicdiplomacy.org/files/legacy/publications/perspectives/CPDPerspectivesLessons.pdf.

Danticat, E. (2013, December 14). Haitian "dreamers" in Dominican Republic shut out of citizenship. *The Miami Herald*.

de Castro, A. (2013, October 28). Dominican Republic has a clear, respectful immigration policy. *Washington Post*. Retrieved from: www.washingtonpost.com/opinions/dominican-republic-has-a-clear-respectful-immigration-policy/2013/11/15/baca2d06-4d56-11e3-bf60-c1ca136ae14a_story.html?utm_term=.bcd3e939b8ca.

de Castro, A. (2014, June 3). Dominican Republic delivers on immigration promise. *The Miami Herald*.

De Moya, M. & Bravo, V. (2018). Unwanted attention: The reputational costs of the Dominican Republic's denial of citizenship for people of Haitian descent. Paper presented at the 2018 International Studies Association Annual Convention, San Francisco, California.

Dominicanos por Derecho (n.d.). Quiénes somos. Retrieved from: https://dominicanosxderecho.wordpress.com/quienessomos/.

Dorfman, L. & Krasnow, I. D. (2014). Public health and media advocacy. *Annual Review of Public Health 35*, 293–306.

EFE Newswire (2014, April 8). Jóvenes de origen haitiano piden ley que reconozca su nacionalidad dominicana. EFE Newswire.

EFE Newswire (2015, April 8). Protesta en Miami contra deportación inmigrantes haitianos desde R.Dominicana. EFE Newswire.

Entman, R. M. (2008). Theorizing mediated public diplomacy: The U.S. case. *The International Journal of Press/Politics 13*(2), 87–102.

Embassy of the Dominican Republic (n.d.). An introduction to the Dominican Republic. Retrieved from: www.domrep.org/gen_info.html#3.

Embassy of the Republic of Haiti (n.d.). Haiti at a glance. Retrieved from: http://haiti.org/haiti-at-a-glance/.

Fiezer, E. (2013, December). Prize-winning Dominican author in war of words over migrant court ruling. *Reuters*. Retrieved from: www.reuters.com/article/2013/12/05/us-dominican-author-immigration-idUSBRE9B401P20131205.

Gantchev, N. (2009). *The cost of activist monitoring: Evidence from a sequential decision model*. Philadelphia, PA: Wharton Business School.

García, S. (2013). La presencia de inmigrantes haitianos en República Dominicana. Retrieved from: www.opd.org.do/images/PDF_ARTICULOS/Politicas_Publicas/la-presencia-de-inmigrantes-haitianos-en-republica-dominicana.pdf.

Garcia-Peña, L. (2013, December 12). Suddenly, illegal at home. *New York Times*. Retrieved from: www.nytimes.com/2013/12/13/opinion/suddenly-illegal-at-home.html.

Gibson, T. A. (2010). The limits of media advocacy. *Communication, Culture & Critique 3*(1), 44–65.

Gilboa, E. (1998). Media diplomacy: Conceptual divergence and applications. *The Harvard International Journal of Press/Politics 3*, 56–75.

Gilboa, E. (2002). Global communication and foreign policy. *Journal of Communication 2*, 731–48.

Gilboa, E. (2008). Searching for a theory of public diplomacy. *The Annals of the American Academy of Political and Social Science 616*(1), 55–77.

Gonzalez, J. (2013, October 23). Racist Carib purge Haitians in D.R. for decades losing citizenship. *Daily News*, p. 17.

Gregory, B. (2011). American public diplomacy: Enduring characteristics, elusive transformation. *The Hague Journal of Diplomacy 6*(3–4), 351–372.

Haitian American Association of New York (n.d.). Our mission. Retrieved from: https://halaony.wildapricot.org/Mission.

Hall, S. (2017) Antihaitianismo: Systemic xenophobia and racism in the Dominican Republic. Retrieved from: www.coha.org/wp-content/uploads/2017/06/Anti haitianismo.pdf.

Hannam, M. A. (2014). Soy Dominicano – the status of Haitian descendants born in the Dominican Republic and measures to protect their right to a nationality. *Vanderbilt Journal of Translational Law 47*, 1123–1166.

Human Rights Watch (2015). We are Dominican: Arbitrary deprivation of nationality in the Dominican Republic. Retrieved from: www.hrw.org/report/2015/07/01/we-are-dominican/arbitrary-deprivation-nationality-dominican-republic.

Inter-American Commission of Human Rights (2015). Situation of human rights in the Dominican Republic. Organization of American States. Retrieved from: www.oas.org/en/iachr/reports/pdfs/dominicanrepublic-2015.pdf.

Jaramillo, L. & Sancak, C. (2007). Growth in the Dominican Republic and Haiti: Why has the grass been greener on one side of Hispaniola? IMF Working Paper, 07/63. Retrieved from: www.imf.org/external/pubs/ft/wp/2007/wp0763.pdf.

Johnson, M. A. (2005). Five decades of Mexican public relations in the United States: From propaganda to strategic counsel. *Public Relations Review 31*(1), 11–20.

Joseph, R. (2015, June 27). Dominican Republic's deportation of Haitians is "akin to apartheid." *Miami Herald*. Retrieved from: www.miamiherald.com/opinion/issues-ideas/article25371358.html.

Joseph, S. M., Irazábal, C. & Désir, A. M. (2018). Trust and hometown associations in Haitian post-earthquake reconstruction. *International Migration 56*(1), 167–195.

Kurlansky, M., Álvarez, J., Danticat, E. & Díaz, J. (2013, November 10). In the Dominican Republic, suddenly stateless. *Los Angeles Times*. Retrieved from: http://articles.latimes.com/2013/nov/10/opinion/la-oe-kurlansky-haiti-dominican-republic-citizensh-20131110.

Kotler, P., Haider, D. H. & Rein, I. J. (1993). *Marketing places: Attracting Investment, industry, and tourism to cities, states and nations*. New York: Free Press.

La solidaridad con los desnacionalizados desborda el Alma Mater de la UASD (2013, December 6). *7 Días*. Retrieved from: www.7dias.com.do/portada/2013/12/06/i153418_solidaridad-con-los-desnacionalizados-desborda-alma-mater-uasd.html#.WsPaVqinFD-.

Laguerre, M. S. (1998). *Diasporic citizenship: Haitian Americans in transnational America*. New York: St. Martin's Press.

Lamb, V. & Dundes, L. (2017). Not Haitian: Exploring the roots of Dominican identity. *Social Sciences 6*(4), 132.

Lee, S. (2007). International public relations as a predictor of prominence of US news coverage. *Public Relations Review 33*(2), 158–165.

L'Etang, J. (2009). Public relations and diplomacy in a globalized world: An issue of public communication. *American Behavioral Scientist 53*(4), 607–626.

Mahieu, R. (2017). "We're not coming from Mars; we know how things work in Morocco!" How diasporic Moroccan youth resists political socialisation in state-led homeland tours. *Journal of Ethnic and Migration Studies*, 1–18.

Manheim, J. B. & Albritton, R. B. (1984). Changing national images: International public relations and media agenda setting. *American Political Science Review 78*, 641–657.

McCalister, J. (2013). Haitians' protest over DR. *Daily News*. Suburban, p. 50.

McKeever, B. W. (2013). News framing of autism: Understanding media advocacy and the combating autism act. *Science Communication 35*(2), 213–240.

Mejía, M. (2015, February 2). Vence plazo del plan naturalización; el gobierno no anuncia prórroga. Retrieved from: www.diariolibre.com/noticias/vence-plazo-del-plan-naturalizacin-el-gobierno-no-anuncia-prrroga-GIDL994471.

Moloney, K. McQueen, D., Surowiec, P. & Yaxley, H. (2012). Dissent and protest public relations. Retrieved from: https://microsites.bournemouth.ac.uk/cmc/files/2013/10/Dissent-and-public-relations-Bournemouth-University.pdf.

OAS (2013). IACHR expresses deep concern over ruling by the constitutional court of the Dominican Republic. Retrieved from: www.oas.org/en/iachr/media_center/PReleases/2013/073.asp.

Oficina Nacional de Estadística (2013). Primera encuesta nacional de inmigrantes en la República Dominicana (ENI-2012). Retrieved from: http://media.onu.org.do/ONU_DO_web/596/sala_prensa_publicaciones/docs/032139500136813 2272.pdf.

Paarlberg, M. A. (2017). Transnational militancy: Diaspora influence over electoral activity in Latin America. *Comparative Politics 49*(4), 541–562.

Pérez, A. (2013). Yo no soy racista, yo defiendo mi patria: Síntomas y efectos nacionalistas en República Dominicana. *Caribbean Studies 41*(2), 245–255.

Pérez, J. T. (2015, June 23). Texto íntegro de la carta que envió José Tomás Pérez al alcalde NY. El Día. Retrieved from: http://eldia.com.do/texto-integro-de-la-carta-que-envio-jose-tomas-perez-al-alcalde-ny/.

Pew Research Center (2015). Hispanics of Dominican origin in the United States, 2013. Retrieved from: www.pewhispanic.org/2015/09/15/hispanics-of-dominican-origin-in-the-united-states-2013/.

Presidencia de la República Dominicana (2013). El Presidente Medina firma el decreto del Plan Nacional de Regularización. Retrieved from: https://presidencia.gov.do/noticias/el-presidente-medina-firma-el-decreto-del-plan-nacional-de-regularizacion?page=0%2C1.

Presidencia de la República Dominicana (2015a). Position of the Dominican Republic government on the report presented today by the OAS fact finding committee to the permanent council of that organization. Retrieved from: https://presidencia.gov.do/themes/custom/presidency/docs/gobplan/gobplan-15/POSITION-OF-THE-DOMINICAN-REPUBLIC-GOVERNMENT-ON-THE-REPORT-PRESENTED-TODAY-BY-THE-OAS-FACT_FINDING-COMMITTEE-TO-THE-PERMANENT-COUNCIL-OF-THAT-ORGANIZATI.pdf.

Presidencia de la República Dominicana (2015b). Haitianos sin papeles en República Dominicana. Retrieved from: https://presidencia.gov.do/plan-de-gobierno/regularizacion-extranjeros.

Presidencia de la República Dominicana (2015c). Haitianos sin papeles en República Dominicana. Retrieved from: https://presidencia.gov.do/plan-de-gobierno/regularizacion-extranjeros.

Presidencia de la República Dominicana (2015d). Gobierno utiliza redes sociales para explicar regularización y documentación. Retrieved from: https://presidencia. gob.do/noticias/gobierno-utiliza-redes-sociales-para-explicar-regularizacion-y-documentacion.

Reconoci.do (n.d.) Moviemiento. Retrieved from: http://reconoci.do/actualidad/.

Rights crisis feared after court ruling (2013 September 27). *Washington Post.* A-Section, p. A09.

Riley, P. (2014). Media diplomacy: Public diplomacy in a new global media environment. In T. A. Hollihan (Ed.), *The dispute over the Diaoyu/Senkaku Islands.* Palgrave Macmillan Series in International Political Communication. New York: Palgrave Macmillan.

Rosendorf, N. (2014). *Franco sells Spain to America: Hollywood, tourism and public relations as postwar Spanish soft power.* New York: Palgrave Macmillan.

Sagas, E. (1993). A case of mistaken identity: Antihaitianismo in the Dominican Republic. *Latinoamericanist 29*(1), 1–5.

Semple, K. (2013, October 18). Dominican court's ruling on citizenship stirs emotion in New York. *New York Times.* Section A, p. 23.

Shumow, M. (2014). Media production in a transnational setting: Three models of immigrant journalism. *Journalism 15*(8), 1076–1093.

Shun thy neighbor (2013). *Washington Post.* Editorial, p. A22.

Signitzer, B. H. & Coombs, T. (1992). Public relations and public diplomacy: Conceptual convergences. *Public Relations Review 18*(2), 137–147.

Tavernier, L. A. (2008). The stigma of blackness: Anti-Haitianism in the Dominican Republic. *Socialism and Democracy 22*(3), 96–104.

The Haitian Community Land Trust (n.d.). About us. Retrieved from: https:// haitianclt.wordpress.com/about/.

Tribunal Constitucional (2013). Sentencia TC/0160/13. Retrieved from: https:// presidencia.gov.do/themes/custom/presidency/docs/gobplan/gobplan-15/Sentencia-TC-0168-13-C.pdf.

Two versions of a Dominican Tale (2013, October 31). *New York Times.* Retrieved from: www.nytimes.com/2013/11/01/opinion/two-versions-of-a-dominican-tale. html.

United Nations Human Rights Council (2013). National report submitted in accordance with paragraph 5 of the annex to Human Rights Council resolution 16/21: Dominican Republic. Retrieved from: http://lib.ohchr.org/HRBodies/ UPR/_layouts/15/WopiFrame.aspx?sourcedoc=/HRBodies/UPR/Documents/ Session18/DO/A_HRC_WG.6_18_DOM_1_Dominican%20Republic_E_Drits. doc&action=default&DefaultItemOpen=1.

United States Department of State (2013). Dominican Republic 2013 Human Rights Report. Bureau of Democracy, Human Rights and Labor. Retrieved from: www.state.gov/documents/organization/220649.pdf.

Wallace, B. (2013, November 14). Here's why a court ruling in the Dominican Republic is spurring international protests. *PRI.* Retrieved from www.pri. org/stories/2013-11-14/protests-are-growing-dominican-republic-tries-strip-citizenship-haitians.

Wallack, L. & Dorfman, L. (1996). Media advocacy: A strategy for advancing policy and promoting health. *Health Education Quarterly 23*(3), 293–317.

We Are All Dominican (n.d.). About us. Retrieved from: https://wearealldominican nyc.wordpress.com/about/.

We Are All Dominican (2013). Open letter to Dominican president Danilo Medina: Voices from the New York diaspora. *Latino Rebels*. Retrieved from: www.latinorebels.com/2013/12/14/open-letter-to-dominican-president-danilo-medina-voices-from-the-new-york-diaspora/.

Wilkinson, S. (2016). Using media to respond to public health emergencies: Lessons learned from Ebola. Retrieved from: www.bbc.co.uk/mediaaction/publications-and-resources/policy/practice-briefings/ebola.

World Bank (2017a, September 29). The World Bank in Dominican Republic: Overview. Retrieved from: www.worldbank.org/en/country/dominicanrepublic/overview.

World Bank (2017b, October 2). The World Bank in Haiti: Overview. Retrieved from: www.worldbank.org/en/country/haiti/overview.

Yun, S. H. (2006). Toward public relations theory-based study of public diplomacy: Testing the applicability of the excellence study. *Journal of Public Relations Research 18*(4), 287–312.

Zaharna, R. S. (2007). The soft power differential: Network communication and mass communication in public diplomacy. *The Hague Journal of Diplomacy 2*(3), 213–228.

Zaharna, R. S. (2011). Relational spheres and the primacy of domestic and diaspora publics in global public diplomacy. Paper presented at the 2011 International Studies Association Annual Convention, Montreal, Canada.

Zaharna, R. S. & Uysal, N. (2016). Going for the jugular in public diplomacy: How adversarial publics using social media are challenging state legitimacy. *Public Relations Review 42*(1), 109–119.

7 Activists' communication and mobilization tactics to find Ayotzinapa's 43 disappeared students

Luis Rubén Díaz-Cepeda, Ernesto Castañeda, and Kara Andrade

Since 2006, Mexico has been going through a rough period where the aim to control the profits from illicit drug traffic by different groups and state actors has caused the murder of at least 234,996 people as of October 2016 (INEGI, 2018) and 30,499 missing people (RNPED, 2018). In 2017, at least 18,898 homicides were attributed to organized crime (Dittmar, 2018). This increased level of violence started with the war on drugs ordered by former President Felipe Calderón Hinojosa (2006–2012) and his strategy of Joint Operations between military personnel and police to enforce the ban on illicit substances. Military involvement continued during Enrique Peña Nieto's administration (2012–2018). In fact, in 2018 the federal government passed the Internal National Security Law that formalized the continued patrolling of the streets by the army; a measure that in 2006 had been announced as temporary.

Since the beginning, activists and those who have suffered directly or witnessed the violent side-effects caused by this strategy have protested the militarization of the country. During this time, some social movement campaigns appeared such as the movement against the militarization of Ciudad Juárez in 2008, the Movement for Peace and Justice with Dignity (Movimiento por la Paz con Justicia y Dignidad, MPJD) in 2011; and the students' movement #Iam132 (#Yosoy132) in 2012. However, thanks to a savvy PR strategy from the activists involved in the Ayotzinapa movement, the demand of finding the students reached levels of mobilizations that far surpassed the previous protests.

The Ayotzinapa movement started when on the evening of September 26, 2014, two of the five buses with student teachers for the Normal rural Isidro Burgos[1] were attacked. Police and unidentified gunmen opened fire for unknown reasons on the buses of students in Iguala, Guerrero. Six people – three passers-by and three students – were shot and killed, more than 20 were wounded, and the 43 students were taken by uniformed police officers and men dressed in military garb (Gibler, 2017). The Attorney General claims that the students were turned in by corrupt local police officers to a drug cartel and they were murdered and incinerated. However, this version was contested by the parents of the students based on reports of several human rights organizations and forensic experts, which claim that there is not enough evidence to support this theory. Hence, the location of the students is still uncertain.

This was not an isolated case in Mexico, yet it gained national and international attention, arguably, this was caused for two reasons. First, the fact that a large number of college students were the victims and second, the use of an effective communication strategy and tactics by the activists involved used an effective communication strategy and tactics. Thanks to their PR strategy, they were able to break the media siege imposed by the federal government and tell the story of the disappeared students attracting national and international attention to the event and to the subsequent behavior of the federal government. Even though mobilization has not accomplished the goal of finding the students, it has arguably added to the further discrediting of Mexico's federal government, and the ruling party – *Partido Revolucionario Institucional* (PRI) – who lost the following mid-term elections. Moreover, José Antonio Meade, the PRI's candidate, came out third in the 2018 presidential election.

Successful PR strategy

The story of Ayotzinapa has rippled out well beyond the borders of their small school tucked in the mountains of Guerrero and into the international media spotlight. In consequence, it is important to understand how the students and teachers of Ayotzinapa experienced and responded to this situation within their community and outside of it, how they subsequently organized around it and the networks that helped make several campaigns to seek justice for the 43 disappeared have global significance.

This chapter demonstrates how the existing communication network of the Teachers' College or Normal Rural School Raúl Isidro Burgos in Ayotzinapa, herein called *La Normal* (Navarro, 2001), made it possible to respond quickly to the crisis of the disappeared students. Then it will focus on how communication became a prominent part of the social movement campaign organization, and how it shaped tactics and strategies for growing the movement beyond Mexico. Access to new information and communication technologies (mobile phones, computers, Wi-Fi-connected cameras) made it possible for *La Normal* to mobilize activist networks beyond their pre-established networks (Bennett & Segerberg, 2012). They were able to create a "logic of connective action" through social networks and this changed the scale of the movement (Bennett & Segerberg, 2012).

The campaigns around the missing students are promoted by the activists in different arenas rather than by only one organization. The role that communication has played in this case aligns with Jo Freeman's three propositions: (1) "the need for a pre-existing communications network or infrastructure within the social base of a movement" which makes "spontaneous" activity possible, (2) this communication network must be "*co-optable* to the new ideas of the incipient movement"; and (3) the presence of one or more "precipitants" or immediate catalysts that spark the fire for the spontaneous action to occur (Freeman, 2003, pp. 22–24).

This chapter relies on data collected through a series of interviews conducted separately by each one of the authors in-person, except where noted, in Mexico and the United States. The interviews we draw on for this chapter are:

- Raúl Romero is a member of the Zapatista movement and Movement for Peace and Justice with Dignity (MPJD) (March 23, 2016).
- Omar García is an Ayotzinapa student and spokesperson of the Ayotzinapa movement (February 22, 2015).
- Julio Cesar Guerrero is a campaign coordinator for the Caravana 43. Phone interview (March 22, 2015).
- Alicia Hopkins, a philosopher, is a member of the Youth in Alternative Resistance Collective (November 9, 2014).
- Raúl Benítez-Manaut is a professor at Mexico's National University UNAM (February 24, 2014).
- Luisa Ortiz Pérez, PhD, is an activist and organizer (March 20, 2015).
- Vidulfo Rosales Sierra is a lawyer from the Tlachinollan Human Rights Center. He works pro-bono on cases for the indigenous and poor people Guerrero, Mexico (March 23, 2015).
- Mark Stevenson is an Associated Press Reporter. Mexico City Bureau. Email interview (February 13, 2015).

Data also comes from the analyses of secondary sources and ethnographic work in activist events. Díaz directly observed key actors in Mexico City during the beginning of the movement (October to December 2014). During this period Díaz attended several organization meetings, marches, and rallies. Castañeda attended a presentation of the report from an international group of experts in Washington DC where he interviewed some of the activists from New York. Andrade conducted a number of trips to Guerrero including visiting the Ayotzinapa Teachers College and shadowing local activists during their community organizing and communication efforts.

History

National context

The war on drugs that former President Calderon (2006–2012) started in 2007 faced strong opposition by some activists because they considered that having the military policing the streets would bring an increase in violence and human rights violations. They were right. By the end of Calderon's administration, there were around 23,000 disappeared and approximately 70,000 dead from drug-related violence from 2006 to 2012 (Stevenson, email interview, February 13, 2015). Enrique Peña Nieto (EPN) was Governor of the state of Mexico (2005–2011) when the protests of a group of farmers from Atenco were violently repressed, and protesters were jailed, hit, and sexually abused. With the election of Peña Nieto as president for the 2006–2012 term, activists were concerned that the militarized strategy not only would continue, but rather would increase, and drug-related violence would intensify. They were right again. According to official reports over 100,000 people were killed during the first five years of EPN administration (INEGI, 2017). These violent living conditions have been protested by diverse activists, who also denounced the high levels of corruption by government officials. This cycle of protest reached a climax with the Ayotzinapa social movement in 2014.

It is important to notice that the Ayotzinapa campaigns could not have reached the participations levels they did, without the previous mobilizations in Mexico (Castañeda, Díaz-Cepeda, & Andrade, 2018), for they created political awareness in those who later would become activists and develop the networks that will sustain the movement (Díaz-Cepeda & Castañeda, 2018). This cycle of mobilization started in Ciudad Juarez with the movement against the militarization of the city,[2] continued with the Movement for the Peace with Justice and Dignity[3] and then with the students' movement #IAm132.[4] All of these movements used new communication technology and social media[5] to spread the message that the government was responsible for the narco-violence. The evidence collected and disseminated by the Normal students and their allies through their PR tactics would change the view that it was all the sole fault of drug lords. This was important because, "Until Ayotzinapa happened, it was hard to convince public opinion that it was also the state that was killing and disappearing people"[6] (Romero personal interview, March 26, 2015).[7]

The night of Iguala

The federal government's version

The evening of September 26, 2014, 43 student teachers were kidnapped. It is still not clear what happened to them. Mexico's federal government claims that policemen took the students to a local cartel, which killed and incinerated them. However, several organizations such as the Interamerican Court of Human Rights claim that the evidence presented by the General Attorney is not conclusive or has been obtained by torturing defendants (GIEI, 2017). The students' parents and their lawyers claim that the military was involved and that the students were being kept at a military base.

Attorney General Jesús Murillo Karam claimed that on Saturday, November 8, 2014 gang members were apprehended and confessed to killing the students and burning their remains for eleven hours in a public municipal dump and then throwing their ashes in the river (Archibold, 2014). In January 2015, Felipe Rodríguez Salgado, a leader of the local *Guerreros Unidos* gang, was arrested and reportedly told investigators that he had been given orders to kill the students because they had connections to rival gang *Los Rojos* (Archibold, 2015). The Mexican government presented this as "the historical truth" of what occurred that night. At the end of January of 2015, the Attorney General made a public statement that detailed how the students "were grabbed by police, handed over to drug gang members, who killed them and incinerated the bodies" (AP, 2015). The government version was broadly reproduced by mainstream media, but it was not accepted by the students' parents, schoolmates, and activists because the version they had from surviving students differed from the official one.

The parents' suspicions of the official version, which were initially portraited as foolish by mainstream media, would later gain scientific support as the Argentina's international forensics team, which was brought in to help identify the remains, stated there was not enough scientific evidence to conclusively prove the theory presented by then General Attorney Jesús Murillo Karam (AP/AFP, 2015). The questions then remained, who took the students? And where were they? Activist Alicia Hopkins argues that Murillo Karam's statements did not have the purpose of answering these questions truthfully, but rather "With this press conference and the support of the political class the federal government wanted to close the case and move on" (personal communication, November 9, 2014). Against the government's predictions, the search for the truth would continue.

The version from one of the Ayotzinapa students

In a noisy greasy-spoon diner near the historical district of Mexico City, 24-year-old Omar García half-sits on the chair, his left leg ready to stand up at any minute and his hand holding the strap of the black backpack resting by his sneaker-clad foot, just barely under the table. It is an early Sunday evening in February 2015, and it has just started to rain. It is getting noisier in the diner, which makes it hard to hear García's quiet deep voice, so I [Kara Andrade] lean in to listen to him. He has short straight black hair, dark brown skin, a wide face with a slight goatee and sad dark brown-eyes that belie his age. His left eye looks slightly swollen and half-open, and there is a small scar on his lips. I ask him if he wants to eat something or to drink some coffee. He shakes his head answering, "No, thanks, I just ate." "I only have about half an hour," he tells me in Spanish. "And then I have another meeting with colleagues" (García, 2015, personal interview). No problem, I tell him. He looks over his shoulder, fidgets a lot in his seat, and lowers his head to think. This is the way his life is now, he tells me; he travels a lot to Mexico City, to other states in Mexico and other countries, meets with people and tells the story of what happened on September 26, 2014, the night when 43 of his school-mates disappeared. Since that night none of the 43 young male students have been seen.

García is a second-year student at the Normal Rural School Raúl Isidro Burgos in Ayotzinapa, a public rural teachers' college in southwest Mexico. He is the spokesperson for the disappeared students in Iguala, and he con-siders himself an activist and most of all, a teacher in training. The story Omar García told Andrade of that night is different from the story the mass media tells. In the evening of September 26, 2014, a group of fresh-man students from the Normal were headed to Iguala to raise funds for a trip to Mexico City to participate in student demonstrations commemorat-ing October 2, 1968, the date of the Tlatelolco massacre of Mexican university students at the hands of the military (Rodríguez, 2014). Students seized five buses to get there together. This was a common practice that is often tolerated and had never been repressed so swiftly and violently before.

For years, he said, the students had been retaining commercial and tourist buses as a public service to the school. During bus retentions, the students would peacefully, with no weapons or any kind of force, ask the bus driver for temporary use of the bus; if the driver agreed, the passengers would be offloaded to other buses and the students would take the addi-tional buses for a few weeks and then return them without any damages. That night, the driver agreed to turn over the bus he was driving as long as he could drop off the passengers he was currently transporting. García says, "We had done that before, many times and the driver would follow-through" (García, March 22, 2015, personal interview). García thinks that the students were tricked by the bus driver because this time things would go differently.

After they arrived at Iguala and the passengers got off, the driver told the students that he would be right back and then locked the doors behind him and did not return. The Municipal Police arrived, and then things grew violent quickly. The students stuck in the bus called for backup. The other 70 colleagues waiting on two buses just outside the city decided to drive in and just as the first bus arrived it was intercepted by patrol cars. One of their colleagues was shot in the head and then García, who was at the school at that time, received a call from another student who said: "The police from Iguala are shooting at us, we have one dead" (García, 2015, personal interview).

Thirty students from the school, among them García, immediately set off toward Iguala to help their colleagues. When they arrived, the scene was quiet, and they were told by the survivors that many of their col-leagues were shoved into seven police cars behind the buses. They did not know how many. Aldo, the one who was shot in the head, was taken away in an ambulance. The few colleagues that remained stayed with the buses to protect the evidence. "The police were still making the rounds there, and the army was at the entrance. They were all there," García says, his left eye twitching (García, 2015, personal interview). When Andrade asked him what happened to his eye, he says the military threw a rock at him on January 13 when the parents of the missing students and other students and teachers from the school tried to gain access to an army base in Iguala (BBC, 2015). He considers this is part of his work as an activist and as a student at Ayotzinapa's teacher's college. They wanted to search for the missing students in the military base where the teachers and students suspected the disappeared were being held or where they suspected the bodies had been burned.

Activists' communication and mobilization tactics

Catalyst for action

What allowed bringing sustained attention to the disappearance of the students in Iguala was that the other students at the school, and its affiliated network, were able to respond to the physical and subsequent disqualifications in the mainstream media by using a pre-established structure of committees, secretariats, and delegated leaders for consensus-based decision-making. One of the main ways this consensus on how to respond to crises was reached was through a General Assembly of teachers, students, and affiliated committee members. The morning after the disappearances happened, García said, the General Assembly met to first establish the facts behind the event and work through the unknowns

> We didn't have a clear count of how many of the colleagues had been disappeared. We thought it was 58, then 57, then after the meeting we knew it was 43, and we thought they were in jail.
>
> (García, 2015, personal interview)

Also present in that meeting were volunteer lawyers, including Vidulfo Rosales Sierra, from the Centro de Derechos Humanos de la Montaña, Tlachinollan A.C. (Tlachinollan Human Rights Center), who works on cases for the indigenous and poor people of Guerrero, Mexico. By then the Tlachinollan Human Rights Center had been working with the school for six months on previous attacks on the students, but nothing of this magnitude (Rosales Sierra, 2015, personal interview). "We had no idea that they were orchestrating a forced disappearance" (García, 2015, personal interview). The decision was made to get the students out of jail, except that when they arrived there were no students to be found.

A series of meetings were then held by the Student Government Association, which is formed by 19 committees; among those are External Relations, Delegates, Political Education, Rural Labor. Each committee has a president, treasurer, speaker, and secretary who serve during one or two-years. Members are nominated by vote or consensus, and once in office each member has to meet with the affiliated student organizations, non-governmental organizations, unions, and other allies.

The educational program at Ayotzinapa's teachers' college includes activist training, which takes six months to complete. Students typically start in August, and by February they are part of the committee, communicating with members, traveling to different places, to different committees, and "learning as you go" (García, 2015, personal interview). García was part of the Political Education secretariat in the role that was delegated to him as the speaker for the Ayotzinapa students.

The Political Education secretariat is where a selected group of students receive an education on leftist ideology and activism training. This training allowed students to have a fast and efficient response to the kidnapping of their classmates. They videotaped the attack, and when policemen took their classmates, students called for a press conference immediately after the event and spread the news with their political allies via WhatsApp and to the general population via Facebook. By doing so, they were able to break the news siege that the state frequently uses to hide this kind of news.

Every member of the External Relations secretariats has a region in Guerrero where they work. Every weekend they have to visit the organizations in their area, help them, check in with them, and see what they need. García states that there is also a list of organizations, schools, and unions beyond Guerrero that the school has maintained relationships with for years and many of which volunteer and provide different types of support for the school. These organizations extend into national and international networks. Among these are State Coordinating Committee of Education Workers of Guerrero, or CETEG, which was the force behind Mexico's democratic teachers' movement, the National Coordinating Committee of Education Workers, or CNTE (Bocking, 2015). Each secretariat is responsible for maintaining contact with all these organizations as they pertain to the secretariat's specific projects and goals through physical visits, the use of mobile phones, emails, telegrams, and social media such as Facebook, Twitter, and WhatsApp. The school also has a pirate short-range FM community radio station that broadcasts daily. By the time the Assembly learned the students were not being held in Iguala's jail the entire network of organizations had already been informed through the various secretariats of the attack on the students through various mediums of communication.

In conclusion, during this first stage of the movement, thanks to the student activists' knowhow and an information strategy that included face-to-face meetings, as well as contact via communication technologies with their political allies, they would later be able to defeat the government strategy of framing the students as criminals and the narrative of these events being an isolated incident where a criminal group had corrupted local police. Through videos taken purposefully by students during the attack, they show how local policemen had participated in the attack and the federal forces located at a driving distance at the very least, had failed to protect the students. These student activists started to point out that the federal government was also responsible. In a few words, by breaking the media siege, Ayotzinapa students and their networks reached a larger audience. Within this audience there were a vast number of people who were also discontent with the EPN administration; they would join the movement. Among these new allies there were some social movements organizations (SMOs) such as Youth in Alternative Resistance (*Jovenes en Resistencia alternative*, JRA), Movement for Peace with Justice and Dignity *(Movimiento por la Paz con Justicia y Dignidad*, MPJD), and Services and Counsel for Peace *(Servicios y Asesoria para la Paz*, SERAPAZ). Members of these SMOs had a lot of experience using social media to promote their causes. They got organized in the Solidarity with Ayotzinapa Committee (Mesa de Solidaridad con Ayotzinapa).

Framing the story

The students' activism training made it possible to mobilize quickly and spontaneously through this pre-existing network of local and national organizations. But how did the story of the 43 disappeared students reach international audiences and how was this story framed in a way that captured so many different types of audiences and the imagination of people who had never even heard of *La Rural*?

The story of the disappeared students resonated quickly with people because they had a better way to communicate their message than previous social movements dud. For example, in Raul Romero's appreciation

> my issue with the activists in Juarez was that they had reached the right conclusion, but they were being terrible in the way of transmitting it to other people and generations; they were not connecting with a larger public.
>
> (Romero, 2016, personal interview)

On the other hand, Ayotzinapa activists were skillful in packing the message in the right way. In consequence, not even days after the disappearances, videos taken by the surviving students on their cellphones were circulated on YouTube to *La Normal*'s participating organization's networks and to media contacts. One of the actions that most resonated with young people and other supporters were the hand-painted portraits of the 43 young male students that figure prominently in every protest. Paradoxically, the most visible figures of the protests are the elderly, sandal-clad peasant parents of the disappeared youths, whose authenticity and genuineness helped mobilize youths. Seeing these elderly, humble peasants angrily shout at top officials, including Peña Nieto, has been a visceral experience for many youths (Guerrero, 2015, phone interview).

These portraits came from a new blog emerged called #Illustrators with Ayotzinapa[8] (*Ilustradores con Ayotzinapa*) that showed the names and faces of the 43 students. It was a blog inviting artists to draw and paint portraits of the missing youths using their student photos. The illustrations went viral, were shared on social media using the hashtag #IlustradoresConAyotzinapa and then the parents marched with these portraits painted on banners and then those portraits were everywhere.

Actvist, Julio Cesar Guerrero, Campaign Coordinator for the Caravana 43, said that these drawings,

> gave a face to the problem. The faces don't represent just the disappeared students, but the thousands of immigrants and citizens who have disappeared in the last few years in Mexico. It's being represented by those 43 students, it's a design for our psyche to understand the urgency and impact of this matter.
>
> (Guerrero, March 22, 2015, phone interview)

Since the beginning of October 2014, tens of thousands marched along Mexico City's main avenue demanding the return of Ayotzinapa's disappeared students (Taylor, 2014). Similar marches took place in November and December 2014. They also spread to other countries as "solidarity" marches and days of action. According to Mark Stevenson, Associated Press Reporter, Mexico City Bureau, "The mobilization has kept the students' disappearances at the forefront of Mexican politics and exposed the issue of the deep penetration of drug gangs into government" (Stevenson, 2014, email interview). These levels of mobilization, which surpassed the previous social movements in Mexico – MPJD, #Iam132 – could be explained by the accumulation of rage, the age and occupation of the disappeared, and their effective PR campaigns.

"The first thing people heard was they were students and people rose up. Students in a public school, *normalistas*, future teachers, that's when things came to a head" (Pérez, 2015, personal interview). Pérez remembers how many people in Mexico City marched and continued to march months later. According to activist and organizer Luisa Ortiz Pérez, a contingent of marchers called *Cariola* or Stroller included mothers with their babies carrying flags and banners saying: "No, not the students, no, not our children! Another 68 No More!" Grandmothers would shout, referring to the students massacred by the Mexican military in 1968 (Pérez, 2015, personal interview).

According to Pérez, the state repression of students triggered something for many people in Mexico because the country has not only been dealing with high levels of narco-trafficking related crime and corruption, but there is also a long tradition of repressing young people which is not forgotten. This repression is something Pérez considers a specific strategy by the state to terrorize an entire community. She witnessed violent repression by the Mexican police and military in Mexico City during marches in support of the Ayotzinapa movement.

> I had never felt fear when protesting for myself or others. The days of the first marches, the violence started. There was heavy violence during the marches, and the police were using the excuse of anarchists having infiltrated the marches to resort to violence, things like hitting baby carriages, hitting women on the head ... [During one of the public vigils being held for the students] it was held in open space, in the Zocalo and they turned off the lights. You know the Zocalo has four entrances and if they close those off no one can move from the inside. There was a vigil at night. They turned off the lights and let loose the police. You can only imagine what happened ... It made us all cry.
>
> (Pérez, 2015, personal interview)

The repression of Ayotzinapa was similar to other movements classified as student movements, such as the night of Tlatelolco in 1968,[9] the break of the National University of Mexico (UNAM) students' strike by Federal forces in 1999,[10] and even previous attacks to the Normal's students by the Federal police.[11] However, one thing that was significantly different was the use of social media to document the marches, vigils, protests, and "die-ins" that were being staged at different schools and public places, as well as subsequent repression. The disappearance of the students was discussed and documented in many ways by different people, captured on video, uploaded to YouTube, Facebook, Twitter and then hashtags were created to follow and comment on those shared moments. Twitter hashtags translated from Spanish to English include "We Are Not a Number" and "I Am Tired" with videos also being filmed by students all over the world showing solidarity. There are recordings of statements such as "We are the 43" and videos narrating the different phases of the complex storyline behind the students' disappearance.

Videos and photography served a vital function of creating testimony and evidence of state repression. Social media then distributed beyond Mexico's border.

> They [the police] couldn't hide behind it and say that they [marchers] were agitators. They were striking, and you could hear and see people saying I was walking out of the metro, or I was there with my colleagues from organizations, NGOs, collectives, mother's groups and they were hitting them, and people recorded them saying things like "Maybe this will make you stop marching, assholes, these students deserved it."
>
> (Pérez, 2015, personal interview)

Pre-existing communication networks

While Ayotzinapa's strongly coordinated actions used high levels of organizational resources to build relationships and mobilize locally and even nationally, the content sharing across social media networks is not something they had anticipated (Bennett & Segerberg, 2012). García, now an avid Twitter user, says that before his colleagues disappeared, he didn't even know what Twitter was. He did not own a cellphone until someone from one of the partnering organizations donated the phone and taught him to use social media on it. Now he has almost 23,000 followers.

Smartphones became essential to the campaign. The parents carry simple cellphones, and they have not been protagonists in online or social media strategies. But others in their networks of support have. Stevenson points out that

> the community police movement (UPOEG) quickly took up their cause and launched an effort to search for the students – an effort that has since expanded to searching for clandestine graves of other victims.
> (Stevenson, email interview, February 13, 2015)

UPOEG search leader Miguel Angel Jimenez-Blanco[12] operated a WhatsApp group chat with journalists, updating them on how many bodies had been found (Andrade, 2015a, 2015b; Andrade, Castañeda, & Díaz-Cepeda, 2017). Similar Facebook and Twitter accounts also exist. The Michoacán self-defense movement in 2013 also began a Facebook page to reach out to the public. The more recent predecessors were the YoSoy132 movement and the use of Facebook pages by anti-drug gang bloggers like ValorPorTamaulipas.[13]

The use of social media for the Ayotzinapa movement has created solidarity and collective identities that go beyond conventional or "brokering" organizations "carrying the burden of facilitating cooperation" of large-scale action networks (Bennett & Segerberg, 2012). Postings across trusted social networks, for example through the use of images like the portraits that become transferable digital memes, allowed for the spread of awareness about the atrocities that took place in Iguala.

Online videos and photos were transmitted under the hashtags #FueElEstado (translated to It Was the State) #EselEstado #NoSomosUnNúmero (We Are Not Just a Number), #YaMeCanse (I Am Tired), #US2tired, #yanoscansamos (We Are Tired) #AyotzinapaSomosTodos (We Are All Ayotzinapa), and #Ayotzinapa. Supporters would often tag pictures of themselves with "I am Ayotzinapa" hashtags and spread them through their online networks. Others created websites or blogs. Supporters created their own personal frames and meanings and claimed their own stake in the movement. In this way Ayotzinapa's original communication network and messages acquired mass appeal throughout Mexico and beyond.

To this day there are more questions than answers, and still, nothing is known with certainty about the disappeared students. The story of their disappearance, however, has gained international attention. The teachers, parents and students of Ayotzinapa sustain the momentum in their state of Guerrero through marches, popular assemblies of local residents and teachers working with labor and teachers' unions, peasant organizations and community-run police movement or *auto-defensas*, the taking of toll booths and the blocking of major highways into an otherwise touristy Pacific-coast area known for beaches and weekend getaways (Asfura-Heim & Espach, 2013).

On a national level they have organized with other student networks inherited from the #YoSoy132 movement of 2012 (Díaz-Cepeda, 2015; Guillén, 2013; Muñoz Ramírez, 2011). Internationally, the campaign has spread to universities in many countries where vigils, protest marches, and actions such as "die-ins" have been staged; songs and poems have been performed on social media. The parents, students, and teacher's plea for justice and accountability by the Mexican government for the Ayotzinapa student disappearances have become part of the demands of other causes and social movement campaigns such as disappeared migrants all over the world, forced disappearances, political prisoners, police brutality in Ferguson, Missouri, the deaths of Michael Brown, Eric Garner, and others at the hands of the police (Tilly, Castañeda & Wood, 2019).

There are also growing international alliances with groups such as School of the Americas Watch, and a coalition of US-based organizations that helped the parents of the disappeared students to organize Caravana43 in March 2015 in which three caravans with a total of 15 parents visited more than 40 cities across the US. "The main aim," the website[14] states, "is to provide an international forum for the parents who have lost their children in a government of systemic violence and impunity." All the financial resources, according to Julio Cesar Guerrero, Campaign Coordinator for the Caravana43, are provided by the coalition members who donate $1,000 to a group account for the parents' travel, food, and other costs (Guerrero, 2015, phone interview).

> We decided from the beginning not to ask for money from anyone. That creates impediments for the project and future actions. It also means negotiating and renegotiating our actions. So, we financed independently.
>
> (Guerrero, 2015, phone interview)

Weaknesses of the movement

While the social media element is its most innovative element, UNAM analyst Raúl Benítez Manaut,[15] saw the pro-Ayotzinapa campaigns having a limited lifespan because of their radical nature, the impractical nature of their request of "You Took Them Alive, We Want Them Back Alive!" and the sporadic resorting to violence.

> They've done things like burning the government building in Chilpanc-ingo and align themselves with groups that are very radicalized, and there's a rejection of that type violence in Mexico. If they continue with that discourse, they will be completely tuned out; they are already being tuned out in Mexico.
>
> (Benítez, February 24, 2014, personal interview)

If they employ similar tactics during electoral campaign times, Benítez Manaut fears there will be full-scale repression by the Mexican police. It would not be the first time the Mexican government would have done this, he warned.

After a brief period of tolerance, by the end of 2014, the Mexican government used their worn playbook strategy to intimidate, isolate, and criminalize. They repressed manifestations in order to make people less likely to attend them. They marginalized the movement by having political leaders constantly claiming that the case was closed, and it was time to move on. For example, national media began covering it less and political leaders such as former president Vicente Fox stated on CNN in Spanish that it was time for the parents to "accept the reality" of what happened to their children (CNN, 2015). Also, they started prosecuting and presenting charges on protesters for damaging public property.

The movement's longevity might also be impacted by the fact that the main organizing entity, *La Normal*, has no monetary resources of its own beyond the contacts and networks that provide it support. So, while social media networks are self-organizing and amplify the message of the movement without a central or "lead" organizational actor, the question is how long can it sustain without those resources? Social Movement Organizations require considerable skill, experience, resources, and professionals who, ultimately, need to be paid for doing the heaving lifting of being a change agent (Freeman, 2003, p. 31).

Despite the popular outrage, political parties and powerful political actors in Mexico ignore Ayotzinapa altogether.

> It has failed to be co-opted by the political players because it's so unstable because it's so fragile and because there's a claim for social justice. Political parties really don't want to have a lot to do with it because it's really dirty.
>
> (Pérez, August 20, 2015, personal interview)

That means it would not be incorporated into any public policy proposal and it would not be debated in Congress, no matter how many people Tweet or Facebook about it.

Nobody wants to touch it because it's nasty stuff. It's drug stuff, it's repression stuff, it's the military, and there are all sorts of mechanisms of co-optation or buying out, and eventually, the main repression will come as well.

(Pérez, August 20, 2015, personal interview)

Thus, despite citizen indignation and widespread mobilization, politicians and state actors have shown little interest in this issue.

Ayotzinapas 43's lessons

This case study is an example of critical public relations theory, as it privileges the perspective of activist and attempts to learn how PR can be used for the benefit of the powerless. As such, it diverges from Excellence Theory assumptions. Excellence Theory is the dominant paradigm in public relations theory (Dozier, Guning, & Gruning, 1995; Grunig & Grunig, 1989). For the most part, this tradition was built from the perspective of resource-rich organizations (Grunig, 1992) that took power as a given. Their staff are concerned not to abuse that power and show Corporate Social Responsibility (CSR), and that organizations should avoid manipulation of the public. Instead, they were to reach mutual understanding by challenging activists via a two-way symmetrical model (Grunig & Grunig, 1997). In the same token PR had been perceived by some activists as an undesirable and unethical "set of techniques for pursuing corporate interests rather than promoting common interests" (Miller & Dinan, 2008, pp. 4–5). In a few words, both scholars and activists considered PR of exclusive use by resourceful organizations.

This paradigm started to break with the worry of peripheral scholars with issues of power and persuasion within PR theory (Coombs & Holladay, 2007; Edwards, 2012, 2016). This concern created a critical public relations theory, which takes into consideration the needs of the powerless; just as the Frankfurt School did back in the 1970s in Sociology (Horkheimer, 1972). Several scholars (Curtin & Gaither, 2005) have called upon researchers to do more thinking on how PR theory can account for power relations and how this knowledge could be used by activists to improve their possibilities of modifying the existing power balance and promote their causes. In Karlberg's words "Researchers should pay more attention to the communicative needs, constraints or practices of citizen groups themselves" (Karlberg, 2009, p. 271).

Timothy Coombs and Sherry J. Holladay (2012) point out that critical public relations theory developed fringe concepts such as power and persuasion/advocacy that may interrupt the colonization of knowledge made by orthodox PR theory. Coombs and Holladay challenge the Excellence Theory's use of Hegel's dialectic method by pointing out that "We need to move beyond description to explore the dynamics of how and why the

Excellence dialectic occurs" (2012, p. 886). Perhaps, the ana-dialectical method developed by Latin American philosopher Enrique Dussel (1974) can conceptually help us to achieve this goal. This means that while Coombs and Holladay make a correct appreciation of Hegel's dialect method, one needs to remember the positive moment of the dialect process: the affirmation of the negation. In other words, it is true that the status quo (thesis) is challenged by social movements (antithesis) and in solving their conflict, they create a new order (synthesis). However, it is often forgotten that for social movements to have enough power to effectively challenge the status quo, they first need to affirm themselves (affirmation of the negation). This affirmation is the positive moment of the dialectic method, the time of activists. This chapter aims then to illustrate the PR tactics and channels used by Ayotzinapa activists to persuade Mexico's government to find the 43 missing students.

Our research shows that similar to other recent social movements such as Occupy (Di, 2015), the Tahrir Square (Tufekci & Wilson, 2012), and South Korea (Choi & Cho, 2017), Ayotzinapa activists used social media to get organized, to disseminate their message, and to announce and call for protests. For the most part, these disruptive tactics were a continuation of the traditional off-line repertory, but enhanced by the use of social media. We found instances of both dissent and protest PR that at their climax jeopardized the stability of Peña Niteo's administration. However, regardless of the efficient use of communication technology and their savvy PR tactics – that allowed activists to mobilize a large segment of the population at an international level – the political class overpowered the protests and diminished the movement.

Conclusion

Our research showed that from the very beginning the mobilization for Ayotzinapa was a complex social movement made up by different SMOs and joined by regular citizens who were outraged by the forced disappearance of the 43 students. Participants had a different level of expertise in the use of PR to promote their cause. The first reaction was made by other students of the *Normal* who were well trained in traditional disruptive tactics such as demonstrations, dies-in, streets closing, and even direct and violent confrontation with the police, but somehow lacked abilities to go beyond their close circle. Yet they purposefully documented the attack, contacted their close allies via WhatsApp, and called a press conference the same night of the events, functioning as "citizen journalists" (Tufekci & Wilson, 2012, p. 373).

As social activists in Mexico City, the center of political life in this country, learned about the events through WhatsApp messages from Ayotzinapa students and their allies, they put their knowledge of social media management to the service of the cause and organized the Solidarity

Committee. It was from this committee that they set the strategy to bring the students back alive. They called for the First Global Action Day and coordinated the different social media campaigns needed. For the most part, these campaigns were made up of dissent tactics, looking to disseminate their ideas and change the government thinking and behavior.

At this early stage, parents had no experience whatsoever. In consequence, they did not play an active role in spreading the message to dissuade Mexico's federal government to find out the truth and their children alive. As parents gained experience, by November 2014, they had become the lead strategy coordinators of the different campaigns. The first (and permanent) campaign has been to find the students alive. Subsequent campaigns were organized to challenge the government's narrative and to free people detained during the protests. These campaigns included a combination of off-line and on-line disruptive tactics such as presenting portraits of the missing students and national and international caravans.

As time passed by and the demands not resolved, at the climax of the movement there was a dissenting PR stage where SMOs involved not only called for new legislation but a new government. On the streets, protesters chanted: It was the State! And since 2014 they got organized on the Popular Citizen Constituent (*Constituyente Ciudadana Popular*, PCC)[16] and the People's National Convention (*Convención Nacional Popular*, PNC)[17] (Díaz-Cepeda, 2016).

It is important to notice that the success of the movement of mobilizing thousands of people at a local, national, and international level was due to a combination of face to face relations and the online connections. The personal webs, prestige, and trust that core activists participating in the Ayotzinapa movement had built over their life brought a network of other activists and their organizations willing and able to mobilize their resources in support of this cause. In Mexico some of these organizations, i.e., Services and Counsel for Peace *(Servicios y Asesoria para la Paz*, SERAPAZ),[18] supplied logistics and a channel of communication with the government. Thanks to Facebook campaigns other organizations, and civil society mirrored their efforts at a national and international level without the need of Ayotzinapa activists or the parents to travel thousands of miles to attend these protests. In fact, a large number of local protests were not coordinated by any central committee, as they were spontaneous or locally organized.

Unfortunately, these efforts and the participation of the Interamerican Court of Human Rights had been fruitless as the EPN administration (2006–2018) insisted in their version that students were killed and incinerated by a criminal organization. The official version recognizes the complicity of local police officers, but it denies any participation of the army and does not allow any investigations in that direction. As of summer 2018, the location of the missing students is still uncertain.

This case study shows evidence for the growing importance of social media networks, new mobile communication technology, and PR tactics around them. However, as Downing (2008) warns, succumbing to techno-logical fetishization is a grave delusion. For while it is vital that the message is spread via social media, it is still necessary that the message resonates with people in the physical world. Where categorical groups (e.g., students) are attacked, contentious politics aims for groups in power to share resources and opportunities with them (Tilly et al., 2019). While new communication technologies help with the diffusion of social justice claims and popular knowledge of a struggle, getting demands met and producing durable change is not any easier than before.

¡Vivos se los llevaron, vivos los queremos!

Notes

1 Normales rurales are rural teachers schools created in the 1920s during President Álvaro Obregón's administration by the Mexican philosopher José Vasconcelos, who served as the Minister of Education. They were established with the goal of bringing social progress to the peasants living in Mexico's country-side through education. Since their launch they are organized in the Mexican Federation of Peasant Socialist Students (*Federacion de estudiantes campesinos socialistas de Mexico*, FECSM) and engage in activism in order to demand better social conditions for the students and the poor (Navarro, 2001). Students follow a socialist and activist approach where they take part in the peasants' struggles, as most of them are peasants themselves.
2 The movement against the militarization of Ciudad Juarez started in 2008 when a small group of activists protested the military strategy of former President Calderon (2006–2012), a strategy that caused the death of over 6,000 people in Ciudad Juarez from 2008 to 2010 during the Chihuahua Joint Operation (Monárrez, 2013, p. 214). As violence increased, more activists joined the movement and Ciudad Juárez became the epicenter of resistance to the war on drugs.
3 On March 27, 2011, the son of Javier Sicilia, a famous Mexican poet, was found dead, along with six other people. In a demand for justice, Javier Sicilia started a caravan from Cuernavaca to Mexico City. His demand for justice and for an end to President Calderon's war on drugs was quickly joined and supported by numerous people and regular social activists. The MPJD toured the country with two caravans. In these two caravans, they had a direct dialogue with the victims of violence, showing that the violence was happening across the country. Despite Calderon's refusal to end the militarization of the country, the MPJD deserves credit for showing that Mexico was going through a human rights crisis.
4 In 2012, the student movement #YoSoy132 translated to "I Am 132," a phrase inspired by the 15M and Occupy movements began when students confronted the Institutional Revolutionary Party (PRI) candidate Enrique Peña Nieto, later to become president of Mexico, about his policies as governor and what the students' considered the Mexican media's biased coverage of the 2012 general election. Using video students spread their messages virally through mainly Facebook and Twitter to 50 cities in the country. This strategy would also help to build transnational links with Mexican students abroad and to gain the support of other international collectives (Gómez-Garcia & Treré, 2014). The #YoSoy132 campaign was successful in mobilizing university students, both online and in street protests, and had an impact in the steps the administration

took with initiatives around education, energy, and telecom reforms in Congress. They were able to organize the first independent debate of the presidential candidates, where the only absent candidate was Enrique Peña Nieto (EPN). It was broadcasted on You Tube and reached a larger audience than the televized ones. Despite all their efforts EPN was voted President of Mexico for the 2006 to 2012 period. Thought with less visibility, EPN continued with the same military strategy and drug related violence not only continued but escalated.

5 See "Yo Soy 132, a Networked Social Movement of Mexican Youth" (Díaz-Cepeda, 2015).

6 Si el estado estaba asesinando a la sociedad y estaba desapareciendo y asesinando no teníamos como comprobarlo hasta que sucedió lo de Ayotzinapa.

7 Raúl Romero (35) is a life-time activist. He has participated in the Zapatista movement and the MPJD.

8 http://ilustradoresconayotzinapa.tumblr.com.

9 Similar to civil rights movements in the United States and Europe during the decade of 1960s, students in Mexico were demanding more democratic conditions in the country. These protests increased and as the Olympic Games in Mexico 1968 were about to be inaugurated (October 12, 1968), the administration of then President Gustavo Díaz Ordaz was in a hurry to end the protest. On October 2, 1968 during a peaceful student manifestation, protesters were shot and many of them were killed or disappeared (to this day the number is unknown). Mass media did not report the attack. Since then October 2 has been commemorate by students, activists, and social organizations as a day of resistance.

10 On April 20, 1999 the assembly of the students of the Mexico National University constituted the Strike Council and closed the University in protest for an increase to the 20 cents tuition fees because this increase violated the right to a free education. The strike continued for nine months until the night of February 6, 2000 when then President Ernesto Zedillo Ponce the Leon ordered the Federal Police to take control of the University facilities. Federal forces continued patrolling the campus until April 23, 2000, violating the autonomy of the University. Main stream media supported these measures and activist students were portrayed as lazy people or even as criminals.

11 On December 12, 2011 two *Normal* students were shot death by the Federal Police during a highway blockade.

12 Miguel Ángel was found death on August 9, 2015. He received several death threats due his involvement in activism. For more on Miguel Angel and his use of communication technology see "Interview with activist Miguel Ángel Jiménez Blanco" (Andrade, Castañeda & Díaz-Cepeda, 2017).

13 www.facebook.com/ValorPorTamaulipas.

14 www.caravana43.com/about.html.

15 President of the non-governmental organization Collective of Analysis of Security with Democracy, A.C.

16 http://nuevaconstituyente.org/.

17 www.tlachinollan.org/convocatoria-vi-convencion-nacional-popular/.

18 https://serapaz.org.mx/.

References

Andrade, K. (2015a). The life and death of Miguel Angel Jiménez, organizer in Guerrero, Mexico. Retrieved from http://pulitzercenter.org/reporting/life-and-death-miguel-angel-jim%C3%A9nez-organizer-guerrero-mexico.

Andrade, K. (2015b). WhatsApp and murder in Mexico. *Latino USA*. Retrieved from http://latinousa.org/2015/12/11/whatsapp-and-murder-in-mexico/.

Andrade, K., Castañeda, E. & Díaz-Cepeda, L. R. (2017). Interview with activist Miguel Ángel Jiménez Blanco. *Interface: A Journal for and about Social Movements*, 9(1), 590–600.

AP. (2015). U.N. Report criticizes Mexico on enforced disappearances. (February 13). Retrieved from www.dailymail.co.uk/wires/ap/article-2952618/UN-body-finds-enforced-disappearances-widespread-Mexico.html.

AP/AFP. (2015). Foreign forensic experts slam Mexico's probe into missing students. (August 2, 2015).

Archibold, R. C. (2014, October 6). 43 Missing students, a mass grave and a suspect: Mexico's police. *New York Times*. Retrieved from www.nytimes.com/2014/10/07/world/americas/43-missing-students-a-mass-grave-and-a-suspect-mexicos-police-.html.

Archibold, R. C. (2015, January 27). Mexico officially declares missing students dead. *New York Times*. Retrieved from www.nytimes.com/2015/01/28/world/americas/mexico-officially-declares-missing-students-dead.html.

Asfura-Heim, P. & Espach., R. H. (2013). The rise of Mexico's self-defense forces. *Foreign Affairs*. Retrieved from www.foreignaffairs.com/articles/mexico/2013-06-11/rise-mexico-s-self-defense-forces.

BBC. (2015). Mexico missing: Protesters try to enter army base. Retrieved from www.bbc.com/news/world-latin-america-30793499.

Bennett, W. L. & Segerberg, A. (2012). The logic of connective action. *Information, Communication & Society*, 15(5), 739–768. doi:10.1080/1369118X.2012.670661.

Bocking, P. (2015). Teachers and parents sustain the struggle for Mexico's missing Ayotzinapa students. *Waging NonViolence*. Retrieved from https://wagingnonviolence.org/feature/teachers-parents-sustain-struggle-ayotzinapa/.

Castañeda, E., Díaz-Cepeda, L. R. & Andrade, K. (2018). Social movements in contemporary Mexico. In C. Tilly, E. Castañeda & L. J. Wood (Eds.), *Social movements, 1768–2018* (pp. x, 194). New York: Routledge.

Choi, S. Y. & Cho, Y. (2017). Generating counter-public spheres through social media: Two social movements in neoliberalised South Korea. *Javnost – The Public Journal of the European Institute for Communication and Culture*, 24, 15–33. https://doi.org/10.1080/13183222.2017.1267155.

CNN. (2015). Fox a los padres de Ayotzinapa: "Ya tienen que aceptar la realidad." Retrieved from https://expansion.mx/nacional/2015/03/17/fox-a-los-padres-de-ayotzinapa-ya-tienen-que-aceptar-la-realidad.

Coombs, W. T. & Holladay, S. J. (2007). *It's not just PR: Public relations in society*. Malden, MA: Blackwell Publishing.

Coombs, W. T. & Holladay, S. J. (2012). Fringe public relations: How activism moves critical PR toward the mainstream. *Public Relations Review*, 38, 880–887. https://doi.org/10.1016/j.pubrev.2012.02.008.

Curtin, P. A. & Gaither, T. K. (2005). Privileging identity, difference, and power: The circuit of culture as a basis for public relations theory. *Journal of Public Relations Research*, 17, 91–115. https://doi.org/10.1207/s1532754xjprr1702_3.

Di, A. (2015). Occupy PR: An analysis of online media communications of Occupy Wall Street and Occupy London. *Public Relations Review*, 41(4), 508–514.

Díaz-Cepeda, L. R. (2015). #Yo Soy 132: A networked social movement of Mexican youth. In N. Knoak & R. O. Donmez (Eds.), *Waves of social movement mobilizations in the twenty-first century: Challenges to the neo-liberal world order and democracy* (pp. 41–58). Lanham, MD: Lexington Books.

Díaz-Cepeda, L. R. (2016). Addressing Ayotzinapa: Using Dussel's analectic method for establishing an ethical framework for complex social movements. In R. Grosfoguel, R. Hernández & E. Rosen Velázquez (Eds.), *Decolonizing the Westernized university: Interventions in philosophy of education from within and without* (pp. 229–242). Lanham, MD: Lexington Books.

Díaz-Cepeda, L. R. & Castañeda, E. (2018). Motivations and activist typologies: Core activists in Ciudad Juarez. *Interface: A Journal for and about Social Movements, 10*(2).

Dittmar, V. (2018). Study: 2017 was deadliest year in Mexico for homicides linked to organized crime. Retrieved form www.insightcrime.org/news/analysis/2017-deadliest-year-organized-crime-related-homicides-mexico/.

Downing, J. (2008). Social movement theories and alternative media: An evaluation and critique. *Communication, Culture and Critique, 1*(1), 40–50. doi:10.1111/j.1753-9137.2007.00005.x.

Dozier, D. M., Guning, L. A. & Gruning, J. (1995). *Manager's guide to excellence in public relations and communication management.* Mahawah, NJ: Lawrence Erlbaum Associates.

Dussel, E. (1974). *Método para una filosofía de la liberación. Superación análectica de la dialéctica hegeliana* (2nd ed.). Salamanca: Sigueme.

Edwards, L. (2012). Defining the "object" of public relations research: A new starting point. *Public Relations Inquiry, 1*(1), 7–30.

Edwards, L. (2016). An historical overview of the emergence of critical thinking in PR. In J. L'Etang, D. McKie, N. Snow & J. Xifra (Eds.), *The Routledge handbook of critical public relations.* New York: Routledge.

Freeman, J. (2003). The Women's Movement. In J. Goodwin & J. M. Jasper (Eds.), *The Social movements reader: Cases and concepts* (pp. 22–31). Malden, MA: Blackwell Publishers.

Gibler, J. (2017). *I couldn't even imagine that they would kill us: An oral history of the attacks against the students of Ayotzinapa.* San Francisco, CA: City Lights Books.

GIEI. (2017). *Informe Ayotzinapa II.* Retrieved from Washington, DC: www.oas.org/es/cidh/actividades/giei/giei-informeayotzinapa2.pdf.

Grunig, J. E. (Ed.). (1992). Activism: How it limits the effectiveness of organizations and how excellent public relations departments respond. In *Excellence in public relations and communication management* (pp. 503–530). Mahwah, NJ: Lawrence Erlbaum Associates.

Grunig, J. E. & Grunig, L. A. (1989). Toward a theory of public relations behavior in organizations: A review of program research. In J. E. Grunig & L. A. Grunig (Eds.), *Public relations research annual* (Vol. I, pp. 27–63). New York: Routledge.

Grunig, J. E. & Grunig, L. A. (1997). Review of a program of research on activism: incidence in four countries, activist publics, strategies of activist groups, and organizational responses to activism. Paper presented to the 4th *Public Relations Research Symposium, Managing Environmental Issues*, July 11–13. Lake Bled, Slovenia. Hillsdale, NJ: Lawrence Erlbaum Associates.

Guillén, D. (2013). Mexican spring?# YoSoy132, the emergence of an unexpected collective actor in the national political arena. *Social Movement Studies*, *12*(4), 471–476.

Hernandéz, A. (2016). *La verdadera noche de Iguala*. Mexico: Editorial Grijalbo.

Horkheimer, M. (1972). *Critical theory*. New York: Seabury Press.

INEGI (2017) *Mortalidad. Defunciones por homicidios*. Concatenated, 2012–2016 [Data set]. Instituto Nacional de Geografía e Informática. Retrieved from www.inegi.org.mx/lib/olap/consulta/general_ver4/MDXQueryDatos.asp?#Regreso&c=28820.

INEGI (2018) *Mortalidad. Defunciones por homicidios*. Concatenated, 2006–2017 [Data set]. Instituto Nacional de Geografía e Informática. Retrieved from www.inegi.org.mx/lib/olap/consulta/general_ver4/MDXQueryDatos.asp?#Regreso&c=28820.

Karlberg, M. (2009). Remembering the public in public relations research: From theoretical to operational symmetry. *Journal of Public Relations Research*, *8*(4), 263–278. https://doi.org/10.1207/s1532754xjprr0804_03.

Miller, D. & Dinan, W. (2008). *A century of spin: How public relations became the cutting edge of corporate power*. London: Pluto.

Monárrez Fragoso, J. E. (2013). Ciudad Juárez, tiradero nacional de muertos: Entre el discurso del guerrero y el caballero. *Debate Feminista*, 205–34. Retrieved from https://core.ac.uk/download/pdf/82594045.pdf.

Muñoz Ramírez, G. (2011). *#Yo Soy 132 Voces Del Movimiento*. Mexico, DF: Ediciones Bola de Cristal.

Navarro, C. (2001). Las normales rurales: Espacios escolares a contracorriente con la política educativa modernizadora. In T. Coll (Ed.), *In anuario educativo Mexicano: Visión retrospectiva*. Mexico: Universidad Pedagogica Nacional/La Jornada.

RNPED. (2018). Registro Nacional de Personas Extraviadas y Desaparecidas. Retrieved from https://personasdesaparecidas.org.mx/db/db.

Rodríguez, R. (2014). Ayotzinapa: A tradition of struggle and resistance. *Permanent Revolution*. Retrieved from http://forum.permanent-revolution.org/2014/11/ayotzinapa-tradition-of-struggle-and.html.

Taylor, A. (2014). Mexico's missing 43. *Photos in Focus*.

Tilly, C., Castañeda, E. & Wood, L. J. (2019). *Social movements, 1768–2018*. New York: Routledge.

Tufekci, Z. & Wilson, C. (2012). Social media and the decision to participate in political protest: Observations from Tahrir Square. *Journal of Communication*, *62*, 363–379. https://doi.org/10.1111/j.1460-2466.2012.01629.x.

8 Reading Gezi Park protests through the lens of protest PR

Barika Göncü, Erkan Saka, and Anıl Sayan

The Gezi Park Protests in Istanbul, Turkey, joined by over 3 million citizens during the summer of 2013, have already created substantial academic literature with the new media usage of activists and protesters being a central topic (Ogan & Varol, 2016; Chrona & Bee, 2017; Saka, 2017b). However, an understudied aspect relates to the activists' use of a series of techniques that could be classified as protest PR (Moloney & McKie, 2015, p. 157) meant to apply pressure on the government and the policy makers and to gain broader support from citizens. Our study demonstrates that although the communication strategies during the protests were spontaneous, the protesters were able to design and implement flexible, timely, and result oriented tactics aiming to interrupt the Government's authoritarian urban policies.

Turkey entered a different political pathway with the conservative Justice and Development Party's (AKP)[1] victory in the 2002 general elections. In the early years of the AKP government, the emphasis was on social reform rather than policies guided by the Islamic roots of the AKP founders. Examples for social reform can be the parliamentary action for EU required political reforms, or the expressed determination to resolve the "Kurdish problem" (Patton, 2007). Following the constitutional referendum of 2010,[2] AKP policies shifted toward a conservative line. Conservative policies and messages on several issues such as alcohol consumption and co-ed habitation were interpreted as restrictions on individual freedom, also signaling the Gezi protests (Göle, 2013, p. 10).

During the same period, the construction sector in Turkey became the locomotive industry. Along with several ambitious construction projects, the Government also had plans to demolish Gezi Park, to be replaced with a shopping mall. Gezi Park was located next to Taksim Square, a gathering venue attached to both political and social symbols. Additionally, the Park was the last remaining green area around the Square. The pedestrianization project of Taksim Square, including the demolishment of the Gezi Park, was launched by the Municipal Assembly in 2011. Yet, the council of Preservation of Cultural and Natural Heritage cancelled some parts of the project in 2012, as a result of which several environmentalist groups and professional bodies started following the issue more closely by establishing a new initiative under the name of "Taksim Solidarity," regularly informing the public about the demolition process.

In the middle of the night of May 27, 2013, construction vehicles entered the Gezi Park to uproot trees. When some activists went to the Park and tried to stop the work in progress, the police forces responded brutally, giving rise to a social media upheaval and a sit-in protest, enhanced by the arrival of more people and some MPs the next morning. On June 1 the police forces retreated from the Park being replaced by an increasing number of individual protesters and NGOs. As the protesters settled in the Park and established a small-scale "protest village" with volunteer-run facilities like a library, infirmary, kitchen, media room, etc., the Park became a center that represented the discontent of different social groups, NGOs, trade unions, and the like, with the policies of AKP. In the days to follow, the Park and the Square became the major center of attention, with supporting visitors from all walks of life. Following the massive police intervention on the evening of June 15, the protesters were drawn out of the Park.

During the 15 days the protesters camped in the Park, they utilized several communication strategies and tactics to legitimize the protests. Events such as marches, rallies or in-park activities converged with digital media tools, resulting in the involvement of people from different social and political backgrounds in the protests. While the in-park activities became the locus point of protesters' solidarity, they also resulted in the embracement of the protests by a wide spectrum of publics. Thus, while the Park and its environs housed an unplanned but strategically coordinated movement in a communicational base, there was also a significant public opinion shift in Turkey. Following the protests, 62.9 pecent of the people in Turkey said Gezi Park should stay as a green area, 49.9 percent thought the Government policies were increasingly authoritarian, and 54.4 percent believed the Government was increasingly intervening in citizens' lifestyle choices (MetroPOLL, 2013).

A report by Social Media and Political Participation Laboratory (Barberá & Metzger, 2013) clearly indicates that the social media traffic during Gezi Park protests was phenomenal, resulting in 2 million tweets on the related hashtags. Social media tools were widely employed not only by the protesters in the Gezi Park but also by citizens in other regions of the country during the demonstrations.[3] In this regard, the significant level of digital literacy skills of the activist groups or NGOs in Turkey is obvious, with also the ability to utilize social media platforms for producing alternative media coverage. Accordingly, research on Gezi protests largely focused on the rise of social media usage (Tufekci, 2014) and how this helped the emergence of a particular public sphere (Sezer et al., 2014), which could better be called a counter public (Warner, 2002) due to its oppositional character. Similarly, Demirhan (2014) focused on Twitter's role in public participation, Arda (2015) worked on virality, and Emre et al. (2014) related humor and social media in protests. In yet another two works Saka investigated the relationship of citizen journalism practices to protests with a particular focus on social media (Saka, 2017a) and pro-government circles' anti-protest usage of trolls (Saka, 2017b; Saka, 2018). In the meantime, two edited volumes worthy of mention did not focus on social media and even media in general: A group of anthropologists pre-pared a special online issue for the *Cultural Anthropology* journal (Yıldırım & Navaro-Yashin, 2013) and Özkırımlı's (2014) edited collec-tion had a political science emphasis. To our knowledge, with the excep-tion of McLeod's (2014) paper, Gezi Park protests were not studied with the objective of highlighting aspects of public relations strategies, tactics or tools used by the protesters, and our study aims to contribute to literature in this respect.

Before presenting our findings on the communication strategies and the tactics of the Gezi Park protesters in the context of protest PR, we will put forward the development of public relations in Turkey in connection to social and political motivations, present a theoretical framework and elab-orate on our methodology.

A brief history of public relations from a societal perspective

The early public relations practices: born to be political

As Edwards (2018) demonstrates, the modern public relations practices have been evolving in relation to modernity, democracy, capitalism, and information technologies in various local contexts. For her, social institu-tions and/or individuals such as states, churches, armies or politicians have utilized public relations as a way of persuasive communication. Therefore, it is clear that political milestones, economic issues, the rise of civil society or information technologies have directly shaped the functions of public relations in a holistic sense. Besides this, local tendencies or interests have also been providing new dimensions and aspects to the practice and the profession, even if they geographically yield a nonlinear historical develop-ment. According to L'Etang (2015, p. 37), public relations histories are not static in character; on the contrary, they are lively histories practically rooted in cultural and social dynamics. Hence, there is also a growing body of literature about the progress of public relations in different geographies (L'Etang, 2013; L'Etang & Pieczka, 2006; Zerfass, Ruler & Sriramesh, 2008; Sriramesh & Verčič, 2003). The development of public relations in Turkey is an example of this historical and geographical nonlinearity and needs to be analyzed through the consideration of the politic and economic agendas of "modern" Turkey.

In the Turkish context; the early public relations practices, which were largely unplanned and non-strategic in character, have often been shaped by different political and economic milestones of the founding years of the Turkish Republic. For instance, during 1930s, the public relations efforts were used for deepening the social influence and prevalence of Western-oriented policies on Turkish society. In order to introduce the modernist reforms, the majority of efforts such as the meetings or gatherings in different cities of Anatolia may be considered as the initial practices of public relations (Erdoğan, 2014, p. 141). Following the founding years, the public relations activities were generally used by different political parties such as the Democrat Party or the Republican People Party for creating voter awareness and support (Kalender, 2013).

The early years of public relations from a societal perspective in Turkey is crucial for several reasons. Whereas the two World Wars led to the use of public relations as a political propaganda tool in countries such as the United States and Britain; in Turkey public relations was used for legitimizing social policies. This is in line with L'Etang's (2015) argument that the histories of public relations are culturally and politically influenced.

Institutionalization of public relations in Turkey

Even though the concept of civil society globally emerged in the 1960s, the idea of the civil society appeared in Turkey only after 1980s as an economic consequences of the military coups of May 27, 1960 and September 12, 1980.

Public relations in Turkey, however, started gaining a modern momentum after the 1960s (Kalender, 2013). This impetus can be related to the new constitution of 1961, and its liberal and democratic contents, which allowed the increasing participation of citizens in deliberative democratic decision-making processes. Yamanoğlu et al. (2013) assert that social developments in Turkey between 1960 and 1980 served as a base for rationalizing public relations. The public relations units in public offices were first established in 1961 under the name of "broadcasting and representation branches." Moreover, in 1964, the Directorate-General of Population Planning predominantly implemented public relations techniques for promoting birth control and family planning. In 1971, The Turkish Public Relations Association was established to enhance professional recognition and solidarity among PR practitioners. The field also underwent a paradigm shift with attention focusing on corporate issues and interests in the aftermath of the decisions taken on January 24[4] and the following 1980 Military Coup (Yamanoğlu et al., 2013).

One of the consequences of the increase in private sector utilization of public relations was the emergence of NGO communications as a balancing force, toward raising awareness on social issues. In fact, the initiation of the NGO power dates back to 1996, when the Second United Nations Conference on Human Settlements held in Istanbul (Habitat II), gave UN recognition to local NGOs (Cohen, 1996). Since then, the effective and systematic communication efforts of the Turkish NGOs have become common practice, with strategic communication campaigns in various specific fields such as politics, education, health, and environment by institutionalized NGOs (Keyman & Icduygu, 2003).

More recently, as a result of increasing social polarization and increasing authoritarianism in Turkey since the last quarter of 2000s (Keyman, 2014), several rallies on social issues or interests were organized under the leadership of different NGOs. A significant example is a rally organized by 21 NGOs coming together as the "Platform of Internet Technologies NGOs," two years before the Gezi Protests. The motto of the rally, in which 60,000 people attended, was "Don't Touch My Internet." Drawing attention to the increasing internet censorship in Turkey, the protest had received broad coverage in various national or international media outlets, including the *BBC*, *CNN*, *Al Jazeera*, *Le Monde*, and *Der Spiegel* (Özyaşar & Aydin, 2014). Another example worth mentioning are the LGBTI Pride Week marches. Held since 1994 against a background of increasing state and local government anti-propaganda, the LGBTI Pride Week marches are recognized for their ability to unite multiple organizations. For instance, for the 2014 march, 19 different NGOs have worked together bringing more than 100,000 participants (Pearce, 2013). These rallies and marches have obviously provided a mental and physical base to Gezi protests.

To conclude, Turkey's context is critical to understand how public relations practically embraced political tendencies and sensibilities in the light of local issues, and how this has led to a nonlinear historical development for the field in Turkey.

From activist to protest PR

The activism in public relations first echoed through the political atmosphere of the 1960s and the 1970s. Yet, even though the initiators were activist groups, PR practitioners using the managerial perspective portrayed activism as an opposing force and considered it the core subject of issues management. As such, issues management clearly focuses more on the impact of social issues on corporate operations, and less on activism and its social consequences. Smith and Ferguson (2010) see the activist public relations as a sort of revisiting of issues management. For them the activist publics have two primary goals: to change and/or improve conditions in relation to specific issues, and to secure continuing support for their activities. Similarly, Holtzhausen (2000) also claims that the function of activist publics in modern societies is to create social change about an issue by primarily utilizing strategic communication efforts. More broadly, Brown (2006) argues, activist public relations concentrates on issues management since it seeks to push forward or legitimize a social issue in the eyes of the society.

In this sense, Demetrious (2006) argues that activism is structurally connected to public relations through an independent, and therefore legitimate, construction of knowledge. In her view, activism is a phenomenon that has also challenged the conventional understanding of the mass media. Hence the changing nature of mass media's complexity from asymmetrical to converged communicational characteristics through the utilization of digital production of media messages have expanded public relations' scope and practices toward a more holistic approach.

Moloney and McKie (2015) see activist public relations as an umbrella concept that includes both protest and dissent PR. The difference between protest PR and dissent PR can be related to the techniques utilized in social movements by the activists. While protest PR focuses on tactics such as marches, rallies, boycotts that are non-partisan PR techniques to create an influence on governmental policies or issues, dissent PR is focused more on the dissemination of ideas to shift prevalent thinking in society. More specifically, Moloney et al. (2013) describe protest PR as persuasive communication that aims to implement "ideas, behaviors and policies into law, regulation and other forms of executive action" (p. 3).

Theoretically, this chapter is based on a protest PR approach, implying that the Gezi Park demonstrations were a social movement, in the course of which activist groups used various tactics aimed at gaining legitimacy vis-à-vis different publics. In this study, we try to shed light on how the activist groups involved adopted public relations strategies and tactics in order to gain support from the public and respond to counter arguments and acts of the authorities. Our aim is to provide insights on how the protesters used protest PR techniques to create awareness in the public sphere for their issues and stances. Given the exploratory nature of the study, qualitative research methods have been used to examine how activist groups utilized public relations strategies and tactics during Gezi Demonstrations. Researchers' ethnographic insights are complemented with in depth interviews, participant observation and secondary resources.

Data gathering took place in two phases. The first phase was carried out during the Gezi demonstrations, between June 3 and June 15, 2013. The second phase including in-depth interviews or second-hand stories was carried out between June 2017 and March 2018. Assessing the consequences of a social movement can take relatively a long time, especially when methodological or communicational interests are considered. In this regard, temporal distance has enabled the interviewees to retrospectively consider their actions. We have limited ourselves to the campaigns that originated in and around Gezi Park itself. Gezi Park protests were quick to expand to many major cities in Turkey, as well as to other parts of Istanbul. Yet, the Park itself and the adjacent Taksim Square remained the major center of the protests. While some of the acts and campaigns examined were recurrent and ongoing, some others were one-off "stunts."

Participant observation was used to better contextualize and elaborate the protesters' points of view. This phase provided us with vivid, emerging and emotionally reactive data. Our field study was carried on during the protests, as a result of our prediction of the significance of the protests for future academic work. All three authors resided in the Park for several days, and participated in rallies, collective acts and forums. Although our participant observation was not in structured or controlled characteristics due to the dynamic nature of Gezi Park protests, it gave us a critical sense to how protesters' goals, strategies or tactics were implemented. Beside this, our extensive field notes also guided in depth interviews.

We have conducted 12 in-depth, semi-structured (based on a 26-items guiding list), interviews with the representatives of major activist groups to explore how particular communication campaigns were orchestrated. It was important to see how activists themselves reacted to events and have consequently developed their strategies. This has also helped us to better understand the group dynamics (Taylor et al., 2004). The interviewees selected were decision-makers and/or leaders of the NGOs participating in the Gezi protests, members of the civil coordination committee, or individuals participating in and actively observing the protests (see list[1]). While the majority of our interviews were face-to-face at locations chosen by the interviewees, two of them were through Skype. All the interviews were recorded and transcribed. The interviews lasted, on average, 45 minutes.

This would be further developed by relying on archival data. Gezi demonstrations triggered a big and heterogeneous archive of (mostly) online material from newspaper archives social media outputs to interviews and activist anecdotal accounts.[5]

Shared goals: saving the trees amidst increasing authoritarianism

For McKie and Xifra (2015), the activist PR strategies are built upon political, economic, and social aims and goals. In the case of the Gezi protests, the initial social aim was to save a green area. Explaining why he joined the protests in the first place, Interviewee 03 said, "We were there to defend a tree. We wanted to keep Gezi as a park." As such, the scale of the protest was small in the beginning. The use of excessive force by the police forces fueled an already accumulating anger and discontent, attaching a second and wider aim for the protests. This is reflected in the account of Interviewee 01, who was an active observer at Gezi:

> Actually, a lot was happening prior to Gezi. Although dispersed in character, there was the mobilization of various environmental initiatives. At the same time, discontent regarding several central and local public policies was growing. Gezi sparkled all this and created a synergy that brought almost everyone together.

As the Taksim pedestrianization project was imposed upon the public without any consultation of the representatives of the civil society, it represented the general conservative and authoritarian attitude of the Government; giving rise to the second major aim of the protesters: to expose and to protest this authoritarianism. According to a comprehensive survey (Konda Research, 2014) the majority of protesters had troubles with the increasingly conservative Government rhetoric, with references to various aspects of secular individual and social choices. "I participated in the Park protests because I was angry at the authoritarian use of state vehicles," Interviewee 07 said.

Collective thinking in site as the base of protests

Towards the establishment of solidarity in and around the Park, nearly all acts, performances or plays emerged through the protestors' collective way of thinking which were issued in park forums during the protests. In a similar sense, Diani (1992) defines the boundaries of a social movement network as "the specific collective identity shared by the actors involved in the interaction" (p. 9). Considering this definition, the collective sense of the protestors created a non-hierarchical dialogue toward the establishment of solidarity in and around the Park. To utilize dialogue as a resisting tool, different social and political groups and NGOs installed stands in the Park, promoting their issues. In a parallel manner, Interview 08 stated the importance of park forums as follows:

> In fact, Park forums were the spaces where the spirit of Gezi Park unearthed. Because we were taking our decisions in there. The ideas were constantly being discussed among the protesters.

As a consequence, forum discussions produced a collective base for realization of PR tactics in the direction of protestors' goals and strategies. For instance, through a common decision, they did not put up their individual flags and/or visual symbols. The only exception, again as a result of common agreement, was the LGBTI flags and colors. By taking these into account, our participative observations also indicate that collective intelligence (Malone & Bernstein, 2015) was one of the key aspects during the protests.

Protesting strategically

It has been shown that communication strategies used by activists could affect public opinion toward activist issues either in a positive or a negative direction (Jahng et al., 2014). The protesters of Gezi adopted four major strategies in communicating the *raison d'être* of the occupation of Gezi Park, and in expressing their vision of a more democratic society: non-violence; encouragement of diversity, solidarity and collective action;

humorous framing; dialogue and collective thinking. These strategies were not predetermined but emerged as reactions to various opportunities and risks in the course of the protests (Frandsen & Johansen, 2015). During our interviews, all the participants referred to the flexible and open nature of the strategies utilized during the protests.

Interviewee 08 said:

> Gezi Park was a dynamic center, where representatives of different political and social groups voiced their stances on both environmental and social issues; so we had to be inclusive in our internal and external communication. Additionally, politicians were constantly using mainstream media to downgrade the protest, and we had to produce prompt responses in line with what we called "Gezi spirit."

Although the Gezi protests were fueled by anger toward the demolishment of the Gezi Park or toward government authoritarianism, the protesters adopted an overall strategy of non-violence (Thomas & Louis, 2013). This strategy can be exemplified through tactics such as forming an unarmed human chain between the park and the police forces, extinguishing the gas canisters thrown by the police in water buckets, and ideological vandalism (Zimbardo, 1970) against vehicles belonging to mainstream media channels perceived to be biased. Thirteen people throughout Turkey died during the protests, and more than 8,163 people were injured (Hapiste Saglik website, 2013). In spite of this death toll resulting mainly from police intervention, the protesters did not proactively engage in violent conduct. The non-violent character of the Gezi protest provided a strategic advantage for the activists. The excessive use of force by the police forces backfired and increased support for the protest (Stephan & Chenoweth, 2008), also evidenced by the finding that one out of every two protesters decided to participate in the protests after seeing police brutality as opposed to a peaceful resistance for not giving away the Park (Konda Research, 2014).

A second strategy was encouraging diversity, solidarity, and collective action as components of democracy. Gezi protests brought together individuals and groups such as leftists, LGBTI individuals, Muslims, soccer fans, nationalists, and secular republicans, who hitherto were not interacting. The participant groups were able to combine their different political or social viewpoints in a relatively coherent manner, constructing "collective action frames" (Benford & Snow, 1992). This strategy also led to the Government's attempts to attach various negative attributes to the protesters (e.g., "non-national," "non-believer") to backfire.

> After Gezi, we met the other half of Turkey, we met with people from different political backgrounds. Since then, our mutual relations have been developing, and getting deeper.
>
> (Interviewee 09)

Interviewee 02 emphasized how the protest was nourished through mutual acceptance and tolerance:

> When I recall Gezi, I remember how people refrained from alcoholic drinks during religious prayers, how we refrained from common phrases of swearing in respect for LGBTI individuals, how everyone tried to use a less sexist language, and how all this projected an inclusive model of co-existence to the society at large.

As a third communication strategy – in harmony with the strategy of non-violence (Sørensen, 2016), the protesters of Gezi adopted "humorous framing" (Hart, 2007), against the serious and authoritarian rhetoric of the Government. The slogans, mottos, symbols, and tactics of the Gezi protest, as well as the tone of voice of the protest in general, was mainly humorous in character. This strategy created an alternative language that facilitated message delivery (Emre et al., 2014), resulting in empathy and support toward the protesters (Branagan, 2007), expressed by Interviewee 12 as follows:

> We were criticizing the divisive and authoritarian language of the Government in a satirical way, translating their repressive expressions and attitudes to a language of humor. This way, everyone out there who had trouble with Government authority felt closer to us.

The protesters at Gezi Park emphasized and underlined dialogue as a fourth communication strategy. Through encouraging dialogue between the diverse groups that participated in the protest, as well as between the protesters and the Government authorities, they were able to (1) formulate a common context to define the issues they promoted (Gutiérrez-García et al., 2015), and (2) propose the inclusion of different viewpoints in resolving social issues. In doing this, the protesters gave the message that understanding different positions and including all parties affected in relevant decisions (Kent & Taylor, 2002) were significant components of democratic processes:

> Inclusion of different points of view enabled groups that are considered somewhat "marginal" to expose themselves. Different groups and individuals had different social visions, and they were encouraged to communicate those openly in the public arena.
>
> (Interviewee 03)

Although unplanned, improvisational and reactive in character, these strategies, along with the connected tactics detailed below, resulted in public support. A barometer survey conducted right after the protesters were deported out of Gezi Park found that two out of every five respondents thought the protesters acted in a democratic manner, and criticized the police forces and the Government for resorting to violence (Konda Research, 2014).

Media tactics

Current ownership patterns in Turkish media date back to early 1980s. Since then as Farmanfarmaian et al. (2018) state:

> Media's symbolic social positioning has been corporate silo-ing, with conglomerate ownership concentrating mass media into the hands of elites ideationally close to the government and who broadly benefit from the status this brings.
>
> (p. 3)

In the early years of AKP's government, there was an observable tension between media elites who aligned with traditional policy elites and the ruling party (Saka, 2009), but as the AKP government under the leadership of Erdoğan settled into power, corporate media structure was shaped to align itself with the new elites. Legal, bureaucratic and financial regulations were imposed effectively to ensure this alignment as corporations that owned media institutions were keen to protect their primary investments in banking, energy, automotive, and construction sectors (Akin & Dogu, 2017). This process of alignment would lead to Doğan Group's retreat from media businesses in early 2018. As pro-government *Demirören* took over "*Hurriyet*, Turkey's most influential newspaper; *Posta*, the most important tabloid; and *CNN Turk*, the last reputable news television station" (Hermann, 2018, March 23), virtually all mainstream media channels would become pro-government.

Although the mainstream media was not totally consolidated as explained above at the time of the Gezi protests, the national media outlets largely neglected the social mobility of protestors. As an ironic example, *CNN TURK*, one of the most followed news channels in Turkey, broadcasted a documentary on penguins on the night of June 2, instead of reporting on the Gezi Park protests. In order to circumvent mainstream media censorship, and to create a dialogue possibility with various stakeholders, a group of activists inside the Park regularly streamed online and named their channel *Çapul TV* after what Prime Minister Erdoğan accused protesters of: "being looters/vandals" (*Çapulcu* in Turkish). Interviewee 06 also described the censorship and *Çapul TV* as:

> During the protest, there was no direct mainstream broadcasting of people living in the park. Due to censorship, protesters had no chance to speak while government officials could continuously comment on

Gezi. This was the starting point of our TV. We wanted to reach out to the public and to create a dialogue environment.

Creating dialogue platforms and mechanisms with various publics, once again, was one of the key strategies of protesters in media relations. As none of mainstream TV channels broadcasted about the protests and few of them sent reporters to create coverage, the protesters used *Çapul TV* to publicize their views and generate a great volume of alternative media coverage. Even though *Çapul TV* was only a web-streaming channel, it attracted national and international media outlets' attention by providing video coverage and effectively shattered mainstream media's silence on protests. Interviewee 06 stated how other media outlets contacted with *Çapul TV* as a news source:

> Since the very first day of our streaming, international media organizations started communicating with us. Our news was also used by the Turkish mainstream media later on. Our reports could be freely used, provided that the source was acknowledged. As Gezi became serious, the mainstream media even came to broadcast us live. We were pleased with that.

As seen, the protestors produced their official "media agency" in the Park, through which they opened up a dialogue channel. Besides reporting on what was actually going on, *Çapul TV* also broadcasted interviews with NGO leaders or individual protesters. Additionally, press releases and press statements, as fundamental texts of public relations, were regularly issued by the Taksim Solidarity through press meetings and via social media accounts, and then used as sources of information by other media outlets. Furthermore, some of our interviewees also mentioned that they had been interviewed by the correspondents from international media outlets.

Performances, plays, and collective acts

According to McKie and Xifra (2015), the activist groups use PR strategies and tactics to achieve their goals (p. 353). Boycotts, demonstrations or rallies as the tactics of activist groups can provoke the public attention through dramatization (Smith & Ferguson, 2010, p. 396). For Sommerfeldt, these activities are "directed at swaying a 'largely indifferent public' who are uninformed about a particular issue" (2012, p. 287). By considering this, the Gezi protesters also organized creative public performances, plays and collective acts to grab the attention of the public (see Table 8.1). For instance, protesters confiscated a construction vehicle to chase a police intervention vehicle, and formed a human chain around Taksim Square to shield the square and the people from police intervention. In response to Istanbul's Governor Hüseyin Avni Mutlu's call for the mothers of Gezi Park protesters to "bring their children home," many mothers instead chose to join their children at the demonstration, forming a "support chain." Another memorable instance came on the eve of Mi'raj, which marks Prophet Muhammad's ascent to heaven: Protesters of secular origin refrained from alcohol and joined in the group prayer led by the Anti-Capitalist Muslims group. This solidarity continued with support for Friday prayers on June 7 and 14. Interviewee 03 described how they attracted the attention of the media during Friday prayers:

> As the Friday prayer was in the daytime, therefore eye-catching, hundreds of journalists came by to observe religious and secular people side by side, praying. After that, our Friday prayers became a media story.

Just as this statement clearly shows how activities in and around the Park captivated the attention of various publics during the protests, it also indicates the creative aspects of the tactics, which were collectively coordinated and organized by protesters. This is also parallel with Harrebye's (2016, p. 25) ideas about creative activism, described as a sort of meta-activism that expedites the strategic and transformative involvement of citizens to galvanize public attention. For him, this is an attempt to revisit the political imagination of modern citizens. When considered through the PR perspective, these tactics that were also based on humorous framing, dialogue, and encouraging solidarity strategies, were of news value for the national and international media outlets as well as various social media platforms. They provided protesters with substantial media coverage in both traditional and digital media. Furthermore, our observations lead us to the conclusion that the humorous and creative characteristics of surprising activities facilitated the involvement of people outside the park.

Table 8.1 illustrates how tactics were located within the strategies described in the previous section. This table does not exhaust all the tactics deployed in protests but provides a credible representation.

Conclusion

In today's world, social movements have critical roles in balancing the power relations in the public sphere. During these, the protestors use a wide array of strategies and tactics in order to attract the attention of various publics. In this sense, the critical public relations literature allows us to consider social movements from a communicational point of view. According to our study, the main aim of the Gezi Park protestors was to save the trees in the park and react against the increasing authoritarianism in Turkey. These aims structured the creativity through which they reflected and acted. In this regard, park forums were the spaces where the communal spirit was born, and provided a collective energy that enabled the realization of protest PR strategies and practices.

Table 8.1 Strategies and tactics of Gezi protesters

Strategies		Tactics	
		One-off events and actions	*Recurrent acts and events*
• Dialogue • Encouragement of diversity, solidarity and collective action			• Forum discussions • Promotional stands of various social groups • Library
• Dialogue • "Humorous framing"	**Media tactics**		• Çapul TV • Gezi Post • Press releases by Taksim Solidarity • Interaction with international reporters
• Encouragement of diversity, solidarity, and collective action • Non-violence	**Performances and plays**	• Piano concert • "Standing Man" protests • Confiscation of construction vehicle	• Morning yoga workshops • Art performances • The "Museum" of Gezi • Art activities for the children
• "Humorous framing" • Non-violence • Encouragement of diversity, solidarity and collective action	**Collective acts**	• Çarşı Fan Group March • Mothers' support chain • Unarmed human chain • İstanbul United • Friday prayers • Mi'raj prayer	• Erasing gender-biased slogans • Refraining from common swearing language • Embracing religious values

In line with their communicational social aims, the activists from a wide political spectrum launched many disparate and at times overlapping communication strategies and tactics. Our chapter demonstrates that the strategies emphasizing non-violence, collective-action, witty humor, and dialogue contributed to an overall empathy toward the protestors. Additionally, our interviewees indicated that these strategies were at the core of the various tactics directed at protesting the increasing authoritarianism in Turkey.

In addition to this strategic point of view, the protestors employed several PR tactics consistent with their collective strategies and aims, to convey their messages. Nearly all interviewees saw these activities as catalysts for their communal solidarity, as well as tools that physically or metaphorically allowed the involvement of various publics in the protests. When secular protestors joined in the Friday prayer, they underlined the possibility of co-existence of differences. When mothers came down to Gezi Park and joined their children, they emphasized the power of inter-generational solidarity. When participant groups refrained from using their symbols and flags, they highlighted the prospect of reconciliation among differences. Therefore, while the protestors were occupying the park, their actions also symbolically occupied the democratic imaginaries of Turkish people from different geographies, generations or social classes.

In this chapter, we argue that the popularity and relative political success of these protests can better be understood through a close reading of these strategies and tactics from a protest PR perspective. On the one hand, these made possible an assemblage of seemingly irreconcilable ideological groups and currents against a strong government. On the other hand, it is this assemblage that made it possible to reach broader sections of society and larger audiences both in Turkey and in the world. We argue that the successful performance of PR techniques has greatly contributed to the visibility, impact and outcome of these protests.

In this sense, the Gezi Park protests and our experience of research, have a contribution beyond highlighting the organic adoption of communication tactics by protesters. This chapter adds to the discussion of conceptualizing the protesters of Gezi as subaltern counter publics (Fraser, 1990), and indicates that the exploration of whether the protests were successful to introduce their points of view to the public agenda in the long run is needed (Sommerfeldt, 2013). Future research could therefore investigate how Gezi Park and Taksim Square as protest sites have influenced the strategies and tactics of the protesters (Feigenbaum et al., 2013), through considering both the physical and symbolic characteristics of the protest space. Finally, our exploration of the Gezi protests from a public relations perspective could also contribute to an enhanced definition of the field as assessed by Edwards (2012). Edwards' elaboration of public relations as a purposeful communication process to promote and strengthen individual, organizational or group agendas has the potential to encourage other studies on the communication practices of relatively informal groups in Turkey, such as local environmentalists, sports fans, and animal rights advocates.

Notes

1　AKP, defining itself as a conservative political party, was founded by Recep Tayyip Erdoğan, current President of Turkey and the former mayor of Istanbul between the years of 1994 and 1998. During Gezi protests, Erdoğan was the Prime Minister.
2　Voters endorsed modifications to Turkey's then current constitution, making the military more accountable to civilian courts and giving the 550-seat Grand National Assembly more power to appoint judges.

3 This report shows that around 90 percent of all the Gezi Park related tweets were posted in Turkey and 50 percent of them were posted in İstanbul. During the Arab Spring, only about 30 percent of people tweeting had come from Egypt. Morozov (2012) implied that most of the uprisings with a strong social media based media relations originated from the US and its foreign affairs plans. He had particularly mentioned the Iranian Presidential Election Protests in 2009. Social Media performance in Gezi Park protests challenges this argument.

4 The "January 24" plan, designed by then Finance Minister and later Prime Minister and President Turgut Ozal, introduced an outward looking approach, shifting the whole focus of the Turkish economy. Ozal's policies included liberalizing foreign trade, streamlining and privatizing state run industries, devaluing the currency, removing price controls and reducing the budget deficit by eliminating government dominance in state run businesses.

5 An ongoing Wiki project aims to collect this archival data: geziarchive.wiki spaces.com.

List of interviewees

- Interviewee 01 – An NGO professional specialized in LGBTI rights and social justice. She was the coordinator of LGBTI and Feminist groups in the Park. Face-to-face. Istanbul, 2017 June.
- Interviewee 02 – One of the core members of Çarşı fan group. He participated the Gezi Park Protests with Çarşı fan group. Face-to-face. Istanbul, 2017 September.
- Interviewee 03 – One of the leaders of Anti-Capitalist Muslims, and an author who works on Islamic theology. He was the coordinator of Anti-Capitalist Muslims during the protests. Face-to-face. Istanbul, 2017 August.
- Interviewee 04 – He is a journalist. He closely followed the Gezi Park protests from the very first day. Face-to-Face. Istanbul, 2018 January.
- Interviewee 05 – A doctor who was responsible for coordinating the issues between different infirmaries in Gezi Park. Face-to-face. Istanbul, 2018 January.
- Interviewee 06 – A journalist who was responsible for the broadcasting of *Çapul TV*. Face-to-Face. Istanbul, 2017 December.
- Interviewee 07 – A professional LGBTI activist. She was one of the coordinators of LGBTI group during Gezi Protests. Face-to-Face. Istanbul, 2018 January.
- Interviewee 08 – He is a journalist. He closely followed the Gezi Park protests from the very first day. Face-to-Face. Istanbul, 2018 January.
- Interviewee 09 – A yoga instructor. She organized the morning yoga sessions in the Park. Face-to-Face, 2017 June.
- Interviewee 10 – A doctor in infirmary who was responsible for treating the protestors. Face-to-Face. Istanbul, 2017 June.
- Interviewee 11 – A member of Çarşı fan group. Face-to-face. Istanbul, 2018 January.
- Interviewee 12 – An active protester who stayed in the Park all through the events. Face-to-face. Istanbul, 2018.

References

Akin, A. & Dogu, B. (2017). NGOs in Turkey's media field: Causes, sources and potentials for development. *Markets, Globalization & Development Review*, 2(2). doi:10.23860/mgdr-2017-02-02-05.

Arda, B. (2015). The construction of a new sociality through social media: The case of the Gezi uprising in Turkey. *Conjunctions. Transdisciplinary Journal of Cultural Participation, 2*(1), 72. doi:10.7146/tjcp.v2i1.22271.

Barberá, P. & Metzger, M. (2013). *A breakout role for Twitter? The role of social media in the Turkish protests* (Rep.). Social media and political participation lab data report.

Benford, R. D. & Snow, D. A. (2000). Framing processes and social movements: An overview and assessment. *Annual Review of Sociology, 26*(1), 611–639. doi:10.1146/annurev.soc.26.1.611.

Branagan, M. (2007). The last laugh: Humor in community activism. *Community Development Journal, 42*(4), 470–481. doi:10.1093/cdj/bsm037.

Brown, R. E. (2006). Myth of symmetry: Public relations as cultural styles. *Public Relations Review, 32*(3), 206–212. doi:10.1016/j.pubrev.2006.05.022.

Chrona, S. & Bee, C. (2017). Right to public space and right to democracy: The role of social media in Gezi Park. *Research and Policy on Turkey, 2*(1), 49–61. doi:10.1080/23760818.2016.1272267.

Cohen, M. A. (1996). Habitat II: A critical assessment. *Environmental Impact Assessment Review, 16*(4–6), 429–433. doi:10.1016/s0195-9255(96)00076-5.

Demetrious, K. (2006). Active voices. In *Public relations: Critical debates and contemporary practice* (pp. 93–107). Mahwah, NJ: Lawrence Erlbaum Associates.

Demirhan, K. (2014). Social media effects on the Gezi Park movement in Turkey: Politics under hashtags. *Social Media in Politics*, 281–314. doi:10.1007/978-3-319-04666-2_16.

Diani, M. (1992). The concept of social movement. *The Sociological Review, 40*(1), 1–25. doi:10.1111/j.1467-954x.1992.tb02943.x.

Edwards, L. (2012). Defining the "object" of public relations research: A new starting point. *Public Relations Inquiry, 1*(1), 7–30. doi:10.1177/2046147x11422149.

Edwards, L. (2018). *Understanding public relations: Theory, culture and society.* Los Angeles, CA: SAGE.

Emre, P. Ö., Çoban, B., & Şener, G. (2014). Humorous form of protest: Disproportionate use of intelligence in Gezi Park's resistance. In E. Zeynep Guler (Ed.) *New Opportunities and Impasses: Theorizing and experiencing politics* (pp. 430–447) Istanbul: Dakam Publishing.

Erdoğan, I. (2014). *Teori ve pratikte halkla ilişkiler.* Ankara: Erk Yayınları.

Farmanfarmaian, R., Sonay, A., & Akser, M. (2018). The Turkish media structure in judicial and political context: An illustration of values and status negotiation. *Middle East Critique, 27*(2), 111–125. doi:10.1080/19436149.2018.1447773.

Feigenbaum, A., Frenzel, F., & McCurdy, P. (2013). *Protest camps.* London: Zed Books.

Frandsen, F. & Johansen, W. (2015). Organizations, stakeholders, and intermediaries: Towards a general theory. *International Journal of Strategic Communication, 9*(4), 253–271. doi:10.1080/1553118x.2015.1064125.

Fraser, N. (1990). Rethinking the public sphere: A contribution to the critique of actually existing democracy. *Social Text, 25/26*, 56. doi:10.2307/466240.

Göle, N. (2013). Gezi – Anatomy of a public square movement. *Insight Turkey, 15*(3), 7–14.

Gutiérrez-García, E., Recalde, M., & Piñera-Camacho, A. (2015). Reinventing the wheel? A comparative overview of the concept of dialogue. *Public Relations Review, 41*(5), 744–753. doi:10.1016/j.pubrev.2015.06.006.

Hapiste Saglik. (2013). *Gezi parkı direnişinde kaybettiklerimiz, 12 kişi*. Retrieved from https://hapistesaglik.com/2013/06/16/eylemde-saglik-gezi-parki-direnisinde-olenler/ (Accessed April 27, 2018).

Harrebye, S. F. (2016). *Social change and creative activism in the 21st century: The mirror effect*. Houndmills, Basingstoke, Hampshire: Palgrave Macmillan.

Hart, M. T. (2007). Humor and social protest: An introduction. *International Review of Social History*, *52*(S15), 1–20. doi:10.1017/s0020859007003094.

Hermann, R. (2018, March 23). Opinion: Turkey's media now have a single owner | DW | 23.03.2018. Retrieved May 8, 2018, from www.dw.com/en/opinion-turkeys-media-now-have-a-single-owner/a-43102278.

Holtzhausen, D. R. (2000). Postmodern values in public relations. *Journal of Public Relations Research*, *12*(1), 93–114. doi:10.1207/s1532754xjprr1201_6. www.metropoll.com.tr/arastirmalar/siyasi-arastirma-9/1731 (Accessed May 2, 2018).

Jahng, M. R., Hong, S., & Park, E. H. (2014). How radical is radical?: Understanding the role of activists' communication strategies on the formation of public attitude and evaluation. *Public Relations Review*, *40*(1), 119–121. doi:10.1016/j.pubrev.2013.11.004.

Kalender, A. (2013). Kavram olarak halkla ilişkiler, dünyada ve Türkiye'de halkla ilişkilerin tarihsel gelişimi. *Halkla İlişkiler*, 2–30. Anadolu Üniversitesi AÖF Yayınları.

Kent, M. L. & Taylor, M. (2002). Toward a dialogic theory of public relations. *Public Relations Review*, *28*(1), 21–37. doi:10.1016/s0363-8111(02)00108-x.

Keyman, E. F. (2014). The AK Party: Dominant party, new Turkey and polarization. *Insight Turkey*, *16*(2), 19–31.

Keyman, E. F. & Icduygu, A. (2003). Globalization, civil society and citizenship in Turkey: Actors, boundaries and discourses. *Citizenship Studies*, *7*(2), 219–234. doi:10.1080/1362102032000065982.

Konda Research. (2014). *Gezi Report: Public perception of the "Gezi protests." Who were the people at Gezi Park?* Available at http://konda.com.tr/wp-content/uploads/2017/03/KONDA_Gezi_Report.pdf (accessed February 12, 2018).

L'Etang, J. (2013). *Public relations in Britain: A history of professional practice in the twentieth century*. London: Routledge.

L'Etang, J. (2015). History as a source of critique: Historicity and knowledge, societal change, activism and movements. *The Routledge handbook of critical public relations* (pp. 52–64). New York: Routledge.

L'Etang, J. & Pieczka, M. (2006). *Public relations: Critical debates and contemporary practice*. Mahwah, NJ: Lawrence Erlbaum Associates.

Malone, T. W. & Bernstein, M. S. (2015). *Handbook of collective intelligence*. Cambridge, United States: The MIT Press.

McKie, D. & Xifra, J. (2015). Expanding critical space: Public intellectuals, public relations, and an "outsider" contribution. *The Routledge handbook of critical public relations* (pp. 349–359). New York: Routledge.

McLeod, M. L. (2014). People power PR: Recasting activists as practitioners. Paper presented to *The European Conference on Media & Mass Communication*. Retrieved from http://iafor.info/archives/offprints/euromedia2014-offprints/Euro Media2014_2493.pdf (accessed May 2, 2018).

MetroPOLL Strategic and Social Research. (2013, June). *Türkiye'nin Nabzı: Gezi Parkı Protestoları ve Türkiye'nin Otoriterleşme-Özgürlük Sorunu*. Retrieved from www.metropoll.com.tr/arastirmalar/siyasi-arastirma-9/1731 (accessed May 1, 2018).

Moloney, K. & McKie, D. (2015). Changes to be encouraged. Radical turns in PR theorization and small-step evolutions in PR practice. *The Routledge critical handbook of public relations* (pp. 151–161). New York: Routledge.

Moloney, K., McQueen, D., Surowiec, P., & Yaxley, H. (2013, March). *Dissent and public relations seminar series*. Retrieved May 8, 2018, from https://microsites.bournemouth.ac.uk/cmc/files/2013/10/Dissent-and-public-relations-Bournemouth-University.pdf.

Morozov, E. (2012). *The net delusion: The dark side of internet freedom.* New York: PublicAffairs.

Ogan, C. & Varol, O. (2016). What is gained and what is left to be done when content analysis is added to network analysis in the study of a social movement: Twitter use during Gezi Park. *Information, Communication & Society, 20*(8), 1220–1238. doi:10.1080/1369118x.2016.1229006.

Özkırımlı, U. (2014). *The making of a protest movement in Turkey: #occupygezi.* Houndmills, Basingstoke, Hampshire: Palgrave Macmillan.

Özyaşar, F. & Aydın, D. (2014). Saving the internet via the internet. In *Media, power and empowerment: Central and Eastern European communication and media conference CEECOM Prague 2012* (pp. 92–97). Newcastle: Cambridge Scholars Publishing.

Patton, M. J. (2007). AKP reform fatigue in Turkey: What has happened to the EU process? *Mediterranean Politics, 12*(3), 339–358. doi:10.1080/13629390701622382.

Pearce, S. C. (2013). Pride in Istanbul. *Societies without Borders, 11*(9), 111–128.

Saka, E. (2009). *Mediating the EU: Deciphering the transformation of Turkish elites* (Unpublished doctoral dissertation). Thesis/Dissertation ETD.

Saka, E. (2017a). The role of social media-based citizen journalism practices in the formation of contemporary protest movements. In *Rethinking ideology in the age of global discontent. Bridging divides* (pp. 48–66). New York: Routledge.

Saka, E. (2017b). Tracking digital emergences in the aftermath of Gezi Park protests. *Research and Policy on Turkey, 2*(1), 62–75. doi:10.1080/23760818.2016.1272268.

Saka, E. (2018). Social media in Turkey as a space for political battles: AKTrolls and other politically motivated trolling. *Middle East Critique, 27*(2), 161–177. doi:10.1080/19436149.2018.1439271.

Sezer, T., Sever, B., Arslan, B., & Arslan, E. (2014). Taksim Gezi Park protests: Public sphere and new media (Turkish, English, American, French and German Press Sample). In *12th International Communication in the Millennium Symposium, Anadolu University, Eskişehir*. Retrieved from www.researchgate.net/publication/272163460.

Smith, M. F. & Ferguson, D. P. (2010). Activism 2.0. In R.L. Heath (Ed.), *The SAGE handbook of public relations* (pp. 395–408). Thousand Oaks, CA: SAGE Publishing.

Sommerfeldt, E. J. (2012). The dynamics of activist power relationships: A structurationist exploration of the segmentation of activist publics. *International Journal of Strategic Communication, 6*(4), 269–286. doi:10.1080/1553118x.2012.686256.

Sommerfeldt, E. J. (2013). Online power resource management: Activist resource mobilization, communication strategy, and organizational structure. *Journal of Public Relations Research*, 25(4), 347–367. doi:10.1080/1062726x.2013.806871.

Sørensen, M. J. (2016). *Humor in political activism: Creative nonviolent resistance*. London: Palgrave Macmillan.

Sriramesh, K. & Verčič, D. (2003). *The global public relations handbook: Theory, research, and practice*. Mahwah, NJ: Lawrence Erlbaum.

Stephan, M. J. & Chenoweth, E. (2008). Why civil resistance works: The strategic logic of nonviolent conflict. *International Security*, 33(1), 7–44.

Taylor, R. R., Jason, L. A., Keys, C. B., Suarez-Balcazar, Y., Davis, M. I., Durlak, J. A., & Isenberg, D. H. (2004). Introduction: Capturing theory and methodology in participatory research. *Participatory community research: Theories and methods in action* (pp. 3–14). Washinton DC: American Psychological Association.

Thomas, E. F. & Louis, W. R. (2013). When will collective action be effective? Violent and non-violent protests differentially influence perceptions of legitimacy and efficacy among sympathizers. *Personality and Social Psychology Bulletin*, 40(2), 263–276. doi:10.1177/0146167213510525.

Tufekci, Z. (2014). Social movements and governments in the digital age: Evaluating a complex landscape. *Journal of International Affairs*, 68(1), 1–18.

Warner, M. (2002). Publics and counterpublics. *Public Culture*, 14(1), 49–90.

Yamanoğlu, M. A., Hızal, G. S., & Özdemir, B. P. (2013). *Türkiye'de Halkla İlişkiler Tarihi: Kurumsallaşma Yılları 1960–1980*. İstanbul: De Ki Basım Yayım.

Yıldırım, U. & Navaro-Yashin, Y. (2013, October 31). An impromptu uprising: ethnographic reflections on the Gezi Park protests in Turkey. Retrieved from https://culanth.org/fieldsights/391-an-impromptu-uprising-ethnographic-reflections-on-the-gezi-park-.

Zerfass, A., Ruler, B. V., & Sriramesh, K. (2008). *Public relations research: European and international perspectives and innovations*. Wiesbaden: VS Verlag für Sozialwissenschaften.

Zimbardo, P. G. (1970). *A social-psychological analysis of vandalism: Making sense out of senseless violence* (1–13, Tech.). National Technical Information Service.

9 Archiving activism and/as activist PR

Occupy Wall Street and the politics of influence

Kylie Message

Introduction: archiving and activism

This chapter examines the activities of the Occupy Archives Working Group, which was one of more than a hundred working groups that existed within and contributed to the 2011 Occupy Wall Street movement that occurred in New York's Zuccotti Park (renamed Liberty Plaza) throughout the period September 17 to November 15, 2011.[1] The remit of the Archives working group was, in the words of co-founder, Amy Roberts, to "ensure that the OWS will own its past. Its mission is to keep OWS historically self-conscious, and guarantee that our history will be accessible to the public" (Roberts, 2011a). Based on recognition that the collections and archives created during a particular action or event as a representation that communicate a particular version of that event, the working group's mission was consistent with Occupy Wall Street's fundamental aim to assert control over their image and the way their image would be used into the future. Indeed, the group's outlook exemplified the shift that was described by journalist, Sarah van Gelder:

> The 99% are no longer sitting on the sidelines of history – we are making history ... The Occupy Wall Street Movement is not just demanding change. It is also transforming how we, the 99%, see ourselves.
>
> (van Gelder, 2011, pp. 11–12)

And yet, while no one could credibly argue that the material culture expressions of protest – the pizza-box signs, messages on placards, t-shirt slogans, artworks and ephemera created by protestors – was not intended to exist as a form of activist PR, the collection of these materials by the Archives working group was not widely supported within the movement. This meant that the activities of the Archives working group, which were based on the premise that their collections and archives are significant forms of self-representation, have not been considered in relation to Occupy's interest in authoring its own history. This chapter seeks to address this oversight, by arguing that the working group's agenda for archiving the movement was a strategic form of activist public relations that targeted two target groups – an external public that would engage with a resultant collection of materials representing Occupy, and internal communities of Occupy activist peers. Discussion of the strategies used to communicate with each of these target groups reveals a disjunct between the Occupy Movement's concern with image control on the one hand, and its suspicion, on the other hand, of the process of self-archiving that was being undertaken by the Occupy Archives Working Group.

This chapter starts from the premise that activist PR is a process of stakeholder management, that Coombs and Holladay (2010, p. 4) call "the management of mutually influential relationships within a web of constituency relationships." While members of the Archives working group did not explicitly articulate their role in public relations terms (a phrase often associated with corporate interest), they were motivated by the intention to maintain control over the way the movement was preserved and subsequently used in collections held by archives, museums, and other repositories. For example, in contrast to the expectation that processes of documentation generate a neutral and objective recording of the "truth" of any event for historical purposes, the Archives working group sought to contribute a form of direct participant action to the movement rather than an objective documentation of it. Their belief that activist archiving could be a manifestation of the social movement guided their pragmatic approach to building a collection that would exist as both a record of, and legacy for, the movement, on the movement's own terms.

However, this attention to creating an image for general (non-Occupy aligned) public consumption was supplemented by the task of making a case to Occupy for internal support of the archive. In other words, although their approach to activism was consistent with Moloney's (2005) argument that a fundamental premise of advocacy is the endeavor to alter the behaviors of others, where "others" are usually defined as a mainstream "general public" and its government offices and representatives (including city, state and national museums and collecting institutions), the target of their internal public relations strategy was a constituent group of peers that included the New York City General Assembly (the primary decision-making forum at Occupy Wall Street). Persuading the General Assembly required "sustained strategic attempts to influence relationships" (Coombs and Holladay, 2012, p. 348), and typically took the approach of educating members about the role that archives can play as an activist-oriented public relation strategy.

The process of communication and strategic relationship building within the internal constituency networks of Occupy Wall Street is valuable to a discussion about activist PR because the long-term preservation of the collection was perceived as being contingent upon funding and approval by the General Assembly. Without this it could not exist, and the legacy of the movement would be left for others to represent.[2] Although collections and archives are widely recognized as representational forms of authority that have historically been associated with propaganda and selective (often governmental) frameworks and agendas (Bennett, 2015), they have not been considered in the context of public relations strategies, or the field of literature that now exists to analyze this form of communication (Coombs and Holladay, 2010; L'Etang, 2016). However, contemporary collections-based research is characterized by an increasing emphasis on relationship building and stakeholder management that is also at the heart of critical literature around activist public relations (Flinn and Alexander, 2015; Message 2018). This chapter brings the stakeholder and constituent focus of scholarship into dialogue with activist public relations and community and agenda-based collections to examine the ways in which the collections and archives created by the Archives working group worked both for and against the Occupy Movement. The first section of the chapter explores how the material collected by the Archives group contributed to Occupy's goal of maintaining authority over its image. I show that the collections provided a positive form of public relations that communicated directly with a general audience who would otherwise become familiar with representations of Occupy authored by staff of public museums, libraries and archives that were also acquiring materials from the site. The second section examines the more complex internal public relations strategies that occurred between the Archives group and the General Assembly.

Authority over image: "external" activism

> Occupy Wall Street Archives Working Group is a collecting initiative, which preserves, safeguards, and makes accessible the records of OWS. It is the repository of the legacy that we will leave for the future generations. Occupy Wall Street Archives Working Group collects ephemera, signs, posters, audiovisual materials, digital files, photographs, oral histories, and artifacts. It stands as evidence of how participatory democracy can work, how culture and politics connect, and how the 99% can come together to generate social and economic change.
>
> (Roberts, 2011a)

The Occupy Archives Working Group created collections that would preserve the continued authority of Occupy Wall Street over its image and legacy. Much of the material culture that was collected was the typical residue of protest that had been created as a form of activist PR to persuade non-Occupy audiences of the legitimacy of their claims. In addition to oral histories and audio-visual records, it included material that was widely represented in news media reporting, was collected by other public museums, libraries and libraries from the US and elsewhere, swept up by Sanitation services for disposal, and/or confiscated by police. Collecting approaches by working group members typically took the form of salvaging material from the site, an exercise that often had to be conducted rapidly. Roberts argued that a broad and multi-focused approach to collecting was appropriate for reflecting the current mood of people within the movement:

> As you know there was a raid on the occupation that started at 1:00 am on Tuesday morning. Fortunately, our archival material was stored offsite. There were many things that we wanted to collect that were destroyed however. That is of course because almost everything was destroyed including the library. I think this highlights the importance of the oral history project. People have been allowed back in the park but not to set up tents or tarps. People are still making signs and I think it is important that we collect these as they reflect people's moods and thoughts about the latest developments.
>
> (Roberts, 2011b)

This approach to collection led working group members (and the broader Occupy movement) to debate the value of archiving material that was ephemeral, often damaged, usually impossible to ascribe authorship for, and difficult at that time to assess as being either representative or unique (a conversation about value attribution that was occurring in external archiving communities as well). There were further concerns that without financial support provided directly by Occupy or through an affiliation with a partner institution, the archives could not be sustained over the long-term, even if they could be established in the first instance. Some members argued in favor of a digital archive over a material one as one way of counteracting the precarious situation they were in (noting this instability was counterproductive to the security an archival repository is supposed to provide).

Many of the typical materials collected, including protest signs, banners and other ephemera are also commonly found in "protest and reform" collections in established museums (including the National Museum of American History in Washington DC and the Museum of the City of New York), libraries (such as the New York Public Library), and archives (the most relevant here is the Tamiment Library and Robert F. Wagner Labor Archives). However, a closer look at the group's mission statement and collections (as described in the statements above) demonstrates an explicit rejection of attempts to "glamorize activism" (which, along with nostalgia, is a characteristic that is often present in larger public collections). In contrast with the highly curated collections of established collecting institutions, the working group's grassroots approach to collecting reinforced the importance of inclusion, and attributing authority to creators and those involved in the movement. This approach showed the falsity of assumptions that activism "is necessarily a homogeneous category" (L'Etang,

2016, p. 207). The group's multifarious approach to collections development also reflected a shift away from perceptions that the student protest movements and social critiques of the 1960s and 1970s contributed to the formation of fixed identities where conservative corporate sponsored PR was defined against radical societal critiques (Coombs and Holladay, 2012). Not only does this dichotomy erroneously pigeonhole activist PR as something defined categorically as that which corporate and government PR is not, it also represents activist PR as a homogenous and singular set of approaches dedicated to progressing an uncontested mission, which it was not.

Rejecting the assumptions and dichotomy that have typically defined activism (and what it is not) opens the way for a new consideration of who the working group's target audience actually was. This approach allows us to suggest that the public-facing collections, which offer a self-representational image of Occupy (as a mainstream-oriented public relation strategy for the movement) are, in fact, less significant than the collections (primarily of documentation, correspondences, records of decision-making and the like) that sought to function as a form of PR generated by activists *for* activists. Rather than representing the disposable products of the movement (signs, banners, and so on and so forth), these collections typically include material that document the experience of living at or contributing to the Occupy movement from the perspective of "insiders." Although much less "glamorous" than the collections of signs, posters, and t-shirts, these collections provide materials related to an "ethnography of infrastructure" that was created as part of the attempt to maintain accountability for and on behalf of the movement.[3]

There were two reasons the collection sought to develop a public relations strategy targeting an ("insider") activist stakeholder group. The first was functional. It sought to provide an open educational resource that could be actively used by other protest movements – such that, for example, placards could be subsequently borrowed, re-used, and returned to the archive (Evans, Perricci, and Roberts, 2014). The second reason was ideological, and related to the working group's commitment to producing a record of internal interactions within Occupy Wall Street that would contribute to continuing accountability within the movement. The collections were, in summary, designed as communication strategies that would advocate for and maintain authority over the image of Occupy. Although they targeted different constituent groups – an external "public" on the one hand, and other activist groups, on the other hand – this comparison shows that they shared the concern with maintaining control over the movement's messages in the short term (representation in current exhibitions and media) and long term (re-use by other activists).

Accountability: internal activism

Stakeholder management and persuasion can also be an internal process, and it was critically important that the Archives working group was able to persuade the General Assembly of the value of the historical record that they were building. It was not, in their view, enough for the movement to hold corporations and government institutions (including museums, libraries and archives) to account. The movement had to itself be accountable for its decisions and actions. Recognizing that they could not possibly capture everything produced within Liberty Plaza, Jeremy Bold, who co-founded the group with Roberts, asked: "What better way to make the archive accountable to the people than to make the people accountable for the archive?" Everyone in the movement, he argued, "should be responsible for thinking historically" (quoted in Samtani, 2011, p. 2).[4] This position was reflected in the second clause of the working group's mission statement:

> Occupy Wall Street Archives Working Group also documents the decision making processes of OWS, of the General Assembly, Coordinators, Think Tank, and Occupiers' meetings, as well as the records of the other subgroups. It guarantees that OWS remain a transparent movement. It ensures the accountability of OWS by documenting our ideas, ideals, strategies, structure, tactics, politics, and culture of OWS and the ways it has helped reshape the political discourse in New York, the nation, and the world.
>
> (Roberts, 2011a)

The group's potential value in terms of keeping other members of the movement accountable (through its production of a collectively authored ethnography of infrastructure) was acknowledged by some other working groups, and frequent discussions within the working group identified the value of retaining meeting notes and minutes as a way of promoting working group transparency in addition to keeping an internal record of decision-making processes for the benefit of future social movements and researchers (Organizational documents – Archives working group, 2011–2012).

However, there remained a lingering perception that a conflict of interest existed between the group's contribution to transparency and its collaboration with external collecting institutions, and the group continued to suffer from a generally held distrust about the association of archives with government institutions. The debates over the role and ownership of the collections demonstrates the point that has been made elsewhere, that Occupy groups (like corporations and institutions) struggled to find the balance between managing their reputation, controlling their image, sharing their messages and identifying and incentivizing conversations with in public sphere representations (Adi, 2015, p. 508). This was certainly the case in regard to disagreements about the most appropriate final location for the collections, which represented an inherent distrust of private and government institutions, staff members and affiliates, including journalists, curators, and representatives from public collecting institutions.[5] As such, the question of where the archives would reside in the short and long term became a divisive and contentious issue within the working group (Evans, Perricci, and Roberts, 2014). The problems associated with maintaining an independent archive were practical as well as ideological:

> [Bold] says he doesn't know how to have that conversation with the General Assembly. "I can't just say, 'Do you want to ship it off to the Smithsonian?'" Roberts says that this is not an option but does see the pressing need for space. "We need somewhere to keep the stuff," she says. "It can't be a basement. It can't be an office hall." ... "We might end up trying to process everything, and then eventually deeding it to Tamiment," Bold says. "But we won't do that without the approval of the movement. The GA [General Assembly] has to decide."
>
> (Quoted in Samtani, 2011, p. 6)

Distrust about the Archives group's reliance on external institutions to provide training, support and expertise for their activities (and the related concern that they could not ensure accountability for the movement because they had "sold out") was exacerbated by decisions made by the General Assembly, specifically its rejection of applications by the Archives group for financial support for core activities, and in its assessment that the Archives Group did not qualify as a form of affective direct action.[6]

Some members of the General Assembly reportedly argued that since the movement was itself ephemeral, what mattered was the occupation as it existed at that time only. They believed that retaining the material evidence was not important. This view compromised Occupy Wall Street's ability to exert control over its legacy, particularly given that other institutions were collecting as frenetically, albeit often selectively, as they could, and usually without developing relationships with Occupiers (Associated Press, 2011; Judkis, 2011; Schuessler, 2012; Helmore, 2015). This point was not lost on working group members who warned that

> There are a lot of other people recording the movement and telling its story, but we want to empower occupiers to help preserve what is being made while their story is unfolding. While some archivists aim to be dispassionate and "objective," our intent was to be more involved in the movement and open about the inherent influence of our actions.
>
> (Evans, Perricci and Roberts, 2014)

Others similarly argued that "the last thing" they wanted was "the historical record of OWS controlled by people who aren't in OWS" (Molenda, 2011 quoted in Erde 2014, p. 82). If we are correct in understanding that activist PR's interest in managing constituent relationships is designed to contribute to a self-replicating and expanding social imaginary, then the lack of support for the Archives group can be seen as having a negative impact on the movement's ability to further influence relationships with constituents that included the institutions that now hold and exert control over Occupy Wall Street collections.[7]

Lack of support by the General Assembly reflected a perception that cultural activities and events including collecting and archives are not sufficiently "political."[8] Distrust in the collection of the images of and from Occupy (that were perhaps viewed as commodities), may have been based on the view that it was a superficial and undesirably institutionalized or consumerist activity, even PR-like in a pejorative sense ("selling out" rather than "capacity building"). There was no acknowledgment by the General Assembly that failure to construct an enduring archive for the moment would mean that the only remaining public representation of the movement would be held in collections not controlled (and in most cases not created) by Occupy Wall Street participants. These risks were also vigorously debated within the Archives group. The lack of interest in using traditional institutions and forms of media to co-opt or subvert mainstream news outlets or sites of representation (including museums, archive and libraries) over the longer term contrasted with the priority for having a current impact. This meant that whilst actions perceived as being immediately "direct" in the sense of being headline-grabbing, such as sending a high profile delegation to Tahrir Square (Roberts, 2011d), were funded, applications for archival resources including banker's boxes and storage space by the Archives group were rejected. The appeal of the immediate effect was evident in enthusiasm expressed for and about the media center, described in the following terms:

> Thanks to the activist habit of *ressentiment*, acquired by seeing protest after protest fail to make headlines, the Occupiers had planned for creating their own media much more than serving anyone else's. There was no place in the encampment more seemingly sophisticated and elite than the jumble of glowing laptops and indiscernible wires around the media center; visitors passed by it awe for this physical manifestation of the age of the hashtag.... This was an important place.
>
> (Schneider, 2013b, p. 40)

Occupy's preoccupation with maintaining its status as headline news shows, in the final instance, that although PR *was* produced by the Occupy Wall Street movement (as a non-homogeneous assemblage of individual and collective participants), the resulting legacy of the movement's communication efforts was not the internally produced archive (that produced, in the end, a kind of anti-institutional ethnography of infrastructure) but the ephemeral material produced for external audiences that the Occupiers, by and large (and certainly many Archives working group members) assessed as being of low enduring value/significance.[9] This result is paradoxical because the life-cycle of the material salvaged from the site by external collectors (and from the Sanitation Department and elsewhere by working group members) was generally intended to be short term but has become the primary representation of the movement. The paradox is that in failing to achieve internal support for the working group's aim to preserve the historical value of the movement for future protesters (by preserving internal documentation), the dominant image surviving of Occupy Wall Street are the collections made by external museums and collections rather than the participants of Occupy Wall Street.[10] In other words, what material collections remain are, ironically, the ephemeral material outputs which, despite not having been significantly valued by the movement, have been collected by and taken to "stand in" (as indexical signifiers) for the movement as a whole by public and government institutions. The internal processes of the movement – which sought specifically to document the challenges and processes as well as the legacy of Occupy Wall Street for the benefit of future activists (i.e., *PR for activists not just by activists*) – are not fully represented by any public collections.[11]

Accessibility: long-term plight of archives

Although the Occupy Archives Working Group sought to source support for an independent archive from within the movement, the task became increasingly difficult. Archives members, Sian Evans, Anna Perricci, and Amy Roberts later explained:

> We wanted to ensure that the experiences that made up the Occupy movement were in fact shared, rather than locked away in a private storage locker. Ultimately, attempts to safeguard the archives outside of an institutional setting amounted to simply making them inaccessible to anyone. The collective spirit of the movement, though outside of any formal institution, will likely become dependent on one for the persistence and access to the materials. That said, some institutional settings are more appropriate than others.
>
> (Evans, Perricci, and Roberts, 2014)

In the end, the working group identified the Tamiment Library and Robert F. Wagner Labor Archives as their generally (but by no means universally) preferred repository. Their preference was based on their understanding of Tamiment as an institution dedicated to the documentation of the history of radical politics, the political Left, social movements, and the labor struggle in New York City. They also noted Tamiment's capacity and resources to adequately preserve the materials, which they could not themselves do independently.

Extended negotiation within the working group ensured, as well as between the working group and Tamiment staff members – two of whom, Chela Scott Weber, Associate Head for Archival Collections, and Michael Nash, Director of the Tamiment (who died in 2012, before the collection was acquired) – had been members of the working group – on issues including intellectual property rights, ownership of material collected from the Sanitation Department and other places following raids and seizures (where authorship could not be determined), and what the deed of gift would look like given that the donation was coming from a community archive whose membership is not standardized, and therefore has no real representation or authority to speak for the group the collection would be identified as documenting. Other less complex but no less significant priorities of the group were the expectation that the collection would be digitized in a timely manner, and that the collection would be available for open access use, partly as a pathway to provide correctives given the concerns over intellectual property, ownership of materials, and the desire not to represent or speak for others. The priority of accessibility was emphasized in negotiations, with the group expressing the strong preference for making the collections open to the public through open house events hosted by Tamiment, at which OWS activists and the general public could review the collection and offer comments, corrections and annotations to the description and organization provided by the Library.

The majority of the ("official") Occupy Wall Street collection was ultimately transferred to the Tamiment Library and Robert F. Wagner Labor Archives in stages (in 2013, 2014, and 2017), however the paper-based archival collections were not accessible for public use until early 2018, while the signs and other three-dimensional materials remain unprocessed and inaccessible (Johnson, pers. comm. 2016).[12] Although I have not had space in this chapter to analyze the working group's relationship with the Tamiment, the exchanges that led to that institution's acquisition of the collections exist as a third set of relationship-building strategies, the dynamics of which were also obviously influenced by both the external and internal forms of activism produced by the Archives working group.

Conclusion

This chapter has provided a discussion about the strategies used by the Occupy Archives working group as a representation of the ways in which activist PR worked for and against the Occupy Wall Street movement. I have shown that while, on the one hand, the aim of the Archives working group was to document the legacy of the movement (extending to maintain control of their image and reputation), they also, even more importantly, identified the collection as a living activist resource. From the outset, "the ideal was always long-term preservation paired with a consistently high level of access" (Evans, Perricci, and Roberts, 2014). Rather than just existing as a commemoration of a past event, the collection was understood as a "living resource" that could shape and influence the views of constituents (within and outside of the movement). It sought to challenge institutional power by modeling an alternative approach to activist archiving that privileged collaboration and relationship building.

Rather than having any pretensions for neutrality (which is a common mistaken presumption made on archives and collections), the working group strongly asserted the value of the archives as being the process of relationship-building that occurs in their production (what I have referred to, following Star (1999) as a kind of ethnography of infrastructure) over the end product (the content held in external collections). This is important in the context of this chapter, which has argued that the desired outcome of the archiving working group – the development of a collection as a living resource – reflects contemporary approaches to critical and community-based archive and museum studies, and employed strategies and a critical emphasis on relationship building that have also been attributed to activist PR strategies.

Acknowledgments

I would like to thank Ana Adi for the invitation to consider activist museum and archiving practices in the context of public relations activism, and referees of an earlier draft for their helpful comments. I am very grateful to the archivists at Tamiment Library for facilitating my access to the collection. I would like to acknowledge my particular gratitude to Amy Roberts, who has helped this work in too many ways to mention, from the provision of further materials and feedback, through to her patient good counsel. It is because of her and other members of the working group that the collection has a future.

Notes

1 104 NYCGA (New York City General Assembly) affiliated working groups are listed at www.nycga.net/documents/GROUP DOCUMENTS (last accessed August 10, 2016, link no longer live). The Archives working group was constituted by a diverse and changing membership of professionally trained archivists, librarians and graduate students in related fields as well as other contributors representing heterogeneous interests, forms of identification, and life experiences.

2 The Archives Working Group was eligible to access a rolling provisional budget of $100 from the movement's General Assembly, which they needed to acquit before they could apply for more. Their (revised) request for $3,940 to cover the basics required for short-term storage and basic, urgent preservation was tabled and rejected at a finance meeting of the General Assembly. Roberts (2011c), "OWS archives budget proposal" (2012).

3 The archives produced by the working group were designed to be "a fundamentally relational concept" that both influenced and were "shaped by the conventions of a community of practice" (Star 1999, p. 382). I interpret these
functions according to Star's (1999) study of infrastructure, where infrastructure is a structural form that exists both in its own right, and as a mere component of a much larger assemblage (in this case, the Occupy Movement) that
itself contributes to an almost limitless field of data beyond that (such as
society). See "Organizational documents – Archives working group"
(2011–2012).
4 "Minutes from meeting with Tamiment" (2012). Extensive debate over the
responsibility for thinking politically as well as historically – in *personal* terms
– also occurred within the group and across the movement, which advocated
for a leaderless horizontal form of organization. Criticisms about the way the
movement reproduced social and political inequalities based on sexual preference and race as well as gender and class were widely articulated, as were concerns that particular individuals or cliques gained dominance, greater authority
or representation in decision-making processes regardless of the movement's
ostensible commitment to consensus. Descriptions about the role and impact of
structural forms of racism, sexism, and privilege on participants are included in
Organizational documents – Archives working group (2011–2012) and in other
reports; see, for example, Ashraf 2011; McVeigh 2011.
5 Members of Occupy were encouraged to declare any institutional affiliations/
connections they had, especially if they intended to use equipment/storage of
that institution for the purposes of any of the Working Groups. Schneider
(2013b) discusses how he negotiated his potential conflict as a journalist participant of Occupy Wall Street).
6 The lack of support for the actions of the Archiving Working Group are summarized by two decisions made by the General Assembly on November 9 and
10, 2011. First, the rejection of their budget request ("I would like to inform
everyone that our budget proposal was rejected by the General Assembly last
night. This was right after a proposal passed without a hitch, for the movement
to spend \$29,000 to send people to Egypt!" (Roberts, 2011d)). Also see minutes
from OWS General Assembly (November 11, 2011, at www.nycga.
net/2011/11/10/nycga-minutes-11102011/#more-3183, link no longer live).
Second, their application (tabled the following day) to move from a Working
Group to an Operational Group, defined as groups that were concerned with
direct action implementation in contrast with other support-focused subsidiary
groups that were ineligible for funding, was rejected after a motion was moved
against including the Archives Working Group:

> James [Molenda] informed me [Amy Roberts] that at last night's meeting,
> that about 8 groups voted against Archives becoming an Operational group
> in the Spokescouncil, which means as of now, we do not have a "Spoke" or
> voice on the Spokescouncil. I think we should continue to function as we
> have. I find this development to be deeply troubling as one of the reasons
> that I was in favor of the Spokescouncil was to improve our ability to work
> with other groups and to have more of a voice not less.
> (Roberts, 2011d; OWS Structure Working Group, 2011)

7 There was significant interest by other museums and libraries in collecting physical material from Occupy Wall Street (and even greater in the creation of
digital archives, which are not the focus of this chapter but see, for example,
Adi, 2015). Representative collections include those held at the Museum of the
City of New York, New York Public Library, Interference Archive (an independent community archive in Brooklyn, New York), as well as nationally, for

example at the Smithsonian Institution's National Museum of American History, in Washington DC.

8 This chapter aims to challenge distinctions between culture and politics by demonstrating the relationship between cultural collections, public relations, activism, and "the political dimensions of struggle and change" (L'Etang, 2016, p. 207). See "Organizational documents – Archives working group" (2011–2012), and also for further analysis, Message (2017).

9 Occupy Archives Working Group members also articulated the view that the material collection was only one element of the record and only important in the context of oral histories and other forms of recording (including online and digital). Perhaps influenced by the movement's preference for and investment in digital media forms of communication, some members were unenthusiastic about the collection of posters and ephemera ("Meeting minutes between Jan–Feb," 2012). There was also a broader ideological preference across the movement for the "occupation of a physical space as an ongoing symbolic critique rather than as focused industrial demand" (Erde, 2014, p. 77).

10 The internal processes of Occupy Wall Street are increasingly becoming subject to critical reflections (Schneider, 2013a; White, 2016) material documentation of such is only starting to become accessible to researchers, as in the case of the Tamiment collections (Occupy Wall Street Archives Working Group Records; TAM 630; boxes 1–4; Tamiment Library/Robert F. Wagner Labor Archives, New York University).

11 While Tamiment Library holds some internal records, its collection is not fully available. Materials donated to Interference Archive in Brooklyn include ephemera, posters (some made by Occuprint member Josh Macphee, who co-founded Interference Archive with Dara Greenwald, Molly Fair, and Kevin Caplicki) and publications, as well as the Born Digital Collection from the Archives working group. Additional records of internal discussions exist digitally or have been kept privately. Research for this chapter has been based on analysis of collections held by the Tamiment Museum and supplementary private collections. These materials and their full analysis are the subject of *Curatorial Activism: Archiving Occupy* (which will be published by Routledge in 2019).

12 The quantity of material audited by the Occupy Archives Working Group as within their stewardship alone was recorded as being up to 50 Linear feet and 400+ signs as at December 12, 2011 (Bold 2012). As at March 2018, the Tamiment Library collection totals 75 linear feet of materials (Tamiment Library/Robert F. Wagner Labor Archives, 2018).

References

Adi, Ana (2015) "Occupy PR: An analysis of online media communications of Occupy Wall Street and Occupy London," *Public Relations Review* 41: 508–14.

Ashraf, Hena (2011) "Claiming space for diversity at Occupy Wall Street," in Sarah van Gelder (ed.), *This changes everything: Occupy Wall Street and the 99% movement*, San Francisco, CA: Berrett-Koehler Publishers, Inc., pp. 33–5.

Associated Press (2011) "Occupy Wall Street becomes highly collectible," *The Mercury News*, December 24. Online at www.mercurynews.com/2011/12/24/occupy-wall-street-becomes-highly-collectible/. Accessed February 21, 2018.

Bennett, Tony (2015) "Thinking (with) museums: From exhibitionary complex to governmental assemblage" in Andrea Witcomb and Kylie Message (eds.), *Museum theory*, Chichester, UK: John Wiley & Sons Ltd, pp. 3–20.

Bold, Jeremy [Jez] (2012) "Minutes from 2012.AUG.2 meeting @ Tamiment" discussion post and attachment, OWS archives Google groups forum, https://groups.google.com/forum/#!topic/ows-archives/C0aKX7dH3L0, August 3, 2012.

Coombs, T.W. and Holladay, S.J. (2010) *PR strategy and application: Managing influence*, Malden, MA: Wiley Blackwell Publishing.

Coombs, T.W. and Holladay, S.J. (2012) "Privileging an activist vs. a corporate view of public relations history in the U.S.," *Public Relations Review* 38: 347–53.

Erde, John (2014) "Constructing archives of the occupy movement," *Archives and Records* 35(2): 77–92.

Evans, Sian, Perricci, Anna, and Roberts, Amy (2014) " 'Why archive?' and other important questions asked by occupiers," in Melissa Morrone (ed.), *Informed agitation: Library and information skills in social justice movements and beyond*, Sacramento, CA: Library Juice Press, pp. 289–306.

Flinn, Andrew and Alexander, Ben (eds.) (2015) *Archiving activism and activist archiving*. Special issue of *Archival Science* 15(4).

Helmore, Edward (2015) "Collecting the art of protest at Brooklyn's interference archive," *Guardian*, October 15. Online at www.theguardian.com/artand design/2015/oct/14/art-of-protest-interference-archive-brooklyn. Accessed February 21, 2018.

Johnson, Timothy (2016) Email to Kylie Message. October 28.

Judkis, M. (2011) "Occupy Wall Street signs: Which should go in the Smithsonian?" *Washington Post*, October 24.

L'Etang, Jacquie (2016) "Public relations, activism and social movements: Critical perspectives," *Public Relations Inquiry* 5(3): 207–11.

McVeigh, Karen (2011) "Occupy Wall Street's women struggle to make their voices heard," *Guardian*, November 30. Online at www.theguardian.com/world/2011/nov/30/occupy-wall-street-women-voices. Accessed March 20, 2018.

"Meeting minutes between Jan-Feb 2012," in "Organizational documents – Archives working group 2011–2013," TAM 630; box 2; Tamiment Library/Robert F. Wagner Labor Archives, New York University.

Message, Kylie (2017) *The disobedient museum: Writing at the edge*, London and New York: Routledge.

"Minutes from meeting with Tamiment" August 3, in "Organizational documents – Archives working group 2011–2012," TAM 630; box 2; Tamiment Library/Robert F. Wagner Labor Archives, New York University.

Moloney, Kevin (2005) "Trust and public relations: Center and edge," *Public Relations Review* 31: 550–5.

Occupy Wall Street Archives Working Group Records; TAM 630; boxes 1–4; Tamiment Library/Robert F. Wagner Labor Archives, New York University.

"Organizational documents – Archives working group 2011–2012," TAM 630; box 2; Tamiment Library/Robert F. Wagner Labor Archives, New York University.

"OWS archives budget proposal." Revised as of January 13, 2012, in "Organizational documents – Archives working group 2012," TAM 630; box 2; Tamiment Library/Robert F. Wagner Labor Archives, New York University.

OWS Structure Working Group, "OWS structure proposal," in "Organizational documents – Archives working group 2011'," TAM 630; box 2; Tamiment Library/Robert F. Wagner Labor Archives, New York University.

Roberts, Amy [Amy R] (2011a) "Occupy Wall Street archive mission statement. docx" discussion post (and attachment), OWS archives Google groups forum, https://groups.google.com/forum/#!topic/ows-archives/V8iofbpsQPo, December 1, 2011.

Roberts, Amy [Amy R] (2011b) "Raid on Tuesday morning," discussion post, OWS archives Google groups forum, https://groups.google.com/forum/#!topic/ows-archives/F4jxN8hD36c, November 17, 2011.

Roberts, Amy [Amy R] (2011c) "Budget fail," discussion post, OWS archives Google groups forum, https://groups.google.com/forum/#!topic/ows-archives/_UOTAyRjM40, November 12, 2011.

Roberts, Amy [Amy R] (2011d) "Spokescouncil," discussion post, OWS archives Google groups forum, https://groups.google.com/forum/#!topic/ows-archives/sDSy_C6dso4, November 11, 2011.

Samtani, Hiten (2011) "The anarchists: Who owns the Occupy Wall Street narrative?" *The Brooklyn Ink*, December 26. Online at http://brooklynink.org/2011/12/26/39230-the-anarchists-who-owns-the-occupy-wall-street-narrative/. Accessed February 21, 2018.

Schuessler, Jennifer (2012) "Occupy Wall Street: From the streets to the archives," ArtsBeat: New York Times Blog, May 2. Online at https://artsbeat.blogs.nytimes.com/2012/05/02/occupy-wall-street-from-the-streets-to-the-archives/. Accessed March 20, 2018.

Schneider, Nathan (2013a) "Occupy, after Occupy," *The Nation*, September 5. Online at www.thenation.com/article/occupy-after-occupy/. Accessed February 21, 2018.

Schneider, Nathan (2013b) *Thank you, anarchy: Notes from the Occupy apocalypse*, Berkeley and Los Angeles, CA: University of California Press.

Star, Susan Leigh (1999) "The ethnography of infrastructure," *American Behavioral Scientist* 43(3): 377–91.

van Gelder, Sarah (2011) "Introduction: How Occupy Wall Street changes everything," in Sarah van Gelder (ed.), *This changes everything: Occupy Wall Street and the 99% movement*, San Francisco, CA: Berrett-Koehler Publishers, Inc., pp. 1–13.

White, Micah (2016) *The end of protest: A new playbook for revolution*, Toronto, Canada: Alfred A. Knopf Canada.

10 Romania's protest

From stakeholders in waiting to activists' becoming PR practitioners

Camelia Crişan

Public relations (PR) is an academic discipline that has fought hard to become recognized and has developed its own theories over the last 25 years (Taylor & Botan, 2004). Thus, it is interesting how PR academics started looking some time ago toward explanatory models and theories from other social sciences (Gower, 2010; Edwards, 2012) to define and understand better their object matter of activity. This to me, a sociologist by formation, feels rather an artificial classification to something that I would simply call social communication. It almost seems that the excellence model in public relations detailed by Grunig, Dozier and Grunig (1994), based on the idea of publics proposed earlier by Grunig (1978) has to be reshaped, changed or transformed. We could argue that PR specialists no longer deal with publics but rather with stakeholders grouped in networks, defined here in terms of Castells' work (2015). In my view Grunig (2009) is trying to cope with this new reality, and employs the term stakeholder along with the one of publics and active publics within a paradigm – as a higher level of organizing the scientific knowledge from a certain domain, stating pre-conditions accepted among a certain school of thought (Kuhn, [1962] 2008). The excellence model, I argue, needs a profound transformation in order to cope with the current realities set forth by digital communication and more specifically by social media, as a tool for networks agglutination. It is, at the same time, particularly intriguing why social labels of different groups like the ones used in the different theories of organizational stakeholders have not made a more consistent way into the public relations models, especially after the numerous discussions in the literature on social license to operate for corporations (Boutilier & Thompson, 2012) and also, corporate social responsibility (Crane, Matten & Moon, 2008; Crisan & Adi, 2016).

In doing so, this chapter focuses on the Romanian #rezist protests taking place in Romania's capital – Bucharest – in the main cities across Romania and in the cities of the world where Romanian diaspora lives (Adi, 2017). Almost 600,000 people participated in the protests, which were the largest street gatherings since the 1989 Revolution, when the dictator Nicolae Ceauşescu was removed from power. The time of these protests was January–February 2017, and they were caused by the Emergency Governmental Ordinance No. 13 (referred to as OUG13) issued by then Prime Minister Sorin Grindeanu's cabinet (Social Democratic Party – SDP), whose official aim was to harmonize the Romanian criminal legislation with the one of the European Union (EU) (Momoc, 2017). However, the public perception of the issuing of the OUG13 was different, namely that it was meant to offer a pardon to the President of the SDP, Mr. Liviu Dragnea, who (as of January 2017) was subject to a criminal lawsuit for abusing his position while serving as President of the County Council Teleorman (South Romania) from 2000 to 2012. Some specific provisions of the OUG13 would have exonerated Mr. Dragnea from being prosecuted. The entire process of this perceived *undercover exoneration* initiated by the Prime Minister for his political boss, has been seen by the citizens as a sham. As an earlier attempt to pass the OUG13 has been blocked by the President of Romania, Mr. Klaus Werner Iohannis, the issuing of the OUG13 only amplified the outrage. In a weekly, ordinary meeting of the Government[1] while the President was there, the Government withdrew the OUG from the list of proposed legislation only for the Prime Minister to convoke another Government meeting later on covering the matter. On January 31, 2018, at 9 p.m., the Government adopted OUG13. The Minister of Justice was sent to host a press conference to defend the passing of this piece of legislation; his performance during the press conference raised questions of whether he was dodging legitimate questions from the members of the press. Meanwhile, in Victoriei Square (the square in Bucharest where the Government building is located) protesters started to gather and shout slogans like: "Another question" (*Alta intrebare*) (with reference to the fiasco press conference organized by the Minister of Justice) (Rogalski, 2017) and "Like thieves, in the night" (*Noaptea ca hotii*) (with reference to the time of the OUG13 adoption).

The OUG13 was published in the *Official Gazette* (to enter into force) the same night but it contained a provision that it would show its legal effects 20 days from its printing. Considering that there were 20 more days until it became compulsory legislation, the protesters gathered every day, despite low temperatures and bad weather, in Victoriei Square to push the Government to withdraw OUG13. At their largest (on February 5) the protests were attended by an estimated 600,000. This was also the day when the Government issued the Emergency Ordinance No. 14 (OUG14), cancelling some of the provisions of OUG13 (referring to the specific case of Mr. Dragnea's trial) and modifying others (Ursu, 2017). The Parliament (which according to the Constitution must approve within some months an Emergency Ordinance), dominated by an SDP coalition, rejected OUG13 and adopted OUG14. The corresponding laws (rejection of OUG13 and adoption of OUG14) entered into force after they were signed by the President. This was a major success for the Romanian protesters who continued in the next months and years, at a lower intensity.

#rezist, as the protests sparked by the OUG13 have ended up being known, has not been the result of a sudden awakening but rather the result of a gradual increase in civic awareness, and of several other street protests successfully. These include stopping a gold mining project in Roşia Montană in 2012, and leading to the fall of the Ponta Government in 2015 in the aftermath of the fire that killed 64 people attending a rock concert in the Colectiv night club (Bortun & Cheregi, 2017). While this chapter will focus mainly on the 2017 protests, it does so by putting them in the context of the larger social movements that have happened in Romania in the last decade.

My approach to understanding Romania's protests from the winter of 2017 is in line with a series of other academics who proposed a different methodological exploration of public relations using theories from the larger domain of sociology, i.e., the Actor–Network Theory (Schölzel & Nothhaft, 2016) as well as Bourdieu's symbolic power theory (Ilhen, 2009; Edwards, 2012; Wolf, 2018). In doing so, I also seek to answer some of the questions raised by Kim and Sriramesh (2009) aimed at explaining the relationship between activists and PR. Specifically, I propose to analyze the Romanian #rezist protests from a theoretical standpoint of the stakeholders' theory (Freeman, Harrison & Wicks, 2007; Fassin, 2009), considering the activists as part of the NGO communities and civic networks (Keck & Sikkink, 1998), rather than PR practitioners. I thus define PR practitioners as individuals who do PR by profession. Also, I define as activists individuals who have been part of setting out the protests. I will further demonstrate, in line with Castells' communication power networks (2015), that activists' motivation has to do with restoring the power balance rather than to communicate about an issue. I argue that the motivation, behavior, and self-identification of some of the initiators and participants in the Romanian protests, including those who work within the public relations field, is little connected to the idea of PR activists, as it has been illustrated in other cases (Toledano, 2016) or by other researchers of the Romanian protests (Adi & Lilleker, 2017). Moreover, the views expressed by the protesters and activists interviewed for this chapter show that, in their opinion, there is a clear difference between how they identify an activist and a PR practitioner, while they all admit that in the pursuit of their goals they engage PR tools.

Publics vs. stakeholders vs. PR practitioners as activists

Since Dutta's (2009) question: "Where are the voices of activists in the public relations literature?" (p. 293), there have been several investigations into how public relations can give more support to the disempowered, the vulnerable, protesters or social movements (Ciszek, 2015; Doan & Toledano, 2018; Fisher, 2018). At the same time, Holtzhausen (2000) calls for an increased participation of public relations practitioners in community activism, and argues public relations practice can be more ethical if practitioners take an activist stance in the organizations for which they work.

(Cited in Holtzhausen & Voto, 2002, p. 60)

Despite these calls for a different and more integrative approach of PR and activism, public relations research is still predominantly related to corporate communication and Grunig's (2009) publics, and too little on stakeholders. In Grunig's view publics "...create themselves and they are motivated to do so by the problems they experience in their life situations" (p. 5) whereas "stakeholders ... define their stakes in an organization; organizations cannot do that for them" (p. 5). As a result, publics, even in their active form are the result of the organizational behavior, while stakeholders are somehow pre-determined. When Philips and Young (2009) challenged the excellence model calling it out for its lack of consideration of internet mediated publics and social networks, Grunig's (2009, p. 6) reply implied that, "...organizations do not need relationships with individuals who are not members of their publics even though these people might be actively communicating and building relationships with each other." Grunig (2009) thus maintained, with a few small changes, the classification of the publics he produced in 1975, where only when an organization's actions have consequences on other parts of society, will the groups organize and become active publics, not before. Publics are thus reactive in nature – active only if provoked and if they become aware of an organizational action – they don't seem to search for information preemptively and anticipate the corporate action and communication.

If one considers stakeholders to be defined as a group of individuals who can influence an organization and who can be influenced by that organization's action, then one considers, along with Freeman, Harrison and Wicks (2007, pp. 113–116) that stakeholders can be: groups with both relatively high cooperation potential and high threat potential (fluctuating stakeholder); groups that have both little cooperation potential and high threat potential (defensive stakeholders); groups with both high cooperation potential and small competition threat (offensive stakeholders); and groups with both low cooperation and threat potential (stable stakeholders). In Freeman, Harrison and Wicks' (2007) view the fluctuating stakeholders may influence the result of a random situation, thus it is imperative for the organization to change the rules of engagement with them. The companies need new strategies and, if the case may be, support programs. Defensive stakeholders are not providing any help, but they can impede the company to pursue its objectives. Current behaviors or a new behaviors with a hint of support may help the company for the time being, but the increase of supportive behavior may be limited in time. The existence of defensive stakeholders is a sign that sometimes people may be more vulnerable in front of friends than in front of their enemies (Freeman, Harrison & Wicks, 2007). Defensive stakeholders may greatly help a company to achieve its objectives and there is a low risk for them be behave in a threatening manner. Perhaps they are tired of trying to regulate a certain behavior, so there is a limited range of options they can try in order to achieve that goal. If risks are low, any strategic program may be tried and exploited for a win. However, new changes in the company's behavior may determine a re-evaluation of their own reaction. They could prove a source of added value and it is possible that the company has not identified their real cooperation or threat-related behaviors. A pro-stakeholder company leadership starts with the awareness that the organization's actions are affecting other people and groups and understanding the magnitude of this influence. In a new version of the stakeholder theory, Fassin (2009) redefines the groups an organization is interacting with, from the point of view of practicing a more efficient management. According to the legitimacy of the stake, the dyad: influence/domination and responsibility, Fassin (2009) puts stakeholders in three categories: real stakeholders, who have in the classical approach real stakes in the company; the pressure groups who are protecting and watching the interests of the real stakeholders – the stakewatchers and the regulators, who have no direct stakes but are imposing rules and exercise an external control (stakekeepers). Listing the parties involved based in functional criteria has as an effect a triangular relation among stakeholders – stakewatchers – stakekeepers.

For each of the three large groups above, there is a subsequent pressure group, and most stakeholders have a corresponding stakewatcher. For instance, Fassin (2009) provides as an example the employees who have as stakewatcher the trade unions, while the government, by law, is a stakekeeper for them. At the same time, Fassin (2009, p. 123) includes the civil society and the communities in a separate group of associated stakeholders, predominantly as a stakewatcher. Media is a distinct stakekeeper and not a stakewatcher, because it can demand from the corporations a socially responsible behavior. Unlike Freeman's model (1994), Fassin's model looks like a solar system which places at its core the management, not the corporation per se, around which the stakeholders rotate like planets, surrounded in their turn by the stakewatchers and stakekeepers. Due to the stakeholders' dynamic character, to the pressures, threats and opportunities from the corporate environments, which can vary in time, the three stakeholders types may easily overlap. From this perspective, some pressure groups, which may be at the same time interest groups, can cooperate with the corporation and may earn the stakeholder status rather than the stakewatcher, while some shareholders may be approached more as stakewatchers than stakeholders. Media may be supportive in some situations and aggressive in others and could be playing a stakekeeper, stakeholder or stakewatcher role successively. In Fassin's (2009, p. 125) view the government is a complex stakeholder, which imposes rules, but it can be treated as a "silent shareholder," as a stakekeeper or a stakewatcher. The benefit of redefining the stake-holders by Fassin (2009) is a step forward toward a better strategic management of stakeholders. We should note the continuity between the stakeholders' model of Freeman, Harrison and Wicks (2007) and the one proposed by Fassin (2009), while the main differences are that by categorizing *ab initio* the stakeholders in the three categories their management can be done more efficiently, the threats and opportunities may be identified earlier and the thus the corporate response can be faster.

It is important to note at this point, that if publics are the result of a social communication process, actors in the process but also a byproduct of a social communication act done by a state or private organization, the stakeholders are – from a managerial perspective – the providers of legitimacy for the organization's actions. This is mostly based on the concept of social license to operate proposed by Boutilier and Thomson (2012), which is referring to a "community's perceptions of the acceptability of a company and its local operations" (p. 1). In order to reach that point, where both its presence and operations are accepted by the community, a company would need to pass several stages of interaction: from withheld/withdrawn to psychological identification, passing after that to acceptance and approval. The process involves empowerment of all stakeholders that make the difference between being granted or being denied the environmental and social license to operate (Borţun & Crişan, 2012). The social license to operate connects the individual or collective action to legitimacy and its results, which are normative – a kind of responsible behavior of the company toward the society. Stakeholder engagement for or against a company's actions is based on their perception that the agency should provide legitimacy to the company's actions, and not vice-versa. They are not created by a company's actions, they are the play-field for the company's actions. Like Porritt's (2007) view on sustainable systems: the economic system can only exist within the social system, and not the other way around. We could then claim that the *stakeholders are activists in waiting* and they activate at the moment when a company or an institution are acting toward receiving a particular social license to operate. But due to the internet and the availability of communication, especially social media, the stakeholders as activists in waiting have the capacity to expand beyond the community borders and act internationally, especially in those situations when those in power (be it corporations or state governments) impose forgetfulness (Keck & Sikkink, 1998), or should we add, use public communication to deceit or to bluntly lie. PR practitioners could qualify in our view as activists in waiting, especially if we define them in line with Holtzhausen and Voto (2002)

> as a conscience in the organization by resisting dominant power structures, particularly when these structures are not inclusive, will preference employees' and external publics' discourse over that of

management, will make the most humane decision in a particular situation, and will promote new ways of thinking and problem solving through dissensus and conflict.

(p. 64)

At the same time, this may always raise an important issue, related to cognitive dissonance (Festinger, 1957, cited in Cooper, 2012) but not so much according to the vicarious dissonance as proposed in the new look of the theory by Cooper (2012, p. 377), where the communicator's admitted hypocrisy leads to multiplying a certain change especially in small groups and in experiments concerning health and wellbeing. It is, however, a thin red line a PR practitioner needs to walk while being inside an organization, and at the same time the advocate of stakewatchers or defensive stakeholders. Borrowing a metaphor from physics, PR practitioners act for organizations like normalizers of pressures in the case of the communicating vessels theory; they mediate power relations through communication, an external form of power breakers (Berger, 2005). We could accept this as a working hypothesis, even if we do it just for the sake of a presumably organizational Socratic dialogue. However, the other side of the argument is a bit more problematic in my view: why would PR practitioners join activist networks to advocate for purposes which may, sometimes, be contradictory to those of organizations and institutions they represent? Is this duality even possible during mass street protests? And to which extent do activists accept this type of involvement?

Activists, social movements and the Romanian winter

This chapter aims to explore these questions by looking at the Romanian protests and how some activists view the PR practitioners who have been part of the movements. What Keck and Sikkink (1998) explain is that

> activists in networks try not to influence policy outcomes, but to transform the terms and nature of the debate ... they frame issues to make them comprehensible to target audiences, to attract attention and encourage action ... they bring new ideas, norms and discourses into policy debates and serve as sources of information and testimony.
>
> (Chapter 1, paragraphs 4–5)

This type of behavior is confirmed by Castells (2015) who argues that movements generally ignore political parties, distrust the media, do not recognize any leadership as well as reject all formal organization "relying on the Internet and local assemblies for collective debate and decision-making" (p. 30). In this rhizome structure, "mass self-communication is based in horizontal networks of interactive communication, that, by and large are difficult to control by government or corporations" (Castells,

2015, p. 33). It means that activists need to find new ways to communicate with each other and with the society to make their cause heard, thus the social media is a strong channel for conveying messages and convincing others to join. Castells argues that the social movements are disputing the social licenses of the other actors to be the stakekeepers, especially when "citizens ... are occupying the medium and creating the message, they overcome the powerlessness of their solitary despair by networking their desire" (2015, p. 35). It is the power used without responsibility or in new areas where social license has not yet been awarded that spark the movements: "the roots are in the fundamental injustice of all societies, relentlessly confronted by human aspirations of justice" (Castells, 2015, p. 38). When they act, networks "connect groups to each other, seek out resources, propose and prepare activities and conduct public relations" (Keck & Sikkink, 1998, Chapter 1, paragraph 13) or through "rumors, sermons, pamphlets and manifestos spread from person to person ... or by whatever means of communication were available" (Castells, 2015, p. 43).

The analysis provided by Keck and Sikkink (1998) and Castells (2015) adds another layer of arguments to my initial statement that stakeholders are activists in waiting. However, if the discussion is now framed in terms of networks of interactive communication, mass self-communication, I wonder where, in this equation, are the publics for whom the PR practitioners are working. It is, in my view, only in the new model of social networks that we can explain how a balance of power can still be reached. This is particularly difficult to understand when publics may not intersect each other or where their overlap is only peripheral. The main difference is that activists, part of social networks engaged in protests, are not looking just to communicate, they want to "prevail over the networks of power" (Castells, 2015, p. 45). If such action is to have success the role of PR practitioners is to *borrow* their means of activity to the disempowered, understanding that they will not necessary be the channel for equalizing the pressure, but mere means to an act of social change.

It is this the context in which I will explain Romania's protests from 2017. Their main root was embedded, in my view, in the first street violent manifestations of 2012. Then, an opinionated exchange of ideas between the then president of the country, Traian Băsescu, and the Head of the Emergency Services/Secretary of State in the Ministry of Health, Raed Arafat, took place during a prime time television show (Hotnews, January 9, 2012), which led to the resignation of the Government (Business Magazin, February 15, 2012). Even the 2012 events were a continuation of several other movements, smaller in scope, mostly conducted by political activists (when President Traian Băsescu was first impeached by the Parliament) (Neagu, April 19, 2008) or led by trade unions (when in 2010 due to the financial crisis the Romanian government decided to reduce all the salaries of the public servants by 25 percent) (Mediafax, May 6, 2010). There were several other issues in 2012: the government had volatile support in the Parliament, due to the President playing a very active role in internal politics, sometimes forcing the limits of the Constitution (as a result then President Traian Băsescu was impeached for the second time by the Parliament (Andrei, July 4, 2012), the first cases of high corruption unveiled by the anti-corruption department where a former Prime Minister (Biro, March 28, 2012) and a couple of MPs were convicted and sent to prison. In 2012, then former Minister of Foreign Affairs described the protesters as the "stupid slum" and afterwards he has resigned together with the whole cabinet (Business Magazin, February 15, 2012).

It is interesting how after the fall of the Government on February 5, 2012, the next social outbursts were already in place: the Anti-Counterfeiting Trade Agreement (ACTA) (Presada, 2012), and a movement growing in Transylvania against the gold exploitation from Roşia Montană. This movement was combined on the internet under the name *United We Save Rosia Montana!* and culminated in September 2013 with large-scale protests, where over 20,000 people attended in Bucharest alone (Ivanov, September 15, 2013). As result of that, the government backed down from the law that would have allowed for gold exploitation in Roşia Montană.

The protests have continued with anti-fracking movements while the internet movement changed its name to *United We Save!*. 2014 came with new protests that have been caused by perceived electoral fraud. 2015 was the year of the tragic accident at the Colectiv night club where due to a lack of compliance with health and safety regulations, fire erupted from fireworks during a rock concert. Concert participants were trapped inside as the flames were expanding. A total of 64 people died and many more were injured. People flocked to the streets once they heard that the hospitals were not properly equipped to handle severe burns and some people died after the accident due to infections (Pojoranu, 2017). To the Facebook group *United We Save* has been added another one, *Corupţia Ucide* (Corruption Kills), and with 25,000 again protesting on the streets, the then Prime Minister, Victor Ponta, resigned.

When OUG13 was passed in the middle of the night, considering the previous successes of street protests, Romanians were quick to flood the streets and show their discontent both in the capital city, in the country and abroad (Ursu, 2017). The movement took the name #rezist and eventually led to the replacement of the SDP government.

The organizers of the #rezist protests used all the arsenal known from PR and communication tools – from appeals on Facebook to mainstream media and humorous post-cards and placards – to convey their message (Armanca, 2017). Street protests continued in 2018, with the SDP's intention to modify the Criminal Codes and put pressure on the independence of the justice system, while the social media movements have transformed from #rezist to #insist.

As mentioned above, the participants in the protests have been diverse, they have lacked visible leadership, but nonetheless managed to attract a record number of people. For the purpose of this chapter alone, my aim is to understand from activists and PR practitioners who have organized and attended the protests how each group perceived the relationship between the use of PR tools, people who participated in the protests, as well as methods and their potential role in shaping message and moods. This made me wonder about the role PR practitioners have played in the protests.

This chapter therefore addresses the following questions:

1 To what extent have activists felt they acted as so-called stakeholders in waiting, rather than publics?
2 Are Romanian activists motivated by communicating a cause or to prevail over power?
3 What are the main differences, in the activists'/protesters' view, between an activist and a PR practitioner?

In order to answer to the above questions, I have conducted in-depth semi-structured interviews with six PR practitioners and activists:[2] B.S. (male, 43), B.I. (female, 29), M.D. (female, 46), N.C. (male, 28), D.T. (male, 40) and G.B. (male, 29), where at least four of them work in PR and communication related fields: B.I. (female, 29), M.D. (female, 46), D.T. (male,40) and G.B. (male, 29). Five of them were from Romania, one is a Romanian living abroad, three of them are from Bucharest and attended the protests in the capital, two of them are from a city in Transylvania and are mostly involved in the local protests and one attended the last protests in diaspora.

The interviews were conducted during March–April 2018, via Skype video and were recorded using Piezzo. The audio files have been transcribed and content analysis has been employed to extract the results.

The interviews featured questions ranging from: their activist history, their motivation to become activists, the reasons why they define themselves as activists (what makes them different from other citizens or participants to protests). Other questions also aimed to uncover whether they – as activists – have used PR tools in their activities, if they feel that there are similarities between PR practitioners and activists or differences and what are those.

For the first question, related to their activist history, the participants responded equally in terms of the trigger for their activism as well as regarding the most significant moments of their activity. B.S. (male, 43), became an activist while listening to *Voice of America* radio station when he was 12–13 years old and thus he discovered that he has an interest in politics. He took part in the 1989 protest and later, during the miners' assault of the University Square, he was arrested and spent a day in jail. Since January 2012 he has been an active participant in all major protests from Romania.

N.C (male, 28) attended the first protest in response to the Copyright Act (ACTA Treaty) when due to some "nasty" provisions related to copyright and piracy, people became scared that they might go to jail for downloading movies from the internet. His first action, a blast email application for the members of the European Parliament, kept on sending automatic emails to everyone. The process was very fast: "There was one MEP who was making a public plea to stop sending her emails because she is invaded and she will vote against the Treaty." In 2012 he attended a "cascade" of protests – against Ponta, against plagiarism, against the President's impeachment etc.

> I was going every day after work and we were trying to gather more and more people ... then Roşia Montană started and I believe that this was the zero moment for the civil society of Romania ... People noticed that you can succeed, if you put continue pressure through protests you can change something.

N.C. soon joined a newly political party. He continued to attend the protests having a lower profile, to be one of the crowd members:

> I was trying not to shout, not to shout directly against the SDP ... so there are no wrong interpretations that my party is there for propaganda.

M.D. (female, 46) started a career in civic art, with painters and artists. As part of that, she started doing political posters, then mind blog campaigns, and after that they got involved in the Roşia Montană movement.

> I started my involvement by producing posters ... one of my colleagues has made the design of the leaf ... then we thought about setting out a Romanian platform for online petitions.

Activism for her is not a hobby anymore, but a daily job:

> When the OUG13 protests started, we had a database with 200,000 members to whom we have send an email and asked them to get on the street.

Based on this experience, she got involved in the production of guides for civil disobedience, how to behave during a protest and while working on that "we thought about how we can call this thing and then the idea came upon us – let's call it Rezist (resist) and the rest is history."

D.T. (male, 40) does not want to be labelled an activist. He wants to be called a citizen because this is the perspective from which he attends the protests. "If citizens don't get involved, things cannot change."

The defining moment for him was a couple of years ago when together with a group of friends he decided to set up an informal group of professionals to get involved in civic activities. One of the "coolest things" they did was to gather around 2,500 people to observe the election processes. They made opinion polls, projects, pins through crowdsourcing. Despite my persistence that such actions are those of an activist, D.T. replied

> In general one is defined according to what one wants to do or what one would do in a perfect situation. In a perfect situation I would like to read, let's say 200 books a year ... If I am a citizen, then I am a 2.0 citizen, I am a person who can provide available resources of time and others, let's say networking to the use of my community.

G.B. (male, 29) become an activist in 2011 when he attended a flashmob for the first time, a simple exercise where young people wrote FREEDOM with letters printed on A4 papers. That was enough to the gendarmes to take them to the police station and give them a fine.

> This is what has activated me, because there was an old law ... one had to declare a protest at least three days in advance, which is a dumb thing, you may not know you will need to protest.

He then started to ask people to meet, at a certain time and place through Facebook, then when people made a habit of it, he donated the event to other organizers. He became an activist and continued to get involved with Roşia Montană and fracking and United We Save.

> I felt I resonated with some of these things, in other cases the decision process of the protest organizers was too slow. I feel I am now a citizen asking for his rights, I am not an activist, or a part of a sub-group, I am an active citizen.

B.I. (female, 29) became aware she was an activist a couple of years ago. She sees a connection between her activism and her activities as a teenager, which included volunteering, writing petitions, and attending flashmobs and public events. While at university, she started attending protests from 2010 in the University Square.

> I cannot recall what my convictions were then, I was not a big fan of president Băsescu and it felt to me that the process [of impeachment] was not very transparent...

B.I. was also involved in the Roşia Montană protests as a member of the Romanian diaspora, and continues to sign petitions, support NGOs. More recently, she has started a local diaspora initiative in the town where she is currently residing. The idea behind this group of citizens who have met while protesting in the streets was to do something more than protest, and

> to make a difference in terms of policies and decisions both in Romania but also in the Diaspora, having in mind the 2020 elections, to have a community we can mobilize to vote, think critically, evaluate the candidates…

And while understanding how important it was to mobilize the diaspora, B.I. understood that it is equally important to connect with Romanian diaspora organizations from other countries as well as with communities from the country. She has undertaken all these activities voluntarily, in her own time and apart from her daily job. In referring to her activity and the diaspora group she is involved with, B.I. states:

> there are people who live here, and even if they are for a short or a long time abroad, they are still very attached to Romania, of what happens there and they want to get involved and they will keep getting involved so they don't feel disconnected of what is going on.

As mentioned in the short biographies out of the six respondents, four have been involved in civic activities event prior to the 2012 street protests, thus the 2017 #rezist movement has come on this prior preparation and awareness.

In terms of the motivation for their actions the interviewees mentioned the following types of categories, which resulted from the verbatim analysis and then clustering their statements, based on content similarity.

All interviewees have mentioned that during their activities they have used PR tools and tactics, to a different extent and variety – from banners and workshops to street flash mobs, discussions, brainstorming etc., but sometimes for different purposes: to provide a means for citizens to contact directly their elected officials (female, 46), to fight – "when you fight someone it is important to define clearly whom you're fighting against and those are at the moment the PSD–ALDE coalition, who is in power at the moment" (male, 40), to produce a kind of political balance and stop a "power-grab" and stop abuses (male, 28), to ask for support of the things you believe in (male, 43), "to wake up as many people as possible … put public pressure when things are not just or wrong or abusive" (male, 29).

With regards differences between activists and PR practitioners, verbatim analysis and then clustering the statements based on the content similarity, I have identified three main categories, each explained by a series of behaviors, different in the case of activists and practitioners.

Table 10.1 Types of motivations of the activists for organizing and attending social protests

Motivations of activists	Statements
Feeling disenfranchised, dissatisfied, powerless, needing social justice	"This method [protest] was the most handy, especially if you feel disenfranchised ... people get out of dissatisfaction, not in an attempt to provide constructive feedback" (male, 28) "... this part of social justice, I think that we all cannot live well, if some of us do not live well or have no chance to live well or better and this is unfair" (female, 29)
Fighting the government and putting pressure on it	"You need to put pressure on the ruling party" (male, 28) "Let's fight, let's live in a democracy" (male, 29) "Nothing happens if you don't get involved ... there is no other way" (female, 46)
Stop the abuses (government, gendarmes, dumb laws)	"To stop abuses ..." (male, 28), "The gendarmes and their abuses have motivated me to get involved and stay involved ... the systematic abuse from the force institutions" (male, 29) "I look around and see how they [government] are passing a dumb law which sooner or later will affect my interests too" (male, 43)
Intrinsic motivations	"I had an intrinsic motivation, to contribute to the wellbeing of the people around me" (female, 29) "I did it out of patriotism ... love for society ... for a better world for me and my children" (male, 43)
Self-actualization/self development	"It something that makes me feel good, to value myself, self-actualization" (male, 40)

From stakeholders in waiting to activism

From the short activist biographies presented by the six respondents, the results are that at least four of them can be included in the *activists as stakeholders in waiting category*, due to the fact that the large protests of the 2000s found them with several other civic actions already completed and already deeming civic duties as incumbent to their normal day to day tasks. Most of the interviewees started their civic engagement while in high school, and when the big street movements started, they were already there, some of them part of the organizing teams – not as a reaction to the event, but in the streets trying to influence the unfolding of events while they were unfolding. They have developed an awareness related to what power structures are allowed or not to do, and were prepared to respond. They were ready to revoke or not grant the license to operate for the government or corporations, anticipating, preparing. In brief, they have not

Table 10.2 Differences between PR practitioners and activists from the point of view of participating in social movements

Differences activists – PR practitioners	Statements
Activists are not PR practitioners nor should they become, they should keep low profiles	"I didn't do it very much [PR tools], to attend flash mobs or to try to be a vector of image to channel stuff" (male, 28)
	"I don't try to put myself in front of a protest, to ride the way ... you need to keep a plurality of voices ... if a movement has no leader it is hard to kill it, it is hard to discredit it ... it is easy to keep the point of a movement on a cause, not on what X person said about that cause and that is the trigger for people's support" (male, 28)
Activists and PR practitioners can develop conflictual relations about a certain a cause/issue	[PR practitioners] "were a bit mono-maniacs, they had a mission, knew what they have to communicate, they had a product – the product was Roșia Montană ... and did not want to be taken out of that product ... while the activists had ideas and wanted to affirm those ideas ... to make them digestible for the public" (male, 43)
Volunteering for activists vs. paid jobs for PR practitioners	"[for doing PR] there is an extrinsic motivation" (male, 28)
	"maybe the reason is [for the difference between PR practitioners and activists], that some are paid for it, others have a cause and believe in it and dedicate their time voluntarily for it" (male, 29)
	"A PR practitioner can do PR for a brand without believing necessarily in that brand, I mean it is a pure professional thing, while an activist, myself as an activist, I can't speak for all activists ... we do it from a very genuine belief, very intrinsic, very emotional" (female 29)
Support for a cause vs. support for a product and results	"PR, as I see it is a matter of companies ... a core of the domain [PR] 90% of the money and activities are for companies ..." (male, 40)
	"for PR practitioners, it could happen that it is an adventure [protests] once in a lifetime, ... he or she has a moment of indignation ... but in general for an activist it is a choice for a lifetime, you keep it going until you retire" (male, 43)

continued

Table 10.2 Continued

Differences activists – PR practitioners	Statements
PR practitioners don't necessary believe in a brand vs. activists are more authentic, dedicated and truthful in supporting their cause	PR tactics would bring you 50 to 100 people, but not thousands, but a PR campaign will not generate a protest. It must be a rather "visceral" reason. "We, the activists, may have a rather colorful speech, but we don't lie" (female, 46)
	"When you do something for the citizens, you are not an employee, a contractor or an entrepreneur, you are more than that … you are an artist. When an artist does something, he believes he's changing the world … PR it's just a job at the end of the day when your communication is commercial" (male, 40)
Both communicate to reach a goal, but activists are willing to take action to a next level	"If you see that communication takes you nowhere you must take it to the next level at some point, and the most direct and simple way to do it is to have a fiscal strike, where people don't pay taxes or a labor strike and then you block the whole country and the you have a leverage – if you don't do our way, the country is blocked" (male, 28)
Activists are partly PR practitioners or could become	"somehow, everything these people do [the activists] to civically influence is a form of PR…" (male, 40)
	"maybe there are not so big differences [between PR practitioners and activists], I just think that it is a label that many would not want to wear [PR]" (male, 28)
	"I think that the PR practitioners are partly activists … but only a part" (female, 29)
PR practitioners use their skills for social interests, thus are partly activists	"I have seen a few brands who tried to promote an idea of activism, this is something I would like, to see more brands doing civic education" (male, 29)
	"…let's use what we know from our work [PR] for the social interest" (male, 40)
	"there may be PR practitioners who truly are activists, or better say, they have the activist drive … having those skills, they were able to direct those North-Korean style choreographies [the Romanian flag – 2017, the leaf – 2012] … but it is something rather at the periphery of the movement" (male, 43)

only reacted to a situation, but they have actively participated, prepared for not allowing certain action to take place. From this perspective, I feel that labelling stakeholders as publics Grunig (2009), even active publics, is both wrong and inaccurate, as publics are formalized once a communicative act has happened. Therefore, in my opinion, calling them "active groups" or "active networks" would be better suited.

With regards my second research question, all our respondents had at least one motivation connected to prevailing over the power structures, they were targeting empowerment and social action through diverse means of communication including, but not exclusively, PR tools. In other words, they had intrinsic motivations – personal development, patriotism, but mostly motivations connected to establishing fair power relations. They have not done it for the benefit of the government or a third party – they wanted to transform the nature of the debate Keck and Sikkink (1998) and to prevail over other forms of power (Castells, 2015).

In terms of the relationships between PR practitioners and activists, the interviewees' opinions are slightly polarized – while some indicate that activists have little or no connection to PR activities and express a dissociation between the roles of activists and those of PR practitioners, others, who have a PR background, view their roles as partly overlapping when it comes to engagement with and participation in social movements.

Overall, there seems to be an agreement among all interviewees that the values, behaviors and content of public relations for companies and social causes are different, i.e., tactics needed to promote a product or a brand are not necessarily useful to promote a cause. Also, personal emotions are stronger when promoting a cause than when promoting a product.

These results are interesting because they show us that the civic actors and the public relation professionals are still part of two different worlds. With a few exceptions, the activists lack trust in PR practitioners, while the PR activists, even if they try their best when doing a corporate job, they still see it as a job, a project, but not an emotional investment. I am not sure that a complete match between a PR practitioner and an activist is possible, but I am confident that a transformation, a change of perspective, may contribute to a larger overlap and an increase in empathy. Such empathy could be first exercised in a company setting, as proposed by Holtzhausen and Voto (2002) or in partnership with non-profit organizations (Toledano, 2016). The other option that would increase the overlap in the intersection between PR practitioners and activists would be for activists to develop a set of skills specifically designed for social actions. For instance, one of the respondents mentioned that several activists from the #rezist movement started their own TV channel, *Rezistența TV* (male, 43). This could be a first step for entering the mainstream media and PR domain.

This might cast some light for a better understanding of activists as publics or/and stakeholders (Grunig, 2009), for how values are constructed and how influence is exercised through social networks (Castells, 2015) and provides some answers to questions raised by PR academics (Kim & Sriramesh, 2009) about the nature of issues that tend to coalesce activists.

Notes

1 According to the Romanian Constitution, the President can attend Government meetings and when he attends, he is presiding over them.
2 The initials are not those of their real names. They are used to connect a point of view with some specific socio-demographic details.

References

Adi, A. (2017) Protester profiles, in *#rezist – Romania's 2017 anti-corruption protests: causes, development and implications* (Adi, A. & D.G. Lilleker, eds.) Berlin: Quadriga University of Applied Sciences.

Adi, A. & D.G. Lilleker (2017) #rezist: Lessons from the Romanian 2017 protests, in *#rezist – Romania's 2017 anti-corruption protests: causes, development and implications* (Adi, A. & D.G. Lilleker, eds.) Berlin: Quadriga University of Applied Sciences.

Andrei, C. (2012, July 4) *Cele sapte motive ale suspendarii presedintelui Traian Basescu. Ce contine documentul USL*, available at www.gandul.info/politica/cele-sapte-motive-ale-suspendarii-presedintelui-traian-basescu-ce-contine-documentul-usl-9813858, viewed on May 20, 2018.

Armanca, B. (2017) Humor as a form of symbolic communication during February 2017 protests in Romania, in *#rezist – Romania's 2017 anti-corruption protests: causes, development and implications* (Adi, A. & D.G. Lilleker, eds.) Berlin: Quadriga University of Applied Sciences.

Berger, B.K. (2005) Power over, power with, and power to relations: Critical reflections on public relations, the dominant coalition and activism, *Journal of Public Relations Research*, 17(1), 5–28.

Biro, A. (2012, March 28) *Motivarea instantei*, available at https://anticoruptie.hotnews.ro/stiri-anticoruptie-11858894-motivarea-instantei-fost-condamnat-adrian-nastase-doi-ani-inchisoare-executare-dosarul-trofeul-calitatii-coruptia-clasei-politice-din-romania-personificata-2004-adrian-nastase-nu-mai-poate-tolerata-ia.htm, viewed on May 20, 2018.

Bortun, D. & B. Cheregi (2017) Ideological meaning in the 2017 Romanian protests, in *#rezist – Romania's 2017 anti-corruption protests: causes, development and implications* (Adi, A. & D.G. Lilleker, eds.) Berlin: Quadriga University of Applied Sciences.

Bortun, D. & C. Crişan (2012) Levels of corporate community engagement. Who should provide the social license to operate, *The Romanian Economic Journal*, 46bis, 41–53.

Boutilier, R.G. & I. Thomson (2012) *Modelling and measuring the social license to operate: fruits of a dialogue between theory and practice*, available at: http://socialicense.com/publications/Modelling%20and%20Measuring%20the%20SLO.pdf, viewed on September 1, 2012.

Business Magazin (2012, February 15) *Cum a plecat guvernul Boc – de la A la Z*, available at www.businessmagazin.ro/actualitate/politic/cum-a-plecat-guvernul-boc-de-la-a-la-z-9238270, viewed on May 20, 2018.

Castells, M. (2015) *Networks of outrage and hope*, 2nd edition. Cambridge: Polity Press. Kindle edition.

Ciszek, E.L. (2015) Bridging the gap: Mapping the relationship between activism and public relations. *Public Relations Review*, *41(4)*, 447–455.

Cooper, J. (2012) Dissonance theory, in *The handbook of theories of social psychology* (van Lange, P.A.M., A.W. Kruglanski & E.T. Higgins, eds.). Sage: London.

Crane, A., D. Matten & J. Moon (2008) *Corporations and citizenship*. Cambridge: Cambridge University Press.

Crişan, C. & A. Adi (2016) A new paradigm: How social movements shape corporate social responsibility after the financial crisis, in *Corporate social responsibility in the post-financial crisis era* (Theofilou A., G. Grigore & A. Stancu, eds.). Palgrave Studies in Governance, Leadership and Responsibility. Cham, Switzerland: Palgrave Macmillan.

Doan, M.A. & M. Toledano (2018) Beyond organization-centered public relations: Collective action through a civic crowdfunding campaign, *Public Relations Review*, *44(1)*, 37–46.

Dutta, M.J. (2009) On Spivak, in *Public relations and social theory: key figures and concepts* (Ihlen, O., B. ban Ruler & M. Fredriksson, eds.). New York: Routledge.

Edwards, L.M. (2012) Defining the "object" of public relations research: A new starting point, *Public Relations Inquiry*, *1(1)*, 7–30.

Fassin, Y. (2009) The stakeholder model refined, *Journal of Business Ethics*, 84, 113–135.

Fisher, M. (2018) Still fighting the good fight: An analysis of student activism and institutional response, *Public Relations Review*, 44, 22–27.

Freeman, E.R., J.S. Harrison & A.C. Wicks (2007) *Managing for stakeholders: Survival, relation and success*. New Haven, USA: Caravan Books Project.

Freeman, R.E. (1994) The politics of stakeholder theory: Some future directions. *Business Ethics Quarterly*, 409–421.

Gower, K.K. (2010) Public relations research at the crossroads, *Journal of Public Relations Research*, *18(2)*, 177–190.

Grunig, J.E. (1978) Defining publics in public relations: The case of a suburban hospital, *Journalism Quarterly*, *55(1)*, 109–124.

Grunig, J.E. (2009) Paradigms of global relations in the age of digitalisation, *PRism*, *6(2)*, 1–19.

Grunig, L.A., M.D. Dozier & Grunig, J.E. (1994) *IABC excellence in public relations and communication management, phase 2: qualitative study, initial analysis: cases of excellence*, San Francisco, CA: IABC Research Foundation.

Holtzhausen, D.R. & R. Voto (2002) Resistance from the margins: The postmodern public relations practitioner as organizational activist, *Journal of Public Relations Research*, *14(1)*, 57–84.

Hotnews (2012, January 9) *Traian Basescu catre Raed Arafat: sa nu cream psihoza ca acest guvern ticalos crea sa distruga sistemul de ambulanta. Daca asta e mesajul, e mincinos si incorect*, available at www.hotnews.ro/stiri-esential-1114 9580-traian-basescu-catre-raed-arafat-nu-cream-psihoza-acest-guvern-ticalos-vrea-distruga-sistemul-ambulanta-daca-asta-mesajul-mincinos-incorect.htm#self, viewed on May 20, 2018.

Ilhen, O. (2009) On Pierre Bourdieu: Public relations in field struggles, in *Public relations and social theory: key figures and concepts* (Ihlen, O., B. ban Ruler & M. Fredriksson, eds.). New York: Routledge.

Ivanov, C. (2013, September 15) *Protest gigantic in Bucuresti impotriva exploatarii de la Rosia Montana cu peste 15.000 de oameni. Protestatarii au blocat tot centrul Capitalei, au marsaluit prin oras si au cerut demisia lui Ponta*, available at www.hotnews.ro/stiri-esential-15584298-rosia-montana-15-proteste-jur-200-manifestanti-adunat-piata-universitatii.htm, viewed on May 20, 2018.

Keck, M.E. & K. Sikkink (1998) *Activists beyond borders*. Ithaca and London: Cornell University Press, Kindle edition.

Kim, J.N. & K. Sriramesh (2009) Activism and public relations, in *The global public relations handbook, revised and expanded edition* (Sriramesh, K. & D. Vercic, eds.). New York: Routledge.

Kuhn, T. ([1962] 2008) *Structura revoluțiilor stiințifice*. Bucharest: Humanitas.

Mediafax (2010, May 6) *Basescu anunta scaderea pensiilor cu 15%, a fondului de salarii cu 25% si a subventiilor*, available at www.mediafax.ro/social/basescu-anunta-scaderea-pensiilor-cu-15-a-fondului-de-salarii-cu-25-si-a-subventiilor-6096508, viewed on May 20, 2018.

Momoc, A. (2017) Particracy against democracy, in *#rezist – Romania's 2017 anti-corruption protests: causes, development and implications* (Adi, A. & D.G. Lilleker, eds.). Berlin: Quadriga University of Applied Sciences.

Neagu, A. (2008, April 19) *19 aprilie 2007 – ziua suspendarii lui Traian Basescu*, available at www.hotnews.ro/stiri-politic-2842037-19-aprilie-2007-ziua-suspendarii-lui-traian-basescu.htm, viewed on May 20, 2018.

Philips, D. & P. Young (2009) *Online public relations: a practical guide to developing an online strategy in the world of social media*. London: Kogan Page.

Pojoranu, C. (2017) The unexpected Romanians: Fighting civic apathy with civic energy, in *#rezist – Romania's 2017 anti-corruption protests: Causes, development and implications* (Adi, A. & D.G. Lilleker, eds.). Berlin: Quadriga University of Applied Sciences.

Porritt, J. (2007) *Capitalism as if the world matters*. London: Earthscan.

Presada, F. (2012) *Case study on the Romanian protests*. Bucharest: The Resource Center for Public Participation – CeRe.

Rogalski, E. (2017) The "revolution of light" came from darkness, in *#rezist – Romania's 2017 anti-corruption protests: causes, development and implications* (Adi, A. & D.G. Lilleker, eds.). Berlin: Quadriga University of Applied Sciences.

Schölzel, H. & H. Nothhaft (2016) The establishment of facts in public discourse: Actor-network-theory as a methodological approach in PR-research, *Public Relations Inquiry, 5(1)*, 53–69.

Taylor, M. & C.H. Botan (2004) Public relations: State of the field, *Journal of Communication, 54(4)*, 645–661.

Toledano, M. (2016) Advocating for reconciliation: Public relations, activism, advocacy and dialogue, *Public Relations Inquiry, 5(3)*, 277–294.

Ursu, R. (2017) In the name of the law, in *#rezist – Romania's 2017 anti-corruption protests: causes, development and implications* (Adi, A. & D.G. Lilleker, eds.). Berlin: Quadriga University of Applied Sciences.

Wolf, K. (2018) Power struggles: A sociological approach to activist communication, *Public Relations Review, 44*, 308–316.

11 Activist PR in Vietnam

Public participation via Facebook to save 6,700 trees

*Nguyen Thi Thanh Huyen and
Nguyen Hoang Anh*

The analysis of this chapter suggests that social media can majorly influence how an organization performs public relations, with public participation in social dialogue emerging as a form of social activism. The authors therefore argue that organizations should closely monitor social media to understand the motivations underlying public discussions to proactively communicate with the public via open dialogue, which would in turn encourage the public to contribute to policy development. The chapter also shows that individuals, groups or existing NGOs can effectively make use of social media to advocate for the issuance or termination of a public policy.

The development of social media has recently led to a paradigm shift from public relations to public engagement. This means that the greater public can be increasingly involved in an organization's decision-making process, altering thus the relationship between the organization and the public by making it more open and transparent. Previously, the dialogue between organizations and the public had focused on interacting mainly through the organizations' websites instead of building relationships through social networks (Taylor & Kent, 2014). Social media has empowered the public to communicate equally with organizations. In other words, social media gave birth to the activist PR movement that organizations could no longer ignore. Social media also drives organizations to adjust their decision-making, which emphasizes listening to social feedback in order to gain support and consensus in policy enforcement phase (Wallinga & Renes, 2013).

With the increasing influence of social media, more and more research concerned with the roles and benefits of social media in establishing, maintaining, and developing relationships between organizations and its public through dialogues emerged (Bortree & Seltzer, 2009; Briones et al., 2011; Waters & Jamal, 2011). Although this is a two-way conversation in which any side could start speaking, studies have been more inclined to approach strategies, tactics, and effects of establishing and maintaining discussion from within the organization than from the public (Cho & De Moya, 2014). In fact, with the explosion of social media, any individual can quickly set up their own channels to start expressing ideas, engaging comments, sharing emotions, or petitioning a certain organization to act responsibly. In effect, the ubiquity and accessibility of social media and social networks enable individuals and activists alike to avoid becoming silenced, marginalized or even harassed. Instead, by becoming the center of social attention and their peer groups, they have more visibility and leverage to instigate noticeable changes (Shaw & Van Leuven, n.d.). This is also the case of a Vietnam online driven protest questioning and contesting the implementation of an urban expansion project aimed at restoring and replacing as many as 6,700 trees in the city of Hanoi during 2014–2015.

Focusing on this case, this chapter analyzes the Vietnamese public participation on Facebook in petitioning the Hanoi city authorities to review the public project. In doing so, we seek to understand why the social network petition was successful. To do so we are investigating both the motivations of the individuals setting up Facebook pages and groups related to the project, and their strategy, if any, and also the groups and pages users' comments and discussions to identify key themes.

The 6,700 trees protection movement

In developing Vietnam, the government has been undertaking numerous urban expansion projects, each with varied environmental implications. Most notably, a project aiming to restore and replace urban trees on both sides of Hanoi streets (referred to here as the re-plant trees project) during 2014–2015 was approved by the Hanoi People's Committee on November 11, 2013. This meant that the city would cut down and replace more than 6,700 rotten, decayed, or otherwise categorized as improper trees on 190 streets in Hanoi and replace them with young trees, of the same species and age.

More than a month before the project was due to be implemented, the Hanoi Department of Construction had made announcements about the project in online newspapers (Vo, 2015). However, many citizens were not aware of the project and therefore surprised to see a series of big trees on many streets abruptly cut down in March 2015. As the result, Vietnamese people started a huge "green protection movement" that has grown from online to offline activities and ended up with the first protest against the plan of the Hanoi People's Committee.

The movement started on Facebook as it allows people to more freely share their opinions and provide personal updates. The government's absence from the platform and its focus on other media channels that it regulates, make Facebook a good platform for public debate independent of governmental oversight. Moreover, almost 50 percent of Vietnam's population of 92 million has an account, which is almost equal to the total population connected to the internet – 53 percent (We Are Social, 2017).

Without a doubt, this makes Facebook the most popular social network in Vietnam.

On March 16, 2015, Mr. Tran Dang Tuan, former Deputy General Director of Vietnam Television, a well-known activist and candidate for the National Assembly, posted an open letter to the President of Hanoi People's Committee on his own Facebook account to petition the city to cease cutting down healthy trees and publicly allow local people to monitor which trees would be cut down on each street, and at the same time consult scientists and listen to public comments. The original post of the petition letter received 6,567 likes, 789 shares, and 588 comments (Le et al., 2016, p. 16). When reused a day later (March 17) by online newspapers, it attracted much more interaction on Facebook. The event culminated when Mr. Phan Dang Long, a spokesman of Hanoi Communist Party Committee, said to journalists in a regular press conference on March 17: "if cutting down trees also required consent from the people, then what is the use of elected government?"[1] (Hong, 2015). This statement incited many negative comments on Facebook. A few days later, some local NGOs revealed the lack of transparency as many newly planted trees were not of the same species as announced.

Many others' creative offline efforts inspired the online discussion. For example, yellow ribbons were tied around trees that would be cut down to mourn for their deaths; many pictures of people hugging trees were taken; public marches such as "Tree Hugs Picnic," "Green Walk," new popular song parodies, themed drawings, etc. were made in order to put pressure on the Hanoi government to stop cutting trees. Notably, on March 17, 2015, the campaign with the goal of collecting 6,700 online signatures on the open letter to the Chairman of the Hanoi People's Committee was initiated on the Facebook page named "6,700 people for 6,700 green trees," whose admin was a housewife in Hanoi. The number of 6,700 signatures was a hint at the 6,700 trees soon to be cut down. As a result, the page collected more than 22,000 signatures from netizens. The mainstream journalists were attracted to the public trend and updated regularly on the green protection activities that made the case become explosive.

Under the pressure of public opinion Hanoi People's Committee issued a decision to stop the project on March 20 in order to have inspections of the sites carried out. Two days later (March 22) the Committee decided to discipline some officials of the Department of Construction arguing that they had many shortcomings in directing and managing the implementation of the project without properly assessing the impacts on the society. On April 13, Hanoi People's Committee reported the inspection results; it indicated that the policy was right, however that there were errors in implementation and especially in communication. This project was officially closed after that and the city started another tree planting project with more consideration of communication strategies.

Social media and the uses and gratifications of public participation

Public participation has been emphasized as a process by which the interests, needs, benefits of the community are communicated, contributed to the decision-making of the government, based on dialogue, two-way communication, mutual interaction with the common goal of better policing (Creighton, 2005; Bleiker, 1994; Susskind, 1999). Public participation is considered one of the most important factors that can affect government decisions, particularly when referring to political, economic, social and environmental issues. However, there is no agreed-upon concept of public participation in the literature. The International Association for Community Engagement (IAP2, 2012) approached the definition of public participation by identifying core values when assuming that the public should have a voice in decisions that might affect their lives. The Co-intelligence Institute (n.d.) also indicates that participation in the process empowers each individual in the community to engage in the formulation and decision-making of government policies. By participating in public discussions on social media on a public issue, the public can find the meaning in their activities, such as a sense of belonging or social responsibility.

Among many studies on public participation, Schroeter et al. (2016) reviewed more than 30 definitions of participatory processes in order to find discriminating criteria for measuring the quality of process and outputs/outcomes. They defined public participation as

> a set of processes that include representatives of different social groups organized by a third party with the purpose of initiating a discourse and cooperative counseling process aimed at informing collective-biding decisions.
>
> (p. 117)

This definition was further operationalized into three criteria for measuring the quality of participation processes, including inclusiveness, information exchange and learning, and influence on the political decision. These main characteristics were connected to eight sub-criteria, such as the platform for communication and *negotiation, equal contribution, exchange knowledge, common base information, transparency, effectiveness, and a shared understanding of impact results*. The social network has many advantages to meet the requirement of these sub-criteria; therefore it is convenient for both the organization and the public to initiate their participation in the social movement.

The term "social movements" refers to a voluntary, purposeful effort by which organizations and individuals act in a rhythmic manner to achieve a sufficiently strong level of influence to create or inhibit social, political, economic or environmental change (Davita & Deric, 2011). Especially in the field of PR, the development of social media has led to the emergence of the new concept, "activist PR" (Adi, 2015; Coombs & Holladay, 2012; Curtin, 2016). There are various approaches to it, with Moloney, McQueen, Surowiec, and Yaxley (2013) proposing a distinction between the terms of "dissent PR," "protest PR" and "activist PR communications" (p. 511) where the latter one includes the former two. In our view, activist PR is when individuals/small groups are using social media as a PR strategy to express their opinions on the injustice of society and create dialogue relationships to connect people and call for change action. Social activists, groups, and individuals can actively choose social networks to communicate with different audiences, encourage them to engage in social movements for the sake of good. Facebook or Twitter can reach more publicity than traditional media. Social network helps individual with the ability to organize without having a leader. Any idea and request will be discussed on Facebook without any meetings or rules. In this sense, Adi's (2015) paper is among the few that analyze this interaction from a PR/communication perspective, investigating how activist groups apply public relations techniques to influence other publics, including the mass media. What Adi's paper, however, is missing is the identification of the motivations for public participation in such activities and discussions. Cho and De Moya (2014) do that by incorporating the Uses and Gratifications theory with message types in public-initiated Facebook conversations. In doing so, Cho and De Moya categorized the themes of public comments on two NGO Facebook fan pages into seven types of public comments/messages: *inquiries, requests, experience, grievance, advocacy, advisory, and self-promotion.* By analyzing these message types more specifically, they could generalize the media users' motivations similarly to the previous studies, such as entertainment, integration or social interaction, personal identity, information, but adding one more new motivation as exchange, which was used when the public ask the organization to help them or others in need (p. 8).

The above studies results inspired and suggested to us a method to investigate the Vietnamese activists' fan pages/groups on Facebook related to the case of 6,700 trees to see if there are similar types of messages and motivations as well as how admins created and managed a huge social discussion on their platforms to achieve their goals.

For this chapter, we have adapted the Cho and De Moya (2014) study methodology to determine the types of messages along with the motivations of network users behind them in order to describe the public trend of interaction. More specifically, content analysis was employed to explore the types of messages that admins and publics posted and commented on the three biggest Facebook fan pages/groups related to the incident, including: "6,700 people for 6,700 trees,"[2] "For a green Hanoi,"[3] and "6,700 trees."[4] An analysis of nearly three months (from March 17 until May 2, 2015) of Facebook conversations initiated by these fan pages/groups revealed the types of messages that the public used in communicating with each other and the local government through social media to achieve their claims of suspension, information transparency, and referendum on the project.

The data were analyzed using the constant comparison method (Glaser & Strauss, 1967). This method involves coding every sentence, assigning a label (or theme) to describe the content coded, and comparing it with the next, thus identifying the themes that emerged from the text (Cho & De Moya, 2014). Following that, the comments were collected and categorized into a list of 11 topics, and then they were grouped into seven categories to prevent the overlap. We divided the sample into two parts and assigned the coding responsibility to two coders. The coder encoded comments according to the topic list and defined the tone of the comment. After coding completion, we worked together to analyze and generalize the themes and the tone of the comment.

We also used in-depth interviews with the Facebook page/groups' admins to learn what had driven them to start the social conversation, whether they understood PR, and how they managed the page/groups to bring change outcomes in the local government policy. We also conducted an in-depth interview with the representative of Hanoi Department of Construction to understand why the project had to be suspended forever and the lessons that they learned from it. All interview results are recorded or saved as written material.

Public interaction on Facebook and message types

During about three months from March 17 to May 2 in 2015, there were a total of 104 entries, 34,754 likes and 7,800 comments on all three studied Facebook page/groups. Among them, the page "6,700 people for 6,700 trees" received the highest number of comments and likes compared to the other two groups. Table 11.1 records the total number of entries, likes, and comments on each and all page/groups.

After reading through many posts and comments, we categorized and coded the pages' entries and comments into seven categories: advocacy,

Table 11.1 Total entries, comments, and likes on three Facebook page/groups, March 17 to May 2, 2015

No.	Page/group	Number of entries	Number of likes	Number of comments
1	"6,700 people for 6,700 trees" page	52	30,067	5,871
2	"For a green Hanoi" group	18	1,456	391
3	"6,700 trees" group	34	3,231	1,538
	Total	104	34,754	7,800

emotion, inquiries, information provision, appeal for action, advisory, and grievance.

The order of presenting the following types of comments is based on decreasing frequency of them on all three Facebook page/groups. The first type of message is *advocacy*, accounting for 40.7 percent of all comments, which refers to comments that support and concur with the idea of suspending the implement the city government's project as well as reject the cutting down trees as in example #1 below:

Thanks to the admins for having launched the movement with the meaningful slogan as "Protect the green, protect the freshness of the living environment." Let's try to be united to stop cutting trees! I personally always support the pure purpose of our better environment.

(Nguyen Thu Thuy, 2015, March 21)

Or comment of responsibility posted by another citizen:

To make a living for myself, I did not pay attention to the case of 6,700 someones is planning, to some people holding papers calling on the street on the past days. It is a shame that without such enthusiastic people, thousands of trees are cut down and then thousands more. I do not have enough money to sit in the car to go to work every day, so I have to ride a motorcycle under the scorching sun of summer without the shade of trees. Today I have brought my whole family to the green walk to cheer and to contribute to the strength of responsible people in the community, with the expectation that this campaign of killing and destroying trees will end. I will be confident enough to teach my little boys about love, their responsibilities to themselves, their families and the community. I love my children and I love Hanoi. I'm proud that I was there today!

(Vu Hung Son, 2015, March 22)

The second type of message types is labeled as *emotion*, accounting for 28.7 percent of all comments, including comments that expressed people's love or tender memories for trees, mournfulness, pain, and also anger when trees on Hanoi streets were cut down even though they were healthy, such as in example #2:

We do not need to synchronize trees of the same species. We love the green trees on the streets of Hanoi that the many previous generations have planted, gave care for us today to enjoy the shade. For decades, even hundreds of years, we can get such beautiful trees. Why such a big problem that people don't have the rights to discuss or consult? Not only can me, but many of you not even imagine a day Hanoi lost the tree lines which have been familiar with many generations.

(Tran Phuong Lien, 2015, March 17)

Or in another comment:

> The killing of such trees is not only wrongdoing with the people of the capital, the people in the country but also with many ancestors have built, poured blood to preserve the capital with thousand years of civilization.
>
> (Nguyen Minh Trang, 2015, March 21)

The third type of message is *inquiries*, including 11.3 percent of all comments, refer to the public's requesting for information regarding the policy, the situation surrounding tree-cutting progress and related issues, such as in example #3 below:

> Is there anyone who has the updated map of trees apart from the one provided by the Hanoi Department of Construction? If not, I can make it with those who can join me!
>
> (Loan Pham, 2015, March 20)

The fourth type of message is information *provision*, accounting for 9.3 percent of all comments. In this type, participants updated on the progress of the tree cutting, shared information on the trees' values to society, contributed consultative ideas in planting trees for sustainable development, and cited examples on tree planting in other countries around the world. A person commented on the group "6,700 Trees" in example #4:

> We should plant along the road, along the fence to make cool shade. The planting area should be large enough because trees grow vertically. If the planting area is narrow the development of root systems will be affected and the tree is easy to fall.
>
> (Nguyen Hong Kien, 2015, March 27)

The fifth type of messages is *call for action*, accounting for 5.2 percent of all comments, refers to publicly initiated calls that aim to connect people and engage them in action to protect the trees as well as the environment, showed in example #5:

> Why cannot every Hanoi lover spend more time to meet at the Hoan Kiem Lake at 9:30 a.m. for the green environment and for the transparency? Members of our group should create an event for everyone to express our attention.
>
> (Phan Dinh Hiep, 2015, April 3)

Advisory is the sixth type of messages, including of 3.3 percent of all comments, shows the contributive ideas or suggestions to save the trees, as in the example #6 below:

In the long run, it is necessary to set up an online tree map system for people to monitor, inspect and protect. Participants contribute information storage. We cannot let the fate of the tree in hands of few people so that it died unjustly as the day before.

(Nguyen Alex, 2015, March 22)

Or:

It is better to send this petition to the National Assembly asking the National Assembly to request the Hanoi People's Committee to discuss the issue before the National Assembly and the people. Many enthusiastic members of the National Assembly will probably force the Hanoi People's Committee to answer.

(Thuy Le, 2015, April 13)

The last type of messages is the *grievance*, presenting in 1.5 percent, included direct complaints or criticisms against the admins of the Facebook site or raise questions about the veracity of information on the tree protection movement which launched on the page/group by its admins. Example #7 showed this:

I do not know why admins have changed the entries so much and deleted many articles or comments. Please be respectful of your fellow members, whether they engage actively or silently. Whoever insults or takes advantages of the politic should be excluded, but if it is the mere opinion of the commentators it shouldn't be erased as we need to respect other different opinions.

(Nhu Quynh de Prelle, 2015, March 30)

Tone, motivations, and the effectiveness of public's comments on Facebook

To find out what motivated people to actively respond to the calling for action by page's admin, we analyzed the tone of the comments, which consists of three properties, including positive, neutral and negative. The positive tone was commented against the removal of 6,700 trees in Hanoi, showing affection for trees, satirizing government and tree-cutting action and calling for other members to join, protect the trees and ask the Hanoi People's Committee to stop cutting trees. Neutral comments provide information, guidance, and advice on planting trees for sustainable development, tree planting and protection experience in other countries. Finally, negative comments express disagreement with the tree protection movement or criticism on the admins and other members of the Facebook page/groups regarding the legal issues pertaining to the movement.

The results exhibited in Table 11.2 show the percentage of positive comments is the majority (73.3 percent), neutral comments accounted for 25.3 percent while negative comments were small (1.4 percent).

Using the Uses and Gratifications theory to analyze the motives of commentators adapted from the study by Cho and De Moya (2014), we found four similar motivations, including information seeking, social interaction/integration, personal identity, empowerment, and a new motivation we called civil responsibility, which expressed the commentator's willingness to contribute for social good. These motivations are attached to the main types of messages analyzed with the examples above. At the same time, the types of messages show that they fit into three indicators to assess the quality of public participation in Schroeter et al. (2016), including inclusiveness (#1), information exchange and learning (#2), and influence on political decisions (#3). Table 11.3 summarizes the results of this finding.

Table 11.2 The user comments' tones, March 17 to May 2, 2015

No.	Page/group	Positive	Neutral	Negative	Number of comments
1	6,700 people for 6,700 trees	4,398	1,269	75	5,742
2	6,700 trees	642	538	22	1,202
3	For a green Hanoi	312	40	5	357
	Total	5,352 (73.3%)	1,847 (25.3%)	102 (1.4%)	7,301 (100%)

Table 11.3 Motivation and the effectiveness of the public participation in the protest against cutting 6,700 trees via Facebook

Motivation	Types of message	Example	Indicator
Empowerment	Advocacy, advisory, grievance	#1, #6, #7	#3
Personal identity	Emotion	#2	#1
Information seeking, exchanging, and learning	Inquiries, information provision	#3, #4	#2
Social interaction and integration	Information provision	#4	#1
Civil responsibility	Advocacy, inquiries, appeal, advisory	#1, #3, #5, #6	#3

A starting point in activist PR in Vietnam

In Vietnam, where the traditional mass media including print, broadcasting, and online newspapers are controlled by the government, this was the first time that a large number of the public used social networks to protest and ask the local government to suspend the implemented policy, which ultimately incited the city government to make concessions. It is no coincidence that people in Hanoi had such a strong reaction. The online influence had spanned beyond discussing, commenting and expressing emotions on Facebook to offline action. For instance, on March 20, 2015, a citizen of Hanoi attracted the public attention by holding the sign "I am a green tree. I am a tree" while standing in a hole on the Le Duan Street, where an old tree had been cut before. His message represented an age-old traditional belief: like people, trees also have souls and voices.

Traditionally, Vietnamese people like to live in harmony with the environment where trees directly help to avoid the heat of the tropical sun. The tree is the symbol, popular cultural code for Vietnamese people as shown in the oft-quoted words of the President Ho Chi Minh: "For the benefit of ten years planting the tree. For the sake of hundred years growing people"[5] or in the lyrics of a famous song by musician Tran Long An (1984) "when thinking about a life, I often remember about the forest."[6] Therefore, the call for protecting the trees on Facebook has received support from a large number of people.

In order to see how PR is understood and applied in this certain case, we interviewed two groups of people, including the administrators of the Facebook page/group, and the representative of the Hanoi Department of Construction, which was the local governmental organization responsible for the re-plant project.

Administrators who set up Facebook pages/groups in this case considered themselves individual activists who spontaneously realized their responsibilities to share the needs of protecting the green value for the city they are living in using Facebook. For example, the page "6,700 people for 6,700" trees was initiated by Mrs. T., a Hanoi home-maker. After reading Mr. Tran Dang Tuan's open letter to Hanoi Peoples Committee, she felt very heartbroken and began the page as an outlet, mainly to share a love for trees, and the importance of trees especially in an urban setting. To her surprise, after 24 hours there were about 10,000 page likes and at its peak, more than 60,000 likes, making the page a space for connecting people, sharing information, and even calling for action. By then many of her friends, members of the page, including journalists, environmental scientists, lawyers, network security specialists, and social activists, joined in a closed group of admins to help plan and run the page.

Among the three page/groups, page "6,700 people for 6,700 trees" is the most successful in attracting public participation during the incident. Based on the effective indicators suggested by Schroeter et al. (2016), through content analysis and interview with its admins, we discovered that the page has created an open space of equality for every people to communicate and contribute without censoring and allowed a free flow of information exchange and learning by its entries and comments in order to create a common understanding of the participation process and results. Therefore, along with other groups/pages, page "6,700 people for 6,700 trees" had influenced the political decision, which brought the Hanoi Peoples Committee to stop implementation of the project forever. As one admin of the page "6,700 people for 6,700 trees" said:

> We do not clearly and systematically understand what PR is. We followed the principle of equally respecting people's opinions to manage the page. For the negative comments of some members who against the idea of our site, our point is not to block but just remind them that their opinion was not welcomed by page's members. This would create a culture of dialogue to make other people know what is good and not good. We respect the freedom of speech of all people, not censorship of comments and try to lead it into dialogue rather than personal excited criticism.
>
> (H. N., Administrator, Facebook page "6,700 people for 6,700 trees," interview in 2017)

The admin of the group "For a green Hanoi" also said that they did not want to censor any comments. However, when some members responded too aggressively, such as instigating violence by inciting people to attack the security forces, separating the political views that ignored the group's biggest goal of protecting the green, they did decide to block these users from the group and also publicly inform and warn others about their decision to ensure the peaceful marches in the center of the city (Administrator Facebook page "For a green Hanoi," interview in 2017).

It is notable that the admins of pages/groups were actively interacting with the public by responding to users' comments. For example, when the public wanted to participate in marching for trees but wondered whether it was legal, the admins of the group "For a green Hanoi" connected them with lawyers to get answers. They also gathered questions from people for the press or shared them, highlighting comments that contained valuable information for the page users. According to one admin of the page "6,700 people for 6,700 trees" in our interview, in the press conference organized by the Hanoi Communist Party Committee on March 17, 2015, they sent 600 questions to journalists, which were gathered and generalized from page's comments, aiming thus to help them to question the organizers. To gain the public trust, the administrator of the page "6,700 people for 6,700 trees" said the following about their way of building credibility:

The identity of the page creator is public so everyone knows who she is. Many people wanted to donate money to help organize the page but we did not accept. All administrators are volunteers. We also did not organize offline activities but only suggested ideas for those who wished to participate in offline activities to create their own small groups to realize. We tried to reply all the hundreds of inbox messages every day. Many people sent us documents like thesis, research paper, etc., so we choose useful information to post on the page or to reply to comments."

(H. N., Administrator, Page "6,700 people for 6,700 trees,"
interview in 2017)

All the pages'/groups' admins are not professional public relations practitioners. Most of them are working in other areas than communication, such as architecture, social work, housework, science, etc. In Vietnam, there are only a few universities that offer public relations programs and many people still do not know about public relations. However, our interviews showed that many Facebook administrators applied good PR insights, including sharing credible viewpoints and providing a peaceful, equal mutual understanding, and respecting environment for commentators when managing their page/groups.

In terms of organizational PR, in our interview, the representative of the Hanoi Department of Construction acknowledged their limitations in understanding PR. In accordance with the regulations of the Ministry of Home Affairs and Ministry of Construction, the Hanoi Department of Construction does not have a functional PR/communication unit. The focal point, that of receiving press information, was assigned to the General Planning office who was tasked with sending one member of staff to implement the decision. Based on the content of information usually requested by reporters, the leaders of the Department of Construction would assign appropriate units to receive and provide information according to their functions and tasks. In 2015 when this case was evolving, the department was not monitoring social media regularly.

Although the project to re-plant trees was key to expanding and improving the city's transportation network, the public communication process of the project was not executed in a timely fashion. At the beginning, the Hanoi People's Committee assigned the Department of Information and Communications to assume the prime responsibility and coordinate with the Department of Construction in disseminating information of this scheme on the media system. However, this task was not implemented effectively due to the limitation in coordinating between state agencies. This caused the Department of Construction to be passive and delayed in the communication of the project. A representative of the Hanoi Department of Construction admitted in our interview that the Hanoi Department of Construction did not actively prepare the communication plan before implementation.

Until the time public opinion was raised against the implementation of the project, the Hanoi Department of Construction and other involved parties in communication responsibility hold press conferences and publicized the content of the project on the official mass media. At this time, the movement against the scheme was formed and reached a climax, therefore it was very difficult for us to soothe the outrage of the public.

(Representative of Hanoi Department of Construction, interview in 2018)

Therefore, the lesson they learned from this case is when constructing and implementing a public project, the organization should communicate and discuss with the public in advance and during the execution period to increase the feasibility of the scheme. In the absence of a functional communication unit, maybe due to lack of regulations, the Department's only option at the time was to rely on other organizations to help them to carry out this responsibility.

At a later stage, since 2016 up to now, when implementing the new project of planting one million trees to 2020, the city has adjusted public relations and communication activities. Hanoi People's Committee has directed the Department of Information and Communication to support the Department of Construction to monitor update and exchange information via email to clarify and resolve urgent issues and to create a more open environment to equally listen to the opinions of the people.

(Representative of Hanoi Department of Construction, interview in 2017)

Conclusion

Social networking has completely changed the way individuals and organizations communicate. Within it, the activist PR may have more power to change the organization's policies. Learning about the message groups, the motivations and the effectiveness of social participation becomes necessary for any organization.

Ordinary people's use of Facebook to stop the implementation of a project in Vietnam has shown that social media can dramatically change the way an organization operates, which then stresses the necessity of an organization to listen more carefully to its publics and their comments regarding its policies and activities. This contains both social and professional values. Accordingly, it proves that individuals or small groups can use social media to mobilize social movements, protect their own interests by paying attention to open, equitable dialogue, and capturing the message's types to understand the motives of the public in order to satisfy their needs. What this chapter also shows is that for the individuals engaging in activism, whether online or offline, the communication of their grievances is not perceived as a public relations or strategic exercise but rather as a core element of negotiating change. This, in a sense, can be good news for PR practitioners in general as it emphasized both the need to build relationships based on an equitable information exchange as well as recognize the value of communication.

For governmental or NGO organization, the case suggests that they should have a two-way dialogue with the public and pay more attention to the opinion of the people, especially not to ignore the voices of individuals in social media. Building online social dialogue will help the organization communicate effectively with the public and, at the same time, taking in public contribution to develop and implement policies. Currently, public participation theories have been mentioned in many studies, but still need to be further researched and refined when examining social media actions, especially in different cultural and political environments.

Notes

1 *"Bây giờ chỉ có chuyện trồng cây mà phải hỏi ý kiến dân! Tôi hỏi thế đất nước bây giờ động đến cái gì đi hỏi dân thì bầu ra chính quyền làm gì ..."*
2 *6700 người vì 6700 cây xanh* – www.facebook.com/manfortree/.
3 *Vì một Hà Nội xanh* – www.facebook.com/groups/vimothanoixanh/.
4 *6700 cây xanh* – www.facebook.com/6700cayxanh/.
5 *"Vì lợi ích mười năm trồng cây, vì lợi ích trăm năm trồng người."*
6 *"Khi nghĩ về một đời người tôi thường nhớ về rừng cây."*

References

Adi, A. (2015). Occupy PR: An analysis of online media communications of Occupy Wall Street and Occupy London. *Public Relations Review*, 41(4), 508–514.

Administrator Facebook page. For a green Hanoi (2017, June, 30). Personal interview.

Bleiker, H. (1994). *A citizen participation handbook for public officials and other professionals serving the public.* 8th ed. Monterey, CA: Institute for Participatory Management and Planning.

Bortree, D. S. & Seltzer, T. (2009). Dialogic strategies and outcomes: An analysis of environmental advocacy groups' Facebook profiles. *Public Relations Review*, 35(3), 317–319.

Briones, R., Kuch, B., Liu, B. F, & Jin, Y. (2011). Keeping up with the digital age: How the American Red Cross uses social media to build relationships. *Public Relations Review*, 37(1), 37–43.

Cho, M. & De Moya, M. (2014). Understanding publics' engagement with non-profit organisations through Facebook: A typology of messages and motivations behind public-initiated conversations. *Prism*, 11(2). Retrieved from: www.prism journal.org/homepage.html.

Coombs, T. W. & Holladay, S. J. (2012). Fringe public relations: How activism moves critical PR toward the mainstream. *Public Relations Review*, 38, 880–887.

Creighton, J. L. (2005). *The public participation handbook: Making better decisions through citizen involvement.* San Francisco, CA: Jossey-Bass A Wiley Imprint.

Curtin, P. A. (2016). Exploring articulation in internal activism and public relations theory: A case study. *Journal of Public Relations Research.* Online first. DOI: 10.1080/1062726X.2015.1131696.

Davita, S. G. & Deric, S. (2011). *Political sociology: oppression, resistance, and the state.* Thousand Oaks, CA: Pine Forge Press.

Glaser, B. & Strauss, A. (1967). *The discovery grounded theory: strategies for qualitative inquiry.* London: Weidenfield & Nicolson.

H. N. Administrator Facebook page. 6,700 people for 6,700 trees (2017, June, 13). Personal interview.

Hong, N. (2015, March 17). Chặt cây xanh Hà Nội không phải hỏi dân. *Vietnamnet.* Retrieved from http://vietnamnet.vn/vn/thoi-su/chat-cay-xanh-ha-noi-khong-phai-hoi-dan-226164.html.

IAP2 (2012). *Core values for the practice of public participation.* Retrieved from www.iap2.org/.

Le, Q. B., Doan, T. H., Nguyen, T. T. N., & Mai, T. T. (2016). *Báo cáo phong trào bảo vệ #6700 cây xanh ở Hà Nội.* Hanoi: Hồng Đức Publishing Houser.

Loan Pham (2015, March 20). Re: Các bạn thân mến! Tuy cơn bão chặt cây đã tạm dừng để rà soát, nhưng không có nghĩa là khả năng cây bị chặt sẽ không tiếp diễn [Facebook comment]. Retrieved from www.facebook.com/manfortree/photos/a.817644334982898.1073741829.817469068333758/819596214787710/?type=3&theater.

Moloney, K., McQueen, D., Surowiec, P., & Yaxley, H. (2013). Dissent and protest public relations. *Papers and discussion from the dissent and public relations seminar series, October–December 2012.* Public Relations Research group: The Media School, Bournemouth University. Retrieved from: https://research.bournemouth.ac.uk/wp-content/uploads/2013/10/Dissent-and-public-relations-Bournemouth-University.pdf.

Nguyen, Alex (2015, March 22). Re: Đến lúc này có 22.020 người đã ký vào lá thư đề nghị. [Facebook comment]. Retrieved from www.facebook.com/manfortree/posts/820720091341989.

Nguyen Hong Kien (2015, March 27). Re: Người ta đang cố tình đổ lỗi cho cây xà cừ, gán cho nhiều thứ tội để cho rằng không phải cây đô thị, và loại nó ra khỏi thành phố [Facebook comment]. Retrieved from www.facebook.com/groups/6700cayxanh.

Nguyen Minh Trang (2015, March 21). Re: Tại Hồ Thiền Quang, Hà Nội. [Facebook comment]. Retrieved from www.facebook.com/manfortree/photos/a.820537408026924.1073741830.817469068333758/820538814693450/?type=3&theater).

Nguyen Thu Thuy (2015, March 21). Re: Các bạn thân mến, từ sáng đến nay Page nhận được rất nhiều thông tin của các bạn về việc tiếp tục chặt cây, chủ yếu ở trước cửa FPT Shop 92 Hai Bà Trưng và phố Lò Sũ, Lý Thái Tổ [Facebook comment]. Retrieved from www.facebook.com/manfortree/posts/820373618043303.

Nhu Quynh de Prelle (2015, March 30). Re: Gửi các thành viên group "6700 cây xanh," Trước hết thay mặt những người khởi tạo group này rất xin lỗi mọi người về hàng loạt trục trặc trên group từ sau khi sự kiện "Green Walk" diễn ra sáng Chủ nhật (March 29, 2015) [Facebook comment]. Retrieved from www.facebook. com/groups/6700cayxanh.

Phan Dinh Hiep (2015, April 3). Re: Nếu bạn nghĩ xuống đường thế đủ rồi, lãnh đạo đã xin lỗi rồi, cứ chờ xem sao [Facebook comment]. Retrieved from www. facebook.com/groups/6700cayxanh.

Representative of Hanoi Department of Construction. (2018, March 3). Email interview.

Schroeter, R., Scheel, O., Rennb, O., & Schweizer, P. J. (2016). Testing the value of public participation in Germany: Theory, operationalization and a case study on the evaluation of participation, *Energy Research & Social Science*, 13 (2016) 116–125. Doi http://dx.doi.org/10.1016/j.erss.2015.12.013.

Shaw, T. & Van Leuven, N. (n.d.). *Activist PR*. Retrieved from https://activist publicrelations.com/.

Susskind, L. (1999). An alternative to Robert's Rules of order for groups, organizations, and ad hoc assemblies that want to operate by consensus. In L. Susskind, S. McKearnan, & J. Thomas-Larmer (eds.), *The consensus building handbook*. Thousand Oaks, CA: Sage Publications.

Taylor, M. & Kent, M. (2014). Dialogic engagement: Clarifying foundational concepts. *Journal of Public Relations Research*, 26, 384–398.

The Co-intelligence Institute (n.d.). *Principles of public participation*. Retrieved from www.co-intelligence.org/CIPol_publicparticipation.html.

Thuy Le (2015, April 13). Re: Đề nghị các bạn ký nhé [Facebook comment]. Retrieved from www.facebook.com/groups/vimothanoixanh/permalink/3743796 76081129/.

Tran Long An (1984). Một đời người, một rừng cây. On *Một Đời Người, Một Rừng Cây* [CD recorded by Trong Tan]), Viet Nam. Retrieved from www.youtube. com/watch?v=dEz44i2cnqA.

Tran Phuong Lien (2015, March 17). Re: Gửi những người bạn của tôi. Gửi những người yêu Hà Nội [Facebook comment]. Retrieved from www.facebook.com/ manfortree/.

Vo, H. (2015, January 26). Hà Nội thay thế 6.700 cây xanh trên phố. *Vnexpress*. Retrieved from https://vnexpress.net/tin-tuc/thoi-su/ha-noi-thay-the-6-700-cay-xanh-tren-pho-3138990.html#ctr=related_news_click.

Vu Hung Son (2015, March 22). Re: Bạn nào không đến được buổi sáng nay thì có thể xem tạm một vài khoảnh khắc ở đây nhé [Facebook comment]. Retrieved from www.facebook.com/manfortree/posts/820921874655144.

Wallinga, D. Van & Renes, R. J. (2013). Social media & the government: Living happily ever after? Retrieved from https://repository.tudelft.nl/islandora/object/ uuid:f837b726-3beb-43c3-9cc8-256f7d458d19/datastream/OBJ3/download.

Waters, R. & Jamal, J. Y. (2011). Tweet, tweet, tweet: A content analysis of nonprofit organizations' Twitter updates. *Public Relations Review*, 37(2), 321–324.

We Are Social (2017). *Digital in 2017: Southeast Asia regional overview*. Available online at http://wearesocial.com/uk/blog/2017/02/digital-southeast-asia-2017 retrieved on February 27, 2017.

12 The beginning of the end

Telling the story of Occupy Wall Street's eviction on Twitter

Photini Vrikki

Occupy Wall Street (OWS) was a protest movement that began on September 17, 2011, at Zuccotti Park, in New York City's Wall Street financial district. The movement put worldwide economic inequality under the spotlight and bred numerous Occupy movements around the globe (Juris, 2012; Gerbaudo, 2012). The New York Police Department (NYPD) eventually evicted OWS from the park on November 15, 2011, with the police circulating immediate eviction notices to everyone residing the park and requesting press passes back from journalists interested in the impending eviction (Rushe, 2011). NYPD's attempts to conceal its actions from the eyes of the mainstream media and the public alike had a reverse effect: it augmented supportive reactions on Twitter and corroborated OWS' claims about structural inequalities in the US.

In this context, this chapter examines new forms of public relations for contemporary social movements as they appeared during the eviction of OWS from Zuccotti Park. To frame these new forms I rely on Lamme and Russell's (2010) observation that there are five motivations that have historically described public relations:

> *profit*, including sales and fund raising; *recruitment*, including customers, volunteers, converts, and employees; *legitimacy*, including individual and organizational; *agitation*, meaning efforts designed to work *against* something or someone; and *advocacy*, meaning efforts designed to work *for* something or someone.
>
> (pp. 335–338)

For them, these five elements work either in combination or individually to fulfill the functions of public relations (Anderson, 2017, p. 4). This chapter rests on the ways three of these motivations worked for OWS: public relations as a practice to *agitate* against mainstream media and the NYPD; to *advocate* for fair treatment for the protesters; and to *delegitimize* the NYPD, by calling the violent eviction as an action that bridged the First Amendment.[1]

Twitter granted OWS' supporters a space to show support, criticize Bloomberg and Obama, react to police violence, and work around the lack of mainstream coverage during the night's events. This unorthodox way for information transmission that "was not synonymous with press relations" (Lamme & Russell, 2010, p. 355) formed a different public relations realm for the movement; one that did not rely on communicating information top-down but rather followed horizontal communication paths between the protesters and their supporters. This chapter aims to explore these PR elements, both theoretically and empirically. In the first part I explore the relationship between public relations and digital technology, and I follow up with a brief discussion of the methodology used, called Narrative Thematic Analysis (NTA). The second part of this chapter discusses mainstream media and the purported violent image usually attributed to social movements such as OWS. It touches on the notion of the *protest paradigm* and how Twitter was used as a PR tool to *agitate* against the negative or non-existent image the press afforded the movement with. The third part reflects on how OWS specifically chose to shift its public relations strategy into social media storytelling, relying vastly on Twitter to *advocate* its *raison d'être* and *delegitimize* the police's actions. The final section analyzes the four "nodal points" (Laclau & Mouffe, 2014/1985, p. 112) of the eviction's narrative: (1) *Honoring the First Amendment*, (2) *Use of force*, (3) *Communication failure of authorities*, and (4) *Arrests*. By telling the story of the eviction through the micro-narratives presented on Twitter this section analyzes the ways in which OWS' eviction day can be seen as a public relations model for the ways in which contemporary social movements can spread information and gather support through Twitter. This chapter aims to fill the gap that exists in the literature on the relationship between public relations, activism, and "the political dimensions of struggle and change" (L'Etang, 2016, p. 207), while it forms an attempt to shed light onto the dynamics of Twitter stories and the ways in which they have shaped the narrative of OWS during its last day on-the-ground.

Public relations and digital technology

As a discipline, public relations has been defined in flexible and numerous ways. More widely, it is understood to be the field that manages the ways in which information is spread between the public and entities such as corporations, governments, and public figures (Grunig & Hunt, 1984, pp. 3–12). However, social and political theorists have often stood against public relations as a tool for good. More specifically, Stauber and Rampton (1995) suggest that public relations is a "cunning" practice; one that preserves and spreads "half-truths" (p. 204), while Chomsky (2013) insists that PR business corresponds with the decline of democracy—suggesting that their practices are deceptive and manipulative for the democratic processes of public sphere. In similar vein, Gower (2007) and McChesney (2013) argue that the power struggle between journalism and public relations has shifted heavily toward public relations, with a clear impact on the ways in which "spin" (Jackson & Hall Jamieson, 2007) is used to depict social events. Gower (2007) has gone even further to suggest that the responsibility lies in the

> marketing mind-set that has developed into a potent force in govern-ment, corporations, and nonprofit groups at the same time that journ-alism has been weakened by budget cuts and increased competition.
>
> (p. xvii)

Nonetheless, Myers (2014) proposes that these discussions "[ignore] a larger, more complex public relations history that exists outside of the cor-porate sphere" (p. 677) such as activist public relations.

In the 90s, before social media networks were even created, Grunig was skeptical as to the ways in which "activists 'do' public relations" and sug-gested that they do not necessarily do public relations "any differently from how other practitioners do it" (1992, p. 299). Indeed, later in the 2000s, Taylor et al. (2001), Vasquez and Taylor (2001) and Roper (2002) agreed that public relations for corporations and for activists did not differ fundamentally. Yet, in an era of social media induced public relations, more questions regarding the differences between what we consider "public relations for activism" and "public relations for corporations" have sur-faced. In Coombs and Holloway's words,

> the development of the Internet offers opportunities for activism that, like the activism of earlier eras, is mimicked and co-opted by corporate public relations.
>
> (Coombs & Holladay, 2012, p. 347)

In their work, Coombs and Holladay argue that in the past decades PR has gone through a transformation, whereby the focus has moved from corpo-rate interests to activism and protests and social movements. For them, PR "holds promise for re-imagining the field and legitimizing the works of activ-ists as an important component in public relations theory and research" (Coombs & Holladay, 2012, p. 347). In the case of OWS, and in this chapter, I investigate the reasons people created and sustained a slightly different and discursive public relations engagement during the movement's eviction; *from* the supporters and activists *to* the supporters and activists in order to *agitate* against mainstream media, *advocate* for the protesters' safety, and *legitimize* the movement while delegitimizing NYPD's actions.

Taylor et al. (2001) propose that "activist organizations have unique communication and economic constraints and may be able to use the Inter-net dialogically" (p. 268). In this instance, OWS constraints were indeed both financial and communicative since they were grassroots, and with no funding available; and communicative, since mainstream media chose to vilify them from the beginning, as this chapter will discuss later. To use the Internet dialogically then became a public relations tool for the movement that helped them render their lack of economic and communicative support less significant. The narratives created on Twitter between the users have given the movement a public relations aura that relied on strategic story-telling. These narratives of advocacy, legitimization, and agitation are the focus of this chapter. Before going into discussing these narratives, the following section outlines briefly the methodology used to trace the PR eviction narrative of OWS on Twitter.

Twitter as Occupy owned media

This chapter adds to further understandings of how Twitter is used as an owned-media platform for OWS and provides insights into the ways in which the OWS story was represented online during its final day on-the-ground (see: Smith, 2010, p. 332). The chapter focuses on these central questions: *How did OWS expressed its eviction story through interwoven narratives on Twitter; and what did the expression of the stories and the responses on the eviction day tell us about the public relations practices of the movement?*

To answer them, I deploy Narrative Thematic Analysis (NTA) as the framework approach that brings together the quantitative and the qualitative discussions concerning social data through the use of narrative analysis (Vrikki, 2017, p. 126). I introduce NTA as a mixed-method approach, intending to draw out issues related to big textual corpora, the sizes of which make them impractical for close reading. NTA informs digital data research by applying a bottom-up perspective on the empirical phenomenon under investigation by forming narratives through tweets. This perspective refines social movement and narrative concepts, reconstructs meanings, and finally proposes a new way of looking at contemporary movements: through their representation on Twitter as narratives.

By using NTA, my goal is to avoid discounting big texts into numbers, as often is the case with social media data. Instead of creating networks, or counting popular words or groups of words, I pick on narrative analysis to interpret:

1 tweets as stories;
2 themes of stories as micro-narratives; and
3 sets of micro-narratives as narratives.

The result—a number of micro-narratives structuring OWS' eviction story on Twitter—accommodates the demand for qualitative frames that can uphold social media data analysis.

Instead of framing theory (Goffman, 1974) I deploy a more discourse-oriented approach for "thematic" analysis to narratives, following Snow et al.'s (1986) emphasis on the importance of discourse. Drawing on the role of discursive elements in social movements from a textual perspective, Snow et al. (1986) stressed the importance of ideology and beliefs in the construction of social movements, and suggested that frames can reclaim the importance of "meaning," or more precisely "the amplification and extension of extant meanings, the transformation of old meanings, and the generation of new meanings" (Snow & Benford, 1992, p. 136). This approach is more relevant to this chapter's objectives as it allowed me to look into, and analyze, the stories of *agitation*, *advocacy*, and *legitimization*, instead of the network or participatory nature of OWS. Through discourse-oriented narrative analysis I examined all the tweets tweeted on November 15 under #OWS and decoded the meanings behind the stories structuring it on Twitter, while drawing upon the frames within which the movement was embedded. The main point of this "thematic" strategy was to create notions, classifications, and theoretical meaning making, which arose from the data through a comparative coding process between theory, interviews and social media data.

More specifically, NTA moves through a series of six quantitative and qualitative analytical steps, outlined in Figure 12.1:

1   Conducting and analyzing interview data.
2   Indexing Twitter data on Excel (e.g., dividing the tweets into the days/hours they were tweeted).

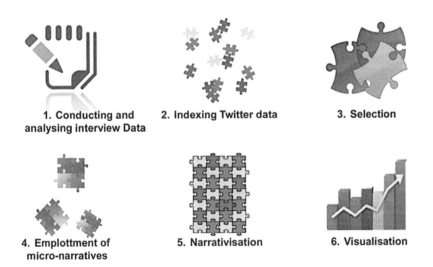

1. Conducting and analysing interview Data

2. Indexing Twitter data

3. Selection

4. Emplottment of micro-narratives

5. Narrativisation

6. Visualisation

Figure 12.1 The analytical steps of Narrative Thematic Analysis.
Source: Vrikki, 2017, p. 119.

3   Selection—for this chapter the selection was for tweets tweeted on the day of the eviction and excluded retweets, tweets with links, photos, and videos on a qualitative level.
4   Emplotment of micro-narratives—in this instance tweets were read and coded under themes that corresponded to their content.
5   Narrativization—here micro-narratives that had similar themes were combined together into single narrative.
6   Visualization, during which the quantitative nature of the narratives from stage 5 were visualized into Excel figures.

Each narrative was formed based on the themes drawn from the interviews and the ways in which these themes could be applied to the emplotment and narrativization of those same thematic narratives onto Twitter data.

This chapter focuses on the analysis of 76,683 originally posted #OWS hashtagged tweets—excluding retweets, tweets with links, photos and videos from the qualitative analysis—tweeted during the last day of the movement on the ground, to bring out the public relations narrative of the movement's story on Twitter during the eviction. The dataset was selected from the database of the Occupy Research project (http://occupyresearch. net), a scheme that contains a significant number of tweets from several 2011 occupy camps and protests. All Twitter datasets on the site, including the one used for this chapter, were collected through R-Shief (www.r-shief. org), using the open Twitter Streaming API between September and December 2011. The dataset is in .csv format and includes more than 1.5 million tweets.[2] For the purposes of this chapter I focus on the micro-narratives that referred to the PR processes of OWS, such as the problematic relationship between mainstream media and the movement, as discussed in the following section.

The ethics of using social media data

When dealing with social media research we usually come across questions regarding ethical use of data and publicly available datasets similar to those collected from Twitter. Recent guidelines from the British Sociological Association mention that "Each research situation is unique and it will not be possible simply to apply a standard template in order to guarantee ethical practice" (2017 p. 11).[3] Relevant research conducted by Williams et al. (2017) suggests that users might be aware that they are using and posting public platforms but may not be expecting that they and the content they produce is used by researchers. We face hence a gap between the expectations of the users and the researcher when it comes to the distinction of data ownership and data ethics (2017, p. 1163).

In order to avoid creating this gap here and because the tweets used in this chapter often contain sensitive content, such as tweets against the police and swearing, I have chosen to anonymize the users and paraphrase their tweets. In this way the content remains the same and at the same time the tweets cannot be traceable back to an identifiable user or any of their interactions. By reconstructing the tweets in such a way I attend to the context of the tweet so as not to change the meaning, while at the same time conserving the emotion of the tweet as conveyed in its original wording.

As researchers, our social contract with our research subjects and data has to provide the necessary ethical parameters to enhance the benefit for research and decrease the harm for people involved or affected by our research. In this context and for this chapter the anonymization of users' handles and the paraphrasing of their tweets lie in the ethics of protection, respect, and privacy.

Mainstream media and the "protest paradigm"

Mainstream media have a big influence onto the ways in which a social movement is represented in the public sphere. While "media relations, arranged interviews, press conferences and press reviews" (Lamme & Russell, 2010, p. 319) were historically used as public relations for social events, OWS quickly sidelined these practices in favor of social media engagement, labelling mainstream media as against them and/or partisan. Indeed, a range of literature argues that our social structures distrust much more non-official news sources, such as social movement actors, than established institutional sources (Hall et al., 1978, p. 58; Chomsky, 2002; McChesney, 2008). And even though not all US media are partisan most of them tend to lean toward their trusted sources and their political temperaments when reporting on protests; usually drawn to "experts" that agree with their own agendas (Herman & Chomsky, 1988; Oliver & Maney, 2000; McCurdy, 2011). Therefore, while "trusted figures" are given more airtime as "credible sources," activists are often forced to use different media practices to counterbalance their chances of getting publicity or for raising awareness about their issues through mediated discussions. This turn is not recent, but it has become even more palpable in the social media era.

The perception that mainstream media are "against" protests has been widely and historically discussed in social movements research, pointing to lack of adequate coverage and criminalizing social action (Halloran et al., 1970; Gitlin, 1980/2003). Many have concurred with the principles of the "protest paradigm"—where protests are covered in such means that their central reason is to "delegitimize, marginalize, and demonize" protest groups (Luther & Miller, 2005, p. 80; McFarlane & Hay, 2003; McLeod & Detenber 1999, p. 5). According to Deacon (2007, p. 119), the "protest paradigm" is merely conveyed and sustained through the "textual and discursive forms" and "rhetorical nuances" of the news articles and reports published about protests. In the "protest paradigm," if incidents of violence break out during a protest, albeit minor, the protest is interpreted through the lens of violence as "the problem," distracting the public eye from the real causes of the protest.

One would anticipate that OWS would fall in a similar "protest paradigm," and indeed, some of the mainstream media's coverage falsely advertised OWS as sharing views with the Tea Party, or inciting violence, and "warfare."[4] This negative coverage gained spreadability when the republican presidential candidate Mitt Romney suggested that OWS protests where "dangerous" and inciting "class warfare";[5] when the *New York Times* writer Charles Blow, described the movement as "a festival of frustrations, a collective venting session with little edge or urgency";[6] and when *Fox News* reported that "the NYPD had taken action to prevent protestors from wreaking havoc" on September 17, 2017.[7] From the condescending voice of Blow, to the imaginary chaotic images of *Fox News*, media had managed to put the emphasis on the conflict between protesters and the NYPD, enforcing the "protest paradigm" and discounting the reasons the movement was created.

In spite of these, the OWS media team tried to befriend the mainstream media, issue statements, conduct interviews, etc., but most of the protesters seemed disillusioned with the press. For instance, Tom suggested that:

> There was a lot of press in NYC, it was very adversarial [...] Like the *New York Post* in NYC—a very conservative newspaper and tabloid, something like the *Daily Mirror* or something in the UK—were always searching for trash on people; we had a lot of conservative publications that were searching for [negative] things.
>
> (Tom, 24, student)

For protesters, the public relations standards of most of the media professionals were based on uncovering the "big story" of the movement, constantly asking for the "specific political ideology" of the movement and its leaders. Aaron, who slept at the park for a few nights, referred to one event where the *New York Post* published a story about a murderer's DNA from a 2004 crime scene supposedly been matched with DNA from a chain used to hold open a subway gate in an OWS protest:[8]

> The New York Post had that front page about the murderer, you know? And where they got their information from? The same way they get all their stories from. There was that NYPD guy who gave it. But if you look at the actual page it was extremely irresponsible [to publish].
>
> (Aaron, 27, student)

Such articles emboldened the "protest paradigm" for OWS and were designed to advance the concept of protesters as extremists, radicals or violent. Aaron's experience conveys what most OWS protesters believed about mainstream media: not as a space for diversified public relations but more as a social entity, or a power structure that was after them. The agitation *against* mainstream media was firmly founded on the nuances and the discursive forms of mainstream media reports about the event.

By assigning OWS with the identity of a "provocative" group, mainstream media wrapped the movement in the cloud of lawlessness and violence. In what follows, I discuss the ways in which OWS came to create a strategic storytelling social media presence both as an attempt to *advocate* against mainstream media reports and NYPD, and as an effort to put forward clear *legitimate* narratives that would *agitate* and organize the public in their favor.

Shifting to a social media storytelling strategy

Considering platforms such as Twitter as bridges between its online and offline representations, OWS used social media storytelling as their public relations strategy. OWS exhibited a delicate understanding of the newsmaking mechanisms and the affordances of social media platforms. Soon after the movement soared and the camp was set at Zuccotti Park, OWS activists realized that social media would play a big role in the movement, and thus invested a lot of their public relations efforts and human resources into communicating their ideas, issues, and concerns through Twitter. Protesters realized that they could sidestep mainstream media and convey their information to the public independently. As Justin explained:

> Social media is just the medium of communication for people that are stepping up and saying we want change; we want something different. It's a medium, it's a tool, and a vehicle for people's voices to be heard […] In other words it subverts the official channels of communication that for so long governments and corporations have relied upon in order to drown any other message.
>
> (Justin, 35, educator)

John went even further to suggest that:

> Social media amplified small voices and brought them to the ears of the populists and to the ears of the people in power. And they are forced to listen to us. And if they don't listen to us, we will just keep on drowning them out, until we revolt. They have to listen to us eventually. They can't ignore all of us. They can't kill all of us. They can't keep us quiet any more.
>
> (John, 27, OWS protester/student)

Adopting social movement storytelling as a synergetic communication practice on Twitter, OWS has become a reminder of the fact that supporters of social movements, activists, and on-the-ground protesters are not abstract actors, but individuals who produce and process stories of their movements on both social media networks and on-the-ground. Rather than seeing Twitter's space in the cyber-utopian term of complete freedom from physical and social or cultural constrains (Turkle, 1995; 2017), I argue here for the significance of social media storytelling for social movements' PR practices. "One reason that perspectives become widely believed is because they are embedded into stories that are told over and over through interpersonal conversation and mass media" argues Heath (1992, p. 57), and this is where Twitter becomes important for OWS' story.

It was not just the fact that social media were an important tool for information transmission that mattered to OWS, but it was also the fact that the tweets told the same story over and over again, allowing the narrative of the movement, and the narrative of the eviction more specifically, to become believable. For Kent (2015) "stories have the power to inform, persuade, elicit emotional responses, build support for coalitions and initiatives, and build civil society" (p. 480). Kent goes on to argue that it is important for public relation stories to "elicit identification, empathy, and memorable situations and experiences" (p. 480). This links to Adi and Moloney's observation on a different Occupy movement, Occupy Bournemouth, which suggested that "It is not only the ability to create and share their own content that makes an activist and protest group successful online but its relevance and its ability to communicate that quality" (2012, p. 119). Narrative culture and strategic storytelling has real and gripping results on movements and their supporters.

Twitter, to some extent, produces and reproduces, stores away and conveys the movement's narratives in a stable but also situation-transcendent space where they are transmitted globally through a new form of storytelling. This new form brings up a "dialogic engagement" that is an "acknowledgement that interactants are willing to give their whole selves to encounters. Engagement assumes accessibility, presentness, and a willingness to interact" (Taylor & Kent, 2014, p. 387). In their "struggle to find the balance between managing their reputation, controlling their image, sharing their messages and identifying and incentivizing conversations online" (Adi, 2015, p. 508), OWS deployed storytelling as a process for public relations that fit best to their processes. In the analysis of the eviction day narrative that follows, I draw from Laclau and Mouffe's (2014/1985) work, which suggests an approach to discursive structure that can be described as "an ensemble of differential positions" (Laclau & Mouffe, 2014/1985, p. 106). Each discourse owns its "privileged discursive points" called "nodal points," which in their turn create micro-narratives before developing narratives (Laclau & Mouffe, 2014/1985, p. 112). To put it simply, OWS' Twitter discourse is read here as a body of multiple micro-narratives, which in their turn form the narrative of the eviction.

Telling the story of the eviction

In the heightened context of the eviction, Twitter worked as a handy and easily accessible tool to circulate information, with strategies in place for maximum amplification of the eviction's non-legitimacy, cause agitation and prolong advocacy for the movement. Such a violent event exerted a strong influence on the structure of OWS' eviction narrative, mirroring the crucial role Twitter had in responding to this violence through thousands of tweets in order to stand *against* the eviction. More specifically, the movement's supporters devoted themselves to building up and spreading their agitation about the eviction on Twitter through stories that reacted to the violent events happening on the ground. Surprisingly, and as we can see from Figure 12.2, given the unexpected police action, the eviction formed the most actively tweeted day of the movement, with 76,683 tweets (including retweets, links, photos, and videos) being tweeted on November 15 under the #OWS hashtag.

What is evident in the analysis of the tweets tweeted on November 15, was the tendency of the users to focus on specific events happening on-the-ground; some of those events were discussed throughout the day, flaring brighter on specific moments, while others were more instantaneous, e.g., the injury of a council member during the eviction, the NYPD raid into the OWS library, or Mayor Bloomberg making an announcement for the eviction, etc. As better viewed in Figure 12.3, the majority of tweets occurred during the first five hours of the day. Other spikes during the day, show how the narrative of the eviction as a whole moved within a spectrum, i.e., tweeting was linked to urgent events taking place and demanding agitation and organization. In order to analyze the big narrative of the eviction we therefore need to look into the smaller narratives, the micro-narratives that constructed it. In what follows I look into the four biggest micro-narratives of the day, focusing on those micro-narratives that had the biggest PR impact on the day's storytelling strategy.

Figure 12.3 further illustrates that most of the tweets were tweeted between the hours of 1 a.m. and 4 a.m. (EST) with later spikes appearing at 8 a.m. and 12 p.m. (EST). By 5 p.m. (EST), activity fell to half of what it was at 1 a.m., and by 9 p.m. tweets tweeting under the #OWS hashtag were in the low 200s. Twitter's activity decline just after the eviction took place, shows not only the agitated character of the eviction stories mediated through the platform, but also how instantaneous advocacy characterized how the story unfolded throughout the eviction hours: it was more important to call out the injustice while it was happening, not after the event. It is hence more interesting to look at what kinds of stories users told on Twitter during the eviction and immediately after the eviction rather than talk about the day as a single event. Similarly to using a magnifying glass to look into the micro-elements of an object, here the analysis focuses on the micro-elements of the narrative, i.e., the micro-narratives that constructed it.

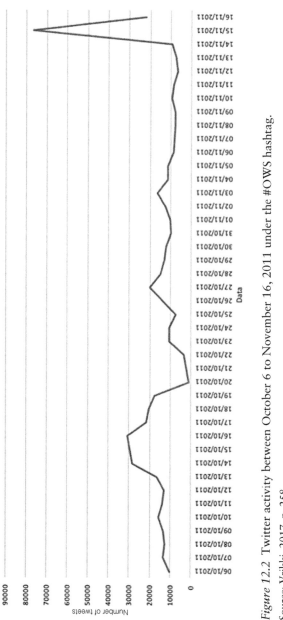

Figure 12.2 Twitter activity between October 6 to November 16, 2011 under the #OWS hashtag.

Source: Vrikki, 2017, p. 258.

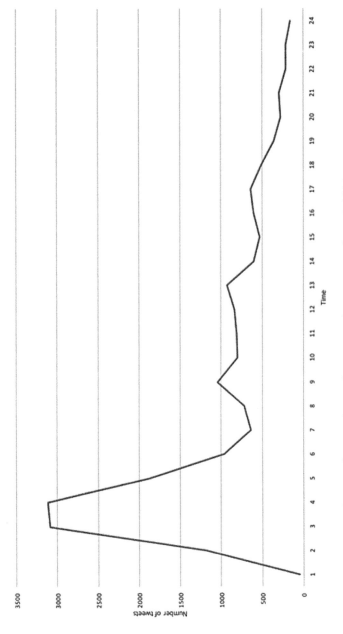

Figure 12.3 The distribution of tweets during the eviction day on November 15, 2011.

Source: Vrikki, 2017, p. 260.

In what follows, I show how the stories structuring the eviction day expose the ways in which Twitter's social space can both preserve sociability but also create communities with shared political ideas (Melucci, 1995) articulated through micro-narratives of instant discursive expression. These narratives work as the public relations storytelling process for the movement, aiming to "influence public behavior" (Lamme & Russell, 2010, p. 284). I first discuss the micro-narrative of honoring the first amendment, before moving into discussing the use of force, the failure of communication between the authorities and the protesters, and the arrests of the protesters in the park.

Honoring the First Amendment

Moving further than the frames of Twitter as a PR ecology game-changer, here, I look into the ways in which tweets served as a participatory political tool for *agitation* that formed the core of the "honoring the First Amendment" micro-narrative. Securing their freedom of the press by covering the eviction themselves and broadcasting it through live-streams, protesters at Zuccotti Park attracted a lot of commentary on Twitter *against* the violent practices of the NYPD. Users commented on what they were watching on live-streams, considering these discursive actions as the ones that secured their freedom of speech and their right to peaceably assemble. There were 1,624 Originally Posted[9] (OP) tweets mentioning live-streams on the day of the eviction, forming almost 8 percent of the whole day's OP tweets ($n = 20,411$), and they formed one of the strongest narratives during the eviction.

In Figure 12.4, we can observe that the peak of the livestream tweets took place during the minutes police were evacuating the protesters from the park; there is also a small rise at 8 p.m. during which Mayor Bloomberg held a press conference, and then several other rises during the day where people were live-streaming marches in support to OWS. At the same time, the figure shows the retweets and tweets with links rising exponentially during the eviction (including photos, videos and links). Similar to the OP tweets, the other two kinds of tweets rise between the first hours of the day, however, we get more photos (of the police entering the park) and links (mostly of live-streams) tweeted between 2 a.m. and 3 a.m. as an immediate agitated response to the abrupt eviction. Stories focused on how people could get information and witness-accounts, describing what was happening on-the-ground, offering advice, or support:

> 01:09 @Jovannaxxxx I just heard "If you refuse to leave the park you will be subject to arrest" on the livestream. It's 1 am, LET THE OCCUPIERS SLEEP. #OWS

> 01:20 @Janetxxxx Livestream from #ows just went down. I am scared for the occupiers. Spread the word. They are only protected if we watch and care!

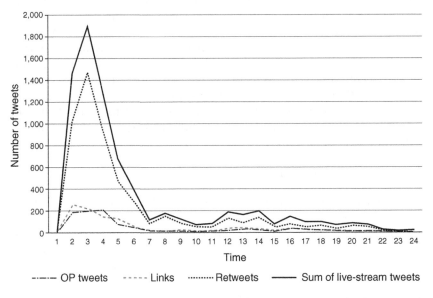

Figure 12.4 The distribution of tweets, retweets, and links tweeted referring to the live-streams.

Source: Vrikki, 2017, p. 263.

> 02:28 @danaxxxx #ows livestream: police & sanitation workers creating a massive pile of people's belongings; stuff they weren't able to retrieve before raid.

A different but similar kind of stories played a major role in supporting the First Amendment narrative, spurring the feeling of "togetherness" between the Twitter community, advocating *for* the movement. Those were the stories of *"The whole world is watching."* Used both as a hashtag and a chant in the park, the phrase voiced the activists' conviction that even the ban of the mainstream media from broadcasting the eviction, live-streams and Twitter still worked as their information and public relations space for OWS. This allowed them to feel like they participated in the on-going events, underlining how despite the use of Twitter as their socializing space, Twitter was still an everyday and reasonably political space where they could show their support by promoting the movement in a different way.

In Figure 12.5, we can observe how the slogan picked up at 3 a.m., at the moment during which the police moved into the park with hoses and bulldozers and the last protesters were zip-cuffed and arrested.

The chant "the world is watching" was a direct call against police brutality, but also worked as a discursive and rhetorical tool for the people

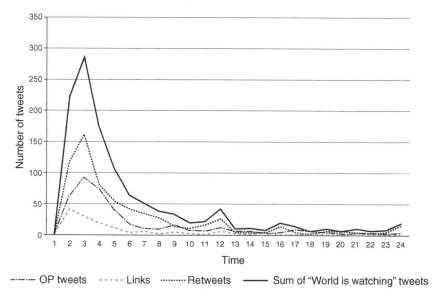

Figure 12.5 The distribution of tweets, retweets, and links mentioning "The world is watching" during the eviction day.

Source: Vrikki, 2017, p. 265.

who believed that if the protest was live-streamed, then the police would not proceed to the eviction, arrests, or use force. It was also a *de-legitimizing* mechanism, blaming the NYPD of bridging the First Amendment:

> 01:09 @CAMTHExxxxxx Stay safe and stay peaceful NYC. #the worldiswatching #ows

> 01:17 @divebuxxxxx The whole world is watching. #ows Stay strong occupiers!

> 04:56 @randomxxxxx #nypd You are fighting for the wrong side. You are the 99% too. Peaceful occupies should not be treated as a thread. The world is watching #OWS

Agitation against the police grew as the events unfolded and the police began disrupting what the protesters considered their legal and civic rights. These stories attacked the US authorities and the NYPD, describing them as dictators and comparing them with authoritarian regimes in the Arab world, further accusing NYPD for overstepping their First Amendment rights:

02:46 @rockrixxxxx Comparing #OWS to Egypt always seemed a little absurd. Then NYPD barred journalists, shut down air space and deactivated cell towers.

03:29 @kerrxxxx when Mubarak does it, he is oppressing his people, when the US does it, they're 'stifling a riot'. #Ows

The intensity of these "oppressive state" stories was rather evident in the ways in which supporters described police's actions as part of a US political context that was not representative of the democratic political system of the country. The parallels drawn with Egypt become more relevant here if we consider the discursive commonalities between OWS and the "Arab Spring." The memories of the revolution taking place in the Arab world influenced a lot of OWS' supporters and gave them reasons to compare what was happening in New York with what had happened in Tahrir Square a few months earlier. It is important, however, to stress that what creates the micro-narrative here is not just the fact that the press was not allowed to access the camp, but it is also that the police blatantly infringed the First Amendment—a law which the USA are proud to hold as their constitution's foundation—by not allowing the journalists to enter the camp during the eviction and hence evading the questions that would arise after the violence and force they used became public.

We can therefore consider some of these discursive acts as mere expression of PR acts with a deep political meaning: first, PR as standing against de-legitimized practices, and second, PR as *advocacy*, focused on specific targets, circumventing the enforced blackout by the police, and the eviction itself. The above stories formed the "Honoring the First Amendment" micro-narrative. Now I will go on to discuss the narratives forming the "use of force" story as one that was strongly present during the eviction day.

Use of force

Considering the disillusionment with the government and the authorities in general, the way users talked about police brutality comes as no surprise. In these new spaces of discursive public relations, we witness a new repertoire of social participation evolving in which the second micro-narrative, the "use of force" micro-narrative, focuses on two main events:

1   the destruction of OWS Library by the NYPD; and
2   the arrest and police-inflicted injury of the council-member Ydanis Rodríguez.

The destruction of a core element of the community, the library, sparked huge outrage on Twitter, lying bare what a community sees as its political stance, authorities and the state may declare it to be a threat. The library consisted of 5,000 books, all donated to the protesters by supporters. The emotional and community links of the OWS with their library were strong, as Claire would later tell me during our interview:

> But you know what angered me most? Not just me, all of us. They came in [the NYPD] and threw all the books we had in The People's library, which so many good people brought to us, to borrow them ourselves or give them to people. And they threw all of them in a dumpster. It broke our hearts.
>
> (Claire, 32, designer)

Recognizing the library as a core communal asset for the group one would assume would require the police to have a more culturally modulated, nuanced, understanding of OWS. However, in the instance of the OWS' evacuation, the police threw all the books of the library away, as a way to dismantle the camp. Following public outrage—partly fueled by Twitter agitation—it was later revealed that the books were transferred to the sanitation department warehouse and could be reclaimed. The resentment toward NYPD was, however, palpable on Twitter:

> 02:59 @joeyxxxx People fight for literacy. NYPD puts it in the dumpsters. #OWS
>
> 04:30 @saramxxxx A media blackout, a trashed library, police violence and arrests. Remind me what century we are in again? #ows
>
> 09:42 @agoxxx Absorbed in my little bound copy of the Constitution this morning, wondering if any like it were in library destroyed by NYPD in #OWS raid

The destruction of the OWS library and the violent removal of the last remaining protesters from the park were promptly followed by the stories about the council-member Ydanis Rodríguez and his police-inflicted head wound. His injury played a big part in the story of the eviction, and more specifically into the micro-narrative of the use of force. As shown in Figure 12.6, the event developed slowly but steadily through the day, with people reporting on the progression of Ydanis' health and expressing their agitation against the police, the NYC authorities, and the way they dealt with Rodriguez:

> 2:43 @Jumaanexxxxxxx I can confirm that @ydanis, a Council Member, has been arrested at #OWS and is bleeding
>
> 02:56 @Dantexxxx NYC council-member Ydanis Rodriguez arrested and is bleeding from head—explain this, NYPD??? #ows

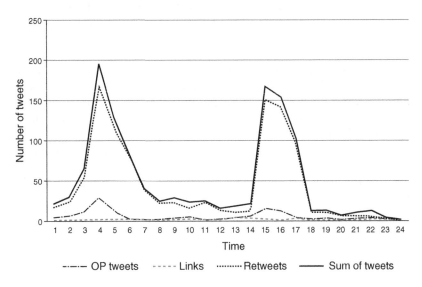

Figure 12.6 Tweets mentioning the injury of the New York councilman Ydanis
    Rodriguez during the eviction day.

Source: Vrikki, 2017, p. 274.

Rodriguez, later sued the city, arguing that he was a victim of police
violence and won. He donated his $30,000 settlement to the Centre for
Constitutional Rights in March 2015.[10] What is, however, noteworthy
here, is that these stories scratch the surface of an important area for
further research. Around the world, people are using social media to
express their agitation with the ways in which police use force to subdue
them. These infrastructures and processes of PR storytelling as a different
way to engage with participatory action than with on-the-ground action
still owns and represents the political struggles of our era. In other words,
these stories tap into essential communication channels that allow messages to be amplified and enter the mainstream. In what follows I will look
into the problematic nature of the relationship between protesters, the
authorities, and the police themselves.

Communication failure of authorities

The first two dominant micro-narratives forming the eviction narrative of
OWS were "honoring the First Amendment" and the "use of force." Now
the discussion will turn toward the problematic and antagonistic nature of
occupiers, the NYPD, Mayor Bloomberg, and President Obama. In this
narrative, we get stories attacking the NYPD, Bloomberg as the master
planner of the eviction who considered the NYPD his personal army, and

Obama as the authority figure who betrayed OWS by allowing the eviction to take place, whom allowed the NYPD to ban the press from the park, and permitted police violence to take place through his inability to control the situation. Hence, here I focus on tweets mentioning specific figures of authority, who were characterized as responsible for this eviction. I look at them through the positioning of failing to communicate and connect with the protesters in a meaningful way and as a clear PR failure from the side of the State that failed to *legitimize* their action. Tweets were calling Bloomberg out for authorizing the eviction:

> 01:44 @CerveauxJuxxxxx Classy move Bloomberg and NYPD. Raiding the park at 1 AM: surely legitimate. #OWS

> 02:16 @DJtightyxxxxxx Dear NYPD & Mayor Bloomberg: it may be 2 am, but 1000s are watching. Is this violent assault really necessary? #OWS

> 03:12 @Steexxxx #NYPD #MayorBloomberg your actions will explode in your face. You think this is over? Not by any chance! #OWS #Zuccotti

Similarly, Obama was accused of blocking the constitutional right of the protesters to assemble and betraying the movement "of change" he called for in his election campaign:

> 02:32 @Smorganxxxx @BarackObama it is a constitutional right of the protestors to assemble and you let the NYPD to breach it? That's pathetic. #ows #p2

> 03:20 @Geoxxxx Mr @barackobama, NYPD is stifling the #OWS in the same way the heartless Egyptian police did so #WTF and f—k your bogus American democracy

> 05:41 @naoxxxx Is this what Obama meant when he said "Hope and Change?" #ows attacked and destroyed by the NYPD.

As the kinds of stories around Obama and Bloomberg developed, more reactions against the lack of communication channels between these authority figures and the movement were put into circulation, and in turn inspired more Twitter users to take action and/or to tweet. Laying out these miscellaneous models of PR engagement sheds light into the understandings of what matters as politics in the contemporary digital world and stresses the need for building better and more legitimate PR channels of communication between social movements, social media, and the authorities.

Arrests

Having started the analysis with the eviction's narrative of "honoring the first Amendment," "use of force," and "communication failure of authorities," and mapped a different use of PR response to urgent events, I wanted to end with one last important and maybe the most significant narrative of the eviction: arresting the last few protesters who remained in the park. A lot of people took on Twitter to protest the arrests and the zip-cuffing of all the protesters who stayed behind to "hold the fort" of the encampment at Zuccotti Park:

> 03:33 @brandonmxxxxxx Around fifty arrests reported close to the kitchen at Zuccotti park. #OWS
>
> 03:34 @inferxxxx Sounds like the NYPD is arresting everyone at Zuccotti Park #Ows
>
> 04:20 @viewofxxxx Sanitation trucks have arrived at the parks and are now cleaning the area "Still making arrests in the park" says a reporter #ows

As we can observe from Figure 12.7, tweets mentioning the NYPD fluctuated throughout the day, but were mostly retweets, while links were low in numbers. Therefore, the fivefold number of tweets being tweeted and retweeted during the hours of 2 a.m. to 5 a.m., illustrates how urgency

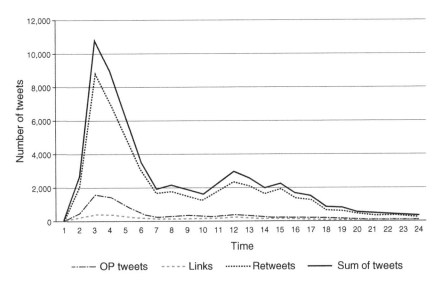

Figure 12.7 The distribution of tweets mentioning the NYPD during the eviction day.
Source: Vrikki, 2017, p. 295.

brings up more advocacy and engagement on Twitter, especially when the urgency is considered an injustice or if there is already someone to blame for and stand against or stand for.

From participation to engagement: Twitter storytelling as PR for social movements

The widespread use of Twitter as a platform that made visible the PR motivations of agitation, advocacy, and legitimization for OWS uncovered at the same time the ways in which the strategic use of digital storytelling by OWS protesters enhance our understanding of the relationship between activism and public relations. Through the micro-narratives of honoring the First Amendment, use of force, communication failure with authorities, and arrests, I sought to counter-argue the dominant assumptions that social media are only platforms of narcissistic utterances (Turkle, 2017). I have instead unveiled how Twitter is used as a tool to expose injustices and abuse during urgent events through storytelling practices that align with PR strategies. Twitter here, becomes the discursive vehicle to voice resistance to injustice and support social movements—particularly during urgent on-the-ground manifestations of violence—a platform to express a shared desire for a need to change the current political system; a system that respects the US constitution and overcomes police brutality.

The PR strategy of storytelling has enabled the protesters to overcome the "protest paradigm" and has affected positively the mainstream reporting of the eviction day. As Poell (2014, p. 716) suggests, "the use of social media brings about an acceleration of activist communication, and greatly enhances its visual character," supporting the argument of Twitter as a storytelling space for social movements such as OWS. Similar to Twitter's description of Earl et al. (2013, p. 459) as "a widely available mobile social networking tool that can be used to reduce information asymmetries between protesters and police," this chapter argued that the miscommunication between protesters and the authorities, including the police, could also be seen as a PR tool between the police and social movements. While Earl et al. (2013) propose that Twitter may be working as a repressive tool for protesters, since there is asymmetrical data information between them and the police, here I have argued that by using PR storytelling users managed to advocate and agitate the public against such repressions.

Social media give a glimpse into a future in which change may not come in the way of new policies and governments, but from the social behavior which is a product of collective storytelling processes: this collective PR action enables people to question dominant approaches and processes and offer individual and collective opinions, either online or on-the-ground, about new ways of conduct with mainstream media and the police. The significance of this narrative, however, lays in its participatory nature: the majority of tweets were sent as the events were unravelling, forming instantaneous stories, and tying together a storyline for the eviction that would have never been possible if the protesters did not have access to Twitter. It would therefore be more practical to talk about this participatory nature of Twitter's narratives as a turn from public relations engagement to participation. In Dahlgren's words,

> Engagement refers to subjective states, that is, a mobilized, focused attention on some object. It is in a sense a prerequisite for participation [...]. For engagement to become embodied as participation and therefore give rise to civic agency there must be some connection to practical, do-able activities, where citizens can feel empowered.
>
> (2009, p. 80)

By forming reactionary micro-narratives on Twitter, users form a different kind of public relations act that relies on shared actions—in this case being agitated and advocating against mainstream media news and the State's actions. The eviction in this respect became a shared experience, in which the will to help and denounce the mainstream media, the NYPD, and the State created a meaningful experience for twitter users; not by just augmenting their participation in the movement but by also enhancing their sense of contributing to public communication strategies. We should, hence be thinking of the social and the PR elements of these platforms as intertwined entities, which work collectively, co-creating content with communicative dimensions.

Twitter's digital dynamics, cultural properties, and PR affordances provide a framework of participation where the mechanisms of social practice can and are being carried out. Indeed, the community of OWS on Twitter became stronger and more obvious during the eviction, since there was a need to show how the emotional connection between the protesters on-the-ground and those online could be translated to building up strong links for their imagined community (Anderson, 1991) and their collective identity (Melucci, 1985). The interaction among distant users' relentless pleas for first-hand accounts about the night, and the on-the-ground protesters' rolling commenting of unfolding events, underlines even further the affordance of Twitter as a springboard for PR communication and social action. This shift, from engagement to participation, demands a rethinking of the meaning of public relations as political action: this re-thinking extends "more mainstream" expressions of public relations (e.g., spread of information) and takes into account notions of political participation expressed or contested in wider social and cultural contexts, such as social media use.

Notes

1 According to the first amendment,

> Congress shall make no law respecting an establishment of religion, or pro-
> hibiting the free exercise thereof; or abridging the freedom of speech, or of
> the press; or the right of the people peaceably to assemble, and to petition
> the government for a redress of grievances.
>
> (U.S. Const. art. I)

2 Please contact the author for access to the dataset. Please note that the dataset
  is in .csv format and needs extraction and computerized handling in order to
  become readable.
3 The new BSA Digital Research Annex is available online at: www.britsoc.co.uk/
  media/24309/bsa_statement_of_ethical_practice_annexe.pdf.
4 For more details see: research undergone by Laya Liu Linjun Fan. Analysis of
  U.S. mainstream media: A case study of news reports on Occupy Wall Street
  Event (2012). Retrieved March 25, 2018, from www.kon.org/urc/v11/fan.html.
5 For more details see: The Young Turks (2011, October 7). Occupy Wall Street
  dangerous—Romney. Retrieved March 25, 2018, from www.youtube.com/
  watch?v=qCnES_JM1fU.
6 For more details see: Blow, C. M. (2011, September 30). Opinion | Hippies and
  hipsters exhale. Retrieved March 25, 2018, from www.nytimes.com/2011/
  10/01/opinion/hippies-and-hipsters-exhale.html.
7 Demonstrators "Occupy Wall Street" to Protest Influence of Money on U.S.
  Politics (September 17, 2011). Retrieved March 25, 2018, from www.foxnews.
  com/us/2011/09/17/demonstrators-occupy-wall-street-to-protest-influence-money-
  on-us-politics.html.
8 See for example: Celona, L. (2012, July 10). Sarah Fox murder scene DNA linked
  to OWS subway vandalism scene. Retrieved March 25, 2018, from https://nypost.
  com/2012/07/10/sarah-fox-murder-scene-dna-linked-to-ows-subway-vandalism-
  scene/.
9 OP tweets are tweets that do not include links, photos, videos, or are retweets. I
  focus on OP tweets here because I'm interested in the discursive notion of the
  stories told, not the spreadability or networks created.
10 See: Barkan, R. (2015, March 30). Councilman arrested at Occupy Wall Street
  donates his settlement cash. Retrieved March 25, 2018, from http://observer.
  com/2015/03/councilman-arrested-at-occupy-wall-street-donates-his-settlement-
  cash/.

References

Adi, A. (2015). Occupy PR: An analysis of online media communications of Occupy
  Wall Street and Occupy London. *Public Relations Review*, *41*(4), 508–514.
Adi, A. & Moloney, K. (2012). The importance of scale in Occupy movement protests: A case study of a local Occupy protest as a tool of communication through
  Public Relations and Social Media. *Revista Internacional de Relaciones Publicas*,
  4(II), 97–122.
Anderson, B. R. (1991/2016). *Imagined communities: Reflections on the origin and
  spread of nationalism*. London: Verso.
Anderson, B. W. (2017). Social movements and public relations in the early twentieth century: How one group used public relations to curtail venereal disease
  rates, *Journal of Public Relations Research*, *29*(1), 3–15.

Chomsky, N. (2002). *Media control: The spectacular achievements of propaganda* (Vol. 7). New York: Seven Stories Press.

Chomsky, N. (2013, August 17). Chomsky: The U.S. behaves nothing like a democracy [transcript of talk]. *Salon.Com*, 1–11.

Coombs, W. T. & Holladay, S. (2012). Privileging an activist vs. a corporate view of public relations history in the U.S. *Public Relations Review*, *38*, 347–353.

Dahlgren, P. (2009). *Media and political engagement: Citizen, communication, and democracy*. Cambridge: Cambridge University Press.

Deacon, B. (2007). *Global social policy and governance*. London: Sage Publ.

Earl, J., McKee Hurwitz, H., Mejia Mesinas, A., Tolan, M. & Arlotti, A. (2013). This protest will be tweeted: Twitter and protest policing during the Pittsburgh G20. *Information, Communication & Society*, *16*(4), 459–478.

Gerbaudo, P. (2012). *Tweets and the streets*. London: Pluto Press.

Gitlin, T. (1980/2003). *The whole world is watching: Mass media in the making & unmaking of the new left*. Berkeley, CA: University of California Press.

Goffman, E. (1974). *Frame analysis: An essay on the organization of experience*. Boston, MA: Northeastern University Press.

Gower, K. K. (2007). *Public relations and the press: The troubled embrace*. Evanston, IL: Northwestern University Press.

Grunig, J. E. (1992). *Excellence in public relations and communication management*. Hillsdale, NJ: Lawrence Erlbaum Associates.

Grunig, J. E. & Hunt, T. (1984). *Managing public relations* (6th ed.). Orlando, FL: Harcourt Brace Jovanovich.

Hall, S., Critcher, C., Jefferson, T., Clarke, J. & Roberts, B. (1978). *Policing the crisis: Mugging, the state and law and order*. UK: Palgrave Macmillan.

Halloran, J. D., Murdock, G. & Elliott, P. (1970). *Demonstrations and communication: A case study*. Harmondsworth: Penguin Books.

Heath, R. L. (1992). Critical perspectives on public relations. In E. L. Toth & R. L. Heath (Eds.), *Rhetorical and critical approaches to public relations* (pp. 37–61). Hillsdale, NJ: Lawrence Erlbaum Associates.

Herman, E. S. & Chomsky, N. (1988). *Manufacturing consent: The political economy of the mass media*. London: Bodley Head.

Jackson, B. & Hall Jamieson, K. (2007). *unSpun: Finding facts in a world of disinformation*. New York: Random House.

Juris, J. S. (2012). Reflections on #Occupy Everywhere: Social media, public space, and emerging logics of aggregation. *American Ethnologist*, *39*(2), 259–279.

Kent, M. L. (2015). The power of storytelling in public relations: Introducing the 20 master plots. *Public Relations Review*, *41*(4), 480–489.

Laclau, E. & Mouffe, C. (2014/1985). *Hegemony and socialist strategy: Towards a radical democratic politics*. London: Verso.

Lamme, M. O. & Russell, K. M. (2010). Removing the spin: Toward a new theory of public relations history. *Journalism and Communication Monographs*, *11*(4), 1–7.

L'Etang, J. (2016). Public relations, activism and social movements: Critical perspectives. *Public Relations Inquiry*, *5*(3), 207–211.

Luther, C. A. & Miller, M. M. (2005). Framing of the 2003 U.S.–Iraq War demonstrations: An analysis of news and partisan texts. *Journalism & Mass Communication Quarterly*, *82*(1), 78–96.

McChesney, R. W. (2008). *The political economy of media: Enduring issues, emerging dilemmas*. New York: Monthly Review Press.

McChesney, R. W. (2013). *Digital disconnect*. New York: The New Press.

McCurdy, P. (2011). The fragility of dissent!: Mediated resistance at the Gleneagles G8 Summit and the impact of the 7/7 London bombings. *Cultura, Lenguaje Y Representación, 9*, 99–116.

McFarlane, T. & Hay, I. (2003). The battle for Seattle: Protest and popular geopolitics in the Australian newspaper. *Political Geography, 22*(2), 211–232.

McLeod, D. & Detenber, B. H. (1999). Framing effects of television news coverage of social protest. *Journal of Communication, 49*(3), 3–23.

Melucci, A. (1995). The process of collective identity. *Social Movements and Culture, 4*, 41–63.

Myers, C. (2014). Reconsidering the corporate narrative in U.S. PR history: A critique of Alfred Chandler's influence on PR historiography. *Public Relations Review, 40*(4), 676–683.

Oliver, P. & Maney, G. (2000). Political processes and local newspaper coverage of protest events: From selection bias to triadic interactions. *American Journal of Sociology, 106*(2), 463–505.

Poell, T. (2014). Social media and the transformation of activist communication: Exploring the social media ecology of the 2010 Toronto G20 protests. *Information, Communication & Society, 17*(6), 716–731.

Roper, J. (2002). Government, corporate or social power? The internet as a tool in the struggle for dominance in public policy. *Journal of Public Affairs, 2*, 113–124.

Rushe, D. (2011). Occupy Wall Street: NYPD attempt media blackout at Zuccotti Park. [Online] *Guardian*. Available at: www.theguardian.com/world/2011/nov/15/occupy-journalists-media-blackout [accessed 19 Apr. 2018].

Smith, B. G. (2010). Socially distributing public relations: Twitter, Haiti, and interactivity in social media. *Public Relations Review, 36*(4), 329–335.

Snow, D. A., Rochford Jr, E. B., Worden, S. K. & Benford, R. D. (1986). Frame alignment processes, micromobilization, and movement participation. *American Sociological Review, 51*(4), 464–481.

Stauber, J. C. & Rampton, S. (1995). *Toxic sludge is good for you: Lies, damn lies and the public relations industry*. Monroe, ME: Common Courage Press.

Taylor, M. & Kent, M. L. (2014). Dialogic engagement: Clarifying foundational concepts. *Journal of Public Relations Research, 26*(5), 384–398.

Taylor, M., Kent, M. & White, W. J. (2001). How activist organizations are using the Internet to build relationships. *Public Relations Review, 27*, 263–284.

Turkle, S. (1995). *Life on the screen: Identity in the age of the Internet*. New York: Simon & Schuster Paperbacks.

Turkle, S. (2017). *Alone together: Why we expect more from technology and less from each other*. New York: Basic Books.

Vasquez, G. M. & Taylor, M. (2001). Research perspectives on "the public." In R. Heath (Ed.), *Handbook of public relations* (pp. 139–154). Thousand Oaks, CA: Sage.

Vrikki, P. (2017). *The story of Occupy Wall Street: Narratives of politics and identity on Twitter*. (Unpublished doctoral dissertation). King's College London, London, U.K.

Williams, M. L., Burnap, P. & Sloan, L. (2017). Towards an ethical framework for publishing Twitter data in social research: Taking into account users' views, online context and algorithmic estimation. *Sociology, 51*(6), 1149–1168.

13 Activist public relations

Moving from frames as objects to framing as a dynamic process

Adam Howe and Rima Wilkes

Studies in political sociology and social movements have engaged with processes very similar to those involved in protest PR, using a social movement framing perspective (SMFP). In this chapter we argue that, while the protest PR literature has clearly paid attention to *frames* (interpretive frameworks or mental schemata that people use to interpret reality in their daily lives), it has yet to fully consider *framing* as a dynamic process. Framing refers to the rhetorical and communicative strategies actors use to reshape the way people view some issue or event. Herein we summarize how protest PR scholars have employed frames and framing. Then, we draw on the case of environmental activism at Clayoquot Sound in British Columbia, Canada, to show how scholars can leverage the SMFP to better explicate the framing processes driving effective protest PR. We focus on this case because of the central role framing played in the conflict. We conclude that activist PR scholars utilizing a SMFP can better empower activists and local communities with informed strategies directed at ongoing processes of effective activist communication.

In 1993 more than 10,000 Indigenous and environmental activists gathered in British Columbia, Canada, at what came to be the largest instance of collective action in Canadian history (Tindall & Robinson, 2017; Doyle et al., 1997; M'Gonigle & Parfitt, 1994). Activists engaged in mass blockades of logging roads into Clayoquot Sound, a pristine part of western Vancouver Island, off the west coast of British Columbia. Clayoquot Sound contains one of the world's last remaining old-growth temperate rainforests and is the ancestral home to the Nuu-Chah-nulth Indigenous people. As a result of this "war in the woods" as it came to be known, over 850 people were arrested (ibid.). The protests were sparked by a decision from the provincial government to open three quarters of the rainforest to wide-scale logging by companies such as MacMillan Bloedel, the largest logging company in British Columbia at the time. Indigenous communities and environment activists took issue with this plan, as it endangered drinking water and land rights for Indigenous communities, and allowed logging companies to use the ecologically damaging practice of clear-cut logging (ibid.). Ultimately, activists were successful in driving almost all major logging corporations – including MacMillan Bloedel – out of British Columbia, allowing local Indigenous communities to form their own logging company (Iisaak Forest Resources) in partnership with a different local logging company (Weyerhaeuser Corp.) informed by more ecologically sound logging practices (FOCS, 2014; Pechlaner & Tindall, 2013).

This case provides a vignette with which to explore the difference between mainstream and activist public relations. Mainstream PR research treats social activism as a threat, and a problem to be solved (Deegan, 2001; Demetrious, 2013; Xu, 2017b). Activists are a threat to corporate reputation and profitability. Thus, from this perspective, the outcome of the "war in the woods" was a disaster – the activist threat to MacMillan Bloedel's reputation and profits was not contained, and the company was forced to abandon its interests in the area. Activist PR scholars challenge the pro-capitalist slant implicit in the mainstream approach, showing how it omits the actions and ideas of activists and affected communities (Dutta 2009). That is, their voices and concerns are marginalized or silenced. To address this gap, rather than focusing on corporate communication, activist PR scholars study PR communication from the perspective of activists (Coombs & Holladay 2012; Zoch et al., 2008a; 2008b). For example, while mainstream PR scholars study how issues are framed in corporate press releases (Choi & Lee, 2017), activist PR scholars study issue-framing in news media or on websites of non-profit activist organizations (e.g., Zoch et al., 2008a; 2008b).

In this chapter we argue that, while the activist PR literature has clearly paid attention to frames, it has yet to fully consider framing as a dynamic process. *Frames* are interpretive frameworks or mental schemata that people use to interpret reality in their daily lives (Benford & Snow, 2000; Taylor, 2000; Snow et al., 1986). The logging protests can, for example, be framed as extremist actions of "eco-terrorists," or as a moral and just duty to protect the sacred environment (Cormier & Tindall, 2005; Doyle et al., 1997). To be effective, frames have to be diffused through culture and across movements. This occurs through face-to-face speech, in the media, online, or through printed materials. *Framing* refers to the rhetorical and communicative strategies actors use to reshape the way people view some issue or event. It involves studying how activists identify the cause or perpetrator of an issue, its victims, and a proscription for its resolution. More importantly, it involves studying how activists mobilize these new interpretations in a "dynamic and evolving process" (Benford & Snow, 2000, p. 614). This process is often contentious, and movement frames are contested by opposing movements, bystanders, the media, or even activists within the movement (ibid.).

In this chapter we summarize how activist PR scholars have employed frames and framing, and outline how the social movement framing perspective (SMFP – Benford & Snow, 2000, p. 614; Hannigan, 2014;

Hänggli & Kriesi, 2012) can be effectively leveraged by activist PR scholars to build on this literature. We show that the SMFP identifies a number of core-framing tasks – diagnostic, prognostic, and motivational framing, as well as frame amplification, bridging, extension, and transformation – that have yet to be fully considered by activist PR literature. Then, using the case of environmental activism at Clayoquot, we show how activist PR scholars can leverage the SMFP to better explicate the framing processes driving effective activist PR. Although to our knowledge no mainstream PR analyses have been conducted on the Clayoquot Sound protests,[1] we focus on the case herein because of the central role of framing processes in environmental activist communications. In this way the protests are an ideal case for exploring the SMFP.

Activist PR

Activists from social movements such as #OccupyWallStreet, the #IdleNoMore Indigenous rights movement, and the broader environmental movement have brought significant pressure to bear on corporate misdeeds and malfeasance. Specifically, activists target activities such as predatory banking, forestry, mining and land development, and industrial pollution, and the destructive and harmful socio-economic conditions that result from these activities (Ciszek, 2015; Coombs & Holladay, 2014; 2012; Zoch et al., 2008a; 2008b).

Mainstream models of PR talk about the threat this kind of activism poses to organizations highlighting "severe disruption, including damage to reputation, sales, profitability, employee satisfaction and, of course, share prices" (Deegan, 2001, p. 2; Demetrious, 2013; Xu, 2017b). One way to mitigate the likelihood of activism is to identify the aims and goals of any challenging group. Corporations may seek to co-opt activists by lobbying or funding NGOs involved in the dispute, or by forming partnerships with stakeholders (ibid.). Thus between 1989 and 1991, MacMillan Bloedel, along with environmentalists, First Nation groups, and logging industry actors participated in a number of coalitions and committees established to foster discussion leading to mutually beneficial agreements. Later in 1991 logging interests also created the B.C. Forest Alliance (the Alliance) – an industry-backed pro-logging organization founded specifically to counter environmentalist media narratives and appear as independent from the industry. The Alliance sought to, and eventually succeeded in, bringing environmentalists to sit on its board; "former Greenpeace president and co-founder Patrick Moore became an Alliance board member and [was] an active spokesman for the alliance…" (Doyle et al., 1997, p. 252).

Activist PR challenges this corporate approach to PR (Coombs & Holladay, 2012). One problem with mainstream PR is that it assumes that power and influence are equally distributed via an "open market" of PR communication (Demetrious, 2013; Deegan, 2001). Activist PR scholars, in contrast, adopt a critical stance to the power struggles between social movements and corporations. They contextualize activism within a capitalist economy and political system that is hostile toward the "activist threat" (Demetrious, 2013). Thus, scholars draw attention to the omission and marginalization of activist voices from mainstream PR communication and research (Xu, 2017b; Ciszek, 2015; Coombs & Holladay, 2014; 2012; Jahng et al., 2014; Smith, 2013; Edwards & Hodges, 2011; Dutta, 2009; Kim & Dutta, 2009; Dozier & Lauzen, 2000; Ihlen et al., 2009; Curtin & Gaither, 2005). In the case of Clayoquot Sound, the formation of the B.C. Forest Alliance was suggested by Burson-Marsteller, the PR firm notorious for its work on numerous high-profile environmental disasters including the Union Carbide poisoning in Bhopal, India, the Exxon Valdez oil spill, and the Three Mile Island (US) nuclear plant disaster. The Alliance was funded by the B.C. forest industry and its links with extensive global capital (Doyle et al., 1997; Marchak, 1983). In response to some fringe violent protest tactics (e.g., the burning of a bridge in the area) the Alliance leveraged their vast resources to engage in counter-PR, in one example publishing news stories describing all of the activists as "eco-terrorists" or "eco-extremists" (Doyle et al., 1997). Such stories overshadowed mainstream activists' views on these tactics, mainly because "societal structures, such as [...] news sources, still favor organizations over activists" (Coombs & Holladay, 2014, p. 66).

This example also highlights the tensions between corporate and activist understandings of public relations. Corporate PR scholars would generally view outcomes that prioritize economic development as successes because they promote social, economic, and political "stability" (Demetrious, 2013; Deegan, 2001). Yet as outlined above, despite the significant amount of power and economic resources leveraged by the B.C. Forest Alliance, by the end of the 1990s the provincial government had approved a set of recommended regulations on logging activity, and logging companies had pulled out of Clayoquot Sound due to reputational and sales damage. Local Indigenous communities acquired logging rights previously owned by these large corporations and formed their own logging company governed by ecologically sound logging practices. Considering this only as a PR failure to be examined for its lessons clearly prioritizes only the corporate capitalist interests and PR activities of corporations. It dismisses any potential for corporate activities do destabilize communities, and denies the possibility that local communities know what is best for them and their resource base.

Much like scholars of social movements and framing, activist PR scholars focus specifically on the PR communication of activists in a "journey of solidarity" (Xu, 2017a; Dutta, 2009, p. 294), and can also engage in dialogue with disadvantaged classes or groups, giving agency and voice to people who are usually categorized by mainstream PR simply as "victims" and subsequently erased from analyses. There is a focus on investigating how movements "gather support for their views from previously unengaged individuals [and] activate those who already agree with [the movement]" (Zoch et al., 2008a, p. 4). This problem "parallels the daily struggle of public relations practitioners trying to engage and inform their publics" (ibid.). In this view PR does not merely provide self-promoting information to publics to "smooth" conflict and manage reputations.[2] Rather, it is a means of persuading or influencing publics toward a particular perspective or interpretation of reality (Coombs & Holladay, 2010, 2012; Moloney, 2005). Activist PR scholars have also investigated how activists leverage social media, websites, and email, showing how use of these platforms expands PR messaging and democratizes activist influence (Weaver, 2016; Coombs & Holladay, 2014; Demetrious, 2013; Zoch et al., 2008a).[3]

However, while activist PR literature considers how activists communicate with and mobilize supporters, it can also benefit from incorporating insights from the social movements literature, which as we show below, is more process oriented with its focus on *framing*. As it currently stands, the theoretical underpinnings of the activist PR communication literature comprise a focus on media and activist *frames* and how these might change public opinion (Borah, 2011, p. 246; Lim & Jones, 2010; Oyer et al., 2010; see also Wilkes et al., 2010). For example, Coombs and Holladay (2012) discussed environmental activism through the 1960s and 1970s, showing how activists were able to influence media stories by providing them with a scenario "where the corporations were cast as the villains in the environmental degradation story" (p. 349).[4] Similarly, Zoch et al. (2008a, 2008b) described PR message design by examining the use of a set of unique frames by activist organizations. They studied frames such as identifying an issue as a current or future threat to specific groups, attributing blame or guilt for an issue to a specific actor, and proposing a remedy or path toward a solution of the issue. Moreover, some of the frames pertained to rhetorical strategies, such as the use of metaphors, visual images, or statistics to frame issues. With this approach, scholars select static frames from a morphology of frames, understood as reified "things."

Overall, framing analyses in activist PR literature either do not approach framing as a dynamic process, or only do so in a limited way. Elucidating the types of frames used in PR communication is important, but largely insofar as it informs us about the broader framing process – the beliefs about reality and the social and cultural values at stake, and how these have been challenged and presented to different publics to affect changes in their interpretation of reality. We argue that this limitation can be effectively addressed by incorporating a coherent sociological social movement framing perspective (SMFP) oriented specifically toward social activism. This would serve to clarify how activists re-framed environmental degradation as they did, the mechanisms implicated in translating media coverage into changes in public opinion, and how this is implicated in mobilizing new adherents. We outline these dimensions in the next section.

Social movement framing

The SMFP moves beyond curating and analyzing static frames, to elucidate a dynamic framing process that involves "signifying work or meaning construction" (Benford & Snow, 2000, p. 614; Hannigan, 2014; Hänggli & Kriesi, 2012). Framing denotes an "active, processual phenomenon that implies agency and contention at the level of reality construction" (Benford & Snow, 2000, p. 614). A central task throughout these processes is for activists to draw from generalized *master frames* – in this case, the "justice" master frame – to construct context-specific *collective active frames* – in this case the "environmental justice" frame described below (Benford, 2013). Master frames are different from collective action frames because they articulate general principles, and are not specific to any particular aspect of life. Other examples include the "equal rights and opportunities," "imperial," or "hegemonic" master frames (Benford, 2013). Collective action frames draw from these principles to articulate mental heuristics or schemata of interpretation that people use to identify and interpret specific life occurrences (Snow et al., 1986, p. 464).

Activists engage with collective active frames through a series of core framing tasks, aimed at encouraging people to become engrossed in a social issue, and spur them to involvement in, and commitment to, a social movement (Taylor, 2000; Snow et al., 1986). There are three core framing tasks: diagnostic framing, prognostic framing, and motivational framing (Benford & Snow, 2000; Snow et al., 1986). Moreover, these are involved in the four core framing processes: frame amplification, frame bridging, frame extension and frame transformation (ibid.). Below, we describe these concepts, illustrate their utility as they apply the Clayoquot Sound protests, and summarize this information in Table 13.1.

In a series of campaigns developed by Friends of Clayoquot Sound (FOCS) – a central organization in the logging blockades – environmental activists drew from the justice *master frame* to construct an environmental justice *collective action frame* (Benford & Snow, 2000; Taylor, 2000; Cable & Shriver, 1995; Čapek, 1993). This collective action frame prioritizes biocentric values and beliefs. A biocentric orientation holds that humans are one among all species on earth and not entitled to any privileged top position on a hierarchy. It holds that nature is not solely for the use of humans, and that humans are dependent on the environment for survival. Thus, it stresses the inherent value of biodiversity, and the importance of preserving a balance with nature. This contrasts with an anthropocentric orientation associated with devotion to growth and prosperity, faith in science and technology, and commitment to the tenants of

Table 13.1 Definition of core framing process and application to Clayoquot Sound protests

Framing process	Definition	Example
Diagnostic framing	Identify and articulate a social/political problem, its consequences/victims, and assign responsibility.	Clear-cutting in Clayoquot Sound by MacMillan Bloedel (and the logging industry in general) will destroy a rare and endangered rainforest, biodiversity, and Indigenous rights.
Prognostic framing	Identify and articulate a potential solution to the problem, and a clear pathway to this solution.	To secure Clayoquot Sound as a protected area, and regulations against the practice of clear-cut logging old growth rainforests. If lobbying fails, engage in collective action/civil disobedience.
Motivational framing	Articulate a clear and strong rationale for people to join the movement and engage in collective action.	It's a moral duty incumbent upon all of us to insure the protection of our forests for a number of reasons: future generations, aesthetics, biodiversity, Indigenous justice, etc. It's up to you!
Frame amplification	Motivate the public to recognize and prioritize a set of values/beliefs/behaviors central to the movement and see how the issue is related to their everyday lives.	The rainforest is home to endangered species, and they are inherently ancient/sacred/beautiful. They have inherent value, and we ultimately depend on them for survival. Greedy corporations are threatening your forests, and your active participation can help prevent it.
Frame bridging	Link one movement/organization with another, structurally unconnected one, based on shared interests/a shared focus. Re-frame the issue to find common ground.	Logging rainforests in Clayoquot Sound violates Indigenous rights. Thus, the environmental movement shares similar goals as the Indigenous rights and environmental justice movements.
Frame extension	Extend the scope of interests/values/beliefs to appeal to issues important to other constituents, but not directly implicated in the primary issue.	Logging rainforests will destroy landscapes and animal populations used by campers, hikers, and hunters, and threaten endangered animal species. We need to protect the rights of hunters, outdoor enthusiast, the tourism industry, and animal rights, by protecting the rainforests.
Frame transformation	Re-frame the issue entirely to appeal to the ideals and experiences of a different/larger audience, that have not "bought in" to your core framing messaging.	Local people employed in the logging industry are not identifying with the anti-logging message. Re-frame the issue entirely: some logging of the rainforest is desirable, so long as it is co-managed with local First Nations and follows practices of selective cutting instead of clearcutting.

capitalist economics – private property, and limited government intervention (Dunlap & Van Liere, 2008).

Activists applied this to the forestry issue, to construct particular frames related to "ancient" and "sacred" forests, their inherent value, and the justice in preserving them. Justice also gets applied through reference to Indigenous rights, which were being transgressed. Thus in the campaigns logging was framed as a threat to Indigenous rights and livelihoods, to the rare existence of a temperate rainforest, to global climate, and to the inherent rights of "nature" itself. Master frames provide the raw material for diagnostic, prognostic, and motivational frames that social movements use in their communications. Diagnostic frames identify problems and attribute blame or guilt to a particular actor; prognostic frames identify a solution to the problem, and a pathway to achieving this solution; motivational frames provide a rationale for joining the movement and engaging in collective action, emphasizing individual agency and ownership of the issue – i.e., moving people "from the balcony to the barricades" (Benford & Snow, 2000, p. 615). In the campaigns activists identified the "victims" of environmental degradation (Indigenous peoples, ancient rainforests, biodiversity), the corporate "perpetrators" causing this injustice (MacMillan Bloedel), the political–economic system that encouraged environmental exploitation (the logging industry and related policies and legislation), and the appropriate pathway(s) to a resolution (civil disobedience, selective cutting, establishing the rainforest as a protected wilderness) (Poletta, 2006; Cormier & Tindall, 2005; Benford & Snow, 2000). They motivated adherents to identify with their interpretation of the issue by appealing to values of justice, conservation, and the need for people to take protection of the forests into their own hands (ibid.).

The values and beliefs in the environmental justice frame are integral to the process of *frame amplification*. This process involves indicating the specific values, beliefs, behaviors or ideals that activists think are worth protecting or promoting and clarifying how a complex issue relates to people's daily lives (Cormier & Tindall, 2005; Benford & Snow, 2000). In the FOCS campaigns, images of trees were used alongside statements underscoring the forest's sacred ancient character. Images of endangered species were shown alongside statements about saving their home – the rainforest. Logging companies were presented as being motivated solely by profits in the context of a capitalist resource extraction industry that decimates priceless ancient rainforests, endangers biodiversity and Indigenous rights in order to satisfy the profit motive and please corporate shareholders. Activists pointed to the importance of direct action by active and engaged citizens, and calls to push government actors to acknowledge biocentric values and engage with Indigenous communities (ibid.). By amplifying these values and beliefs through the environmental justice frame, FOCS motivated people to identify with the movement, and demand justice through democratic participation.

Clayoquot activism also exemplified *frame bridging*. Bridging involves linking two interpretive frames or organizations that are ideologically congruent regarding a specific issue, but structurally unconnected (Benford & Snow, 2000). For example, environmental activist groups often seek to reframe local issues as national, international or global issues, forming bridges with other movement organizations to garner broader support (Brummans et al., 2008). The FOCS campaigns effectively linked the Clayoquot protests with a number of other national and international movements/interests, namely the Indigenous rights movement, the protection of wild salmon (a key interest to coastal communities in B.C.), movements for the protection of global rainforests and the animals/biodiversity within them, and the broader environmental movement concerned with the negative social effects of climate change.

The campaigns engaged in *frame extension*, a process whereby a movement extends its primary interpretive framework to encompass interests, values, or beliefs that are incidental to the primary objectives of the social movement but central to other publics (Benford & Snow, 2000; Snow et al., 1986). One example of frame extension would be extending rainforest biodiversity to the protection of wild salmon. In the FOCS campaigns, activists extended their framing by highlighting negative consequences of logging the rainforest that were unseen/unknown by potential adherents, such as the potential loss of "nature" that is used for leisure activities.

Finally, activists also engaged in *frame transformation*. Frame transformation is necessary when activists realize that existing framing activities are ineffective and that a more fundamental shift in interpretation is necessary (Benford & Snow, 2000; Snow et al., 1986). Activists "reframe the issue ... to tailor it to the ideals and the lived experience of the larger target audience" (Cormier & Tindall, 2005, p. 5). In the case of Clayoquot Sound activists began speaking of the value of selective cutting (logging of a small number of trees in a demarcated area) as a less destructive alternative to clear cutting, transforming the anthropocentric frames of the forestry company toward a more biocentric interpretation (ibid.).

Conclusion

Challenging dominant values and beliefs, and motivating support from the public are core dimensions of activist communication. Explaining the processes whereby activists communicate their grievances and claims to the public is imperative in accounting for successful instances of activist PR. Not only does this center the interests of activists and affected communities in the analysis, but it also provides a useful buffer from the predominant corporate approach to PR research. Herein we have outlined the challenge made by activist PR scholars against mainstream approaches to PR. We demonstrated a gap in activist PR literature, insofar as scholars have not fully leveraged a social movements framing perspective (SMFP) in analyses of activist PR communication.

The SMFP is a core framework in the sociological social movements literature (e.g., Danaher & Dixon, 2017; Earl & Garrett, 2017; Ketelaars et al., 2017; Tindall & Robinson, 2017; Williams, 2016; Brown, 2014; Hadler, 2013; Alkon et al., 2013; Cormier & Tindall, 2005; see also Snow et al., 2014 for overview). In line with the activist PR literature the SMFP also provides a framework for considering the universe of *frames* used by activists. More importantly, it facilitates studying the dynamic and contentious ongoing processes of influence at the core of social movements – *framing*. Activists engage in these processes to motivate movement support and participation, and to change the public's interpretations of issues and events related to the movement.

We argue that these framing processes are the raison d'être of activist PR. While a small number of studies have made inroads toward integrating a SMFP (Anderson, 2017; Coombs & Holladay, 2012; Zoch et al., 2008a; Zoch et al., 2008b), we argued that the literature needs to be expanded upon. Drawing on the SMFP we demonstrated some useful avenues for expanding activist PR literature toward more process-oriented framing analyses. This involves studying the master frames that inform activist PR, and how this communication engenders frame amplification, frame bridging, frame extension, and frame transformation.

We did so with an analysis of the conflict over Clayoquot Sound in British Columbia, Canada. We argued that Indigenous and environmental activists drew on the environmental justice collective action frame and engaged in the core framing tasks outlined above, to transform how the public interpreted clear-cut logging practices. The predominant frame was that clear-cut logging was a necessary and unfortunate by-product of industry. In response activists mobilized diagnostic, prognostic, and motivational frames as well as frame bridging, extension, amplification, and transformation in the context of an environmental justice collection action frame. Through effective ongoing communication such as the FOCS campaigns, activists challenged and even transformed the dominant corporate framing of logging the rainforests, and successfully mobilized adherents to create the largest instance of collective action in Canadian history.

Finally, we conclude by noting the normative consideration that should underlie any such project related to activist PR framing. Framing remains a "fractured paradigm" in the PR field more generally (Entman, 1993; Lim & Jones, 2010). That is, PR framing literature does not have a "general statement of framing theory" (Entman, 1993, pp. 51) to guide and cohere analyses. Therefore, it is reasonable to expect that mainstream PR scholars would also draw from the social movement framing perspective; partly to unify this fractured landscape, partly to further inform corporate PR strategies in opposition to activism. There is also the question of whether it is "good" for corporate PR practitioners to be better equipped in "solving" the activism problem – an evaluation that depends on the standpoint of the evaluator. However, as most genealogies of public relations argue, activism and corporate PR dialectically learn from one another (e.g., Coombs & Holladay, 2012, p. 348). This might ultimately make the potential moral hazard of further empowering corporate PR insignificant. Activist PR scholars utilizing a SMFP can better empower activists and local communities with informed strategies directed at ongoing processes of effective activist communication.

Notes

1 Perhaps the most extensive analysis related to the Clayoquot Sound protests that involves PR is Doyle et al.'s (1997) discussion about controversial PR firm Burson-Marsteller, which in 1991 helped form a central counter-movement front-organization representing B.C. logging interests called the B.C. Forest Alliance. The authors highlight how in the context of corporations taking "a more active [PR] stance on environmental questions" (pp. 245), B.C. logging corporations, through the Alliance, engaged in a counter-movement PR campaign. The authors use this as a case to study the openness of B.C. media to oppositional PR activities, finding news media to be relatively "open, pluralistic, and diverse [offering] valuable openings for social movements struggling to contest dominant meanings" (p. 266).
2 Publics are identifiable groups that form in response to some issue or situation, and whose opinion can affect the success of organizations (Coombs & Holladay, 2014, p. 31).
3 Local or grassroots activists such often lack power to access "legacy" media (radio, television, and newspaper), which is an important resource in any successful PR campaign. Online communication is inexpensive, open, non-mediated, and allows organizations to dissemination information quickly to wider audiences (Zoch et al., 2008a).
4 Further, as with other analyses in the PR literature, they focused on how frames generally impact "the public good" or "public opinion" (García, 2011; Lim & Jones, 2010; Entman, 2004; Brewer, 2003).

References

Alkon, A. H., Cortez, M., & Sze, J. (2013). What Is in a Name? Language, Framing and Environmental Justice Activism in California's Central Valley. *Local Environment, 18*(10), 1167–83.

Anderson, W. B. (2017). Social Movements and Public Relations in the Early Twentieth Century: How One Group Used Public Relations to Curtail Venereal Disease Rates. *Journal of Public Relations Research, 29*(1), 3–15.

Benford, R. D. (2013). "Master Frames." In David A. Snow, Donatella della Porta, Bert Klandermans, & Doug McAdam (Eds.), *The Blackwell Encyclopedia of Social and Political Movements.* Oxford, UK: Blackwell.

Benford, R. D. & Snow, D. A. (2000). Framing Processes and Social Movements: An Overview and Assessment. *Annual Review of Sociology, 26*(1), 611–39.

Borah, P. (2011). Conceptual Issues in Framing Theory: A Systematic Examination of a Decade's Literature. *Journal of Communication, 61*(2), 246–63.

Brewer, P. R. (2003). Values, Political Knowledge, and Public Opinion about Gay Rights: A Framing-Based Account. *Public Opinion Quarterly, 67*(2), 173–201.

Brown, G. (2014). Does Framing Matter? Institutional Constraints on Framing in Two Cases of Intrastate Violence. *Mobilization: An International Quarterly, 19*(2), 143–64.

Brummans, B. H. J. M., Putnam, L. L., Gray, B., Hanke, R., Lewicki, R. J., & Wiethoff, C. (2008). Making Sense of Intractable Multiparty Conflict: A Study of Framing in Four Environmental Disputes. *Communication Monographs, 75*(1), 25–51.

Cable, S. & Shriver, T. (1995). Production and Extrapolation of Meaning in the Environmental Justice Movement. *Sociological Spectrum, 15*(4), 419–42.

Čapek, S. M. (1993). The "Environmental Justice" Frame: A Conceptual Discussion and Application. *Social Problems, 40*(1), 5–24.

Choi, J. & Lee, S. (2017). Managing a Crisis: A Framing Analysis of Press Releases Dealing with the Fukushima Nuclear Power Station. *Public Relations Review, 43*(5), 1016–24.

Ciszek, E. L. (2015). Bridging the Gap: Mapping the Relationship between Activism and Public Relations. *Public Relations Review, 41*(4), 447–55.

Coombs, W. T. & Holladay, S. J. (2010). *PR Strategy and Application: Managing Influence.* Malden: Wiley-Blackwell.

Coombs, W. T. & Holladay, S. J. (2012). Privileging an Activist vs. a Corporate View of Public Relations History in the U.S. *Public Relations Review, 38*(3), 347–53.

Coombs, W. T. & Holladay, S. J. (2014). *It's Not Just PR: Public Relations in Society (2nd ed.).* Chichester Wiley Blackwell.

Cormier, J. & Tindall, D. B. (2005). Wood Frames: Framing the Forests in British Columbia. *Sociological Focus, 38*(1), 1–24.

Curtin, P. & Gaither, T. K. (2005). Privileging Identity, Difference, and Power: The Circuit of Culture as a Basis for Public Relations Theory. *Journal of Public Relations Research, 17*(2), 91–115.

Danaher, W. F. & Dixon, M. (2017). Framing the Field: The Case of the 1969 Charleston Hospital Workers' Strike. *Mobilization: An International Quarterly, 22*(4), 417–33.

Deegan, D. (2001). *Managing Activism: A Guide to Dealing with Activists and Pressure Groups.* London: Kogan Page.

Demetrious, K. (2013). *Public Relations, Activism and Social Change: Speaking Up.* London: Routledge.

Doyle, A., Elliot, B., & Tindall, D. (1997). "Framing the Forests: Corporations, the B.C. Forest Alliance, and the Media." In W. K. Carroll (Ed.), *Organizing Dissent: Contemporary Social Movements in Theory in Practice, 2nd ed.* (pp. 240–68). Toronto: Garamond Press.

Dozier, D. M. & Lauzen, M. M. (2000). Liberating the Intellectual Domain from the Practice: Public Relations, Activism, and the Role of the Scholar. *Journal of Public Relations Research, 12*(1), 3–22.

Dunlap, R. & Van Liere, K. D. (2008). The "New Environmental Paradigm." *The Journal of Environmental Education, 40*(1), 19–28.

Dutta, M. J. (2009). "Theorizing Resistance – Applying Gayatri Chakravorty Spivak in Public Relations." In Ø. Ihlen, B. van Ruler, & M. Fredriksson (Eds.),

Public Relations and Social Theory: Key Figures and Concepts (pp. 278–300). New York: Routledge.

Earl, J. & Garrett, K. (2017). The New Information Frontier: Toward a More Nuanced View of Social Movement Communication. *Social Movement Studies*, 16(4), 479–93.

Edwards, L. & Hodges, C. E. M. (Eds.) (2011). *Public Relations, Society & Culture*. New York: Routledge.

Entman, R. (1993). Framing: Toward Clarification of a Fractured Paradigm. *Journal of Communications*, 43(4), 51–8.

Entman, R. (2004). *Projections of Power: Framing News, Public Opinion, and U.S. Foreign Policy*. Chicago, IL: U Chicago Press.

Friends of Clayoquot Sound (FOCS). (2014). Ancient Forests: Overview. Retrieved from http://focs.ca/campaigns/ancientforests/.

García, M. M. (2011). Perception is Truth: How U.S. Newspapers Framed the "Go Green" Conflict Between BP and Greenpeace. *Public Relations Review*, 37(1), 57–9.

Hadler, M. (2013). Aligned Frames? The Basis of Political Actions against Offshoring in West Virginia and Austria. *Sociological Spectrum*, 33(1), 57–72.

Hänggli, R. & Kriesi, H. (2012). Frame Construction and Frame Promotion (Strategic Framing Choices). *American Behavioral Scientist*, 56(3), 260–78.

Hannigan, J. (2014). *Environmental Sociology*. Oxon: Routledge.

Ihlen, Ø., van Ruler, B., & Fredriksson, M. (Eds.) (2009). *Public Relations and Social Theory: Key Figures and Concepts*. New York: Routledge.

Jahng, M. R., Hong, S., & Park, E. H. (2014). How Radical is Radical? Understanding the Role of Activists' Communication Strategies on the Formation of Public Attitude and Evaluation. *Public Relations Review*, 40(1), 119–21.

Ketelaars, S., Walgrave, S., & Wouters, R. (2017). Protesters on Message? Explaining Demonstrators' Differential Degree of Frame Alignment. *Social Movement Studies*, 16(3), 340–54.

Kim, I. & Dutta, M. J. (2009). A Subaltern Studies Approach to Crisis Communication. *Journal of Public Relations Research*, 21(2), 142–64.

Lim, J. & Jones, L. (2010). A Baseline Summary of Framing Research in Public Relations. *Public Relations Review*, 36(3), 292–7.

M'Gonigle, M. & Parfitt, B. (1994). *Forestopia: A Practical Guide to the New Forest Economy*. British Columbia: Harbour Publishers.

Marchak, P. M. (1983). *Green Gold: The Forest Industry in British Columbia*. Vancouver: University of British Columbia Press.

Moloney, K. (2005). Trust and Public Relations: Center and Edge. *Public Relations Review*, 31(4), 550–5.

Oyer, S., Saliba, J. K., & Yartey, F. (2010). More Words, Less Action: A Framing Analysis of FEMA Public Relations Communications during Hurricanes Katrina and Gustav. *Public Relations Journal*, 4(2), 1–13.

Pechlaner, G. & Tindall, D. B. (2013). "Changing Contexts: Environmentalism, Aboriginal Community and Forest Company Joint Ventures, and the Case of Iisaak." In D. B. Tindall, R. L. Trosper, & P. Perreault (Eds.), *Aboriginal Peoples and Forest Lands in Canada* (pp. 260–78). Vancouver: University of British Columbia Press.

Poletta, F. (2006). *It Was Like a Fever: Storytelling in Protest and Politics*. Chicago, IL: University of Chicago Press.

Smith, M. F. (2013). "Activism." In R. L. Heath (Ed.), *Encyclopedia of Public Relations* (pp. 6–8). Thousand Oaks: SAGE.

Snow, D. A., Rochford, E. B. Jr., Worden, S. K., & Benford, R. D. (1986). Frame Alignment Processes, Micromobilization, and Movement Participation. *American Sociological Review*, 51(4), 464–81.

Snow, D. S., Benford, R., McCammon, H., Hewitt, L., & Fitzgerald, S. (2014). The Emergence, Development, and Future of the Framing Perspective: 25+ Years Since "Frame Alignment." *Mobilization: An International Quarterly*, 19(1), 23–46.

Taylor, D. E. (2000). The Rise of the Environmental Justice Paradigm: Injustice Framing and the Social Construction of Environmental Discourse. *American Behavioral Scientist*, 43(4), 508–80.

Tindall, D. B. & Robinson, J. L. (2017). Collective Action to Save the Ancient Temperate Rainforest: Social Networks and Environmental Activism in Clayoquot Sound. *Ecology and Society*, 21(1), 1–40.

Weaver, C. K. (2016). A Marxist Primer for Critical Public Relations Scholarship. *Media International Australia*, 160(1), 43–52.

Wilkes, R., Corrigall-Brown, C., & Myers, D. J. (2010). Packaging Protest: Media Coverage of Indigenous People's Collective Action. *Canadian Review of Sociology*, 47(4), 327–57.

Williams, S. J. (2016). Hiding Spinach in the Brownies: Frame Alignment in Suffrage Community Cookbooks, 1886–1916. *Social Movement Studies*, 15(2), 146–63.

Xu, S. (2017a). Crisis Communication within a Community: Bonding, Coping, and Making Sense Together. *Public Relations Review*, 44(1), 84–97.

Xu, S. (2017b). Discourse of Renewal: Developing Multiple-Item Measurement and Analyzing Effects on Relationships. *Public Relations Review*, 44(1), 108–19.

Zoch, L. M., Collins, E. L., & Sisco, H. F. (2008a). From Communication to Action: The Use of Core Framing Tasks in Public Relations Messages on Activist Organizations' Web Sites. *Public Relations Journal*, 2(4), 1–23.

Zoch, L. M., Collins, E. L., Sisco, H. F., & Supa, D. H. (2008b). Empowering the Activists: Using Framing Devices on Activist Organizations' Web Sites. *Public Relations Review*, 34(4), 351–8.

14 Digital media, journalism, PR, and grassroots power

Theoretical perspectives

Marina Vujnovic and Dean Kruckeberg

Introduction

This chapter analyzes similarities and differences between journalism as activism and activism as it is currently understood in the public relations literature. Comparative analysis of activist practices in these two related fields is necessary at this time because digital, online communication tools that are used by activists tend to blur the lines between these professions. Brunner (2017) observes that, in the market-driven digital media environment and with the availability of various communication tools, the lines are blurred between editorial content and advertising, public relations, and marketing. We believe that digital media tools challenge ethics and definitional standards of these professions and that ethical standards are particularly challenged by the activist practices that are occurring in both public relations and journalism.

Comparative analysis helps us to understand, not only what activist practices look like in both journalism and PR, that is, how similar or different they are, but also how these practices challenge the ethics of both professions. This chapter does not attempt to provide conclusive evidence; rather, its goal is to engage in exploratory research by sorting through existing literature to uncover, not only definitional complexities of activism in journalism and in public relations, but also what practices can be considered activism and what kind of ethical challenges scholars and activists may face in the context of the digital market economy. In addition, this chapter attempts to explore the connections among protest PR, activist PR, and dissent PR, focusing on the unprecedented potential of an expanding network terrain in which new communication tools are being used and created by activist groups and public relations practitioners worldwide. We ask what are the types of activities that these terms are describing and whether making distinctions among them helps us to understand these practices. We further ask who engages in these types of PR practices and who benefits. Is it individuals, corporations, governmental bodies, and nongovernmental organizations, or perhaps all of them? Through an examination of the existing literature, we hope to provide at least some answers to these questions.

In the past 20 years or so, a large number of scholars have examined what is most commonly termed as activist PR in US public relations scholarship. However, more questions than answers exist when it comes to what activist PR looks like in practice and how it is similar or different from Protest PR and Dissent PR. A recent resurgence of interest in exploring these variations in PR, both definitionally and practically, is not coincidental. The emergence of the Internet and networked communication and the use of digital media have enabled the production of communication tools that are used by numerous social actors to accelerate and to expand their grassroots power. Hence, this chapter's goal is to discuss the place of activism and activist practices within the traditional professional paradigms of journalism and public relations. Further, we provide a theoretical discussion of activism in journalism and in public relations and include some example or cases found in the scholarly literature. Finally, we tie our findings to questions that have guided our examination of this topic and provide a critical discussion to both illuminate and to complicate contemporary discussions on the topic. We pose several questions for future research in the hope that continuous critical examination and research on this important topic will contribute to a better understanding of activist practices in public relations and, more importantly, to understand their potential for igniting social change.

Activism in journalism and public relations in the context of the dominant paradigms

Much of the recent literature on alternative forms of journalistic and public relations practices has focused on so-called activist practices and activism itself, particularly as the latter relates to the emergence of new networked communication technologies and their potential to redefine the fields (Deuze & Witschge, 2018; Russell, 2016; Coombs & Holladay, 2012a; Coombs & Holladay, 2012b). In the core of this debate is the effort to break away from the modernist view and interpretation of these fields and their practices. Deuze and Witschge (2018) argue that the "modernist dream of consensus and coherence [in journalism] is a fallacy" (p. 166). Additionally, they emphasize that the traditional focus on newsroom work of journalists limits our understanding of journalism. They advocate looking beyond a traditional organizational professional focus, even while recognizing that newsrooms are still relevant sites of journalistic practice. As such, newsrooms are not islands that are isolated from other institutional units and systems, but rather are a part of the networked system that impacts the work of journalists in both non-material and material ways. Similarly, in public relations, a growing number of critical scholars have identified the dominance of an organization-centric modernist view of public relations (Coombs & Holladay, 2012b) that places both the origin and an understanding of the practice within a tight corporate framework.

Similar parallels can be drawn in terms of the dominant occupational ideologies that stem from a functionalist approach by which journalism and public relations must be seen as distinct professional categories in media and communication. For instance, Kruckeberg (1998) argued for public relations as a specialized field with its own values, ethical standards, and professional parameters distinct from other communication or business fields.

In journalism, a large body of literature examines the existence of similar professional parameters that focus on objectivity, non-bias, truth-seeking, and ethical standards that would assure the ideal of service to the public and democracy (Schudson, 2008; Zelizer, 2004). Even though these paradigms are still very strong in the mainstream profession and literature (Deuze & Witschge, 2018), there is a call to rethink those professional ideologies for reasons that include a changing communication field, challenges of the post-industrial economy, and a growing number of activist and pressure groups that have evolved, partly as a result of availability and the potential of networked technology, to name a few.

Activism is a challenging concept for both professions precisely because of their overemphasis on mainstream practices, dominant ideologies, and institutionalized forms. To better understand the theoretical and practical places of activism in both professions, we turn to a discussion of journalism and public relations scholarship on activism. In journalism scholarship, we particularly pay attention to the term advocacy. In public relations, we look at the body of literature on activism as it has developed in the context of a growing body of critical public relations research. Through our discussion, we provide examples from the scholarly literature in the hope that these examples can help us shed light on activist practices, particularly those that—albeit not exclusively—are emerging in the digital age.

Journalism and public relations: advocacy and activism

Even though journalism has devoted more scholarship to alternative forms of journalism than perhaps has public relations, there is still an overwhelming focus on a dominant journalism paradigm that prioritizes knowledge that emerges from the examination of organization (newsroom)-centered, professionally driven practices. Discussion of advocacy in journalism as a form of activist practice has always had a place in the public and scholarly domains. Advocacy and activism, however, are often seen in opposition to the dominant journalistic paradigm, primarily that emphasizes objectivity and neutrality (non-bias). Even opinion-journalism that lives within the dominant paradigm is seen as a fact-based dissection of an issue to show which side is closer to so-called truth, rather than the open advocacy for an organization, individual, or public interest.

Derrick (2012), in a discussion of journalists' involvement in innocence projects (exoneration through DNA testing of those wrongly convicted), argues that there is a fine line between journalism and advocacy and asks whether reporters who work with innocence projects could still be considered journalists? However, some argue that advocacy, and even activism, has always been an intrinsic part of journalistic practice. Feldstein's (2006) overview of the history of muckraking investigative journalism posits that, in the interest of the public good, muckrakers are the challengers of those who abuse power. Journalists who practice muckraking are characterized as dissidents, revolutionaries, and reformers. However, Feldstein (2006) concludes that such journalism is likely to remain an exception rather than a rule. It is clear, though, that activism and reform are in the center of this celebrated, yet now rarely practiced, style of journalism.

A type of journalism in which advocacy and activism aren't as clearly defined is public journalism. Although journalists should bring citizens into the process of democracy by offering, not just facts, but rather a platform for public debate and action, it is not clear what is the actual role of journalists after data potentially turns into action. Voakes (2004) argues that in the core of the public journalism proposition is the role of the journalist to identify what is in the public good. He traces both sides of the public journalism debate, outlining views of those who criticize and those who support public journalism. However, the so-called common good or public good is not easily identified, especially around political issues. This is particularly true today when public life is inundated with partisan views and sensational gossip-mongering that was reflected in the news media coverage of, for instance, the 2016 US presidential campaign. Untrue stories such as the Pope endorsing Trump for president or the conspiracy theory known as Pizzagate, which alleged that several members of the Democratic party ran a human trafficking ring in several US restaurants, are just a few examples of what seems to be a sea of similar partisan-driven stories that emerge almost daily (Taub, 2017). Little civility is left in civic debate.

One strand of journalism, however, which is called advocacy journalism, embraces advocacy as an intrinsic part of the profession, rather than as a practice that makes journalists potentially labeled as not-journalists. Advocacy journalism is considered to be anathema in the mainstream journalism paradigm. In fact, advocacy is one of those terms that are most often used to differentiate public relations from journalism (Fisher, 2016). Advocacy journalism is sometimes considered an umbrella term for any type of journalism in which journalists argue for a cause (taking sides on an issue) or in social activism. Waisbord (2008) attempted to understand advocacy journalism in an international context. He concluded that there must be a distinction between traditional advocacy journalism, in which journalists take sides and argue for a cause, and civic advocacy journalism, in which various groups use journalistic tools and media to further their causes and agendas. In the core, however, is advocacy for the common good and social change. The newest debate that includes issues of advocacy and journalism, which is no less controversial than are the debates already outlined here, is whether journalists can be activists. Olesen (2008), in his study of the Danish Cheminova debates, places a question mark after his statement, that is, activist journalism? His study showed that journalists who produced an investigative journalism documentary, even though they didn't have an activist agenda in mind, managed to place a pesticide issue, that is, a pesticide produced by the Cheminova chemical industry, high on the public agenda and in the core of public debate, something that civil society organizations were not able to do because of their lack of access to traditional media. Olesen (2008) argues that those are "activist-like" activities and roles, rather than activism, and proposes that the journalist be viewed "as part of a complex field of democratic publicity" (p. 247). In other words, he proposes that journalists and media are active participants in shaping politics and issues, rather than they are simply conduits of public debate. He still feels uncomfortable calling this shaping of public issues and politics activism.

Olesen (2008) inadvertently poses another question, that is, are journalists taking up advocacy because they are members of the elite with media power at hand? Rather than providing more access to civil society organizations to argue for causes that are in the interest of the public, journalists themselves engage, if not in activism, then at least in activist-like roles. We argue that in the core of this issue is the need to understand journalism and media's often elite position that has the power to both include and exclude voices, taking on activist-like activities because they are in position to do so.

Russell's (2016) recent book, *Journalism as Activism*, is not shy in asserting that, yes, journalists can and sometimes should be activists, in addition to understanding activists who use traditional journalistic tools and various new communication tools as journalists. She champions stories of four "new-style activist journalists" (p. 116), and "members of the media vanguard" (p. 137), that is, Bill McKibben, Glen Greenwald, Tim Pool, and Juliana Rotich. Notably, all of these journalists work outside of traditional newsrooms. However reasonable her proposition sounds in the context of the networked digital communication and media terrain, it is precisely the traditional newsroom that still stands very much as a gatekeeper to an idea of journalists engaging in activism. A good example is Jose Antonio Vargas, a journalist, filmmaker, and activist who is a Pulitzer Prize winner for his breaking news coverage on the Virginia Tech shooting in 2008, which he performed with a team of journalists at *Washington Post*. His journalistic accomplishments in the mainstream press are notable, and the quality of his journalism had never been questioned. However, in 2011, after he had revealed his status as an undocumented immigrant in his essay in *New York Times Magazine* (Vargas, 2011), he immediately came under fire for taking a firm stance on undocumented immigration and for advocating for the Dream Act, which is a pathway for citizenship for as many as 1.8 million undocumented immigrants. As was indicated in an interview that he had given shortly thereafter on NPR's Fresh Air, professional journalists felt unease that Vargas would call himself a journalist after he had openly advocated for immigration reform and had formed an advocacy group. The question he received from Michelle Norris in this interview implies that being an advocate and journalist is dichotomous: "You're a former journalist at this point, or do you still consider yourself to be a journalist? You're an advocate, and it's sort of hard to be both" (*Fresh Air*, NPR, 2011, July 7). Vargas replied that he is a journalist, but this kind of questioning of whether advocacy can exist alongside journalism shows an uneasy relationship among advocacy, activism, and journalism. It is, perhaps, an expectation that the professional paradigm of journalism places on journalists not to engage on behalf of any particular idea, group, or individual, putting advocacy and journalism in a contentious relationship.

Unlike in journalism, advocacy in public relations is considered essential. Yet, somewhat surprisingly so, the relationship between public relations and activism has historically been contentious. Many have identified the organization-centric Excellence Theory, which was first conceptualized by Grunig and Hunt (1984) as the dominant paradigm in public relations research and practice (Botan & Hazleton, 2006; Benecke & Oksiutycz, 2015), where the first discussion of activism as activist publics had emerged. Excellence Theory's emphasis on the ideal of two-way symmetrical communication necessarily places activist publics (together with that activism) in opposition to organizational goals. Activism is seen as an unwelcome challenge with which organizations must begrudgingly deal, even if at times activists' efforts pressure organization to make a positive change (Grunig, 2001).

This implies that activist publics have the power to impact organizations through media. But it is important to note that scholars such as Fisher (2016) and Olesen (2008) argue that civil society organizations (CSOs) as activist groups have limited impact on media. Even when CSOs' efforts are recognized by the media, the gatekeeping function seems to work against placing critical issues that are promoted by activist organizations on the media agenda. It is, indeed, the modernist, functionalist worldview that centers on the organization's needs and benefits that have made activism almost a dirty word in public relations (Demetrious, 2013; Coombs & Holladay, 2012b; Benecke & Oksiutycz, 2015; Holtzhausen, 2007; Holtzhausen & Voto, 2002; Ciszek, 2015). For instance, Ciszek (2015) writes, "Within functional perspectives, activists are obstacles the organizations must navigate" (p. 447). Additionally, Coombs and Holladay (2012a) identified that the modernist, organizational perspective in which scholarship on activism first emerged "is about unequal power between organizations and publics" (p. 881).

It is within critical public relations theory that activism has been embraced as a theoretical concept and practice to be valued. Indeed, Coombs and Holladay (2012b) have argued that activism is one of three central concepts of critical public relations, with the other two being power and persuasion. They observed that, even though historically activists were first to use the tools that we now call public relations, corporations "appropriated and refined the concept" (Coombs & Holladay, 2012b, p. 349) and placed it within organizational parameters. One of the reasons they cite why public relations suffers from a negative image is the lack of a full understanding of its origins. We would further argue that, in addition to corporate appropriation and redefinition of activism as something negative, the professionalization of PR practice (similarly to what is seen in journalism) has contributed to understanding activism as an unwelcome challenge to the mainstream professional and organizational structure in which professionals operate.

It is important to note that activism in public relations, similarly to that in journalism, has been identified as a practice of public relations within an organization as well as organized practices of individuals outside of the organizational corporate structure. Holtzhausen and Voto (2002) developed a postmodern view of activism within the traditional organizational structure, arguing that public relations practitioners are agents of change. They believe that public relations practitioners in a postmodern view of PR "will act as activists" (p. 57). It is through ethical decision-making and resistance to power that public relations practitioners, among other responsibilities, will act as the voice of dissent within the larger organizational structure. Holtzhausen (2000) called for public relations practitioners to be actors in social change, engaging in community activism as well as activism within their organizations. This was a novel idea at the time, even though Karlberg (1996) called on more research in public relations that would examine the use of public relations among activists. The idea that public relations practitioners would be activists and voices of dissent within the organizational structure was challenging the dominant paradigm in which public relations practitioners are loyal first and foremost to the organization (Dozier & Lauzen, 2000).

Vujnovic (2004) examined the role of the public relations practitioner in the organizational context and questioned whether the practitioner should sit in the dominant coalition, precisely because of the pressures of organizational loyalty that hinders the ability of the PR practitioner to serve as a dissenting voice for the organization. She argued for the role of public relations practitioner as an ombudsman who could advocate and fight for both organizational and publics' interests. This is similar to Holtzhausen and Voto's (2002) argument in which public relations practitioners as communication specialists can serve as organizational advocates for concerns voiced by various external publics.

Since then, a growing literature in public relations has focused on activists and activism, and critical public relations scholars have contributed to lively discussions (Coombs & Holladay, 2012a). Activism in the public relations literature has been examined in areas such as issues management (Jaques, 2006) and, more recently, in how activists have used online media (primarily social media) and the Internet and which public relations tools did they utilize (Adi, 2015; Adi & Miah, 2011; Adi & Moloney, 2012).

There is also recent recognition of activists' use of tools of public relations historically. For example, Alwood (2015) described the role of public relations in the gay rights movement from 1950 to 1969, while Spatzier (2016) examined both journalism and the public relations practice of an Austrian activist, Bertha von Suttner, in the late nineteenth century. Indeed, Coombs and Holladay (2012b) said that a lack of focus on studies in which contributions of activists to public relations are examined is a "glaring omission" (p. 352) in the public relations literature, especially that which is concerned with the history of US public relations. Those afore-mentioned examples are certainly filling in some of this void.

Additionally, some literature exists on digital public relations activism/dissensus. Owens and Palmer (2003) describe public relations tactics that have been used by anarchists to mount a counter-public relations publicity campaign against the negative perceptions of anarchists that were prevalent in the mainstream media, while Derville (2005) argues for the relevancy of recognizing differences between activist groups in a study of tactics used by radical activist groups. Weaver's (2010) study of New Zealand activist group, Mothers Against Genetic Engineering (MAdGE), showed a type of activist/dissent public relations that she termed carnivalesque protest and defined as a particular "genre of activist public relations which articulates conflict with, and resistance to, dominant discourses on controversial issues" (p. 35). Finally, Veil, Reno, Freihaut, and Oldham (2015) outline a case of a social media hijacking in which one activist, Vani Hari, used a hoax to get her followers to hijack the *Kraft Foods* Facebook page, pressuring that company to remove potentially harmful chemicals from its food. This use of online hijacking as a form of pressure by an activist group was a successful campaign and only one of the various campaigns that also included more traditional public relations strategies.

The obvious question here is whether such radical pressure tactics violate ethical standards. We ask that question ourselves, but argue that a hoax, even if potentially unethical, is a viable strategy to motivate action. In all of these examples, impact on society and change in social, political, and economic life seem to be motivating factors.

Moloney, McQueen, Surowiec, and Yaxley (2013) offered two new terms, dissent and protest PR, to describe public relations techniques that hold paramount a change in civil life and political economy. Those who practice Dissent PR and Protest PR also wish to impact policy. They define dissent PR as

…the dissemination of ideas, commentaries, and policies through PR techniques in order to change current, dominant thinking and behavior in discrete economic, political and cultural areas of public life.

(p. 3)

In the core of this definition is support for the ideas of public intellectuals and the promotion of new thinking. Protest PR is its follow up. It uses persuasive communicative techniques as well, but the goal is implementation and action. Moloney and McKie (2016) define Protest PR as, "techniques such as marches, rallies, stunts, strikes, boycotts and lawsuits to create influence on policy makers" (p. 157).

In some ways, Moloney et al.'s (2013) goal is to attempt to differentiate Dissent PR and Protest PR from activist public relations. However, Moloney and McKie (2016) clearly see both terms as a subset of activist PR. They also make two important points: (1) that public relations is per se a neutral, ideology-free technique, although the message is not value-free; and (2) that Dissent PR and Protest PR are not to be associated with left-wing causes only.

We fervently agree with that. Ample evidence exists of groups from the right-wing, conservative side of the political spectrum successfully utilizing what we see as examples of Dissent PR and Protest PR. An example is Citizens United, a conservative non-profit which dissent PR work led to a landmark, yet controversial, constitutional campaign and corporate law in 2010 that allowed organizations in for-profit and non-profit sectors to use their funds to advocate for the election or defeat of any candidate. Their campaign began prior to the 2008 elections with a 90-minute documentary, *Hillary: The Movie*, which posed the questions whether showing this movie was electioneering communication and therefore illegal under then-Bipartisan Campaign Reform (Barnes, 2009). Another example is a Tea Party movement that utilized what we could call protest PR tools that led to the election of many ultra-conservative individuals to the US Congress. The core issue in the public relations literature is what constitutes ethical public relations methods. For instance, hacking, pressure tactics, and hoaxes would, for the most part, be considered unethical. In many ways, public relations still grapples with embracing persuasion as a type of ethical public relations method. Hence, techniques that activists use in an organizational context, as well as outside of organizations, to put pressure on organizations and policy makers challenge mainstream public relations even further. Indeed, activist PR raises important ethical questions that will surely result in vehement debate among public relations scholars and practitioners for years to come. We will return to this discussion later. Now, however, we would like to turn to the blurring lines between journalism and public relations in the context of the digital network economy and why it is particularly relevant for a discussion on activism.

Digital networked economy, blurring of the lines between journalism and public relations in activism and beyond: continued debate

We have attempted to outline activism in both journalism and public relations as it is defined in the existing literature. In this part of the chapter, we will address some questions and problems that we had presented at the onset and pose some new ones as they have emerged in our reading of the literature. The scope of these questions is beyond our ability to address in one chapter. However, we want to at least touch upon some issues, not only recognizing them, but keeping the discussion in the scholarly community alive, and to propose potential paths to scholarly research that could emerge from such a discussion. Therefore, we suggest that scholars could find these questions useful as point of departure to build knowledge on this important topic. Most of the questions are definitional ones. For example, how does digital communication, including digital labor, redefine what is journalism and what is public relations today? Do the terms Activist PR, Protest PR, and Dissent PR help us to better understand public relations practices and techniques that are being used by individuals and organizations who seek social and policy change? What is dissent in Dissent and Activist PR, and how is dissent tied to the digital economy? What are these techniques like, who uses them, and does digital communication blur, not only definitional lines between journalism and public relations, but also between journalistic and public relations practice and techniques? Through the examination of the literature, we've also become curious about the relationship of activist journalism and public relations to social movements?

Finally, an important question that underlines much of the discussion in the literature about what are acceptable journalistic and public relations methods and practices is the question of ethics itself. Even though journalism is a much older practice than is public relations, both are predicated on strong ethical professional standards. Professional paradigms and standards in both professions guide what types of communication methods and tools are considered acceptable. Public relations and journalism struggle with the same issues when it comes to activism and dissent in which unorthodox tools, such as hacking, pressure tactics, and hoaxes, might be needed, are efficient, and, hence, acceptable. Thus, we ask if those individuals who are outside of these mainstream professions, for example, professionals who have dissented or citizens and groups that utilize tools of journalism and public relations to further their causes, are bound by the ethical standards of these professions. And, if answer is yes, are ethics embedded in the tools, themselves? In other words, would a hoax be more acceptable as an activist tool for public relations and journalism if we didn't view it through the lens of professional standards? Does the goal justify the means? Does the use of such tools and techniques that ultimately generate change and that arguably lead to common good validate those tools as acceptable in the practices of public relations and journalism? Finally, is there a need to make clear distinctions between what tools are acceptable for the practice of journalism and what separate tools are acceptable for the practice of public relations? The need for such clear distinctions seems to be strongly embedded in the traditional understanding of these professions and in the existing literature.

To tackle these issues and questions, let us return to some of the discussions we have already outlined. Spatzier's (2016) examination of definitions of journalism and public relations argues that both disciplines focus on the functioning of society. She further elaborated that scholars have defined journalism and public relations as "a system that produces and deploys issues for public discourse" (p. 788). If we define public relations and journalism from outside of the dominant paradigms in which public relations is focused on propagating particular interests through information and in which journalism serves the function of unbiased presentation of information for the public good, little or no difference between the two can be seen (Spatzier, 2016). Indeed, our examination of activism in public relations and journalism shows that tools and techniques that journalists and public relations practitioners use today, and have used in the past, are often shared. This is in opposition to strong professional paradigms that argue for the need to clearly distinguish amongst the tools used in these professions. Spatzier (2016) showed the historical example of Bertha von Suttner, who fought for rights of women in the late nineteenth century, using journalistic writing as a public relations tool and public relations activities within her journalism. Spatzier (2016) further writes that, in the 1980s in Austria, public relations was seen as a journalistic field, that is, as "organizational journalism" (p. 788). In the United States, an example of a muckraking journalist in the late nineteenth and early twentieth centuries is Ida B. Wells, an anti-lynching and women's rights activist and journalist who used public relations tools to further her causes. These are certainly early examples of how activism tends to blur the lines between journalism and public relations. Olesen (2008), using a modern-day example of Danmarks Radio's documentary production that exposed how workers for Cheminova, a large Danish chemical producer, handled pesticides without proper protection, argues that, even when activism is not a goal of journalistic production, activist-like activities tend to bring journalism closer to the field of publicity. He argues for a "view of journalists as part of the complex field of democratic publicity" (p. 247).

We've already outlined that advocacy is a key, yet controversial, term in journalism. Advocacy has been arguably the biggest differentiator between journalism and public relations in the scholarly literature. Yet, in our examination of the literature, we also found that advocacy has been a part of journalism practice from its naissance. It was with the birth of the professional ideology of objectivity and neutrality that advocacy had become a dirty word in journalism.

In public relations, advocacy defines the field. However, advocacy consists of persuasion, and persuasion has been seen as a derogatory term in mainstream public relations (Coombs & Holladay, 2012a). However, through our examination of the literature, we have found that persuasion and advocacy are emerging as the major tools of communication in the digital age. Our examination of the literature on Protest PR found that pressure techniques are, in some circumstances, considered valid public relations tools for activists. It is considerably more difficult to say whether pressure as a public relations tool would be acceptable to traditional public relations practitioners, even when they choose to serve as dissenting voices for their organizations.

While we've noticed the convergence of journalism and public relations in terms of tools and techniques that are used in the digital networked economy, they, nevertheless, seem to be differently impacted by this convergence. Lloyd and Toogood (2015) argue that public relations thrives in the digital economy. Corporations and other organizations don't depend on news media access as much as they had been. At the same time, journalism has experienced a significant cut in its workforce. In part because of this, journalism is becoming more dependent on the content that is produced by public relations practitioners and citizens, and it's not surprising that this content might contain more advocacy.

The digital economy and what Deuze and Witschge (2018) call "permanent instability inside the news industry" (p. 177) under the conditions of the late capitalist post-industrial economic system further reinforce the idea of blurring the lines between these two professions. More scholarship is needed that would take into consideration the intricacies of informational and digital labor and how these affect journalism and public relations. With the rise of artificial intelligence and the growth of the use of robots in online communication, the need for discussion and an understanding of digital work and digital labor is growing. While differentiating between digital work and digital labor using Marxist theory, Fuchs and Sevignani (2013) point to dependency on free labor of platforms such as Facebook. We argue that, as work in newsrooms become more dependent on unpaid labor through, for example, internships or labor that might become dependent on artificial intelligence, journalists increasingly become digital workers whose goal is to promote news stories to members of the public utilizing various social media more so than they are reporters chasing facts.

Thus, it could be argued that, in the digital economy, a major aspect of journalists' work of today is PR. This is true even for mainstream journalism. And, at the same time, public relations practitioners, perhaps more so than ever, engage with tools that are typically used by journalists. This is particularly true when activism in the networked communication and media space is involved.

Following our reading of the literature, we are also interested in learning who engages in activism and whether activism is inherently political regardless of its origins. We can differentiate between various types of activism, for example, corporate activism, political party activism, and consumer activism, but it is undisputable that in the core of activism are politics. L'Etang (2016) argues that activism is not a homogenous category. Rather, activists come from various ideological backgrounds and involve political struggle. She argues that "PR literature on activism has tended to ignore the political dimensions of struggle and change" (p. 207). González-Bailón, and Wang (2016) use the term "networked politics" and "networked discontent" (p. 95) to refer to collective action in the digital age. We found in our examination of dissent and protest that PR falls within the studies of collective action in the digital age, primarily looking at the use of social media to identify protest campaigns and its strategies and tactics (Adi, 2015; González-Bailón & Wang, 2016).

In our examination of the literature, we at times questioned the need for the use of dissent PR and protest PR terminologies and the attempts to differentiate the two with activist PR. We side with Moloney and McKie (2016) that dissent PR and protest PR are subsets of activist PR. We agree with Adi (2015) that there is a need in the PR literature to look at activist PR, corporate, and protest PR and compare them in the strategies and tactics that each uses. She found similarities in the ways in which activists in these categories communicate online: to reach their supporters; to advocate for issues, products or causes; and to engage with opponents.

Moloney and McKie (2016) argue that PR has always been "a neutral set of communicative tools" (p. 154). If we, indeed, accept that communicative tools are ideology- and politics-free communication, especially as defined in activism, is not. Adi (2015) noted power struggles within the protest movements. We would suggest that Protest PR, whether in the context of social movements or not, should also examine the political dimension of communication and should note both the journalistic and PR tools that are used to further political goals. Dissent PR, on the other hand, should take into account the structural and economic obstacles to dissemination of information in traditional communication channels and digital networked channels. González-Bailón and Wang (2016) point out that "protest communication networks are fragmented" (p. 102) and are more similar to traditional channels of communication than was previously thought in that diffusion and dissemination of information are made difficult and less fluid. While there is much discussion on the role of digital networked communication platforms in mediating collective action, it is important to note that traditional media platforms still play an important role in activism. A good example since the mid-twentieth century is US conservative media's activism through the use of talk radio and activist and mainstream television networks that activists have managed to create to "popularize the idea of liberal media bias" (Hemmer, 2016, p. xii). Conservative media activism as a grassroots movement propelled, among other things, the birth of the Tea Party movement, which has resulted in the transformation of American politics. This also supports the idea set forth by scholars of Dissent and Protest PR that activism and dissent isn't simply a leftist project.

Finally, we come back to the question of ethics. In a world in which the dissemination of disinformation is a growing practice, and in which it is ever more difficult to discern information from disinformation, what role do techniques such as deceit play into Activist, Dissent, and Protest PR strategies? Is deceit justified if the ultimate goal is the common good? Moloney and McKie (2016) think that PR that uses deceit shouldn't "attract esteem" (p. 156). However, Veil et al. (2105) argue that a hoax is a "viable, albeit potentially unethical, strategy to motivate action" (p. 103). As the United States is enveloped in a discussion of the consequence of Russian hacking into the 2016 Presidential election, the radical activist actions of Russian individuals and organizations, which are likely connected to the Russian government, are overwhelmingly criticized as negative, even disastrous, for democratic processes and institutions. Would, from an activist standpoint, these hoaxes, dissemination of fake information, and inciting other activist responses as viable dissent and protest tools be justified? These are the kinds of questions that scholars of communication will need to continue to grapple with as we outline and study various ways in which online tools and protest communication networks are used. Perhaps, if we say that the common good justifies the means, there still might be various definitions of what constitutes the common good and what is the common interest, which distinctions become considerably more difficult to discern in a highly politically polarized world.

Conclusion

To conclude, we believe that activism as a broader category should be analyzed, comparatively whenever possible, in both traditional and digital networked settings. Activism within the journalism and public relations professions should be studied comparatively alongside studies that examine how activist groups use journalistic and public relations tools. Perhaps deceit, hoax, and online platform hijacking are more acceptable protest tools for grassroots activists than for the activists who emerge within the professions of journalism and public relations in which ethical standards guide most of their practices and philosophies. Similarly, communication tools, strategies, and tactics need to be studied comparatively in traditional media and online settings, including discussions of economics, power, and politics. Only through a more comprehensive, comparative, and historically grounded study of activism, as well as of activist-like practices and the role that communication plays in its emergence and evolution, will we be able to understand activism's complexities and nuances. That knowledge will help us to understand, not only who activists are, how they emerge, and how they contribute to change, but more importantly what role communication plays in social change. Lastly, those kinds of studies will help us better gauge the roles that journalism and public relations play in social change. We understand that the task that we have set for ourselves and for other scholars is not an easy one, but, as communication scholars, we believe that any study of social change and its components is incomplete without a comprehensive, comparative, and historically grounded study of communication.

References

Adi, A. (2015, June). Occupy PR: An analysis of online media communications of Occupy Wall Street and Occupy London. *Public Relations Review*, 41(4) 508–514. Retrieved from http://dx.doi.org/10.1016/j.pubrev.2015.06.001.

Adi, A. & Miah, A. (2011). Open source protest: Human rights, online activism and the Beijing 2008 Olympic Games. In S. Cottle & L. Lester (Eds.), *Transnational protests and the media* (pp. 213–224). New York: Peter Lang.

Adi, A. & Moloney, K. (2012). The importance of scale in Occupy movement protests: A case study of a local Occupy protest as a tool of communication through public relations and social media. *Revista Internacional de Relaciones Publicas*, 4(II), 12–97. Retrieved from http://dx.doi.org/10.5783/RIRP-4-2012-05-97-122.

Alwood, E. (2015). The role of public relations in the Gay Rights Movement, 1950–1969. *Journalism History*, 41(1), 11–20.

Barnes, R. (2009, March 15). "Hillary: The Movie" to get Supreme Court screening. *Washington Post*. Retrieved from www.washingtonpost.com/wp-dyn/content/article/2009/03/14/AR2009031401603.html.

Benecke, D. R. & Oksiutycz, A. (2015, December). Changing conversation and dialogue through LeadSA: An example of public relations activism in South Africa. *Public Relations Review*, 41(5), 816–824.

Botan, C. & Hazleton, V. (2006). Public relations in a new age. In C. Botan & V. Hazleton (Eds.), *Public relations theory II* (2nd ed., pp. 1–20). Mahwah, NJ: Lawrence Erlbaum Associates.

Brunner, B. (2017). Introduction. In B. Brunner (Ed.), *The moral compass for public relations* (pp. 1–15). New York: Routledge.

Ciszek, E. L. (2015). Bridging the gap: Mapping the relationship between activism and public relations. *Public Relations Review*, 41, 447–455. http://dx.doi.org/10.1016/j.pubrev.2015.05.016.

Coombs, T. W. & Holladay, S. (2012a). Fringe public relations: How activism moves critical PR toward the mainstream. *Public Relations Review*, 38, 880–887. doi:10.1016/j.pubrev.2012.02.008.

Coombs, T. W. & Holladay, S. J. (2012b). Privileging an activist vs. a corporate view of public relations history in the U.S. *Public Relations Review*, 38, 347–353. doi:10.1016/j.pubrev.2011.11.010.

Demetrious, K. (2013). *Public relations, activism and social change: Speaking up.* London: Routledge.

Derrick, J. C. (2012, Winter). The fine line between journalism and advocacy: Are reporters who work on innocence projects still journalists? *The News Media and The Law*, 36(1), 22–24.

Derville, T. (2005, November). Radical activist tactics: Overturning public relations conceptualizations. *Public Relations Review*, *31*(4), 527–533.

Deuze, M. & Witschge, T. (2018, February 18). Beyond journalism: Theorizing the transformation of journalism. *Journalism*, *19*(2), 165–181.

Dozier, D. & Lauzen, M. (2000). Liberating the intellectual domain from the practice: Public relations, activism, and the role of the scholar. *Journal of Public Relations Research*, *12*(1), 3–22.

Feldstein, M. (2006). A muckraking model: Investigative reporting cycles in American history. *Press/Politics*, *11*(2), 105–120. DOI: 10. 1177/1081180X06286780.

Fisher, C. (2016). The advocacy continuum: Towards a theory of advocacy in journalism. *Journalism*, *17*(6), 711–726.

Fresh Air, NPR. (2011, July 7). Coming out as an "undocumented" immigrant, an interview with Jose Antonio Vargas, Special Series: Voices in immigration debate. National Public Radio. Retrieved from www.npr.org/2011/07/07/137648605/a-journalist-comes-out-as-an-illegal-immigrant.

Fuchs, C. & Sevignani, S. (2013). What is digital labour? What is digital work? What's their difference? And why do these questions matter for understanding social media?. *tripleC*, *11*(2), 237–293.

González-Bailón, S. & Wang, N. (2016, January). Networked discontent: The anatomy of protest campaigns in social media. *Social Networks*, *44*, 95–104. Retrieved from http://dx.doi.org/10.1016/j.socnet.2015.07.003.

Grunig, J. E. (2001). Two-way symmetrical public relations: Past, present, and future. In R. L. Heath (Ed.), *Handbook of public relations* (pp. 11–30). Thousand Oaks, CA: Sage.

Grunig, J. E. & Hunt, T. (1984). *Managing public relations*. New York: Holt, Rinehart and Winston.

Hemmer, N. (2016). *Messengers of the right: Conservative media and the transformation of American politics*. Philadelphia, PA: University of Pennsylvania Press.

Holtzhausen, D. R. (2000). Postmodern values in public relations. *Journal of Public Relations Research*, *12*(1), 93–114.

Holtzhausen, D. R. (2007). Activism. In E. L. Toth (Ed.), *The future of excellence in public relations and communication management* (pp. 357–379). Mahwah, NJ: Lawrence Erlbaum Associates.

Holtzhausen, D. R. & Voto, R. (2002). Resistance from the margins: The postmodern public relations practitioner as organizational activist. *Journal of Public Relations Research* *14*(1), 57–84.

Jaques, T. (2006). Activist rules and the convergence with issues management. *Journal of Communication Management*, *10*, 407–420.

L'Etang, J. (2016). Public relations, activism and social movements: Critical perspectives. *Public Relations Inquiry*, *5*(3), 207–211.

Lloyd, J. & Toogood, L. (2015). *Journalism and PR: News media and public relations in the digital age*. Oxford, UK: I.B. Tauris & Co. Ltd in association with the Reuters Institute for the Study of Journalism, University of Oxford.

Karlberg, M. (1996). Remembering the publics in public relations research: From theoretical to operational symmetry. *Journal of Public Relations Research*, *8*(4), 263–278.

Kruckeberg, D. (1998, Summer). The future of PR education: Some recommendations. *Public Relations Review*, *24*(2), 235–248.

Moloney, K. & McKie, D. (2016). Changes to be encouraged: Radical turns in PR theorization and small step evolutions in PR practice. In J. L'Etang, D. McKie, N. Snow, & J. Xifra (Eds.), *The Routledge handbook of critical public relations* (pp. 151–161). London and New York: Routledge.

Moloney, K., McQueen., D, Surowiec, P., & Yaxley, H. (2013, March). Dissent and protest public relations. Papers and discussion from the Dissent and Public Relations seminar series, October–December 2012. Bournemouth, UK: Public Relations Research Group, The Media School, Bournemouth University, 1–14. Retrieved from https://research.bournemouth.ac.uk/wp-content/uploads/2013/10/Dissent-and-public-relations-Bournemouth-University.pdf.

Olesen, T. (2008). Activist journalism? The Danish Cheminova debates, 1997–2006. *Journalism Practice, 2*(2), 245–263. DOI: 10. 1080/17512780801999394.

Owens, L. & Palmer, K. L. (2003). Making the news: Anarchist counter-public relations on the World Wide Web. *Critical Studies in Media Communication, 20*(4), 335–361.

Russell, A. (2016). *Journalism as activism: Recording media power.* Cambridge, UK: Polity.

Schudson, M. (2008). *Why democracies need an unlovable press.* Cambridge, UK: Polity Press.

Spatzier, A. (2016). One woman – Two sides of the same coin? Journalism and public relations: The case of Bertha von Suttner, Austria. *Public Relations Review, 42*(5), 787–791.

Taub, A. (2017, January 11). The real story about fake news is partisanship. *New York Times.* Retrieved from www.nytimes.com/2017/01/11/upshot/the-real-story-about-fake-news-is-partisanship.html.

Vargas, J. A. (2011, June 22). My life as an undocumented immigrant. *New York Times Magazine.* Retrieved from www.nytimes.com/2011/06/26/magazine/my-life-as-an-undocumented-immigrant.html.

Veil, S. R., Reno, J., Freihaut, R., & Oldham, J. (2015, March). Online activists vs. Kraft Foods: A case of social media hijacking. *Public Relations Review, 41*(1), 103–108.

Voakes, P. (2004, Fall). A brief history of public journalism. *National Civic Review, 93*(3), 25–35.

Vujnovic, M. (2004). *The public relations practitioner as ombudsman—A reconstructed model.* Unpublished master's thesis. Cedar Falls, IA: University of Northern Iowa.

Waisbord, S. (2008). Advocacy journalism in a global context. In K. Wahl-Jorgensen & T. Hanitzsch (Eds.), *The handbook of journalism studies* (pp. 371–385). New York: Routledge.

Weaver, C. K. (2010, March). Carnivalesque activism as a public relations genre: A case study of the New Zealand group Mothers Against Genetic Engineering. *Public Relations Review, 36*(1), 35–41.

Zelizer, B. (2004). *Taking journalism seriously.* London: SAGE.

15 The activist reformation of PR in the attention economy

Thomas Stoeckle

For grassroots activism, the attention economy is both opportunity and risk: while it has become quicker and easier to generate a groundswell of momentum, it has also become harder to sustain that momentum. At the same time, public relations – understood as purposive, persuasive strategic organisational communication – is finding itself affected by, and required to adapt to, changes in its environment. The worlds of activism and PR blend in the concept of activist PR, with the forms of dissent PR, and protest PR. The former encourages action, whereas the latter provides alternative viewpoints and challenges established thinking.

Historically, the dynamics between activism, dissent and protest have led to reform. The idea of an activist reformation of PR in the attention economy is one that considers the yin and yang of the liberation and suppression of dissenting voices through social media; it is one that considers protest and counter-protest movements from the perspective of their social context; it looks at concepts of PR as evolving from modernist, excellent models, to critical, postmodern positions, and then towards a metamodern idea, conceding that positions have become blurred as the present media ecosystem allows and enables more volatility and fluid alignments. PR in this understanding operates outside a managerial straitjacket, as strategic communication that supports and drives organisational objectives by enabling stakeholder relationships in an increasingly complex and uncertain environment.

Introduction

We look to the past to understand the present. With that understanding, we look to the future. In 2017, we celebrated the quincentenary of the start of the Protestant Reformation, usually considered to have been triggered by Martin Luther's making public his Disputation of the Power of Indulgences, the 95 Theses. Many draw comparisons between then and now.[1] The invention of the printing press in Europe[2] by Johannes Gutenberg in the 1440s led to fundamental changes in society, in politics, in the sciences. For the first time, the exclusive power of written, reproducible knowledge was taken from the ruling classes – the aristocracy and the clergy – and made accessible to the masses. This led to the "typographic man" (McLuhan, 1962), arguably brought about the Reformation[3] and the Enlightenment, and ultimately enabled modernity (Hassan & Sutherland, 2017).

This analogy of a technological revolution transforming power structures in society is often applied to our modern times.[4] The internet and social media have created a networked public sphere (Benkler, 2006; Fuchs, 2014) where reaching sizeable audiences is no longer a prerogative of large organisations (Demetrious, 2011). In the beginning, this was seen as a liberation, a fundamental shift in the way individuals and organisations interact. Also, from the perspective of Excellence Theory, the leading functional paradigm of PR (Botan & Hazleton, 2006; Edwards, 2012), the conversational role and function of social media was seen as transformative, enabling two-way symmetrical interaction between organisations and their publics – defined as "Best Practice" in Excellence Theory (Macnamara & Zerfass, 2012).

Coombs and Holladay (2012) discuss how this perspective was extended to describe activism as a force to drive organisations towards an orthodox ideal of excellence, however "it is at the discretion of the organization that activist concerns are considered at all" (p. 884). Only once concepts such as power, persuasion and advocacy – which have no place in the "symmetrical worldview" (p. 882) – have been re-introduced into PR theory, is there room and scope for alternative, critical viewpoints that are "significantly more capable of addressing activist advocacy and concomitant issues" (p. 880). Scholars such as Holtzhausen (2012) and Demetrious (2013; 2016) have developed their arguments based on the conclusion that the concept of activism can help advance critical ideas and critical theory-led thinking in public relations, and bring them into the mainstream (Coombs & Holladay, 2012, p. 884).

We live in an era where concepts and phrases such as fake news and post truth have entered the mainstream of public discourse. What used to be seen as verifiable facts selected and presented by professional gatekeepers are now viewed as opinion. We describe the conditions and consequences – intended as well as unintended – of our attention economy,[5] based on a monetisation of computer-mediated data extraction and analysis that critics call surveillance capitalism (Zuboff, 2015).

This chapter looks at the challenges and opportunities arising for PR as a discipline affected by, and required to adapt to, changes in its environment. Moloney and McKie (2016) see opportunities for an "activist turn" in their reflections on the various turns in scholarly writing and thinking in PR. They describe a field that is ideologically neutral and continuously evolving, and where "techniques cross over from activist PR to mainstream business PR" (p. 151). Their perspective of PR as "used by partisans of all stripes" (p. 155) is instructive for a discussion of activism that is increasingly taking place both on the left, and on the right. Moloney and McKie describe activist PR as consisting of the two concepts of dissent PR and protest PR. Whereas protest PR is giving voice to issue-focused activist groups and encourages action, dissent PR is about the dissemination of alternative viewpoints and challenges to established thinking (p. 157).

These new perspectives on activist, dissent and protest PR also lend themselves to a renewed discussion about the need for reformation in PR (Demetrious, 2016). Following the historical example, activism, dissent and protest might lead to reform.[6]

This chapter will explore some of these arguments and conclude with a suggestion to reframe PR in social theory that moves beyond both modernist, and postmodern perspectives, and towards the more open and flexible idea of metamodernism (Akker, Gibbons, & Vermeulen, 2017) with a new understanding and a new language to describe our current historical moment. The idea of an activist reformation of PR in the attention economy, then, is one that considers the yin and yang of the liberation and suppression of dissenting voices through social media; it is one that considers protest and counter-protest movements from the perspective of their social context; it looks at concepts of PR as evolving from modernist, excellent models, to critical, postmodern positions, and then towards a metamodern idea, conceding that positions have become blurred as the present media ecosystem allows and enables more volatility and fluid alignments.

Social media and global conversations

The Cluetrain Manifesto optimistically alluded to the conversational capabilities of the Internet (as well as to Luther's 95 Theses):

> A powerful global conversation has begun. Through the Internet, people are discovering and inventing new ways to share relevant knowledge with blinding speed. As a direct result, markets are getting smarter – and getting smarter faster than most companies.
>
> These markets are conversations. Their members communicate in language that is natural, open, honest, direct, funny and often shocking. Whether explaining or complaining, joking or serious, the human voice is unmistakably genuine. It can't be faked.
>
> (Levine, Searls, Weinberger, & Locke, 2000, p. xi)

We know a lot now about the manifold ways in which it can be faked (Wardle & Derakhshan, 2017). The Cluetrain Manifesto was published one year after Google was founded, five years before Facebook, and seven years before Twitter. With the benefit of hindsight, and the experience of almost 20 years since the Manifesto, we now know that algorithms that help optimise search results, recommendations and any other way to catch peoples' attention online can be manipulated, and have often unintended consequences (O'Neil, 2016; Schneier, 2015).

Collister's (2016) critical analysis of algorithmic public relations high-lights challenges related to resource access, a "renewed economic influ-ence in the computational communication environment" (p. 365) with the "potential to exert a post-hegemonic power embedded in the material substrata of communication" (p. 367). At the same time, however, the new communication networks have created new opportunities for social movements. The internet enables and advances non-hierarchical and reciprocal communication. Those communication networks are increas-ingly wireless and formed through the interactions of portable smart devices.

Castells (2015) described a new social structure, in which the social movements of the twenty-first century are being formed (p. 248). The idealism of the early days of the internet, with an end of business as usual, empowerment of the individual, and curbing the power of corporations, has made way for apathy, cynicism and more polarised debates, at least in part enabled through the structural conditions of the internet (Pariser, 2011). Now we talk about attention economy (Wu, 2016) and surveillance capitalism (Zuboff, 2017), and Tufekci's optimistic take on attention being "oxygen for movements" (2017, p. 30) also means that it can and will provide the same oxygen for counter-movements. The following section looks at the role of attention in more detail.

Attention is the new oil

The aforementioned journalist and academic, John Naughton, describes humanity as worshipping at the "Church of Technopoly" in the introduc-tion to his 95 Theses about Technology (Naughton, 2017). He reminds his readers that the purpose of a thesis is to start a discussion and thus calls his Theses assertions "to get people talking", rather than conclusions or convictions. He takes a broad view from exponential progress of techno-logy (Thesis 3), to digital markets being "winner takes all" (Thesis 9), all the way to digital technology changing the structure of our brains (Thesis 90), and finally in Thesis 95, that we should be aiming for Intelligence Augmentation (IA), rather than Artificial Intelligence (AI).

Thesis 17 states that "In an age of digital abundance, attention is the really scarce resource". Naughton references this prescient statement from Herbert Simon in 1971:

> In an information-rich world, the wealth of information means a dearth of something else: a scarcity of whatever it is that information consumes. What information consumes is rather obvious: it consumes the attention of its recipients. Hence a wealth of information creates a poverty of attention and a need to allocate that attention efficiently among the overabundance of information sources that might consume it.
>
> (Simon, 1971, p. 40)

When we look at the conditions of the attention economy (Davenport & Beck, 2001; Wu, 2016) from the vantage point of public relations (Galloway, 2017), then our focus is on increasingly fragmented, perpetually distracted (Wu, 2016) publics (or audiences) and their relationship to organisations: as empowered, informed and connected, but also manipulated stakeholders who make meaning through selection, exercising agency through interpretation (Webster, 2016). Scholars also discuss information overload and continuous partial attention as characteristics of the attention economy (Jenkins, Ito, & boyd, 2016; Standing, 2016). Davenport and Beck, who popularised the phrase through their 2001 book *The Attention Economy*, discuss the psychobiology of attention from the perspective of management and performance: "Anyone who hopes to manage attention successfully must understand the way our nature prioritizes our mental focus" (p. 58).

For PR practitioners, their "ability to monetize their expertise correlates crucially to their ability to generate attention for clients and employers" (Galloway, 2017, p. 969). Beyond a more passive role of consuming information, social media participants have become creators, re-users and sharers of content in a public networked environment. This brings into view concepts of public that range from the traditional (based on the common interest of a mass audience as part of the public sphere)[7] to the modern (based on networks of interconnected individuals). Online interactions generate data, which is used in an ecosystem of targeting and advertising services to track the movements and behaviours of audiences in order to finetune product and services. This "21st century Faustian pact" (Zuboff, 2015, p. 83) from the perspective of the user is less a value exchange, and more an extractive operation: social media platforms such as Facebook and Google provide free services for users in return for personal data which are sold to advertisers.

Again, this brings to mind the yin and yang of modern communication ecosystems. The optimistic take is one of open structures with a fine-tuned, varied diet of media. Pessimists see closed structures suppressing dissonant voices and enabling growing polarisation of opinions (Webster, 2016, p. 132). Wu (2016) makes the point that every modern marketplace has contests on two intertwined levels: merit or quality, and attention. While you can't have one without the other, the contest for attention comes first and therefore "winning the attentional games is a powerful strategy", as Wu concludes, in open societies the danger is not so much suppression of voices, but a drowning out of dissonant views, creating a "constant risk of the contest for attention coming to dominate the contest on the merits" (p. 267). The following section will first look at the historiography of public relations, and the various concepts applied to explain the evolution of the field. Subsequently, it will link present concepts with the idea of activist, protest and dissent PR in the attention economy.

From symmetry and excellence to critical theory and consilience

Grunig and Hunt's seminal 1984 publication, *Managing Public Relations*, is not only the foundational work for what became the leading paradigm of public relations theory. It is also "one of, if not *the*, best-known histories of public relations" (Holtzhausen, 2012, p. 72). The historical perspective has indisputable merit; however, it needs to be understood and interpreted in the context of its time. Grunig and Hunt's discussion of the origins of PR in the press agentry and publicity model (from the 1850s onwards), followed first by the public information model (from around the 1900s), then the two-way asymmetric model (from the 1920s), and finally the two-way symmetric model (from the late 1960s) needs to be read in that way. Some scholars are critical of the seemingly linear historiographic perspective of continuous betterment, away from the propaganda before and during World Wars I and II, and towards excellence and symmetry (Kenny, 2016; Laskin, 2009).[8]

Macnamara's (2016) recent review of key literature and international research studies on leading concepts in the field led him to conclude that "public relations has to make space for new theories and models to continue the process of knowledge construction that is necessary for disciplinary progress" (p. 344). Public relations, both as a profession, and as an academic discipline, is a field with many influences, many different currents and subfields. To do this pluralistic and ever evolving environment justice, recent analyses apply the concept of consilience, aiming for multidisciplinary consensus (Marsh, 2017), they acknowledge the "balkanisation"[9] of strategic communication (Botan, 2017) which includes PR as a subfield, and they conceive of PR as both interdisciplinary and multidisciplinary, existing in a "world of convergences" (Brown, 2015).

In her critical reflection on the present and the future of the field, Edwards (2012) stated "the increasingly varied nature of PR research, with multiple paradigms employed by scholars to explain the characteristics and effects of PR" (p. 7). This open perspective is a necessary condition for the reformation of PR, including activism, internal and external dissent, and protest. It represents progress from excellent PR towards critical and co-creative PR as it shifts the focus from organisational needs and optimisation of processes to reach publics, towards the co-creation of meaning between publics (Botan, 2017).

This chapter therefore recognises two distinct schools of thought: on one side, the Grunigians (Moloney, 2006)[10] or "symmetrists" (Brown, 2006, p. 207), and on the other, representatives of a postmodern (Holtzhausen, 2012), critical approach (L'Etang & Pieczka, 1996). The argument for a reformation of PR in the attention economy, and the inclusion of concepts of activist, dissent and protest PR, favours the latter over the former.

For many years the leading paradigm in PR scholarship, Excellence Theory with its four models of public relations (Grunig & Hunt, 1984; Grunig, Grunig, & Dozier, 2006; Grunig, 2013), is increasingly seen as limiting for the future of the field (Edwards, 2012). Over the last three decades, a counter-movement has been forming to challenge this "meta-narrative".[11] It has become increasingly vocal and confident in staking its claim.[12] In scoping *The Public Relations of Everything*, Brown (2015) does not hesitate to

> acknowledge Jim Grunig, PR's paradigm shifter, without whose extra-ordinary, prodigious and influential scholarship I would have had no shore from which to push away in my "radical" skiff.
>
> (p. 13)

Critical theory applied to PR is seen as a "conceptual canopy covering an array of diverse but interlinked perspectives" (Moloney & McKie, 2016, p. 151). Openness is key, as Holtzhausen (2012) observed in introducing her postmodern approach to PR theorising:

> Theories are not objective and all-knowing but rather represent one way of looking and explaining. Theories are the products of specific contexts. If contexts change, so do theories.
>
> (p. 17)

This brings to mind a quote famously attributed to John Maynard Keynes: "When the facts change, I change my mind. What do you do, sir?" Theory needs to underpin and inform practice. It needs to be empirically useful, rather than normatively correct, to help us establish which frameworks and concepts of public relations are most effective in describing our world which increasingly blends a physical with a digital lifeworld – one of the characteristics of the attention economy. Van Akker and Vermeulen (2017) refer to the various protest movements of the early 2000s and 2010s in their outline of metamodernism as a social theory for our times. With net-worked structures and modes of organisation (Castells, 2015), those move-ments were (and are) both subject and object of modern public relations (Demetrious, 2013). In the following section, this relationship between activist movements and public relations will be explored further.

The role and theory of activist PR in society

The story of protest PR is often told as a personal story. The Turkish-born activist and scholar Zeynep Tufekci centred her book *Twitter and Tear Gas* (2017) around personal experience, from the Zapatista uprising in Chiapas in Chile in 1994, the WTO protests in Seattle in 1999, to the Arab Spring in 2011 and being present during the failed Turkish coup in 2016.

Exploring the "dialectic and co-evolving landscape of threat, leverage, and challenge between social movements and the powerful" (p. 269), her analysis focused on how the networked public sphere creates new risks and new opportunities, both for social movements, and for those in power (p. 274). The need for attention and publicity on all sides of the equation only strengthens the need for a refined and reformed understanding of public relations as a bridging function.[13]

The sociologist Manuel Castells wrote his analysis of activism and social movements in the internet age, *Networks of Outrage and Hope* (2015), in large part based on observations of, and interactions with social activists and participants in movements such as the Indignados in Spain. His concept of social change draws on Habermas, as well as on descriptions of both social, and neural networks. For him, social change occurs in the dynamic between individuals and the neural networks of their brains, and the social and communication networks of groups (p. 247). Both Tufekci, and Castells are proponents of a digital commons, a digital public sphere that enables the formation of networked groups and collective action, as opposed to platforms that operate as privatised walled gardens with the main purpose of selling data for targeting to advertisers (Wu, 2016).

Holtzhausen and Demetrious, in their respective works on activism and PR, draw on personal experience and involvement with environmental activism in Australia (Demetrious, 2011; 2013), and with the long process of dismantling apartheid in South Africa (Holtzhausen, 2012). Rhetorical and critical scholars in particular look at the role of PR in creating, maintaining and evolving the public sphere, especially the social and cultural "meaning-making between organizations and publics, as they develop, co-create, negotiate, and maintain their relationships with one another" (Toth, 2009, p. 48). The critical lens focuses on the social construction of these relationships, the processes of discourse and meaning-making in the attention economy, and consequently on the role of power and privilege as a "dysfunction of societies and the organizations that disproportionately shape them" (Toth, 2009, p. 57). Some see this dysfunction in corporate activism and political lobbying in particular in the US, where business interests seek to sway political and regulatory decision-making, with little or no interference by the public (Kavanagh & Rich, 2018).

Offering a perspective on public involvement in such communication and decision-making processes via activist groups, Demetrious (2013) states a "deep and enduring hostility to activists and the role they play in civil society" (p. 26). Given that PR "manufactures discourse to control and manipulate the meaning making process", to overcome these "foundational contradictions between public relations and democratic theory" (p. 33) and to involve social movements in a more equal societal discourse, she concludes with Moloney (2006, p. 6) that "it is time for the legitimacy of the unity of 'public relations' to be contested and arguments for its reform to move beyond a 'classical pluralist' framework" (p. 31).

Demetrious centres her argument on an understanding of activism as a driver for occupational reform in PR, in an attempt to "move understanding of public relations beyond the marketplace to its relations towards society as whole" (p. 7).

Hers is a worthy and ambitious goal, and one that appears to be more easily achievable in some markets, than in others (Demetrious is Australian, and she teaches at Deakin University in Victoria). Occupational reform is an essential and integral part of the reformation of PR, and its progress from theoretical concept to practical implementation will depend on broad support in a field that is highly diverse, and more focused on practitioners' day-to-day requirements, than standardised global practices.[14]

Holtzhausen (2012) identifies activism as the "postmodern agency of public relations" and goes on to conclude that "public relations as activism is a necessary condition for a just society" (p. 30). The relationship between activism and power is described as rhizomatic, that is enabling independent and uncontrolled growth in a micropolitical sense, as opposed to the static power structures of macropolitics (Deleuze & Guattari, 1987).

In the same vein, Castells called the Indignados movement a "rhizomatic revolution" (Castells, 2015, p. 113ff.).

These positions, developed from the perspective of activism (as form of) PR, move us along pathways to "define PR in a way that better reflects the plurality of views in the field" (Edwards, 2012, p. 23), and away from what is seen as limited systems thinking, "the modernist focus on specialization, bureaucracy, mistrust, and disempowerment" (Pieczka, 2006, p. 385). The aim, then, is to (re)define the PR of activism and social movements as a part of a post-symmetric "reformation".

This analysis is not meant to duplicate L'Etang's (2016) "interpretation of public relations history and historiography viewed through a focus on activism and social movements" (p. 28), but rather to build on her suggestion that "that public relations histories should be repositioned and embedded within histories of broader societal shifts" (p. 28). These shifts in Western democratic societies find their expression in rising support for populist opinions and parties – often explained either through the "economic insecurity", or the "cultural backlash" thesis (Inglehart & Norris, 2016), in the rise of the Precariat (Standing, 2016), and also more broadly in a networked public sphere which provides a fertile breeding ground for social movements (Castells, 2015; Tufekci, 2017).

What is required is social theory that is fit for purpose, i.e. capable of describing and explaining the complex world around us in ways that help us make sense of it (Ihlen & Verhoeven, 2009, p. 326). For activism, protest and dissent PR in particular, the focus needs to be more on the effects, as opposed to how PR is done. This requires profound and varied, multi-disciplinary analyses of PR's changing role in a changing society (Bentele & Wehmeier, 2009; Ihlen & Verhoeven, 2009). It will need to address issues of agency, leadership and power, as well as progressive (in the sense of moving forward) and conservative (in the sense of protecting and retaining) positions. This will include activism, protest and reformation, as well as counter-activism, counter-protest and counter-reformation.

Couldry and Hepp (2017), building on the classic argument of the Social Construction of Reality (Berger & Luckmann, 1966), assert that "social theory is no longer viable, unless it has been, in part, transformed by media theory" (p. 3). Social movements as "imagined collectivity" are evolving from "collective action" to "connective action" (Bennett & Segerberg, 2013), with new opportunities, as well as new risks for creating shared identity under the conditions of "deep mediatization" (Couldry & Hepp, 2017) – the power of algorithms, fragmentation of audiences, and changing definitions of media. The impact on our social sphere is such that online platforms have become virtual versions of public spaces where the social is being enacted (p. 2).

This "enactment of the social" renewed the focus on the role of organisations, their publics and the evolving and increasingly complex web of relationships with their environment. Botan (2017) addresses this complexity through the concept of co-creation, where publics and organisations continuously develop the mutual understanding of their relationship, irrespective of differences in perspective.

In his model of co-creational strategic communication, activism is central to the formation of publics, the definition of issues, and – critically – the resolution of issues:

> The cocreational perspective suggests that, since publics define issues, those issues can only be resolved when publics say they are resolved.
>
> (p. 101)

In modern communication management parlance, this would give activists a "stake" in the process.

Starting from Ihlen and Verhoeven's (2009) view of five phases of PR history – "the public is damned or ignored (1865–1900); the public is informed or served (1900–1918); the public is educated or respected (1918–1945); the public is known (1945–1968); and the public is involved (1968–today)" (p. 324) – the concept of public involvement posits that in order to understand the evolving role of PR in modern societies, characterised by continuously increasing complexity and rapid change,[15] it needs to be studied not just from a managerial and instrumental perspective, but also (and increasingly more so) as a social phenomenon: "its practice needs to be understood in relationship to societal (macro), organizational (meso), and individual (micro) properties" (Ihlen & van Ruler, 2009, p. 1). Moreover, the use of different, comparative approaches in social theory, with a range of paradigms and research methods, is a sign of growing maturity for the field (Ihlen & van Ruler, 2009; Ihlen, van Ruler, & Fredriksson, 2009). In recent years, scholars have been calling for multi-paradigmatic

(Bardhan & Weaver, 2011), pluralistic (Toth, 2009), even polyparadigmatic (Botan & Hazleton, 2006) approaches to match the field's multilayered demands. In particular Marsh's (2017) concept of consilience – a multidisciplinary consensus spanning the humanities, the natural and the social sciences – offers a promising framework for such research.

And this multidisciplinary consensus is necessary at a time when change in society, in the information and communication ecosystem is happening at such accelerating speed that descriptions and evidence-based, empirically derived theoretical concepts can barely keep up. For the function and practice of PR, as well as for the academy, this creates conditions that are conducive for reform, if not reformation.

Metamodernism – social theory for a reformed activist PR?

Discussions of PR and social theory usually start with modernism and its association with liberalism and humanism. Holtzhausen (2012) identifies them as the root for the "underlying values of the work of James Grunig ... and his contemporaries and the subsequent focus on two-way symmetry as a communications approach in the field" (p. 22f.). In the same context, Brown (2015) credits Edwards Bernays with setting in motion the "progressive wheel ... of modernist and evolutionary historiography of PR" (p. 83). For many critical scholars of PR, postmodern discourse theory offered a path away from the modernist, functionalist worldview of society (and PR's role in it), and towards perspectives of "public relations' potent role in relation to discourse and to identity formation, and to agency" (Demetrious, 2013, p. 8).

In their 1997 work *The Postmodern Turn*, Best and Kellner describe in much detail the shift from modern to postmodern, as "decisive rupture with previous ways of life, bringing to an end the modern era" (p. xiii). They described the process of "embarking on a voyage into novel realms of thought and experience" (p. ix) [...] "a transdisciplinary space [which] reflects our position that social reality can be analysed most adequately through multiple methodological and theoretical perspectives" (p. xii). Today, in spite of the important contributions in particular by Holtzhausen,[16] postmodernism is generally regarded as a concept in need of rejuvenation, as Moloney and McKie (2016) argued. Nevertheless, they conceded that "Although few in the PR academy have publicly enrolled to make it a lasting turn within the field, PR postmodernists have assisted in making PR more critical" (p. 192).

Something new and different is required, beyond both the modern utopia, and the postmodern dystopia. A social theory that is fit for the purpose of describing and explaining our complex and fragmented world, accommodating concepts of PR as supporting and managing activism and social movements as meaningful and constructive contributions to modern society. In their seminal introduction to metamodernism, Vermeulen and Van Den Akker set the scene:

> Our description and interpretation of the metamodern sensibility is
> therefore essayistic rather than scientific, rhizomatic rather than linear,
> and open-ended instead of closed. It should be read as an invitation
> for debate rather than an extending of a dogma.
>
> (Vermeulen & Van Den Akker, 2010, p. 2)

Their deliberate lack of epistemological commitment, together with the
refutation of the "syntactically correct but semantically meaningless term
post-postmodernism" (p. 3) makes this a promising attempt, not least
given the present societal and planetary challenges, including a growing
sense of uncertainty and unpredictability.

Most importantly, the perspective of metamodernism is towards the
future, and towards new and different questions, which require new and
better answers. Vermeulen and Van Den Akker describe the critical, skeptical distance that millennials keep from intellectually and politically rigid
positions. Instead, they attach themselves fluidly and reversibly to movements both on the political Left, and the political Right, motivated at least
in part by utopian longings (Vermeulen & Van Den Akker, 2015, p. 58).

Given PR's own somewhat fluid theoretical state, the concept of metamodernism represents an as yet unexplored transdisciplinary field with rich
potential to provide better answers. It allows turning the conceptual dichotomy of activism and counter-activism, protest and counter-protest, activists and corporations into a dialectic of thesis and antithesis, with
reformation as the synthesis to help PR find its place in this new, continuously evolving environment of the attention economy.

Conclusion

In this chapter, we looked at the Reformation as an example for societal
transformation and change through activism and propaganda, relative to
its social, cultural, political and technological conditions, triggers and
drivers (in particular the impact of the printing press). The transformations
and changes that we are experiencing in the digital attention economy are
in many ways analogous. Modernist theories of PR, for many years the
dominant paradigm, no longer seem fit for purpose. Critical and postmodern perspectives of PR have become increasingly influential. Research
and theorising related to activism and social movements have been a key
factor in this development.

However, recent political events and subsequent analyses of roots and
causes point to emergent and evolving challenges that call for new and
different models and concepts of activist, protest and dissent PR theory
and practice. The new models and concepts will help overcome activists'
struggles with the role and function of PR, as it will be re-imagined, if not
reformed to meet the challenges of an ever more uncertain world where
fundamental principles such as trust, informed dialogue, a shared sense of

reality are being put to the test. The conditions and effects of the attention economy, of surveillance capitalism, the power and the often unintended consequences of algorithmic content selection and decision-making on social platforms will require, if not continuous, reviewing, reframing and reforming of approaches.

Promising approaches all share similar characteristics of openness and recognition for the need to conceptualise and implement multi- and transdisciplinary solutions, across the widest possible range of theory, fields of research, and scientific tradition. As first modernism, and then postmodernism "was the future once", now the time may be right for metamodernism, a concept that is "essayistic rather than scientific, rhizomatic rather than linear, and open-ended instead of closed" (Vermeulen & Van Den Akker, 2010, p. 2). Not least in light of viable alternatives, this would provide an adequate theoretical framework – what in German intellectual tradition would be called "theoretischer Überbau" – for a reformed, re-imagined theory and practice of activist PR in the attention economy.

Notes

1 Cambridge professor and technology commentator, John Naughton, has published his 95 Theses about Technology online (http://95theses.co.uk/). They get continuously updated in an attempt to trigger conversations about the future of the networked world (Naughton, 2017). In another play on the 500th anniversary of the Reformation, a group of UK economists nailed their 33 Theses for an Economics Reformation to the doors of the London School of Economics, on 12 December 2017 (www.opendemocracy.net/neweconomics/33-theses-economics-reformation/).

2 It must be acknowledged that movable type printing started in China in the seventh century AD (McLuhan, 1962). For the purposes of this chapter, however, the focus is on Gutenberg and the history of printing in Europe.

3 Scholars attribute the momentum and impact of the early Reformation to Luther's vision and adeptness in using the new medium of print, as well as his role as its dominant propagandist (Edwards Jr., 2004). The term propaganda itself is also closely associated with the Reformation: in an attempt to counter the growing Protestant movement in the early seventeenth century, Pope Gregory XV established the Sacra Congregatio de Propaganda Fide – to communicate and propagate the Catholic faith (Tilson, 2006; Brown, 2014).

4 In Twitter and Teargas, Zeynep Tufekci discusses the false dichotomies of human vs technology, utopia vs dystopia etc. with regard to the printing press, as an analogy for modern network technology enabling social movements:

> The story of the printing press should serve as a warning about the dialectical nature of technological-historical transformations; the very technology that enabled the mass printing of indulgences to enrich the Catholic Church led to their opportunistic profusion, feeding the outrage that led to new rebellions against the Church. These rebellions used this same technology for their own purposes but even more effectively, touching off centuries of struggle.
>
> (Tufekci, 2017, p. 263f.)

5 The term attention economy was popularised by Davenport and Beck (2001). In recent years, it has increasingly been discussed in a critical context (see for example Webster, 2016; Wu, 2016).

6 Reformation and protest are historically, linguistically, and etymologically closely related, not least through the Reformation leading to the formation of Protestantism. Supporters of the cause of Martin Luther protested to the ruling powers of church and state on various formal occasions. The term protestant derives from their formal entreaties at the Diet of Speyer in 1526 (Chadwick, 2001).

7 The concept of public sphere goes back to Jürgen Habermas (1989). For example, Demetrious (2013) based her historic understanding of "the triangulation of news as commodity, the idea of a mass audience, and public opinion as a corollary of democracy" (p. 15) on the German philosopher's ideas.

8 In this worldview, the scandal involving UK communication firm Bell Pottinger in 2016, as well as the revelations in 2017 and 2018 about political PR firm Cambridge Analytica are seen as anomalies, and the firms caught red-handed are ostracised as black sheep. An article on the independent liberal media platform open Democracy recently discussed this issue from a different perspective, highlighting the risks of "privatising military propaganda": www.opendemocracy.net/uk/brexitinc/adam-ramsay/cambridge-analytica-is-what-happens-when-you-privatise-military-propaganda.

9 Synonymous with fragmentation (not just political), see https://en.wikipedia.org/wiki/Balkanization.

10 In his foreword to Routledge's *New Directions in Public Relations and Communication Research* book publication series (of which this book is part), editor Kevin Moloney states that

> Its remit is to publish critical and challenging responses to continuities and fractures in contemporary PR thinking and practice, and its essential yet contested role in market-orientated, capitalist, liberal democracies around the world. The series reflects the multiple and inter-disciplinary forms PR takes in a post-Grunigian world; the expanding roles which it performs, and the increasing number of countries in which it is practised.

11 In her postmodern interpretation of Public Relations as Activism, Holtzhausen (2012) applies Lyotard's concept of the metanarrative ("a system of meaning that tries to include all other narratives in an effort to legitimate itself" (p. 125)) to Grunig's work: "The concept of symmetry has arguably become the most dominant theoretical approach in public relations and can be described as one of the field's true metanarratives" (p. 66).

12 This school of thought in public relations theory is often described as post-symmetric, as it challenges the dominance of Excellence Theory with its ideal of two-way symmetric communication. It can be traced back to the late 1980s, when young scholars started questioning the foundations of the functional normative paradigm. Over the years, this has created a broad church of critical scholarship, involving disciplines across the humanities, social and natural sciences. Anthologies and handbooks include (L'Etang & Pieczka, 1996; Heath, 2001; Heath, Toth, & Waymer, 2009; Ihlen, van Ruler, & Fredriksson, 2009; Edwards & Hodges, 2011; L'Etang et al., 2016).

13 Tufekci is also one of the most vocal and regularly quoted critics of the potential negative societal effects of social media, including the consequences of algorithmic content selection optimising for ad targeting.

14 In a recent PR Conversations exchange, Kevin Ruck and Heather Yaxley raise similar points, quoting various pieces of industry research indicating that professional development remains an area for improvement. www.prconversations.com/professional-pr-development-why-bother/.

15 It is perhaps justified, in the wake of Brexit and Trump, to introduce a sixth phase, 'the public is unpredictable' (2016 onwards). Whilst a number of scholars have recently submitted comprehensive 'post-symmetric' works (Brown, 2015; Botan, 2017; Marsh, 2017), not enough time has passed for in-depth, data- and theory-led research into the implications for modern PR.

16 Moloney and McKie (2016) call her "the most prominent PR postmodernist" (p. 191).

References

Akker, R. v. & Vermeulen, T. (2017). Periodising the 2000s, or, the emergence of metamodernism. In R. v. Akker, A. Gibbons, & T. Vermeulen (Eds), *Metamodernism. Historicity, affect, and depth after postmodernism* (pp. 1–20). London and New York: Rowman & Littlefield.

Akker, R. v., Gibbons, A., & Vermeulen, T. (Eds) (2017). *Metamodernism. Historicity, affect, and depth after postmodernism.* London and New York: Rowman & Littlefield.

Bardhan, N. & Weaver, C. K. (Eds) (2011). *Public relations in global cultural contexts: Multi-paradigmatic perspectives.* New York: Routledge.

Begley, S. (2017). *Can't. Just. Stop. An investigation of compulsions.* New York: Simon & Schuster.

Benkler, Y. (2006). *The wealth of networks.* New Haven, CT: Yale University Press.

Bennett, W. L. & Segerberg, A. (2013). *The logic of connective action.* Cambridge: Cambridge University Press.

Bentele, G. & Wehmeier, S. (2009). Commentary: Linking sociology with public relations – some critical reflections in reflexive times. In O. Ihlen, B. van Ruler, & M. Fredriksson (Eds), *Public relations and social theory. Key figures and concepts* (pp. 341–362). New York: Routledge.

Berger, P. L. & Luckmann, T. (1966). *The social construction of reality. A treatise in the sociology of knowledge.* London: Penguin.

Best, S. & Kellner, D. (1997). *The postmodern turn.* New York and London: Guilford Press.

Botan, C. H. (2017). *Strategic communication theory and practice. The cocreational model.* New York: Wiley & Sons.

Botan, C. & Hazleton, V. (2006). Public relations in a new age. In C. H. Botan & V. Hazleton (Eds), *Public relations theory II* (pp. 1–18). Mahwah, NJ: Lawrence Erlbaum.

Brown, R. E. (2006). Myth of symmetry: Public relations as cultural styles. *Public Relations Review, 32*(3), 206–212.

Brown, R. E. (2014). The strategic heart: The nearly mutual embrace of religion and public relations. In B. St John III, M. O. Lamme, & J. L'Etang (Eds), *Pathways to public relations. Histories of practice and profession* (pp. 11–27). London and New York: Routledge.

Brown, R. E. (2015). *The public relations of everything. The ancient, the modern and postmodern dramatic history of an idea.* London: Routledge.

Castells, M. (2015). *Networks of outrage and hope. social movements in the internet age* (2nd ed.). Cambridge: Polity Press.

Chadwick, O. (2001). *The early reformation on the continent.* New York: Oxford University Press.

Collister, S. (2016). Algorithmic public relations: Materiality, technology and power in a post-hegemonic world. In J. L'Etang, D. McKie, N. Snow, & J. Xifra (Eds), *Routledge handbook of critical public relations* (pp. 360–371). London and New York: Routledge.

Coombs, W. T. & Holladay, S. J. (2012). Fringe public relations: How activism moves critical PR toward the mainstream. *Public Relations Review*, *38*, 880–887.

Couldry, N. & Hepp, A. (2017). *The mediated construction of reality*. Cambridge: Polity Press.

Davenport, T. H. & Beck, J. C. (2001). *The attention economy. Understanding the new currency of business*. Boston, MA: Harvard University Press.

Deleuze, G. & Guattari, F. (1987). *A thousand plateaus. Capitalism and schizophrenia*. Minneapolis, MN: University of Minnesota Press.

Demetrious, K. (2011). Bubble wrap: Social media, public relations, culture and society. In L. Edwards & C. E. Hodges (Eds), *Public relations, society & culture. theoretical and empirical explorations* (pp. 118–132). London and New York: Routledge.

Demetrious, K. (2013). *Public relations, activism, and social change. Speaking up*. New York and London: Routledge.

Demetrious, K. (2016). Sanitising or reforming PR? Exploring "trust" and the emergence of critical public relations. In J. L'Etang, D. McKie, N. Snow, & J. Xifra (Eds), *Routledge handbook of critical public relations* (pp. 101–116). London and New York: Routledge.

Edwards Jr., M. U. (2004). *Printing, propaganda, and Martin Luther*. Minneapolis, MN: Fortress Press.

Edwards, L. (2012). Defining the "object" of public relations research: A new starting point. *Public Relations Inquiry*, *1*(1), 7–30.

Edwards, L. & Hodges, C. E. (Eds) (2011). *Public relations, society & culture. Theoretical and empirical explorations*. London and New York: Routledge.

Fuchs, C. (2014). Social media and the public sphere. *tripleC*, *12*(1), 57–101.

Galloway, C. (2017). Blink and they're gone: PR and the battle for attention. *Public Relations Review*, *43*(5), 969–977.

Grunig, J. E. (2013). Furnishing the edifice: Ongoing research on public relations as a strategic management function. In K. Sriramesh, A. Zerfass, & J.-N. Kim (Eds), *Public relations and communications management: Current trends and topics* (pp. 1–26). New York: Routledge.

Grunig, J. & Hunt, T. (1984). *Managing public relations*. New York: Holt, Rinehart & Winston.

Grunig, J. E., Grunig, L. A., & Dozier, D. M. (2006). The Excellence Theory. In C. H. Botan, & V. Hazleton (Eds), *Public relations theory II* (pp. 21–62). Mahwah, NJ: Lawrence Erlbaum.

Habermas, J. (1989). *The structural transformation of the public sphere*. Cambridge, MA: MIT Press.

Hassan, R. & Sutherland, T. (2017). *Philosophy of media. A short history of ideas and innovations from Socrates to social media*. London and New York: Routledge.

Heath, R. L. (Ed.) (2001). *Handbook of public relations*. Thousand Oaks, CA: Sage.

Heath, R. L., Toth, E. L., & Waymer, D. (Eds) (2009). *Rhetorical and critical approaches to public relations II*. London and New York: Routledge.

Holtzhausen, D. R. (2012). *Public relations as activism. Postmodern approaches to theory & practice*. London and New York: Routledge.

Ihlen, O. & van Ruler, B. (2009). Introduction: Applying social theory to public relations. In O. Ihlen, B. van Ruler, & M. Fredriksson (Eds), *Public relations and social theory. key figures and concepts* (pp. 1–20). New York: Routledge.

Ihlen, O. & Verhoeven, P. (2009). Conclusions on the domain, context, concepts, issues and empirical avenues of public relations. In O. Ihlen, B. van Ruler, & M. Fredriksson (Eds), *Public relations and social theory. Key figures and concepts* (pp. 323–340). New York: Routledge.

Ihlen, O., van Ruler, B., & Fredriksson, M. (Eds) (2009). *Public relations and social theory. Key figures and concepts*. New York: Routledge.

Inglehart, R. F. & Norris, P. (2016). *Trump, Brexit, and the rise of populism: Economic have-nots and cultural backlash*. Cambridge, MA: Harvard Kennedy School Faculty Research Working Paper Series.

Jenkins, H., Ito, M., & boyd, d. (2016). *Participatory culture in a networked era*. Cambridge: Polity Press.

Kavanagh, J. & Rich, M. D. (2018). *Truth decay. An initial exploration of the diminishing role of facts and analysis in American public life*. Santa Monica, CA: Rand Corporation.

Kenny, J. (2016). Excellence theory and its critics: A literature review critiquing Grunig's strategic management of public relations paradigm. *Asia Pacific Public Relations Journal, 17*(2), 78–91.

Laskin, A. V. (2009). The evolution of models of public relations: An outsider's perspective. *Journal of Communication Management, 13*(1), 37–54.

L'Etang, J. (2016). History as a source of critique: Historicity and knowledge, societal change, activism and movements. In J. L'Etang, D. McKie, N. Snow, & J. Xifra (Eds), *Routledge handbook of critical public relations* (pp. 28–40). London and New York: Routledge.

L'Etang, J. & Pieczka, M. (Eds) (1996). *Critical perspectives in public relations*. London: International Thompson Business Press.

L'Etang, J., McKie, D., Snow, N., & Xifra, J. (Eds). (2016). *Routledge handbook of critical public relations*. London and New York: Routledge.

Levine, R., Searls, D., Weinberger, D., & Locke, C. (2000). *The Cluetrain Manifesto. The end of business as usual*. Cambridge, MA: Perseus Books.

Macnamara, J. (2016). Socially integrating PR and operationalizing an alternative approach. In J. L'Etang, D. McKie, N. Snow, & J. Xifra (Eds), *Routledge handbook of critical public relations* (pp. 335–348). London and New York: Routledge.

Macnamara, J. & Zerfass, A. (2012). Social media communication in organizations: The challenges of balancing openness, strategy, and management. *International Journal of Strategic Communication, 6*(4), 287–308.

Marsh, C. (2017). *Public relations, cooperation, and justice. From evolutionary biology to ethics*. London and New York: Routledge.

McLuhan, M. (1962). *The Gutenberg Galaxy. The making of typographic man*. Toronto: University of Toronto Press.

Moloney, K. (2006). *Rethinking public relations. PR propaganda and democracy* (2nd ed.). London: Routledge.

Moloney, K. & McKie, D. (2016). Changes to be encouraged: Radical turns in PR theorisation and small-step evolutions in practice. In J. L'Etang, D. McKie,

N. Snow, & J. Xifra (Eds), *Routledge handbook of critical public relations* (pp. 151–161). London: Routledge.

Naughton, J. (2017, October). Retrieved from 95 Theses about technology: http://95theses.co.uk/?page_id=20.

O'Neil, C. (2016). *Weapons of math distraction: How big data increases inequality and threatens democracy*. New York: Crown Publishers.

Pariser, E. (2011). *The filter bubble. What the internet is hiding from you*. London: Viking.

Pieczka, M. (2006). Paradigms, systems theory and public relations. In J. L'Etang, & M. Pieczka (Eds), *Public relations. Critical debates and contemporary practice* (pp. 333–358). Mahwah, NJ, and London: Lawrence Erlbaum Associates.

Schneier, B. (2015). *Data and Goliath: The hidden battles to capture your data and control your world*. New York: W.W. Norton & Company.

Simon, H. A. (1971). Designing organizations for an information-rich world. In M. Greenberger (Ed.), *Computers, communication, and the public interest* (pp. 40–41). Baltimore, MD: Johns Hopkins University Press.

Standing, G. (2016). *The precariat. The new dangerous class*. London: Bloomsbury Academic.

Tilson, D. J. (2006). Devotional-promotional communication and Santiago: A thousand-year public relations campaign for Saint James and Spain. In J. L'Etang & M. Pieczka (Eds), *Public relations. Critical debates and contemporary practice* (pp. 167–186). Mahwah, NJ and London: Lawrence Erlbaum Associates.

Toth, E. L. (2009). The case for pluralistic studies of public relations. In R. L. Heath, E. L. Toth, & D. Waymer (Eds), *Rhetorical and critical approaches to public relations II* (pp. 48–60). London and New York: Routledge.

Tufekci, Z. (2017). *Twitter and tear gas. The power and fragility of networked protest*. New Haven & London: Yale University Press.

Vermeulen, T. & Van Den Akker, R. (2010). Notes on metamodernism. *Journal of Aesthetics & Culture, 2*, 1–14.

Vermeulen, T. & Van Den Akker, R. (2015). Utopia, sort of: A case study in metamodernism. *Studia Neophilologica, 87*, 55–67.

Wardle, C. & Derakhshan, H. (2017). *Information disorder: Toward an interdisciplinary framework for research and policy making*. Strasbourg: Council of Europe, DGI(2017)09.

Webster, J. G. (2016). *The marketplace of attention. How audiences take shape in a digital age*. Cambridge, MA and London: The MIT Press.

Wu, T. (2016). *The attention merchants. The epic struggle to get inside our heads*. London: Atlantic Books.

Zuboff, S. (2015). Big other: Surveillance capitalism and the prospects of an information civilization. *Journal of Information Technology, 30*(1), 75–89.

Zuboff, S. (2017). *The age of surveillance capitalism: The fight for a human future at the new frontier of power*. New York: PublicAffairs.

Index

Page numbers in **bold** denote tables, those in *italics* denote figures.

For Product Safety Concerns and Information please contact our EU representative GPSR@taylorandfrancis.com Taylor & Francis Verlag GmbH, Kaufingerstraße 24, 80331 München, Germany

Printed and bound by CPI Group (UK) Ltd, Croydon, CR0 4YY
01/05/2025
01858416-0006